THE MENTAL FLOSS
HISTORY
of the
WORLD

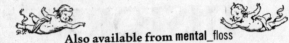

Also available from mental_floss

mental_floss *presents: Condensed Knowledge*

mental_floss *presents: Instant Knowledge*

mental_floss *presents: Forbidden Knowledge*

mental_floss*: Cocktail Party Cheat Sheets*

mental_floss*: What's the Difference?*

mental_floss*: The Genius Instruction Manual*

mental_floss*: Scatterbrained*

mental_floss *presents: In the Beginning*

mental_floss *presents: Be Amazing*

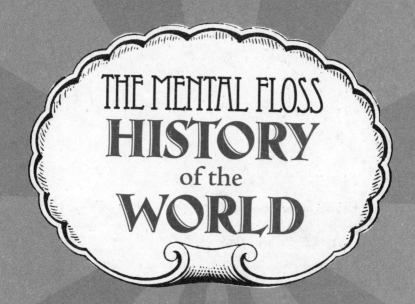

THE MENTAL FLOSS HISTORY of the WORLD

AN IRREVERENT ROMP THROUGH CIVILIZATION'S BEST BITS

ERIK SASS **and** STEVE WIEGAND
with WILL PEARSON *and* MANGESH HATTIKUDUR

HARPER

NEW YORK · LONDON · TORONTO · SYDNEY

HARPER

A hardcover edition of this book was published in 2008 by Collins.

THE MENTAL FLOSS HISTORY OF THE WORLD. Copyright © 2008 by Mental Floss LLC. All rights reserved. Printed in the United States of America. No part of this book may be used or reproduced in any manner whatsoever without written permission except in the case of brief quotations embodied in critical articles and reviews. For information address HarperCollins Publishers, 10 East 53rd Street, New York, NY 10022.

HarperCollins books may be purchased for educational, business, or sales promotional use. For information please write: Special Markets Department, HarperCollins Publishers, 10 East 53rd Street, New York, NY 10022.

FIRST HARPER PAPERBACK PUBLISHED 2009.

Designed by Emily Cavett Taff

The Library of Congress has catalogued the hardcover edition as follows:

Sass, Erik.
   The Mental floss history of the world/Erik Sass and Steve Wiegand with the editors of Mental floss.—1st ed.
      p.   cm.
   ISBN 978-0-06-078477-5
   1. World history.   2. Civilization—History.   I. Wiegand, Steve, 1951-   II. Mental floss (Durham, N.C.)   III. Title.

D23.S28 2008
909—dc22   2008015936

ISBN 978-0-06-184267-2 (pbk.)

09   10   11   12   13   WBC/RRD   10   9   8   7   6   5   4   3   2   1

CONTENTS

Acknowledgments
vii

Introduction
ix

CHAPTER 1:
AFRICA AND AFTER
(60,000 BCE–1500 BCE)
1

CHAPTER 2:
CHAOS AND CONTROL
(1500 BCE–500 BCE)
33

CHAPTER 3:
ATHENS, ALEXANDER, AND ALL THAT
(500 BCE–0 BCE)
65

CHAPTER 4:
THERE'S NO PLACE LIKE ROME
(Except China, Persia, India, Mexico, and Peru)
(1 CE–500 CE)
95

CHAPTER 5:
THE NOT-REALLY-THAT-DARK
(Unless You Lived in Europe) AGES
(500–1000)
125

CHAPTER 6:
THE FAIR-TO-MIDDLIN' AGES
(Even If You Lived in Europe)
(1000–1300)
155

CHAPTER 7:

RENAISSANCE, ANYONE?
(And How About Genocide and Slavery?)
(1300–1575)
187

CHAPTER 8:

WAR AND SLAVERY
(And, Uh, Enlightenment)
(1575–1750)
221

CHAPTER 9:

THE AGE OF LIBERATION, FRAGMENTATION, STAGNATION, AND PLAIN OL' NATIONS
(1750–1900)
255

CHAPTER 10:

THE EMPIRES STRIKE OUT
(1900–1930)
293

CHAPTER 11:

TO THE BRINK OF THE ABYSS
(1931–1962)
325

CHAPTER 12:

ONE WORLD
(1963–2007)
359

THIS JUST IN:

IF YOU THOUGHT THE LAST DEPRESSION WAS GREAT . . .
395

APPENDIX:

OH YEA, CANADA
399

Index
403

About the Authors
419

ACKNOWLEDGMENTS

To paraphrase Yogi Berra, Steve and Erik would like to thank mental_floss editors Will Pearson and Mangesh Hattikudur for making this book necessary, along with HarperCollins editor Stephanie Meyers for making it (we hope) readable.

Steve would also like to thank his sister, Deborah Daly, for her encouragement and interest in what's been going on in the world for the last 20,000 years. And, of course, his wife, Ceil, and daughter, Erin. Just for putting up with him.

Erik would like to thank his parents, Karen and Steve, for reproducing and imparting their love of learning, and his older brother, Adam, for listening to his constant prattle with the appearance of interest. For demonstrating that reading and writing about history can actually be interesting, he owes a debt of gratitude to Mary-Therese Pasquale-Bowen, Colonel Dan "D.A." Allen, USAF (Ret.), and Duke history professors Malachi Hacohen, Kent Rigsby, Peter English, and Kristin Neuschel. Special thanks as well to Justin and Juliet Schwab for their Classical expertise.

Will and Mangesh would like to thank Cathy Hemming for her wise counsel, Steve Ross for his confidence in mental_floss, and the entire Collins crew for their enthusiastic support. But most of all, we'd like to thank Stephanie Meyers for being the greatest editor in the history of editors. And we've clearly been studying our history.

INTRODUCTION

BY ERIK SASS

We know that 99 percent of "history," as *they* teach it, is mind-numbingly boring. And we're sorry about that; we can't change what happened in your youth.

But this book is about to make history, by making history interesting. Why? Because history is an edge-of-your-seat thrill ride with all the makings of a Hollywood blockbuster. You want action? We got action. Sex and violence? Plenty of both. Psychopathic mass murderers? Psychopathic mass murderers *run* history! And the best part is, it's all real.

In the following pages, you'll read about babies on opium, chicken-flavored beer, cosmetic testicle beads, undercover czars, and gin as a way of life. We've also got multibillion dollar heists, secrets from Central American jungles, a duchess who rode through town naked to get her husband to lower taxes, and Roman orgies so scandalous that even the Romans were scandalized.

Of course, if it's the serious stuff you crave, we've got that, too. From the religion that gave birth to Christianity (we're not talking Judaism), to why the Black Death may not have been *such* a bad thing, to the lurid details of how a country of 300 million people wasn't just conquered, but conned into thinking it was their idea, there's no shortage of substance.

A natural question about any single-volume history of the world should be: "Is everything here?" The straight answer is: no. Not that we didn't try. Sadly, HarperCollins rejected our original 500 million-page manuscript as "overenthusiastic" and "hard on the back." (Whether it would have been marketable as the first book visible from space is still up for debate.) And while this version does omit a few details, we think we did alright. There's a wealth of fun facts here, and maybe three-quarters of the "important" stuff. Luckily, there's a surprising degree of overlap.

On that note, some people claim history is a serious business, and we could lay some solemn jive on you, like "those who do not know their history are doomed to repeat it."* Unfortunately, that's not necessarily true. As you'll see in the following pages, history is full of people who knew plenty about history, but kept on repeating the same stupid mistakes again and again anyway.

But that doesn't mean the past isn't worthwhile in its own right. History is funny, thrilling, heartbreaking, transcendent. There's laughing and gasping, crying, and so much more. And history gives us hope. Because maybe those solemn historians were right: with a little luck, maybe we *will* learn something that helps us dodge the next bullet.

So we encourage you to read, enjoy, and try to pay attention. Because there is going to be a quiz when you're finished. It's called the future.

* In the words of George Santayana

1
AFRICA AND AFTER
(60,000 BCE–1500 BCE)

If there's one thing you can say about human beings, it's that we're *always* hungry. When modern humans (*Homo sapiens sapiens*) left Africa to conquer the globe more than sixty thousand years ago, they settled near sources of food, and those areas that produced more food became more populated. Some groups found forests with game to hunt, while others wandered grasslands, tending herds of cows. In Stone Age Mexico, coastal peoples subsisted on shellfish for thousands of years, leaving a huge heap of clam shells 240 feet long, 90 feet wide, and 21 feet tall.

Another thing about us: we don't like to share. Tribes constantly battled for territory, and some were pushed into less friendly environments—but nomads made the best use of limited resources. Arabs conquered the vast Arabian Peninsula by taming the camel, a hardy desert animal that carried them between lush oases. Central Asians took to horse- and sheepherding, ranging across thousands of miles in search of rare good pastures. Inuit learned to build homes out of ice.

But in terms of calories per acre, grain cultivation feeds many more people than fishing, hunting, or raising domestic animals. Grain cultivation began around 9000 BCE and soon spread around the world, and places that grew grain experienced a population explosion (oh yeah, apparently we also like to have sex . . . *a lot*). Soon, there was so much food that some people could stop working in the fields and specialize in crafts. Expert potters, weavers, and masons were soon followed by tailors, leather tanners, miners, and other trades. Yes, that includes "the world's oldest profession."

Around 8000 BCE, the world's first civilizations—defined as people living in cities—began appearing. The craftspeople lived together in encampments for safety against rival groups and for convenience of trade. Cities also became centers of government—in most cases, likely a hereditary monarchy descended from old tribal authority.

Little is known about the world's first governments, but they were probably dominated by a single family or clan passing authority from generation to generation, with a dominant man becoming ruler each time. In prehistory, governments along matriarchal (woman-centered) or communal (leaderless) lines may have existed, but by the beginning of recorded history, these had been snuffed out. Each of the world's first civilizations was ruled by one man, a king. Men have hogged the remote ever since.

The king's job was simple: to protect his followers. In general, the people believed that the king's authority came from the immortal gods, so kings were closely associated with religion from the get-go. In some places the king was also the high priest, in charge of sacrificial offerings and ceremonies intended to bring good harvests. In other places, the king worked closely with the high priest or employed soothsayers to help divine the future.

While rival kings could cause trouble, the biggest enemy facing early civilizations was nature itself, which operated at the will of invisible gods. Droughts, floods, and other natural disasters could destroy crops, bringing starvation and misery. Translation: If everyone had enough to eat, the gods were happy with the leader; if there wasn't enough to eat, well . . . It's no surprise that across the "civilized" world, each ruler's first act was to store grain against hard times.

To make this food-insurance system work, kings ordered their subjects to turn over some grain during good times, which could be distributed again in an emergency. Grain was stored in huge stone or mud-brick silos, called granaries. Priests were in charge of keeping track of which grain had come from which landowner.

To help remember the grainy details, priests invented writing. Recording quantities, names, and dates on clay tablets in turn led to accounting and banking. Soon regular people began quantifying goods such as livestock, tools, and luxury items. As writing spread to society at large, merchants, bankers, and scribes joined the other craftsmen who lived in cities. Writing led to the first commercial contracts (e.g., "for these four pigs, you bring me two cows in three days"—we're not saying it was glamorous).

However, not every culture chose to settle down and farm. The differences between cities and nomadic groups created a lot of friction. For one thing the cities' accumulation of wealth, in the form of surplus grain and other goods, naturally attracted attention from people living a more marginal existence outside the cities. Nomads often enjoyed a tactical advantage over city folk, and men from the wilds, skilled in horse-mounted warfare, have long terrified the simple farmer on the outskirts of town. The nomadic threat still exists today—but by 1500 BCE, the power of settled societies based on farming was already uncontestable. The history of civilization is their story.

·············· **WHAT HAPPENED WHEN** ···············

2,500,000 BCE	*Homo habilis*, earliest protohuman ancestor, uses stone tools in Africa.
2,000,000 BCE	Various protohuman ancestors spread out across the planet.
1,500,000 BCE	Hominids master fire.
300,000 BCE	Neanderthals live in Europe.
150,000 BCE	The Sahara is a lush grassland.
130,000 BCE	Modern humans, *Homo sapiens sapiens*, appear in Africa.
60,000 BCE	*Homo sapiens sapiens* spread out over the planet.
10,000 BCE	Polar ice caps begin to melt, raising sea levels four hundred feet.
9000 BCE	The Natufian culture domesticates wheat, inventing agriculture.
7500 BCE	The world's first cities emerge at Catal Huyuk and Jericho.
5,300 BCE	The Sahara has become a desert.
5000 BCE	Catal Huyuk and Jericho are mysteriously abandoned.
4500 BCE	The first Sumerian cities, Eridu and Ur, are founded.
4000 BCE	The first cities are founded in Egypt.
3100 BCE	Egypt is united by the pharaohs and becomes the world's first state.
3000 BCE	China's first civilization begins (Longshan culture).
2600 BCE	Harappan civilization flourishes in the Indus River Valley.
2530 BCE	Egyptians complete the Great Pyramid of Cheops.

2200 BCE   Babylon is founded by the Amorites.

1900 BCE   China's first royal family, the Xia dynasty, rules.

1750 BCE   Abraham leaves Ur for Canaan.

1700 BCE   Harappan civilization disappears.

1600 BCE   Indo-Europeans establish Hittite and Mitanni kingdoms
in Mesopotamia.

·············· **SPINNING THE GLOBE** ················

The Highly Fertile Crescent

The *first* large-scale settlements in the world were Jericho, in modern-day Israel, and Catal Huyuk, in modern-day eastern Turkey. Both were founded around 8000 BCE(ish), in the western half of the "Fertile Crescent," a rich agricultural belt straddling the Middle East whose eastern region includes Mesopotamia (present-day Iraq). These settlements were like a "first try": they never grew as large as the civilizations that followed them, eventually fading and disappearing under mysterious circumstances.

Between 8000 BCE and 7000 BCE, Jericho probably had about two thousand inhabitants, living in rectangular houses with plaster walls and floors and encircled by protective stone walls. The people appear to have practiced some form of ancestor worship, venerating skulls adorned with seashells. Catal Huyuk was larger: The oldest layer yet discovered, covering thirty-two acres, dates to about 7500 BCE, when it probably had a population of six thousand. Catal Huyuk connected a network of villages stretching hundreds of miles around, and was a major center of religion and trade. It was inexplicably abandoned around 5000 BCE.

Jericho and Catal Huyuk were followed by a collection of city-states in Mesopotamia that were all part

SLAP HAPPY

At the Akitu festival marking the New Year, the kings of Babylon had a special responsibility: getting slapped so hard their momma felt it. The ritual was part of a ceremonial purification of the city. According to protocol, the king would enter the temple of Marduk, Babylon's chief god, and tell the god that he hadn't done anything wrong in the last year—for example, slapped the cheek of any of his subjects. The high priest then slapped the king but good; if the king's eyes teared up from this unjust punishment, he was telling the truth, and Marduk approved him to rule for another year.

Sargon the Great was the first in a long line of people with the same idea: conquering everything. But like most of the others, his amazing success was fleeting.

Legend has it that Sargon's mother was a "changeling," meaning either a demon or a prostitute, who gave birth to the future conqueror around 2350 BCE. According to Sumerian stories, in his youth, Sargon served as the royal cup-bearer for the king of Kish, named Ur-Zababa. Believing Sargon was favored by the goddess Inanna, Ur-Zababa tried to have him killed, but Sargon escaped. He built up a following among local tribesmen, founding a new city, Akkad, as his capital, and then went on the warpath. After conquering all of Sumeria, including Kish (sweet, sweet revenge), Sargon symbolically washed his sword in the Persian Gulf—Sumeria's southernmost boundary—to symbolize his total control over the area. Still hungry for power, he headed north to conquer Assyria, Lebanon, and southern Turkey, before finally turning east to conquer Elam, in Persia (now Iran).

A clever ruler, Sargon understood the importance of trade and of controlling the long-distance trade routes between cities. His empire dominated the trade routes connecting the Harappan civilization of India to Sumeria, Egypt, and the Mediterranean basin. These trade routes made Sargon and his successors fabulously wealthy.

Sargon tried to continue his empire by placing his children in positions of power, but after his death, key territories rebelled against one of his sons, Rimush, who was then assassinated by his brother Manishtushu. Sargon's short-lived empire was finished.

of the Sumerian civilization. The big players were Eridu and Ur, founded between 4500 and 4000 BCE, Uruk and Lagash (3500 BCE), Kish (3200 BCE), and Nippur (3000 BCE). Though these cities quarreled endlessly, they shared a common language, culture, and religion.

These cities were small by modern standards: the largest, Uruk, had at most sixty thousand to eighty thousand inhabitants at its height. Even so, there was constant friction between them, as neighboring farmers feuded over property boundaries. When things got bad enough, the cities went to war. Sumerian kings eventually created standing armies, but in the early days, conflicts were probably spontaneous, with town meetings turning into angry mobs. Warriors could be armed with spears, clubs, and good old-fashioned rocks.

Politically, each city-state was ruled by a *lugal*, or "big man"—in other words, a king. His main responsibility was divvying up water for irrigation. Because water was scarce, city governments served as guardians of the water supply, and were responsible for organizing mandatory work teams a couple of times a year to maintain irrigation canals and dams.

The "big man" served alongside the high priest of the city's cult, who officiated at religious ceremonies and collected offerings for the gods. In Ur, the locals worshipped a sun god called Utu or Hadad, the boss of a pantheon that also included Inanna or Isthar, the goddess of fertility, spring, storms, love, and marriage, and Ereshkigal, her twin sister, the goddess of death.

The most important religious festival was the spring planting festival, also marking the Sumerian New Year. It lasted twelve days, during which the priests purified themselves, presented animal sacrifices, and supervised the king's prayers for divine assistance. The festival also involved visits by "gods" on river barges and mock battles representing the struggle between good and evil. Like all good holidays there was plenty of time for banquets and parties.

As agriculture spread, so did civilization, and before long, new players arrived on the scene. In what is now western Iraq, the Amorites, distant (and apparently more ambitious) relations of the Sumerians, founded a great city, Babylon, by 2200 BCE. Babylon grew far larger than the first generation of city-states, and before long it dominated the older urban centers of Sumeria. Babylon had a population of more than two hundred thousand at its peak in 1700 BCE, when it was the center of regional trade and manufacturing. Like their predecessors in Sumer, Ur, and Uruk, the people of Babylon built a giant ziggurat—a stepped pyramid with a temple on top—bringing them closer to their gods for religious ceremonies.

NOT SO FRIENDLY NEIGHBORS

While Babylon reigned supreme in the second millennium BCE, trouble was brewing. In the area north of modern Baghdad, around 1900 BCE, a fierce tribe called the Assyrians established their own civilization along the Tigris River, centered on the cities Assur, Nineveh, and Nimrud. Far more warlike than their southern neighbors, the Assyrians pretty much lived to fight, and they had a couple of big advantages. They had learned how to domesticate horses, and the secret of making iron tools and weapons that were sharper and deadlier than the Babylonians' bronze weapons. In 1500 BCE, the Assyrians were still just a bunch of hicks and Assyria was a backwater of Mesopotamia—but they were organized, ambitious, and itching for a fight. Watch this space!

Egypt:
Winner of the World's First
Mega-State Contest

Egypt is often pictured as the world's first civilization, but its cities got rolling a little later than Sumer, sometime after 4000 BCE. Still, a couple of hundred years is loose change at this point in human history—and if it's a contest of size, Egypt wins hands down. Around 3100 BCE it became the world's first mega-state, unifying almost five hundred miles of territory from the Mediterranean Sea to the first cataract (waterfalls) on the Nile River. The pharaohs who ruled Egypt were the most powerful men in the world, and their power lasted far beyond that of the Sumerian kings.

Egypt was unified by a semi-mythical king (or kings) named Menes, who founded the First Dynasty as well as Egypt's capital, Memphis, just south of the Nile Delta. There are stories of conflict between the people of northern Egypt and southern Egypt, but the Nile united them. Egyptian culture and religion centered on the river, whose rhythms structured Egyptian society for thousands of years. (Currently the giant Aswan Dam controls the floods.) During the winter months, snow fell in Ethiopia, where the Nile begins in the mountains. In the spring, when the snow melted, the floodwaters rose to cover the surrounding "flood plains" at the bottom of the Nile Valley, in Egypt. When the Nile finally retreated a month later, it left a thick layer of

NAME THAT GOD

Among the active gods, Ammon's power was represented by Ra, the sun god, with a human body and the head of a falcon, wearing a crown shaped like the sun. Ra crossed the sky in a golden ship every day, then descended into the underworld at night, where he fought and defeated Death before reappearing the next morning. He was the patron god of the pharaohs, symbolizing power.

The first god of death (yes, there was more than one) was Anubis, depicted with a human body and the head of a jackal. He was the chief god of funerals, weighing the hearts of the dead to determine whether they had behaved justly while alive. The second god of death, Osiris, replaced Anubis as chief god of the underworld sometime before 2000 BCE. His story is truly bizarre: after a rival god killed Osiris and chopped him into pieces, Osiris's sister and wife(!), Isis, reassembled the whole body except for Osiris's penis, which she replaced with a wooden replica. The Egyptians worshipped the dead Osiris, wooden package and all. Isis was the "mother goddess," usually depicted wearing a crown of cow horns and holding a sun disc. She was the patron goddess of the royal throne, closely associated with the power and dignity of the pharaohs.

silt—fertile farmland. This made Egypt the breadbasket of the ancient world.

The Nile could also be incredibly destructive when it flooded, so it's no surprise that Egyptians believed it had divine power. The Nile *was* the universe, controlled by gods who required prayers to avert their wrath. The first god was a primordial spirit named Ammon, representing the chaos that existed before the universe was formed. He was an invisible father who held the power of creation—in fact he created himself (ah, paradox). His name means "the Hidden One." Fittingly, he usually stayed in the background.

Each pharaoh was a representative of a single divine spirit, which transmitted itself from pharaoh to pharaoh. This is an important area where Egypt differed from Mesopotamia. In Mesopotamia, the "big man" ruled alongside a high priest, while in Egypt the pharaoh was both ruler *and* high priest, *and* a living god to boot.

After the pharaoh died he required magnificent funeral rites to ensure his resurrection in the afterlife. The practice of building pyramids as crypts for dead kings began around 2700 BCE, with the stepped pyramid built for Pharaoh Djoser in Saqqara. There were some mishaps along the way. The most famous screw-up is the bent

SURPRISINGLY ORDINARY EATS

So what did ancient people actually eat? The best source of information about ancient food comes from Egypt, where ancient Egyptians turned wheat and barley into porridge and also baked a bread that was something like modern-day pita. Sometimes the Egyptians added figs, honey, butter, or oil infused with herbs to the bread for flavor. Beer was an important source of nutrition, consumed at every meal along with bread.

Ordinary Egyptians made butter, and seem to have made some kind of cheese, though it's unclear what its consistency was, or what it tasted like. Vegetables included beets, cucumbers, sweet onions, radishes, garlic, turnips, chickpeas, beans, leeks, lentils, and lettuce. They also ate meat, though this was for the most part food for the rich, and a relatively rare treat for the lower classes. Upper-class Egyptians ate beef, mutton, antelope, gazelle, ibex, and hyena. (They wouldn't eat pork, which they believed carried leprosy.)

The poor had more access to domestic and wild fowl, including duck, goose, heron, quail, pelican, and crane. Fish were plentiful in the Nile, and probably constituted the main source of protein in poor people's diets. Popular species included perch, catfish, and mullet. For dessert, Egyptians liked sweet fruit such as figs, dates, pomegranates, grapes, and watermelon.

pyramid of Snefru, built at Dahshur around 2600 BCE: apparently the designers realized the sides were too steep halfway through, and reduced the angles dramatically, resulting in the odd eight-sided structure that's still visible today.

The largest pyramid ever built is the Great Pyramid: 481 feet high, 756 feet on each side, containing about 2.3 million blocks of granite weighing 2.5 tons each, with a façade of 144,000 white limestone blocks, which were later removed for use on subsequent pyramids. The pyramid was built between 2550 and 2530 BCE, for the pharaoh Khufu, known in Greek as Cheops. The massive structure, covering a total of 13 acres, probably took 100,000 workers 20 years to complete—and to this day, we're still not sure exactly how.

India:
What Harappaned to the Harappans?

Not much is known about Harappan civilization, which blossomed around 2600 BCE along the Indus River in present-day Pakistan and India. But in some ways it is the most impressive of all early cultures because Harappan cities were incredibly well-organized.

Mohenjo-Daro is a good example. Like the cities of Sumeria, this city was built out of mud-brick and wood. It probably had about thirty-five thousand inhabitants, and they clearly valued cleanliness, building a sewage system, aqueducts to bring fresh water to neighborhood fountains, and a communal bath, where an underground furnace provided hot water. Wide streets were planned in a grid formation, with "zoning" separating residential and commercial activities. Mohenjo-Daro had a large granary, a public well, and a citadel with an impressive "castle" structure. There were also two large assembly buildings for town meetings.

To this day, no one has deciphered the Harappan written language, which had about four hundred characters that appeared on large public "sign boards" and on clay and bronze tablets. To create documents, scribes carved sentences or phrases into stone seals, then pressed the seals into the wet clay. Bronze documents were reserved for special ceremonial use.

Harappan religion is also something of a mystery, although there are hints of a cult centered on bull worship, including the image of a man with bull horns, or a bull horn headdress, seated in the lotus position. Archaeologists have also found small statuettes of round-bellied women—possibly symbols of a fertility goddess. The Harappans buried their dead with their heads pointing north, and included pots of food, tools, and weapons for use in the afterlife.

In its nine-hundred-year existence, Mohenjo-Daro was totally re-built six or seven times after being destroyed by floods. The entire Harappan civilization probably disappeared around 1700 BCE be-cause of massive flooding, foreign invaders (possibly "Indo-Euro-pean" tribes), or both.

China:
Building Walls, Making Pots, Sacrificing Children

The first Chinese cities emerged as part of the Longshan culture, a Stone Age civilization that existed from roughly 3000 BCE to 1500 BCE, with about fifty separate city-sites distributed along the Yellow River. The Longshan people surrounded their cities with deep moats and large walls made of rammed earth. Some cities had walls more than four miles long. Indeed, ever since then, Chinese cities have boasted impressive fortifications—and in fact, the Chinese word for "city" (*cheng*) comes from their word for "wall."

Early Chinese religion centered on worship and veneration of an-cestors, who held a place in a larger cosmology where a supreme god presided over lesser gods representing the sun, moon, wind, rain, and other forces of nature. Priests used "oracle bones" bearing inscrip-tions to learn the will of the spirits, writing a question and then heat-ing the bones in a fire until they cracked, providing a "yes" or "no" answer. The inscriptions on oracle bones are the first evidence of writ-ten language in China.

The Longshan culture produced exquisite black pottery, includ-ing fragile wine vessels, bowls, and incense burners. Some of these clay creations are as thin as eggshell, yet have miraculously survived to the present day. Like other early civilizations, the people of Long-shan included these works of art in the graves of the wealthy to make things easier for them in the afterlife.

During this period, Chinese society was already organized around the patriarchal clan—the male-centered extended family that domi-nates Chinese culture to the present day. The Longshan culture also left evidence of big gaps in wealth: of fifteen hundred burials in the Taosi cemetery, just nine male burials included large numbers of pre-cious objects, while the rest contained virtually none.

> A capital city should be square on plan. Three gates on each side of the perimeter lead into the nine main streets that crisscross the city and define its grid-pattern.
> —*Book of Diverse Crafts*, China, a text recording ancient wisdom

China's first hereditary monarchy, the Xia Dynasty, was widely thought to be mythical until the discovery of the Erlitou culture, a Bronze Age civilization that followed the Longshan culture. According to one of the first written histories, around 2200 BCE, Gun, the father of the founder of the Xia Dynasty, built "a city to protect the king and the people." However, his attempts to control massive flooding ended in disaster. His son, Da Yu, managed to control the flooding (presumably from the Yellow River) by following the advice of his advisor, Boyi, who suggested channeling rather than blocking the water. Later Yu wanted to abdicate in favor of Boyi, but Yu's son Qi killed Boyi and seized power himself, establishing the Xia Dynasty. Thus China's first hereditary dynasty was founded on disobedience, murder, and injustice.

> We must recall that all life evolved from water. Many creatures still live in water. All creatures drink water. Our bodies are predominantly water; the layers that make us human are thin. We may need the air of heaven, the nourishment of the earth, but we also need the quenching power of water.
> —*I Ching*, mystical Chinese text, c. 2800 BCE

The Xia were replaced by the Shang Dynasty around 1750 BCE (there was probably some overlap), by which time China's first cities were well established. Archaeologists believe they have discovered Xibo, the capital of Shang, in modern Henan province. As part of their religion, the Shang sacrificed humans right and left: in one Shang city, archaeologists discovered 852 human sacrifices to dedicate new buildings. Meanwhile kings were buried with thousands of sacrificial victims to serve them in the afterlife. Sacrifices included, but were not limited to, elephants, rhinos, buffalo, oxen, sheep, deer, dogs, tigers, and children.

Australia:
Where You Can Get Away From It All

For anyone trying to avoid the rest of the human race in the ancient world, Australia was your best bet. Beginning about ninety-nine million years ago, the continent began drifting away from Antarctica, India, and Africa (which were joined together in a supercontinent, Gondwanaland) and by thirty-nine million years ago, it was more or less isolated.

The ancestors of today's aborigines migrated southward from Asia across landmasses that would later become the separate islands of Indonesia, New Guinea and Australia when sea levels rose at the end of the last Ice Age, twelve thousand years ago. The rising water isolated

Australia's bizarre animals evolved in isolation for millions of years, acquiring characteristics found nowhere else on earth. For example, the young of marsupials such as kangaroos and koalas gestate in an external pouch on the front of the mother's body. The duckbill platypus seems to combine a bird's bill with the body of a beaver; a sharp spur behind each leg is tipped with incredibly toxic poison. (Don't *ever* play with a platypus.) Then there's the kiwi, the small flightless bird native to New Zealand; kiwis are just weird. And don't forget the ancient world's "megafauna"—animals much larger than their relatives today—including the ten-foot-tall kangaroo with vicious claws, a "marsupial lion," and the six-thousand-pound super wombat. (Hey, that's a great name for a band.) The extinction of these animals is associated with the arrival of humans in Australia around 50,000 BCE.

the aborigines on Australia, basically cutting them off from other humans for thousands of years.

Australia wasn't always a desert. Archaeologists have found evidence of freshwater lakes and a large inland sea in the central part of the country. A Stone Age culture lived on these shores between 45,000 and 40,000 BCE, subsisting on fishing, hunting, and gathering. Some kind of human habitation continued until 20,000 BCE, when the sea dried up. Today's aborigines are probably related to this extinct culture.

The aborigines developed a unique religion centered on the "Dreamtime," when archetypal animals and mythic heroes created the Universe; giant cosmic snakes and lizards are thought to have played a role in creating the landscape, and are associated with certain features of the terrain. All existence can be traced back to the first primeval creators, and all beings in nature are therefore related to one another in a vast cosmic network. Aboriginal beliefs have been credited as forerunners of modern ecological science.

· · · · · · · · · · · **WHO'S UP, WHO'S DOWN** · · · · · · · · · · · · · · ·

Wheat: UP

Archaeologists say that human beings domesticated wheat about eleven thousand years ago—but did wheat actually domesticate *us*? Bizarre as it sounds, it's a question that has evolutionary biologists scratching their heads.

After the last Ice Age ended, the planet warmed up and there was abundant rainfall. In the typical Stone Age hunter-gatherer society, men went hunting while women gathered fruit, vegetables, tubers, and herbs growing in the wild. One group of people in what is now present-day Syria and Lebanon, the Natufians, harvested grain from wild wheat fields using pottery sickles (which broke all the time, leaving archaeological clues).

The wheat grew well by itself because the world was a lush paradise very different from today. But that paradise didn't last. About thirteen thousand years ago a cold snap called the Lesser Dryas caused a drought. This was bad news for the Natufians: as plant life shriveled up, the climate changes hit wild wheat fields hard. Harvests shrank dramatically, and there was probably mass starvation.

Hunger is a great motivator, so eventually the Natufians discovered ways to maximize wheat harvests. They carefully set aside a portion of each harvest as "seed grain" to plant the next crop, and they also figured out the basics of pollination and cross-breeding. By breeding certain plants selectively, they encouraged desirable traits such as bigger seeds, more seeds, and less chaff (the inedible fibers that have to be filtered out).

But who was really wearing the pants, humans or wheat? In the good old days the Natufians were seminomadic, wandering through forests and wild wheat fields. But when fertile areas contracted during the drought, the Natufians settled down permanently to focus on their most important food resource. Wheat cultivation also changed gender roles and the structure of family and society, as men gave up hunting to work in the fields (traditionally women's work). Then property and ownership were invented to allow farmers to divvy up land.

All this effort had a single goal: making sure the wheat plants survived and reproduced. Natufian-style agriculture spread quickly, triggering the formation of civilizations in Jericho, Catal Huyuk, Sumer, and Egypt. Since then, thanks to mankind's tender loving care, wheat now covers a much larger percentage of the globe than when it grew wild. Take the United States: unknown before Spanish colonists introduced it in the sixteenth century, wheat now occupies forty-seven million acres of land. That's almost seventy-five thousand square miles! From the perspective of evolutionary biology, wheat made out like gangbusters—and we're doing all the work.

Jews: NOT DOWN YET

Most early human religions were polytheistic (multi-god), meaning that worshippers had to guess the mood of a particular god or goddess, then try to influence it by sacrificing precious objects, animals, or even people. Too much attention to one god would arouse the jealousy of the others, who also had to be placated with prayer and sacrifice.

But what if it were all controlled by one all-powerful God? With one God, it's a lot easier to figure out if you're on the heavenly naughty list: if things are good, God's happy with you. If things are bad, you have some work to do.

That's (sort of) the revolutionary idea behind Judaism, the world's first and longest-lived monotheistic (single-deity) religion. Abraham, the founder of Judaism, was a Sumerian prince who answered a call from God to leave the city of Ur, where he was living, and settle in the land of Canaan (modern Israel and Palestine) sometime around 1750 BCE. In return for worshipping just one God—that would be Him—God said he would make Abraham's descendants into a great people. With his wife (also half-sister) Sarah, Abraham obeyed God's command and trekked about five hundred miles west, to the Promised Land of Canaan.

But God didn't really make it *easy* on his chosen. When he doubted Abraham's commitment, he ordered him to sacrifice his oldest son, Isaac, on a stone altar in the desert. At the last minute, convinced of Abraham's faith, God changed his mind and said that Abraham could sacrifice a ram instead, leading to another of Judaism's brilliant innovations: no more human sacrifices. Human life was too valuable for such bloodthirsty displays. (Animals were not so lucky, however.)

THE JEW CREW BELIEVED IN A FEW—WHO KNEW?

When they finally got around to writing stuff down, the Jews talked a good game about always having been monotheists . . . but it's not quite that simple. According to some scholars, the Hebrews finally embraced monotheism long after Abraham, as a way to unite against their neighbors the Canaanites. In fact, evidence suggests that the early Hebrews worshipped the Canaanite gods Ba'al and El and the goddess of birth and mercy, Asherah. But the best evidence comes from the Bible itself, in Psalms 82:1: "God has taken his place in the divine council; in the midst of the gods he holds judgment." And the First Commandment, "You shall have no other gods before me," doesn't state that other gods don't exist.

But the new rules of sacrifice still didn't make being Abraham's children any easier. When Abraham had a son named Ishmael by his Egyptian maid Hagar, his jealous wife, Sarah, convinced him to banish both mother and son to the desert—a virtual death sentence. But God protected them, and Ishmael became the "father of the Arab people." (*Ishmaelite* is an archaic term for "Arab.")

The combination of horses and chariots gave Indo-Europeans—also called Aryans or Caucasians because of their proximity to the Caucasus Mountains—a big advantage over opponents still fighting on foot. Between 2200 and 1500 BCE, the nomadic Indo-Europeans left their homeland in southern Russia and conquered a wide swath of Europe, the Middle East, and Asia. Aside from horses, their principal wealth was herds of cattle, and everywhere they went there are stories of cattle rustling and warfare to steal enemies' herds.

One of their first conquests was Persia, or Iran—in fact, *Iran* comes from the Farsi word for "Aryan." In Mesopotamia the Indo-Europeans clashed with the native Semites, the ancestors of today's Jews and Arabs, creating the Hittite and Mitanni empires around 1600 BCE. The Hittites were a powerful, well-organized state whose chariot-mounted warriors terrorized Egypt. They reigned supreme until the rise of the Semitic Assyrians, who also knew something about the horse and chariot thing.

AND WHY NOT MAKE UP HISTORY?

Sometimes a little knowledge can be dangerous. In the nineteenth century, European racists claimed that the Indo-Europeans were "white" conquerors who subdued "inferior" Semitic and Asiatic peoples. In the twentieth century, Adolf Hitler said that the "racially pure" descendants of Aryans were blond-haired, blue-eyed Germans, who therefore had a right to conquer and dominate their neighbors. These racist visions have almost nothing to do with historical reality. Because Hitler hated Russians, he said that the Aryans must have come from Thule, a mythical Island near Iceland (say wha?). There's also no real way to know what the Aryans looked like for sure, with no human remains. And they probably weren't racially superior: they just got around a lot faster because they had horses.

Two thousand miles to the east, different Indo-European tribes arrived in the Indus River Valley around 1700 BCE. The demise of Harappan civilization around the same time may have resulted from these invasions. The Indo-Europeans became the new bosses of India, cementing their rule with a strict "caste" system dividing society into an elaborate hierarchy. They dug in their heels on the top three rungs of the ladder, dominating the priesthood, nobility, and merchant class. Over time, intermarriage lessened racial distinctions, but the caste system remained.

Meanwhile the Hellenes—the people who became the ancient Greeks—migrated into the peninsula from the Balkans between 2100 and 1600 BCE. The Mycenaean civilization they created is named after Mycenae, an important city located southwest of Athens.

Mediterranean Residents: DOWN

Imagine a wall of water 10 stories high moving toward you at 450 miles per hour. Terrified? Now you know how the Stone Age inhabitants of the Mediterranean basin must have felt around 7000 BCE when the largest tidal wave in human history struck without warning. This super-tsunami wiped out coastal settlements along thousands of miles of coastline in Europe, Asia, and Africa. Although there are no casualty estimates, the death toll could have been in the millions.

Geologists believe the tidal wave was caused by a volcanic eruption by Sicily's Mount Etna that dumped 6 cubic miles of rock into the sea at more than 200 miles per hour. The force of this impact liquefied the seabed, triggering a giant submarine mudslide. The resulting 130-foot-tall waves reached the farthest parts of the Mediterranean basin in about three and a half hours. Because the sea has only one outlet, at the narrow straits of Gibraltar, tidal waves probably bounced back and forth from one side of the basin to the other for some time, like ripples in a giant pond.

Archaeologists have found the remains of a Neolithic fishing village at Atlit-Yam, on the eastern shore of the Mediterranean, which was obviously abandoned in a hurry. How can the archaeologists tell? Fleeing for their lives, the fishermen left their half-gutted catch to be buried under a mountain of mud, which preserved the fish remains for thousands of years.

Drinking: UP

Luckily for them, most ancient peoples had some kind of wine—meaning an alcoholic beverage stronger than beer, made from grapes or other fruit. Wine-making probably began shortly after 6000 BCE, when people started using clay to make pottery that was fired in ovens to create a hard, durable material for storage. Clay pots were used to store fruits and vegetables, and the first wine may have been the result of accidental fermentation of grapes or grape juice.

The earliest evidence of wine-making comes from the Zagros Mountains of northern Iran, where archaeologists excavated a kitchen with six clay jars that were being used to make some sort of wine between 5400 and 5000 BCE. One 2.5-gallon jar contained a yellow residue they believe is the remains of white wine made from green grapes.

Wine-making spread fast. The Sumerians were making wine by at least 3100 BCE, and clay seals depict Sumerian aristocracy enjoying small cups of wine along with beer served in clay jars—history's first double-fisters. Grapes weren't native to Egypt, but they were probably imported from Syria. Clay jars containing wine were included in Egyptian burial offerings, and by the second millennium BCE, there were five distinct "brands" of wine from Delta vineyards that dead pharaohs could sip in the afterlife.

On the other end of Asia, Chinese legend says that around 2100 BCE, Emperor Yidi invented a method for fermenting millet to make "yellow wine." In burial sites in Anyang and the Yellow River Basin, archaeologists found clay vessels dating to the Shang Dynasty that amazingly still contained actual liquid wine. The Shang-era wines were flavored with herbs, flowers, and tree resin.

And of course the ancient Greeks of the Minoan and Mycenaean civilizations were big fans of wine. Archaeologists have discovered a foot press for mashing grapes on Crete that is dated to about 1600 BCE. Greek legend is replete with references to the role of wine in the lives of gods, heroes, and ordinary mortals. Intoxication with wine may have facilitated shamanistic rituals, and extreme intoxication may have produced visions akin to those produced by hallucinogenic drugs such as peyote or mushrooms. A prominent example is the cult of Dionysus, the Greek god of wine, whose followers held ritual orgies where they tore live bulls apart with their teeth and bare hands.

– Comparative Religion –

Hey, Who Put All This Crap Here?

Early cultures had no friggin' idea where the universe came from, but this didn't stop them from making up some fairly bizarre explanations, which weirdly share more than a few similarities. In fact, so many details are shared between cultures that they suggest the existence of a primeval myth that originated with our earliest ancestors. Anyway, let's start at the beginning, with the Old Testament (even though it actually followed the Sumerians, but they can't stop us—because they're dead).

"In the beginning God created the heaven and the earth. And the earth was without form, and void; and darkness was upon the face of the deep. And the Spirit of God moved upon the face of the waters. And God said, Let there be light: and there was light." So far, so good. God

CRAZY ALTERNATIVE "SCIENCE" TIMELINE

For the sake of objectivity, mental_floss now presents an alternative timeline of the origins of the Universe based on the findings of so-called "physical scientists."

20 BILLION YEARS BCE: The Singularity. No one can really explain it.

20 BILLION YEARS BCE + 1 SECOND: Protons and neutrons form. Specifics still TBD.

20 BILLION YEARS BCE + 3 MINUTES: The nuclei of hydrogen and helium form from protons and neutrons.

19 BILLION YEARS BCE: Stars begin to form clusters called galaxies.

5 BILLION YEARS BCE: Our sun is born.

4.6 BILLION YEARS BCE: Our Earth forms from solar debris (which explains a lot).

4.53 BILLION YEARS BCE: Our Earth and a quasi-planet, Theia, merge and then separate messily, creating the moon.

4.4 BILLION YEARS BCE: Life forms in tide pools. Good luck suckers—you'll need it!

then says, "Let us make man in our image, after our likeness," and places his creation, Adam, in the Garden of Eden. Noticing Adam is lonely, God makes Eve from one of Adam's ribs to keep him company. It all goes awry when a malicious snake, Satan, talks Eve into eating an apple from the forbidden (yet curiously unguarded) Tree of Knowledge. Long story short: Adam also takes a bite, they become aware of sex, God boots them from the Garden, and humanity is doomed to suffer forever because of their ill-considered snack. Sounds reasonable, yes? Sure it does.

In the earlier Sumerian version, the universe begins as watery chaos in the form of Nammu, the goddess of the sea, who gives rise to the male sky, An, and the female earth, Ki. Their son, Enlil, becomes boss of the Sumerian pantheon by separating his parents and seizing control of his mother. (Freud, eat your heart out!) He and the other gods fashion human beings from mud mixed with the blood of a sacrificed god—"in their own image" kinda. Humans live as nomads at one with nature until Ninurta, the goddess of birth, tells them to build cities and fill the world with their descendants. (This may parallel Adam and Eve's departure from their natural state in Eden.)

In the Greek creation myth, the universe also begins as dark void, "Chaos," totally empty except for a giant black bird named Nyx. She lays a golden egg—it's unclear where, since the universe is a void, but . . . whatever—the egg then hatches and gives birth to Eros, the god of love. The upper half of the shell becomes the sky, Uranus, the lower half the earth, Gaea. Their descendants eventually become the gods, and eventually the chief god, Zeus, sends the titans

Prometheus and Epimetheus to create human beings and animals, telling them to give both special powers. However, Epimetheus gives all the powers to the animals, leaving nothing for humans, so Prometheus steals divine fire from Mount Olympus and gives it to men—far more power than they needed, allowing them to rule all the other animals.

The egg idea is a popular one, for obvious reasons. The Chinese creation myth says that the formless chaos of the universe slowly congealed into a black egg containing a human-like creature, Pangu, generally pictured with horns and fur (resembling the Greek god Pan). When Pangu hatched, he separated the two halves of the egg with a giant axe, making earth and heaven, which correspond to the two principal energies, yin and yang. When Pangu died, his breath became the sky, his eyes the sun and moon, his blood the rivers, and his body the land itself.

And Enough with the Flooding, Already!

Most cultures also have stories about a "great flood" sent by angry gods to destroy mankind in the distant past. In Western civilization the most well known example is the story of Noah in the Bible. When God got fed up with mankind's disobedience and wickedness, he chose Noah and his family to perform a special mission: to build a huge boat (an ark) to hold breeding pairs of every animal to repopulate the world after the deluge.

In the Sumerian version, the god Enki warns the king of Shuruppak, Ziusudra, that the gods have decided to destroy the world with a flood. Enki tells Ziusudra to build a large boat, where the king rides out the week-long flood. He prays to the gods, makes sacrifices, and is finally given immortality. According to Sumerian histories, the first Sumerian dynasty was founded by King Etana of Kish after this flood.

> *Aboard ship take thou the seed of all living things.*
> *That ship thou shall build;*
> *Her dimensions shall be to measure.*
> —Sumerian flood myth

According to the ancient Greeks, the mythical demigod Prometheus warned his son, Deucalion, that a great flood was coming, and instructed him to build a giant waterproof chest to hold himself and his wife, Pyrrha. The rest of humanity was drowned, but Deucalion and Pyrrha rode out the nine days of rain and flooding in their chest. As the flood subsided, they washed up on Mount Othrys, in northern Greece. Zeus told Deucalion and his wife to throw stones over their shoulders, which became men and women to repopulate the world.

Finally, Hindu mythology tells of a priest named Manu, who served one of India's first kings. Washing his hands in a river one day, Manu saved a tiny fish, who begged him for help. The grateful fish warned Manu that a giant flood was coming, so Manu built a ship on which he brought the "seeds of life" to plant again after the flood. The fish—actually a disguise for the chief god, Vishnu—then towed the vessel to a mountaintop sticking up above the water. Sound familiar?

Though it's impossible to know if these stories refer to the same actual event, a couple of historical events are plausible candidates. The most compelling explanation is the huge rise in sea levels that occurred at the end of the last Ice Age, beginning about twelve thousand years ago (10,000 BCE). The melting of the polar ice caps raised sea levels almost four hundred feet around the world—which must have made quite an impression.

········· **SO LONG, AND THANKS FOR ALL THE** ... ·········

Pretty Horses

Ten(ish) miles per hour while running—that's the top speed humans could travel before they tamed horses. Few other animals can support the weight of a man while moving at speeds of up to forty miles per hour, or carry him thousands of miles without collapsing from exhaustion. A human being on a horse has huge advantages in speed and mobility, so it's no surprise that the first people to tame horses also conquered the world.

Horses first evolved in North and South America about fifty-five million years ago, before migrating across the Bering Strait land bridge to Asia, Africa, and Europe. Around 8000 BCE a series of mass extinctions, probably due to the arrival of Native Americans, killed off large mammals in the Americas, including woolly mammoths, sabertooth tigers, and horses. In the meantime, rising sea levels submerged the land bridge, so horses couldn't migrate back to the Americas.

The earliest evidence of domesticated horses dates to around 4500 BCE. The first people to domesticate horses lived around the Caspian Sea, in the Ural or Caucasus Mountains of southern Russia. They tamed a subspecies of the common horse called the tarpan, native to the area around the Black and Caspian seas. By around 2000 BCE, they had invented horse-drawn chariots. Sometimes they sacrificed horses and chariots together in burial offerings for their dead chieftains.

Sharp Objects

In early human history, our only material for toolmaking was stone, which was pretty easy to find. Thus, the "Stone Age," which is actually divided into three periods. In the Paleolithic (Old Stone Age), humans chipped off pieces that were used as crude blades. In the Mesolithic (Middle Stone Age), the tools got more sophisticated, with craftsmen producing specific shapes, such as triangles and trapezoids, which were probably used with wooden arrows or axe handles. These led to refined tools such as double-edged arrowheads and highly polished axes during the Neolithic (New Stone Age).

The next step came when our clever ancestors figured out how to take nuggets of copper metal, which exist in nature, heat the metal to high temperatures, and then shape it into a blade or other useful shape by pounding it with rocks. The first copper implement on record dates to 6000 BCE, from a culture now known as the Old Copper Complex, which existed in modern-day Michigan and Wisconsin. Knowledge of copper-working arose independently in the Middle East, Asia, and Europe beginning in the fifth millennium BCE. Archaeologists call the period from 4300 to 3200 BCE the Copper Age, or Chalcolithic.

Though copper tools were a big improvement over stone, copper blades bent easily and lost their edge on hard surfaces. Then, around 3200 BCE, metalworkers in Susa, Iran, discovered that copper became much stronger when it was melted and mixed with another metal, tin. The resulting alloy, bronze, was stronger than either metal in its pure form.

Bronze gave ancient armies—the Sumerians, Egyptians, and Shang Dynasty Chinese—a big advantage over opponents armed with stone or copper weapons, cutting through enemies like a warm bronze knife through human butter (gross, but true). These weapons were produced in royal foundries (metal workshops) controlled by government officials. Because deposits of tin and copper don't usually occur in the same area, demand for bronze led to some of the world's first long-distance trade.

Sharp Flying Objects

Throwing rocks at animals and people is fine if you're a juvenile delinquent or a feral child, but if you're looking to do more than annoy your enemies, you're going to need something like a bow and arrow.

How early humans hit on this ingenious invention is a mystery, but it was a huge breakthrough. A taut bowstring could propel objects faster and more accurately than an unarmed man, giving the user a huge advantage in warfare and the hunt.

The earliest arrows on record, which were tipped with flint arrowheads, date to between 9000 and 8000 BCE, during the late Paleolithic (Old Stone Age), from the Ahrensburg Valley north of Hamburg, Germany. The oldest bows found come from nearby Denmark, where they were preserved in a bog. These five-foot elm bows probably had animal skin or plant fiber strings, though no one knows for sure.

During the Mesolithic (Middle Stone Age, beginning around 8000 BCE), arrows got longer—up to four feet—and probably went farther as bows became more powerful. By the Neolithic period, bows were made mostly of yew, a wood that is both strong and flexible, especially when soaked in water and heated. A Neolithic "caveman" whose body was preserved by ice in the Swiss Alps, nicknamed Oetzi (also Ötzi), carried an unfinished bow and bowstrings made of flax, a plant fiber. Around the same time, the Natufian culture of ancient Palestine and Syria used mechanical straighteners to make their arrows more accurate.

THE ICEMAN COMETH

Born around 3300 BCE and preserved in an Alpine glacier, Oetzi looked like just another poor dead bastard to modern observers. The body, discovered by hikers in 1991, was first thought to be a recent murder victim by Austrian authorities; actually, he was murdered ages ago. The Austrians damaged Oetzi as they pried him out of the ice with a jackhammer, letting passersby carry off various objects as souvenirs. Later, crowds touched the mummified body at the inquest, damaging it permanently with bacteria. The icing on the wake? It turns out the body was actually discovered on Italian soil, precipitating a not-so-minor diplomatic dispute. Oetzi is now on display at the South Tyrol Museum of Archaeology, in Bolzano, Italy.

By the time the world's first enduring civilizations popped up around 4000 BCE, bows and arrows were in use everywhere, and archers were an important part of organized armies. The ancient Egyptians' main opponents, the Hittites, were experts with the bow and arrow, pairing one or two archers with a driver in a horse-drawn chariot beginning in the eighteenth century BCE. Around the same time, the Assyrians created a larger, heavier chariot that could hold an archer, a driver, and two shield-bearers. The most revolutionary development came from Central Asia, where Indo-European nomads combined archery with another skill, horseback riding, sometime in the second millennium BCE. A man on horseback equipped with a bow and arrow was even more mobile, and deadlier, than an archer paired with someone else driving a chariot. When the Assyrians picked up on this skill, bad things happened to their neighbors.

Whatever Floats Your Boat

It doesn't take a genius to notice that wood floats, and a big enough piece of wood can support the weight of living things. Plants and animals have migrated across thousands of miles of salt water by hitching rides on tree trunks. With a little creative thinking, early humans discovered they could, too.

The first boats weren't too complicated: they were simply large tree trunks hollowed out with a stone or metal blade to make a space for rowers to sit. People in what are now the Netherlands, Denmark, Germany, and Finland were making dugout canoes around 9000 BCE. Some specimens from Denmark dated to around 5000 BCE are more than thirty feet long. They were probably used for cod fishing, whaling, and trade. They could also serve as coffins and funeral pyres for important people such as chieftains—a custom continued by the Vikings.

The design was so simple and effective that it was developed independently by different cultures all around the world. In Japan, people of the Jomon culture were using dugout canoes by 7500 BCE. In Africa the oldest dugout canoe on record comes from Nigeria, where it was carved around 6000 BCE. Tall trees in tropical forests allowed ambitious boaters to carve some huge canoes. The Taino people of the Caribbean made boats more than 90 feet long, manned by 80 rowers, and in Africa some dugout canoes were up to 120 feet long.

The undisputed masters of the dugout canoe are the Polynesians, who get the prize for greatest distance traveled. Their typical seagoing dugout was "just" thirty to sixty feet in length, but it could carry families and livestock thousands of miles across the open ocean. People from Southeast Asia began fanning out across the islands of the South Pacific around 1500 BCE. One wave of settlement jumped from New Guinea to Samoa—a distance of twenty-five-hundred miles. Then, between 400 and 700 CE, the Polynesians did it again, making another twenty-five-hundred-mile trek from Samoa to Hawaii. The Polynesians regularly traveled back and forth between islands for long-distance trade. To navigate these huge distances they created detailed maps made of twigs, seashells, and stones that showed the positions of islands, currents, and stars.

The Goddess of Beer

One of the first things humans did with grain was ferment it to make alcohol. Beer was a source of nutrition, with the bonus of giving drinkers a buzz. There's evidence of Sumerians brewing a primitive beer as far back as 3000 BCE. In fact, they liked beer so much that it got its own patron goddess, an important figure called Nin-Kasi, and a lot of the information we have on the Sumerians comes from religious texts devoted to her.

The first mention of Nin-Kasi appears around 2900 BCE. Her name means "Lady Who Fills the Mouth" or "She Who Satisfies the Desires." She was the brewer of beer, but also the beer itself. The deity of beer was a goddess because most Sumerian brewers and tavern keepers were women, and most early brewing took place in the home. Siduri, one of the minor goddesses in the Sumerian pantheon, was a tavern keeper.

Indeed, it wasn't just humans who liked beer: the gods and goddesses were also big fans. According to Sumerian myth, Enki, the god of springs and well water, got drunk with Inanna and gave her some of his most important powers—a move he later regretted. The gods also passed around a beer jug at their banquet in Babylon to celebrate the founding of the city.

WE LIKE TO PARTY

There's no question the ancient Sumerians used beer to get drunk and go wild. They were very open about it, even leaving documents depicting their drunken activities. A clay placard from around 1800 BCE found in Babylon depicts a woman drinking beer from a jar with a straw while having sexual intercourse. And a poem in praise of Nin-Kasi from around the same time reads, "I feel wonderful, drinking beer, in a blissful mood."

The Great-Granddaddy of Rock 'n' Roll

Music might be the biggest mystery of the ancient world. Archaeologists have found musical instruments and depictions of people playing them, but it's hard to figure out what the music sounded like. To make things even more mysterious, most early music was probably unaccompanied singing.

Our first musical instrument is ourselves: we can sing (well, some of us) and clap our hands or stomp our feet for percussion. A lot of early music probably consisted of prayers chanted by a priest, or the ritual recitation of oral history by an older member of the village passing along stories from previous generations. As in contemporary religious ceremonies, there may have been "call and response" parts where the audience repeated key phrases or answered "questions."

The first actual musical instrument on record in China is a bone flute at least seven thousand years old, followed by "pan" pipes and bronze bells. In ancient Egypt the female relatives of royal officials played the harp and sang at ceremonies honoring gods and dead people. Beautiful female singers also entertained the wealthy at banquets. Meanwhile making instruments was a prestigious leisure activity enjoyed by the rich and powerful: the coronation inscription of Pharaoh Thutmose III says he made "a splendid harp wrought with silver, gold, lapis lazuli, malachite, and every splendid costly stone."

There's a lot less information about the music of ordinary people, though we have some clues. In Egypt, women would chant to pass the time while grinding grain. In Sumeria, regular folks would unwind at taverns with an early form of beer and entertainment provided by female musicians—possibly also prostitutes. One seal from around 2500 BCE found in Ur depicts a man and woman drinking beer while a woman plays a bull-headed lyre.

Looking Dope

Alongside wheat, hemp was probably the first plant cultivated by humans for its useful properties—and no, they weren't using it to get high. Hemp fiber stripped from the stems of the plant is a strong, durable material for making clothes. In fact, the oldest evidence of human handicraft (other than stone tools) is a piece of hemp cloth from Catal Huyuk, in Turkey, that's about ten thousand years old.

Paleobotanists (scientists who study ancient plant remains) believe hemp originated in Central Asia, somewhere in a range covering Afghanistan, Tibet, and Kazakhstan. With human help, hemp

YOU DON'T WANT TO SMOKE THAT . . .

So what is the difference between marijuana and hemp, anyway? First of all, here's what they have in common: both are varieties of *Cannabis sativa*, and both smell like, well, weed. The main difference is their history of human cultivation. Marijuana was bred to maximize its narcotic properties for thousands of years, while hemp was bred to maximize its useful fibers. Thus the plants are literally opposites within the *Cannabis* genus. Marijuana plants tend to be short, measuring eight to ten feet tall at most, with large reproductive buds containing up to 20 percent tetrahydrocannabinol (THC). Meanwhile, hemp plants can grow to twenty-five feet tall, with never more than 1 percent THC.

Note: Even though George Washington advised farmers to "make the most of the hemp seed and sow it everywhere," American farmers are still being locked up for growing the plant!

spread east and west simultaneously, arriving in China by 10,000 BCE, Mesopotamia by 8000 BCE, Europe by 1500 BCE, and India by 800 BCE. Over time, human cultivation led to the creation of distinct biological strains in these different areas.

Hemp spread because it was incredibly useful. Around 2500 BCE in China it replaced much weaker bamboo fiber as material for bowstrings, with Chinese royalty and nobility devoting large amounts of land to hemp cultivation. There's "ghost" evidence that China actually beat Catal Huyuk on the hemp cultivation timeline: marks left by knotted hemp cords appear on Chinese pottery twelve thousand years old, though the hemp itself burned away.

From ancient times newly crowned emperors of Japan have worn special hemp clothing when they perform a special ceremony called *Daijosai*, which confirms their new position. In the *Daijosai*, the emperor offers sacrifices to Amaterasu, the female goddess of the sun in the Shinto religion. The sacrifices include grains, livestock, and silkworms, representing Amaterasu's authority over food and clothing. Clothing the emperor in hemp—source of both food and clothing—is a sign of respect for the goddess.

..... AND THANKS, BUT NO THANKS, FOR ... .

A Hole in the Head

Have you ever had a headache so bad you wanted to bore a hole in your skull to let the evil spirits out? No? Well, then it's a good thing you didn't live five thousand years ago, because that was an accepted and very popular medical technique.

The practice, called trepanning, has been around since at least twelve thousand years ago. Neolithic shamans, or medicine men, treated various ailments—possibly including migraines, brain tumors, and insanity—by boring a hole about the size of a half-dollar coin in the rear or top of the skull. Evidence of the practice has been found all over the world, with trepanned skulls discovered in Asia, Europe, Africa, Australia, and North and South America. It was apparently a favorite treatment: at one Neolithic burial site in France, 40 out of 120 skulls had been trepanned.

Amazingly, many subjects survived the procedure, which was performed using a sharp rock and no anesthetic. In fact, the patients may have demanded it: some disorders affecting the brain, such as hematomas, create a feeling of intense, excruciating pressure inside the skull, and trepanning may work to relieve this symptom. Even more remarkable, some skulls found had multiple bore holes, meaning the procedure was performed several times.

The popularity of trepanning continued long after the end of the Neolithic period. It was still standard practice in ancient Greece, when the physician Hippocrates wrote a manual for performing the operation correctly. Roman doctors would grind up the pieces of bone they extracted through trepanning for use in medicines to treat other ailments. Trepanning was practiced in Europe as late as the eighteenth century.

Grave Robbing

Despite the elaborate security precautions, virtually every single tomb in the Egyptian pyramids was looted by grave robbers. And the robbers weren't just looking for gold and jewels: they wanted it *all*, meaning dozens of mummies were looted along with their treasures.

At the pyramid of the Pharaoh Khfare, sacrilegious thieves replaced the mummy with animal bones. Even the "Father of Pyramids," Khufu's Great Pyramid at Giza, was looted—particularly ironic because Khufu had ordered extra security measures for his pyramid after his father's tomb was robbed. Khufu's designer, Ankhaf, changed the location of the royal burial chamber midway through the giant project, and included several false or "dummy" chambers to confuse grave robbers.

Robbing pyramids was a large-scale undertaking, calling for hundreds of men to bore through tons of stone. At the pyramid of the Pharaoh Djedefre you can still see the passage grave robbers tunneled through the stone to get at the pharaoh's burial treasure. A long tunnel at the tomb of Senusret I, whose twists and turns evade granite blocks intended to frustrate robbers, suggests that the robbers were familiar with the pyramid's design—maybe from an inside source.

The thieves grew bolder as time went on: in the pyramid of Pharaoh Huni, at Meidum, sloppy tomb robbers left behind a small wooden hammer propping up the stone lid of the pharaoh's sarcophagus. Even more audacious, the thieves who looted the pyramid of Senusret III left

YOU MIGHT NEED TWO SPOONFULS OF SUGAR . . .

Who knew that mummies had medicinal properties? Actually, they don't. And they can be incredibly toxic. But that didn't stop stupid people from grinding them up and using them to "cure" incurable diseases. From the twelfth to the nineteenth centuries CE, wealthy, not-so-bright Europeans paid top dollar for "mummia" to make tea or eat straight up for any variety of ailments, including epilepsy, paralysis, bruises, and migraines.

behind crude graffiti depicting themselves on the walls of the royal burial chamber, an apparent taunt to the descendants of the dead pharaoh.

It's unclear if royal priests were actively involved in the looting of the pyramids, or were merely incompetent. However, there's some evidence of deceit. When the tomb of Queen Hetepheres, the wife of Snefru, was robbed during the reign of her son Khufu, the priests in charge of reburying the pharaoh's mother interred an empty casket to cover up the fact that they couldn't find her body . . . and they never told Khufu the truth.

Keeping It in the Family

In the ancient world, it was all about banging your sister . . . if you were rich enough. Cultural anthropologists say there is a universal "taboo" against incest, with every culture in the world condemning sexual intercourse between family members—but the rulers of the ancient world clearly didn't get the memo.

You might think religious authorities would frown on incest, but it's pretty hard to condemn what the gods themselves are doing. In the Mesopotamian pantheon, the chief god Enlil slept with his mother, Ki, to create life, and his brother Enki did him one better: he slept with his daughter, with the granddaughter thus conceived, and then with his great-granddaughter from that relationship!

No surprise, then, that the Sumerian royal family was pretty relaxed about family members knocking the boots. To preserve royal blood and keep power in the family, it was standard practice for Sumerian princes to marry their half-sisters by their father. But there was a double-standard: incest among regular folks was strictly forbidden, with punishments ranging from exile to being burned alive.

The Egyptians really went to town. Again, the gods led the way: the god of death and resurrection, Osiris, was married to his sister,

AS LONG AS IT'S IN THE NAME OF GOD . . .

The practice of incest carried over from Sumerian culture into early Judaism. Abraham, the founder of Judaism, was a Sumerian prince who gave up the good life to preach his vision of a single all-powerful god. But he didn't give up Sumerian royal habits: his wife, Sarah, was also his half-sister. Of course there's plenty of incest to go around in the Old Testament. When it looked like the Jewish people were in danger of extinction, the daughters of Abraham's nephew, Lot, got their father drunk and conceived two children by him.

Isis. And just for fun the Egyptians threw necrophilia into the mix: after she reassembled the dead body of her brother-husband, Isis impregnated herself with his semen and gave birth to Horus, who succeeded Osiris as ruler of Egypt.

By the time of the pharaohs, men were firmly in control of the family, but royal blood was still passed by the women. Incestuous marriages helped preserve royal blood, keeping property in the family. The Egyptians' attitude is clear in their written language of hieroglyphics. The word *sister* could also mean "lover," "mistress," or "wife"!

The pharaohs didn't hesitate to marry their sisters (and daughters) and conceive children with them. Because they possessed royal blood, the daughters of the pharaoh weren't allowed to marry beneath their position—which pretty much eliminated any prospects besides good ol' dad. One of the greatest Egyptian pharaohs, Ramesses II, married four of his own daughters: Bintanath, Meritamen, Nebettawi, and Hentmire. Bintanath is known to have borne him at least one child.

· **BY THE NUMBERS** ·

125,000	estimated world population 100,000 BCE
1–10 million	estimated world population 10,000 BCE
100 million	estimated world population 3000 BCE
300 million	estimated world population 1000 BCE
12	number of subspecies of the genus *Homo* (man) that existed before the arrival of *Homo sapiens sapiens*
1	Number of women living in 150,000 BCE to whom all human mitochondrial DNA can be traced
20	average human life expectancy 100,000 years ago
22	average human life expectancy in Sumeria 5,000 years ago
75	average American life expectancy in 2006
5'1"	average height of a human male 10,000 years ago
5'9"	average height of an American man today
1,500	average daily caloric intake of Stone Age shell fisherman 10,000 years ago
2,700	average daily caloric intake of a contemporary American man
1 in 2	chance that a newborn child would die before the age of five, 10,000 years ago

133	number of times the word *smite* appears in the Old Testament
190	number of times the word *wrath* appears in the Old Testament
3,000	number of years Egypt was ruled by the pharaohs
170	number of pharaohs in that period
31	number of dynasties that ruled Egypt in that period
20,000	number of inscribed clay tablets found in the royal library at Ur

2
CHAOS AND CONTROL
(1500 BCE–500 BCE)

IN A NUTSHELL

If you're a "glass half empty" type of person, you might say human history has been an endless series of disasters, with sporadic breaks to let us catch our breath. And even the optimists among us have to admit that this era was a catastrophe. In fact, it got so bad that some historians call it the ancient "Dark Ages."

Just when it looked like everything was calming down in the wake of the Indo-European invasions, it all went to hell again around 1500 BCE. Leading the way were mysterious peoples who attacked established civilizations across Europe and the Middle East. Some of these groups were Indo-European, but their invasions are distinct from the Indo-European or "Aryan" migrations that began almost a thousand years earlier. For the most part, the reasons for their migrations are unknown.

In the Middle East, a group of seafaring invaders known only as the Sea Peoples invaded Egypt and the Hittite Empire of central Turkey around 1200 BCE. The Sea Peoples were the most serious threat faced by either kingdom—in fact the Hittites collapsed. But nobody knows exactly where they came from, or why they suddenly invaded. Eventually the threat receded, but the chaos they created led to the rise to power of an extraordinarily cruel group of conquerors known as the Assyrians.

Meanwhile, to the west, the Mycenaean civilization of Greece was overthrown by foreigners (or were they?) known as Dorians. These invaders from north of Greece soon controlled most of the Greek peninsula. The Dorians and the Sea Peoples may have been one and the same, but there's no way to be sure, as so little is known about them.

Although they're not usually included in histories of the other barbarian upheavals of the time, the Jews fled Egypt during this period. They established a Jewish kingdom in Canaan, their Promised Land, but soon discovered that their neighbors there, the Assyrians and Babylonians, were even less friendly than the Egyptians.

And far to the south, sub-Saharan Africa saw the migration of the

Bantu people from modern-day Nigeria into the rainforests of Central Africa—and beyond. Like the Assyrians in the Middle East, the Bantu were helped by iron weapons, which gave them a tactical advantage over Stone Age peoples from the Congo River to South Africa.

The chaos didn't affect every part of the planet. During this same time, China enjoyed a long period of stability under the Zhou Dynasty, and Central America saw the flowering of its first civilization, the Olmecs, who created a glittering urban culture with traditions later embraced by the Mayans and the Aztecs.

·············· **WHAT HAPPENED WHEN** ··············

1550 BCE Volcanic explosion of the island Thera devastates Mediterranean.

1500 BCE The Jews leave Canaan for Egypt.

1300 BCE Olmec civilization begins.

1235 BCE Athens founded.

1200 BCE Sea Peoples attack Hittite kingdom and Egypt; Dorians invade Greece; Jews flee Egypt.

1122 BCE China's Zhou Dynasty founded.

1000 BCE Kingdom of the Jews divided. Zoroaster is born (probably). Bantu expansion begins.

900 BCE Olmecs begin building pyramids.

783 BCE Assyrians conquer Jewish kingdom of Israel (Canaan).

771 BCE Western Zhou Dynasty ends.

750 BCE Dorian kingdom of Sparta founded.

729 BCE Assyrians conquer Babylon.

671 BCE Assyrians conquer Egypt.

625 BCE Assyrian empire collapses.

607 BCE Babylonians burn Jerusalem, kidnap the Jews.

554 BCE Cyrus the Great seizes power in Persia and Medea.

539 BCE Cyrus occupies Babylon and frees the Jews.

The Sea Peoples:

Somewhere in the Mediterranean . . .

The trouble started with a bang: the eruption around 1550 BCE of a Greek island in the Aegean Sea called Thera. The island was blown out of existence by an explosion that threw more than 16 cubic miles of debris into the air and sea, triggering a massive tidal wave. At least 120 feet tall, the wave ripped across the Mediterranean, probably killing hundreds of thousands of people. This catastrophe may be the basis for the legend of Atlantis.

In the wake of the tsunami, a loose confederation of southern European tribes, the Sea Peoples, began migrating into the eastern Mediterranean. Some historians think the Sea Peoples originally lived in the Balkan Peninsula, but they may also have come from southern Italy and Sicily; one subgroup, the Denyen, were probably Greek. The Sea Peoples had no written language, and left no hints as to where they came from. Civilizations such as Egypt spent most of their time fighting the Sea Peoples. From their written records, we know they knew the names of some of these enemy tribes—Peleset, Tjeker, Shekelesh, and Weshesh—but that was about it.

The first civilization to go was the Minoan culture of Crete, which actually may first have been wiped out by the tidal wave. Archaeologists have found the remains of wrecked ports and stone walls that were knocked over by the water. In the wake of the disaster, Crete was resettled by the Sea Peoples as they fanned out across the eastern Mediterranean.

The Sea Peoples hit the Hittite empire to the east, then Egypt to the south, around 1200 BCE. Records from these areas paint a picture of aggressive foreigners who greedily plundered gold and precious objects. They seemed to be both pirates and refugees. By all accounts they were fierce warriors. One Egyptian description remembered, "No land could stand before their arms . . . They laid their hands upon the land to the ends of the earth . . ."

According to Hittite records, the attackers massed their ships off the southwest tip of Turkey, raiding coastal cities and then heading inland to attack core territories. The assault was sudden and unexpected: at one coastal city in Syria named Ugarit, the governor received a letter on a clay tablet warning of the foreign invaders, but Ugarit was destroyed before he could react.

The Sea Peoples' attacks led to the collapse of the Hittite empire, weakening it so much that the Hittites' rivals from northeast Turkey were able to capture and burn the capital, Hattusas, around 1200

BCE. Then the Sea Peoples headed south, sweeping across the modern countries of Lebanon and Israel before slamming into Egypt.

The first serious attack came in 1208 BCE, when four groups allied with tribes from Libya launched an all-out assault on the Nile Delta. Egypt's struggle with the Sea Peoples lasted more than thirty years, defining the reigns of seven pharaohs, devastating the kingdom's economic center, and almost causing a civil war. After many battles, the Egyptians had the situation under control by 1175 BCE. Ramesses III said he scored two decisive victories over the Sea Peoples on land and sea, then forced the Peleset tribe to settle in Egyptian-controlled Palestine, where they became known as the Philistines (both names probably come from "Peleset"). But in reality this might just be PR spin: the Peleset probably settled voluntarily, and then simply refused to leave. As the Philistines, they were remembered in the Old Testament as a foreign people who used iron weapons, destroyed Jewish holy places, and stole sacred objects.

> They were coming toward Egypt, with all in flames . . . But the heart of this god, the lord of the gods, was prepared . . . I organized a fleet in the Nile Delta as strong as a wall . . . They were completely equipped both fore and aft with brave, well-armed fighters, Egypt's best, like roaring lions upon the mountains . . .
> —Ramesses III, on fighting the Sea Peoples

Although Ramesses III triumphed over the Sea Peoples, Egypt never fully recovered from the damage. A series of bad harvests resulted in economic chaos, and late in his reign Ramesses III discovered a conspiracy against him by his wife, Queen Tey, and son, Pentewere. They were tried for treason and executed along with more than forty senior officials. The coup was averted, but the weakened kingdom would be easy prey for new empires rising in the east.

The Dorian Invasion:
Return of the Heraclidae

While the Sea Peoples were busy spanking the Hittites, foreigners called Dorians invaded the Bronze Age Mycenaean civilization of Greece. The northerners arrived in Greece around 1200 BCE, and because they came from the same area as the Sea Peoples, historians speculate that the two were related.

The Dorians' origins are mysterious, with most information coming from Greek mythology. According to their own oral history, the Dorians were descendants of the mythical hero Hercules (*Heracles*, in

Greek). Hercules, the story goes, was robbed of his kingship in southern Greece by an evil Mycenaean king, Eurystheus. Seeking allies, Hercules traveled to northern Greece, where he performed superhuman tasks to make the area safe for human habitation, such as killing monsters. While he was there he also impregnated dozens of local princesses, and his various offspring founded a group of noble families collectively known as the Heraclidae. The Dorians claimed that they were descendants of Hercules, finally returning to reclaim his rightful inheritance in southern Greece.

This mythological story, called the "return of the Heraclidae," seems to hint at real historical events. But this is all speculation, because the Dorian invasion was the beginning of a Greek "Dark Ages" that left few historical clues. The large cities such as Mycenae, Thebes, and Tiryns shrank and even disappeared. Traditional arts such as pottery, weaving, and sculpture withered, and Greek society reverted to small-scale farming and animal herding. As long-distance trade routes collapsed, bronze tools and weapons were replaced by those of iron. Most important, written language vanished for about five hundred years—meaning we know very little about this part of Greek history. It's too bad, because this period saw one of the most important developments in the history of Western civilization: the founding of the "classical" Greek city-states.

Athens:
Rockin' Democracy

Native Greek "Hellenes" founded Athens around 1235 BCE—conveniently just in time for the Dorian invasion. The Hellenes of Athens seem to have resisted the northern barbarians in many ways—for example, Athenians always distinguished their dialect, "Ionian," from "Doric" Greek, which they considered rough and primitive.

The people of Athens pushed back against their own aristocrats by establishing governments elected by the people, although they had to proceed cautiously at first. In the eighth century BCE, the regular people reached a compromise with the aristocrats to get rid of the king, replacing their hereditary monarchs with elected "archons," selected from the aristocracy. Then the Athenians slowly limited the power of the aristocrats: at first the archons ruled for ten years at a time, but in 683 BCE their term was reduced to one year.

Many of Athens's democratic traditions were formalized in a constitution in 590 BCE by a wise leader named Solon. Later, in the sixth century BCE, under the leadership of an ambitious politician named Cleisthenes, the Athenians finally established a system of collective rule by all the male citizens, called "democracy"—from the Greek words *demos* ("people") and *kratos* ("power"). Any citizen could vote in the assembly, and aristocrats had no special privileges, though they retained their wealth—and with it, great power.

The Athenians were very protective of their democracy because the aristocrats occasionally staged coups to overthrow it. When they were in charge, the aristocrats formed an "oligarchy," or government by a small group relying on repression. The aristocrats pursued policies that angered regular Athenians—for example, giving themselves sweetheart deals from the public funds. (Shocking, we know.)

From humble origins as a sleepy "one-horse town," Athens slowly grew into a cosmopolitan city of farmers, sailors, and merchants who built a system of trade alliances dominating the Aegean Sea. Beginning in the ninth century BCE, they sent colonists to the west coast of Anatolia (Turkey), across the Aegean Sea. These settlers founded "Ionian" Greek colonies, culturally related to Athens, which generally followed Athenian leadership. During this time, other Greek cities were also establishing colonies around the Mediterranean Sea, led by Corinth and Argos.

The Athenian army was composed of "hoplites," citizen-soldiers responsible for arming themselves with a helmet, spear, and small shield. Although their equipment was about as good as that of the Spartans, on land the Athenians were no match for their warlike southern neighbors. They didn't have much time to practice, while the Spartans did nothing but.

> An Athenian is always an innovator, quick to form a resolution and quick to carry it out. You, on the other hand, are good at keeping things as they are . . . While you are hanging back, they never hesitate; while you stay at home they are always abroad . . . And so they go on working away . . . seldom enjoying their possessions because they are always adding to them. In a word, they are by nature incapable of living a quiet life or allowing anyone else to do so.
> —An emissary from Corinth, in front of the Spartan assembly, comparing Sparta with Athens

The Athenians' strong point was their navy. The navy was made up of galleys powered by sails and oarsmen, called triremes ("three-fitted" in Greek, referring to the three lines of oars stacked on top of each other). The triremes were about 120 feet long, rowed by 170 oarsmen sitting on benches of three different heights. The ships were equipped with long bronze underwater "beaks" for ramming enemy ships.

Athens began investing in ships in the sixth century BCE, and by 480 BCE it had the most powerful navy in the Greek world. Some wealthy citizens paid to build entire squadrons. However, the poor citizens who manned the oars sometimes went on strike, paralyzing the fleet.

Sparta:
One Badass City-State

That sort of thing would never be possible in Sparta. The Dorian invaders who conquered the southern Greek city of Messenia in the eighth century BCE set up a rigid class system separating a tiny group of "citizens" from a giant population of native "helots," who worked in slavery-like conditions. The system became even more brutal after the helots tried to revolt in the seventh century BCE. By the fifth century BCE, there were about ten thousand citizens versus perhaps two hundred thousand helots. The Spartan hierarchy was incredibly strict: helots had no political rights or freedom of movement, and gave up half of every harvest to the Spartan overlords.

> They would gladly eat the Spartans raw.
> —Xenophon, on Spartan helots

The Spartans were equally hard on themselves, creating a military society with one goal: training invincible soldiers to control the helots. Spartan life centered on military preparation. Weak and deformed newborn children were exposed to the elements and left to die by order of the state. Boys entered military school at the age of seven, where their first task was to weave a mat of coarse river reeds they would sleep on for the rest of their lives. They were forced to run for miles while older boys flogged them, sometimes dying of exhaustion, and were encouraged to kill helots as part of a rite of passage. At age twenty, after thirteen years of training, the surviving young men finally became soldiers. They served in the Spartan army until age sixty, living in communal barracks, where they shared meals and bunked together.

They were allowed to marry but rarely saw their wives until they "graduated" to "equals," at age thirty. Ironically, this gender separation helped Spartan women accumulate property and power. Women are believed to have owned about 40 percent of Sparta's agricultural land and were at least sometimes responsible for managing the labor of helots, making them far more "liberated" than other Greek women.

The Spartans created one of history's more unusual governments. Somewhat like in Athens, all male citizens age thirty and up formed

The basic story of Homer's *Iliad* is pretty well known: the beautiful Helen is "kidnapped" by Paris, the prince of Troy. Enraged, her husband, King Menelaus, calls on his allies, the Mycenaean Greek kings, to punish the Trojans and get his wife back. But this war was probably just one part of the broader upheavals caused by the Sea Peoples and Dorians around the same time. So who's who in this big mess? (Keep in mind that all these theories are based partly on Greek mythology, which freely mixes fact and fiction.)

One theory says that the Dorians and the Sea Peoples were both related to the Trojans. This could make sense, because Hercules, the Dorians' heroic ancestor, also had a son with Queen Omphale of Lydia—a Trojan ally in western Turkey that was sometimes confused with Troy itself. The ancient Greeks also said that the Phrygians (another group often confused with the Trojans) migrated to Asia Minor from Thrace (Bulgaria). Several groups claiming descent from Hercules could have migrated from Thrace into Asia Minor and Greece simultaneously.

But...what if this is all backward? Could the *Greeks* be the Sea Peoples? This makes at least as much sense: after all, it's the Greeks who sail across the sea, besiege Troy, and burn it to the ground in classic Sea People fashion. Also, one of the common "nicknames" for the Greeks is the *Danaoi*, meaning "descendants of Danaos," an early mythical hero—and scholars believe that these people are the same as the Denyen, one of the Sea Peoples mentioned by the Egyptians.

If the Greeks are the Sea Peoples, what about the Dorians? According to one Greek myth, when the Mycenaean Greeks were off fighting the Trojans, the Dorian descendants of Hercules were reclaiming their "rightful inheritance" in southern Greece; in other words, when the Mycenaeans were out of town, the Dorians sneaked in and stole their stuff. But according to another legend, the "return of the Heraclidae" happened a full eighty years *after* the Trojan War ended. So there's that.

What *really* happened? Probably some combination of all the above: the Sea Peoples may have been a mix of Greeks, Trojans, Dorians, and a bunch of other folks who lived in the area, fleeing multiple catastrophes and creating even more catastrophes as they did so (the "cascade" or "big friggin' mess" theory). But it's anyone's guess!

an assembly. But that's where the similarities ended. In Sparta, the assembly picked a council of twenty-eight nobles, all over the age of sixty, to advise not one but two kings. This dual-kingship was hereditary, but if the rulers were incompetent, they could be deposed by the real bosses of Sparta—a group of five powerful men called ephors, who were elected annually by the assembly, leading it in wartime, when the kings were away.

Phoenicians:
History's First Globetrotters

Generally speaking, the ancients were pretty lousy sailors: in small wooden ships, with only the position of the sun and the shore to navigate by, they were safest staying off the open sea altogether. But there was one exception: the Phoenicians.

The Phoenicians came from among the oldest Semitic tribes, and created a civilization on the Mediterranean's east coast. Expert sailors, they plied regional trade routes connecting the metropolitan centers of Egypt and Mesopotamia to olive oil, wine, marble, tin, and agricultural products from North Africa and Europe.

To help them cross hundreds of miles of open water, the Phoenicians may have invented the astrolabe, a complex device modeling the movements of the sun and stars that was later credited to a Greek inventor. Contemporaries noted the Phoenicians' ability to sail at night and out of sight of land, which allowed them to deliver in-demand goods to urban marketplaces twice as fast as their competitors.

Despite their huge impact on the Mediterranean basin's economy and culture, the constantly feuding Phoenician cities remained weak and divided. This made them easy targets for their neighbors, especially Egypt. The pharaohs first conquered Phoenicia around 1500 BCE, as a buffer against the Indo-European Hittite Empire in central Turkey. But by 1400 BCE, the pha-

THE UNITED STATES OF PHOENICIA?

In the 1840s, American fraudsters planted silver-plated copies of Carthaginian coins across North America, claiming the Phoenicians had discovered the New World about seventeen hundred years before Columbus!

raohs had lost control of the region to Hittite chariot armies advancing from the north.

In the long run, being weak may have had its benefits. The Phoenicians probably acquired their great sailing expertise after being conquered by the Sea Peoples, who arrived in this area around 1200 BCE. The Phoenicians emerged as a major sea power by about 1100 BCE, with a golden age lasting until 800 BCE—a period that saw the founding of the major Phoenician colonies, including Carthage, which created its own "Punic" Empire (the word is derived from *Phoenician*) covering Algeria, Tunisia, Libya, Sicily, and Spain.

In their heyday, the Phoenicians sailed farther than any other ancient people. From their bases in modern-day Syria, Lebanon, and Israel, Phoenician merchants reached Britain and the Canary Islands, some seven hundred miles off Spain's Atlantic Coast, by the eighth century BCE. Around 600 BCE, a Phoenician fleet sailed around Africa from east to west at the command of the Egyptian pharaoh Necho II—an incredible feat. And a trove of Phoenician coins in the Azores suggests the Phoenicians located those mid-Atlantic islands by 200 BCE.

Bantu? Us, Too!

Today almost all Africans living south of the equator—some 400 million people—speak one of 450 languages in the "Niger-Congo" linguistic family. The name of the largest subgroup, Bantu, simply means "people" in most of these languages. But the Bantu in question didn't arrive in the southern half of Africa until the first millennium BCE.

Although there are no certain dates, the Bantu expansion seems to have begun by around 1000 BCE, when people from Nigeria migrated to the south and east, settling the rain forests and plains country of Cameroon, the Congo River Basin, and the African "Great Lakes" region (Tanzania, Rwanda, and Burundi). By 0 BCE, they had reached Zambia and Angola, more than two thousand miles to the south.

The Bantus' unstoppable spread was driven by a population boom resulting from agriculture, and from military superiority due to iron weaponry. The first evidence of large-scale land clearing for agriculture in the Bantu homeland in Nigeria dates to about 3000 BCE. The "proto-Bantu" cultivated native fruits and vegetables, including yams, melons, coconut, and oil palms, and grains such as rice, millet, and sorghum. These early tribes also imported domestic cows, goats, and pigs from Mediterranean cultures to the north, across the Sahara Desert. It was probably demand for more farmland and pastures that drove the Bantu migrations.

But the conquest of new lands was made possible only by their

WE'RE NOT RACIST, WE'RE JUST ... OKAY, WE'RE TOTALLY RACIST

The apartheid government of South Africa used the word *Bantu* to refer to South Africans who spoke Bantu-derived languages (about 80 percent of the population), giving the word a pejorative meaning that it still carries today. By using the word, white racists also suggested that the Bantus were themselves "foreigners" in South Africa, with the implication that whites had just as much right to rule the country as they did—a classic divide-and-conquer tactic from British colonial times. Unsurprisingly, nobody bought it.

knowledge of ironworking—refining, heating, and shaping iron ore. This required the invention of special high-temperature furnaces made from stone and clay, often built on hilltops, with tall "reverse chimneys" taking advantage of wind as a natural bellows (to make the fire hotter). In the twenty-first century, these furnaces dot the open grasslands south of the Sahara Desert, the "savannah," with some of the earliest examples dating to around 1500 BCE in central Niger (north of Nigeria). Iron working had spread to southern Nigeria and northern Cameroon by around 800 BCE.

Iron tools made agriculture more efficient and allowed the clearing of thick tropical forests, while iron weapons gave the Bantu a huge combat advantage over Stone Age tribes. Their hapless opponents were pushed into increasingly marginal terrain, eventually ceding all the prime land to the Bantu. The descendants of these original Bantu-defeated natives still live in isolated Stone Age cultures today, including the pygmies of the Congo rain forest and the bushmen of the Kalahari Desert.

The Bantu expansion across Africa probably wasn't all violent: anthropologists point out that languages can be spread through trade and peaceful migration, too. It's true that today Bantu speakers have varied ethnic backgrounds, suggesting that intermarriage and peaceful cultural exchanges did occur. But once again, because they left no written records, it's hard to know exactly what happened.

One thing's for sure: Bantu-derived languages are complicated as hell. Like most European languages, each word has a "gender"—but rather than European languages' traditional three genders (masculine, feminine, and neuter), Bantu languages have ten to fifteen. That means ten to fifteen different rules for modifying a noun depending on its place in a sentence! Nonetheless, English managed to pick up a number of Bantu words, including *banjo, bongos, jumbo, mambo, marimba, safari, samba,* and of course the always popular *zombie*.

China:
Gettin' Some Mo' Zhou

The Zhou (pronounced "Joe") Dynasty was a mixed blessing for China. On the one hand, the early

---

FOWL PLAY

Kings have given up their power for all kinds of stuff: women, money, wine, etc. But how about a pretty bird? According to legend, King Zhao was lured into Chu territory with the promise of seeing a rare bird. Being a nice guy, the king of Chu guaranteed Zhao's safety during the visit, and being incredibly naïve, Zhao believed him. Only after crossing into Chu did Zhao realize it was a trap. He died trying to flee across the Han River in a leaky old boat.

kings of Zhou united China in a feudal (well . . . sort of feudal) system. But subsequent kings got greedy. They created a centralized bureaucracy and a tax-collection system that threatened the regional nobles. As we'll see later, this was a recipe for disaster (after disaster after disaster).

There are actually two phases of the Zhou Dynasty: the first, "Western" phase, so-called because it was ruled from the western capital of Hao; and the second "Eastern" phase, after the capital was moved to the eastern city of Luoyi. The first phase was all good, and the second phase was pretty much crap.

The Western Zhou Dynasty began in 1122 BCE, when the Ji family united central China through warfare, colonization, and political maneuvering. This family kept the area around the Yellow River Valley locked down with a robust military of fourteen divisions in two main detachments: the "Six Armies of the West" and the "Eight Armies of Chengzhou." To back up the military might, the Ji also claimed the "mandate of heaven"—meaning that God was on their side.

To run the whole thing, the kings of Zhou eventually created bu-

EMPEROR JIMMU: LEGEND . . . OR PERFECT BABY NAME?

The legendary first emperor of Japan, Jimmu (660 BCE–585 BCE), ruled around this time—but as with other parts of the world, in Japan it's almost impossible to know anything for sure about this period, because nobody wrote anything down.

Almost all the information about Jimmu is based on Japanese mythology. Jimmu is believed to be a descendant of the sun goddess Amaterasu—the supreme divinity of the Shinto pantheon—as well as the sea god Ryujin. His name meant "divine might."

He was born in Takachiho, a rural town on the island of Kyushu, in southern Japan. This was too far from central Japan, so Jimmu's brother Itsuse, who wanted to rule Japan, sailed across Japan's Inland Sea to modern-day Osaka. Here, Itsuse was killed in combat with a hostile local chieftain, and Jimmu became the head of his household.

To defeat the hostile chieftain, Jimmu decided to attack from the west, rather than the east, so the afternoon sun would blind his opponents. With help from Amaterasu, Jimmu defeated the local chieftain and gained the submission of his people.

According to tradition, lunar New Year's Day also marked the first day of Jimmu's reign, and is now celebrated as Japan's founding day. The founder of the Yamato Dynasty was remembered and revered for his peaceful reign, a time of mythical idyll when Japan was untroubled by outsiders or internal strife.

reaucratic institutions for tax collection, the administration of justice, and important projects such as flood control and road building. Unfortunately, these efficient systems competed with the local nobility, who saw their grasp on power—and their reason for being—gradually being undermined.

The decline began with a catastrophic military defeat during the reign of King Zhao: the annihilation in 1024 BCE of the Six Armies of the West by the neighboring Chu, a semi-barbaric kingdom. After Zhao's death, the state bureaucracy continued to function, but it was only a matter of time before someone challenged the Ji family's control.

That moment came in 771 BCE, when a very angry father-in-law burned Hao to the ground. The Marquis of Shen, a powerful noble, stormed the capital after King You ditched his daughter, the queen, for a concubine. The marquis proclaimed his grandson Ping Wang the new king, and they moved the whole operation to the eastern city of Luoyang. The Zhou dynasty continued, but it was officially circling the drain, ruling in name only. Within a few hundred years, the nobles stopped even pretending to acknowledge the king's authority.

Mesoamerica:
Ol' School Olmecs

Around 1300 BCE, on the other side of the world, a brand-new civilization emerged in the tropical lowlands of southeast Mexico. The Olmecs were the first native civilization to develop in Mesoamerica—the isthmus connecting North and South America. Their influence spread in all directions, and they are considered the "mother culture" of the Maya, Zapotec, Toltec, and Aztec civilizations. Among other things, the Olmecs started the classic practices of pyramid building and human sacrifice.

As in other parts of the world, the birth of civilization was linked to agriculture, a population boom, and the formation of cities. Mesoamerica's staple crop was (and still is today) corn. Corn was domesticated by 4000 BCE in western Mexico, and by 1400 BCE, cultivation had spread to the river valleys of the Olmecs' homeland, near modern-day Veracruz.

Olmec cities probably developed from groups of villages united by powerful chiefs, who then became kings. At its height in 800 BCE, one of the largest Olmec cities, La Venta (its Spanish name—the Olmec name is lost) probably had a population of about fifteen thousand, including skilled potters, basket makers, weavers, masons, and carpenters. Jewelers made exquisite jade ornaments for the rich and powerful, who also adorned themselves with colorful quetzal feathers. The Olmecs never invented the technology to make metal tools, remaining a Stone Age civilization.

The first Olmec cities were centered on raised earthen mounds topped by temple structures. Beginning around 900 BCE, the Olmec replaced these with the stone pyramids that are still standing today. Aside from the pyramids, the most impressive Olmec ruins are colossal heads, each weighing twenty tons or more, carved out of volcanic basalt hauled from quarries more than fifty miles away. Archaeologists speculate that the heads are portraits of Olmec kings.

The Olmec religion revolved around a pantheon of gods and goddesses with combined human and animal features. A main god was pictured as a jaguar or sometimes a jaguar-serpent, with power over earth, rain, and fire. There was also a mother goddess, a bird god, and a "Feathered Serpent," a snake with quetzal plumage, which would appear again and again in Mesoamerican religions. Every human was felt to have an animal spirit, and all animals represented some mythological character or cosmic force. The jaguar was the most important.

The Olmecs began a number of traditions that endured for thousands of years. They built courts for a ball game that seemed to serve some religious or ceremonial purpose. In the game, two players or teams would face off wearing stone belts, which they used to maneuver a ten-pound rubber ball into a small stone ring above the court. The Olmecs also practiced human sacrifice: archaeologists believe the losers of this ball game were decapitated to please the gods!

But it wasn't all fun and games with the Olmecs. Like the Maya, they were close observers of the cosmos who invented an extremely precise "Long Count Calendar" based on a fifty-two-year cycle with numerous subcycles—more accurate than calendars in Europe, Asia, or Africa including some used thousands of years later. By 650 BCE they had invented a written language for record keeping, and they may also have invented the number zero—usually attributed to the Maya—as part of their calendar system.

− Shaking Up the Compass −

East Meets West

People like to throw the phrase around, but when did East meet West? The Middle East (the West, in this case—yes, it's confusing) is separated from China (the East) by two thousand miles of Central Asian mountain ranges and deserts. Given all those obstacles, it's hard to know exactly when the two areas got in touch for the first time.

But this is one area where archaeologists get a little help from fashion: one of the first trade goods to make it from China to the Middle East was silk. That's no coincidence. In addition to feeling like a little slice of heaven on earth, silk is incredibly light and easy to carry. Wealthy people in the Middle East were willing to pay its weight in gold for the incredible luxury fabric.

The Chinese knew they had a good thing going when they wove the first silk-like cloth in the third millennium BCE. The fine thread produced by native Chinese silkworms (*Bombyx mori*) that were fed on mulberry leaves was so smooth and soft that the kings of China established silk manufacturing as a royal concession. Archaeologists discovered the remains of silk manufacturing, including half a silk cocoon, dating back as far as 2600 BCE.

However, the first evidence of silk in the Middle East comes from the mummy of a middle-aged Egyptian woman who died around 1000 BCE. The use of a silk scarf or bandana in her hair is a clear indicator of her wealth and status. From Egypt, demand for silk spread to the rest of the Mediterranean basin, and by 600 BCE, an epic caravan route named for the fabric, the Silk Road, connected Babylon to China. The Persians wore silk underneath their armor, and it's probably the luxurious "Amorgian" fabric referred to in *Lysistrata*, a Greek comedy from 411 BCE.

As in following millennia, it's unlikely that any merchant actually traveled all the way from China to Egypt along the route later called the Silk Road. Instead, dozens of local traders probably made "short hops" (still very long, even by modern standards) to the next city or trading post along the route, Western merchants met Chinese merchants to exchange goods in modern-day Afghanistan and far western China. Over the course of several years, this trade relay finally brought the luxury fabric six thousand miles.

North Meets South

Silk traders weren't the only ones making long journeys during this period. A number of biblical and non-biblical sources tell of a historic visit to the court of King Solomon by the Queen of Sheba. No one is quite sure where Sheba was, but we can be relatively confident that *someone* visited Solomon, because she made a huge impression: some *major* bling.

According to Bible scholars, King Solomon ruled from 971 BCE to 931 BCE, presiding over a Jewish golden age before the kingdom of Israel split in two. At the crossroads of Africa and Asia, the little kingdom straddled a number of strategic trade routes. That's probably how the Jews came into contact with the land of Sheba.

They're still debating the exact location, but most historians agree that Sheba was either in modern-day Yemen, south of Saudi Arabia, or just across the Red Sea in Ethiopia, home to the oldest civilizations of east Africa. The Ethiopians claim the "Queen of Sheba" as the ancient Queen Makeda, and Sheba may actually refer to an Ethiopian kingdom that controlled Yemen as well.

The Queen of Sheba visited Solomon, according to the Bible, because she'd heard about his great wisdom and desired to test his knowledge and judgment. But the queen clearly intended to do more than administer a quick quiz, in light of the ludicrous luxury items she brought with her. In addition to spices, gems, and valuable hardwoods, she apparently rolled up in Jerusalem with 4.5 tons of gold, which she gave to Solomon as a *gift*. Of course Solomon, not to be outdone, showered her with an equal amount of bling to take back with her to Sheba—but not before she converted to Judaism.

The pair got along so well it's no surprise the visit got intimate: according to Ethiopian legend, Solomon seduced and impregnated Sheba, whose son, Menelik I, became the first emperor of Ethiopia. Thousands of years later, this story allowed Ethiopia's Christian kings to claim descent from King Solomon.

·········· **WHO'S UP, WHO'S DOWN** ··············

Monotheism: UP

A cosmic battle between good and evil ends on the Day of Judgment. As the world is consumed by fire, the Savior returns to defeat evil once and for all, and the souls of the good rise to join him—while the souls of the wicked are condemned to burn forever in Hell. Sounds familiar, right? Just hold your spiritual horses: this isn't Christianity. It's Zoroastrianism, an ancient faith that's still practiced today by Indian believers called Parsis.

Zoroaster himself was a prophet who probably lived around 1000 BCE, along the Ditya River, in far eastern Iran. Zoroaster's teachings likely arrived in Medea, the most powerful kingdom in Iran, courtesy of nomadic tribesmen and long-distance traders.

According to Zoroaster, the existence of evil in the world is due to a mistake made by the first humans shortly after God (Ahura Mazda) created the universe. Ever since then the world has been a battleground between good and evil (or "the truth" and "the lie"), with human beings playing a central role. For good to win, humans must strive to be virtuous, doing acts of charity and holding true to their faith in spite of earthly temptations. According to legend, after receiving this revelation at the age of thirty, Zoroaster himself was tempted to renounce his faith by the devil, Angra Mainyu, but resisted.

The resemblance between Christianity and Zoroastrianism is no coincidence. During the chaotic times of Jesus Christ, the Middle East was permeated with the vivid imagery of Zoroastrianism, including its appealing vision of the just receiving their eternal reward—even if they suffered while on earth. Jesus Christ and his early Christian followers might not have consciously borrowed from Zoroastrianism. But it would have been hard to escape the influence of this ancient religion.

While many details of Zoroaster's life and teachings do sound a lot like Christ's, or vice versa, other parts are different: for example, instead of going to Heaven after the apocalypse, Zoroaster said the spirits of the good would be reincarnated in a new world created by God—which sounds more like Hinduism.

In Zoroastrianism, symbols of God include the sun, called the "Eye of Ahura Mazda," and fire, the sign of His presence on earth. To this day, Parsi places of worship are known as "fire temples," and fire has an important role in their ceremonies. This led outside observers to mistakenly label Parsis "fire worshippers." Parsi priests dress in flowing white robes symbolizing purity, and receive a silver mace capped with the head of a bull when they are inducted into the priesthood.

Appalling Viciousness: UP, THEN DOWN
Throwing babies on spears? Skinning people alive? All in a day's work for the Assyrians, who were truly "mad, bad, and dangerous to know." Since at least 1800 BCE, the Assyrians had been brooding violently in their homeland on a stretch of the Tigris River in northern Iraq. They got their big break when the invasions of the Sea Peoples upset the regional pecking order. After the collapse of the Hittite empire in 1200 BCE, the Assyrians embarked on a series of conquests stretching fifteen hundred miles from Egypt to the Persian Gulf.

Previously, Middle Eastern armies used horses to pull chariots, and the Assyrians were quick studies in chariot combat. But they also became expert fighters while riding on horseback. Assyrian horsemen were armed with spears, swords, and bows and arrows. They also invented battering rams to subdue walled cities.

They were not nice people. By their own account they routinely slaughtered the inhabitants of conquered cities, turning them into ghost towns. King Ashurnasirpal II bragged that he cut off the limbs of captured soldiers, then impaled, flayed, and burned them alive; in fact, he was so proud of this that he decorated his palace with art depicting such scenes. King Esarhaddon built pyramids of skulls outside cities he destroyed. And in 689 BCE, after Babylon launched an ill-advised rebellion, King Sennacherib thoughtfully leveled the city by opening the irrigation canals and flooding it.

Needless to say no one much cared for the Assyrians, who maintained control by keeping a monopoly on the supply of iron weapons. For the same reason they also jealously guarded their horses. But in the end, iron and horses couldn't save the Assyrians from their own barbaric cruelty. A reputation for brutality worked fine as psychological warfare when they were strong—but when the Assyrians were weakened by internal divisions, everyone revolted.

A Babylonian uprising in 625 BCE, led by a native prince named Nabopolassar, led to the total collapse of the Assyrian empire, with all the conquered peoples rising against their brutal masters. But there was plenty more brutality on the way. The new Babylonian bosses had picked up some of the Assyrians' worst habits—as the long-suffering Jews were about to find out.

Jews: DOWN, UP, DOWN, UP (Ech, I'm *Farmisht*, Already!)

The Jews found themselves in trouble in Egypt in this period, and in even more trouble trying to leave.

After wandering south into Egypt around 1500 BCE, the Jews settled east of the Nile River Delta and got on fairly well with the Egyptians—at first. But at some point the Egyptians turned on their guests, enslaving them and forcing them to build two palace cities for the pharaoh—probably Ramesses II (1279-1213 BCE). In an even more unfriendly gesture, according to the Old Testament, Ramesses II then ordered every newborn Jewish male to be drowned.

Rather than kill her son, one Jewish mother built a small boat of reeds and floated the child into the Nile River. Her son washed up in a clump of river reeds, where one of the pharaoh's daughters found him and decided to raise him as her own son; *Moses* may come from the word for "son" in ancient Egyptian.

Raised in the pharaoh's household, Moses was rich and culturally Egyptian—but still sympathetic to his people's plight. In fact, one day he killed an Egyptian slave master who was being cruel to Jewish slaves. After the murder, he was forced to flee the royal court to become a shepherd in the desolate Sinai Peninsula. There God appeared to him in the form of a burning bush and commanded him to lead the "Israelites" to freedom.

But the new pharaoh (probably Merneptah) wanted to keep the Israelites as slaves. So God got serious, hitting Egypt with ten "plagues," each nastier than the last, including turning the Nile into blood, and releasing swarms of frogs and locusts and diseases that killed off Egyptian livestock. The tenth plague was the deal breaker, killing every Egyptian firstborn male.

To stop the divine punishments, the Egyptians drove the Israelites out of Egypt, which was great, since they were seriously ready to leave by this time. After forty years of wandering in the desert, the Israelites finally succeeded in conquering the Holy Land, then called Canaan, under Joshua, an apprentice of Moses and a talented military commander. The Jews reclaimed their Promised Land with a vengeance, dividing the land and cities among the thirteen tribes of Israel.

When Joshua died, the Israelites were ruled by a series of "judges," who traveled the land explaining Jewish law and settling legal disputes. However, in history's first recorded instance of kvetching, the Israelites became dissatisfied with the judges' leadership. They demanded that the fourteenth judge, Samuel, appoint a king so the Israelites could be like other nations. Despite personal reservations, Samuel picked a military hero named Saul to become the first king of the Jews.

Saul scored a big victory against the Philistines—but later turned out to be just a tad crazy. As he came unhinged, he relied more and more on David, a young shepherd whose harp playing soothed him when he was feeling off kilter. He even allowed David to represent the Israelites in one-on-one combat with the Philistines' best fighter, a giant named Goliath. Miraculously, David killed Goliath with a single stone from his slingshot.

BECAUSE WOMEN REALLY ARE BETTER AT MULTITASKING . . .

Unusual for this male-dominated society, one of the Hebrew judges was a woman: Deborah, who was also a prophet, poet, and victorious military leader. The story of Deborah, who held court under a palm tree near the desert, suggests a bigger role for women in early Jewish history. To this day Jews trace religious descent through the mother's line (much like ancient Egypt)—another hint of matriarchal organization in early times.

Unfortunately, the Jews' tribal rivalries continued to paralyze them after Saul died. Around 1000 BCE, the kingdom of the Jews was divided in two, and the weakened, divided kingdoms were no match for fierce northerners who first showed up around 900 BCE—the Assyrians, followed by the Babylonians, who took a page from the Assyrian playbook (*It Takes a Village to Raze Another Village*).

The Babylonian king Nebuchadnezzar wanted to rebuild the Assyrian empire, except this time with Babylonians in charge. In 607 BCE, he burned Jerusalem, including the fabulous Temple of Solomon, as an example to other small kingdoms not to resist him. Then, to make further resistance impossible, he kidnapped the entire Jewish population and moved it to Babylon. The Jews' infamous Babylonian exile lasted more than fifty years, until they were rescued by a visionary leader from the east, Cyrus the Great of Persia.

Open-mindedness: UP

Persia was the great-granddaddy of world empires—a huge realm stretching three thousand miles from Greece to India. The Persian empire united many different regions and societies under the rule of one man, the Great King, or king of kings. The founder of the Persian empire, Cyrus the Great, learned from the Assyrians' mistakes and adopted an open-minded style of government that made Persia a success.

Cyrus himself was a follower of Zoroaster. But basically he never met a religion he didn't like: as long as the local priests supported his authority, he'd perform whatever bizarre rituals they required.

When Cyrus was born, the Persians were vassals of their neighbors, the Medes, who fancied themselves more civilized than their country cousins in good ol' Pars (the Persian heartland). But civilization is a mixed blessing. Wandering the mountain valleys of Iran on horseback, the Persians stayed close to their nomadic roots, which gave them a big combat advantage.

Sensing widespread resentment against the Medes over high taxes,

EVERYTHING THEY NEED TO KNOW, THEY LEARNED IN THE ZAGROS MOUNTAINS

According to Herodotus, the early Persians were simple, virtuous people who taught their sons just three things: to ride a horse, to use a bow and arrow, and to tell the truth.

Cyrus organized a rebellion against his own grandfather, the Medean king Astyages, in 554 BCE. As king, Cyrus showed a light touch, treating the Medes as equals of his Persian subjects. Astyages's Medean soldiers then joined his army, making possible the great conquests that followed. In fact, so many of Cyrus's troops and administrators were Medes that his "Persians" were actually known to contemporaries as "the Medes." But then, ancient chroniclers were hardly precise (and neither are we).

Next, Cyrus hit the rich kingdom of Lydia, in central Turkey, ruled by the fabulously wealthy king Croesus. Actually Croesus started it: he was afraid Cyrus was going to conquer Babylon, which he wanted for himself. Before attacking Persia, across the Halys River, however, Croesus (a rather neurotic king) sought reassurance in the worst place possible—the Oracle of Apollo at Delphi. There he received a prophecy he thought was encouraging: "If Croesus crosses the Halys, a great empire shall be brought down." So Croesus attacked Cyrus in 547 BCE.

But Cyrus quickly turned the tables on him: the next year, in a daring mid-winter campaign, he introduced the Lydian cavalry to Central Asian camels. The Lydian horses bolted, terrified of the unfamiliar animals, and the Persians captured the Lydian capital, Sardis, as well as Croesus, with his huge treasure. The empire Croesus destroyed was his own (cue ironic trombone sound effect).

Next stop: Babylon. Luckily for Cyrus, King Nabonidus—a commoner who'd seized power in a coup—was utterly incompetent. He foolishly alienated the important Babylonian priesthood by refusing to honor Marduk, Babylon's chief god. Even worse, he spent most of his time in faraway cities, rebuilding temples to other gods, which was pretty much the ancient version of a Jerry Springer throwdown.

While he was out of town, Nabonidus left his son Belshazzar in charge, but Belshazzar wasn't particularly interested in affairs of government. According to the Bible, a disembodied hand wrote a supernatural message on the wall of Belshazzar's palace reading, "You have been judged, and found lacking, by the Persians." The hand was right. In 539 BCE resistance in Babylon crumbled, and Cyrus entered the city as a liberator, without a drop of blood spilled. Nabonidus and Belshazzar were arrested and died in captivity.

Cyrus was ready to play by the rules. His first act was a visit to the temple of Marduk, where he made extravagant sacrifices and distributed bribes to the priests. Marduk's approval of Cyrus then became part of Persian propaganda: Cyrus later boasted that Marduk had chosen him to be "king of the whole world."

Cyrus also returned sacred objects stolen by the Babylonians from different subject peoples around the Middle East, earning huge good-will from his new constituents. In his most famous act of toleration, he freed the Jews, held prisoner in Babylon since being kidnapped fifty years before, and gave them funds to rebuild the temple destroyed by Babylon's King Nebuchadnezzar. Cyrus also returned the gold vessels used in temple ceremonies that Nebuchadnezzar had stolen.

Cyrus's successors continued the imperial expansion at full throttle. Under his remote cousin Darius, the Persian empire reached its zenith. Modeling his enlightened government on Cyrus, Darius (another "the Great") followed local customs wherever possible. This local sensitivity helped mask the efficient centralized administration he created. Darius divided his huge empire into twenty "satrapies," or provinces ruled by "satraps," or governors. Each satrapy paid a certain amount of gold and silver as tribute to the Great King every year, and had to supply a certain number of troops in wartime. To combat corruption and keep the satraps under control, Darius employed the "Great King's Eyes"—spies who made secret inspections and then reported back to him.

NOT CHOSEN, BUT NOT TOO BAD, EITHER

Even though he wasn't Jewish, Cyrus is remembered by Jews as one of "God's anointed," a "messiah" or "savior" (but not *the* Messiah/Savior). In ancient times, the Jews recognized virtuous gentiles who followed the most important injunctions—against idol worship, murder, adultery, and so on—as "righteous gentiles" or "righteous among nations," meaning they would be admitted to Paradise even if they didn't observe the sabbath. In modern times the state of Israel created an award for the "Righteous Among Nations" to recognize gentiles who had helped Jews escape the Holocaust.

Persian domination was stable, and their empire, covering most of the known world, seemed destined to last forever. There was just one small problem: a feisty group of people living on the far western fringe of the empire who called themselves the Greeks . . .

········ **SO LONG, AND THANKS FOR ALL THE** . . . ········

What Happens in Vegas . . .
Human beings have been degenerate gamblers since pretty much day one, and we have the archaeological evidence to prove it: dice. The first dice, made from the heel bones of hoofed animals, were used by Stone Age people around

forty thousand years ago. Variants of these "natural" dice—called astragali by archaeologists, from the scientific name of the heel bone—were used all over the world for thousands of years.

Then, around 1500 BCE, an Egyptian gambler made the first "cubic" dice. While astragali produced respectably fair (i.e., random) results when tossed in the air, the ancient Egyptian gamer understood that a perfectly square object, with faces of identical size, should be even more random. The first Egyptian dice were made out of ivory—the start of an unfortunate trend that continued until the invention of plastic, costing many unlucky elephants their tusks (and lives).

The Egyptian dice were used to play a game with religious overtones called Senet, in which competing players tried to maneuver their "souls" (pieces) into the afterlife. Despite its spiritual bent, the game was probably an occasion for betting—and the Egyptians had plenty of other games of chance if they ever got bored with Senet. In fact, gambling became such a problem that the pharaohs banned it, sending offenders to do hard labor in the royal quarries. Like most other attempts to control gambling throughout history, the royal decrees probably didn't have much of an impact.

Around 900 BCE, the Etruscans of northern Italy were using dice that pretty much resembled modern dice, with opposite sides containing markings that added up to seven: one and six, two and five, three and four. By this time, contemporary dice from other parts of the Mediterranean were being made from a variety of materials including bronze, agate, onyx, marble, rock crystal, amber, alabaster, and porcelain.

Of course, just as some humans have always been gamblers, some gamblers have always been cheats. Archaeologists excavating the ancient city of Pompeii—which was covered in ash by a volcano in 79 CE—found numerous sets of dice, including several loaded pairs.

Tamales (con Salsa!)

In addition to an incredibly precise calendar and the number zero, the Olmec people of Central America also invented the delicious tamale—a thick piece of dough made from ground corn, which can be used to wrap and cook an endless variety of tasty ingredients. Mexican restaurants everywhere owe the Olmec a major round of *gracias*!

The basic stone tools for grinding corn—the mano and metate—date back to pre-Olmec times, with archaeological evidence from before 1500 BCE. Women used the cylindrical mano like a rolling pin, to crush corn kernels on the curved surface of the metate. However, the "classic" tamale probably didn't emerge until after 1000 BCE,

TAKE YOUR VITAMINS

Niacin deficiency leads to a danger-ous disease called pellagra, which usually kills its victims after four or five years of painful skin lesions, diar-rhea, and dementia. Fun, no?

when a clever cook in Guatemala discovered the secret to getting the full nutritional value from corn: the kernels must be cooked with lime or wood ash to release the vi-tamin B_3 (niacin), which is critical to human health.

Since a plain tamale is rather dull, the Olmec probably experi-mented with various sauces to spice it up, thus inventing the precur-sors to modern salsa. Although there's no physical evidence of salsa making, archaeologists and ethnobotanists (scientists who study agriculture) do know that the Olmec cultivated tomatoes, chiles, corn, and beans, thus providing plenty of ingredients for a proto-salsa.

The main show, of course, was the filling inside the tamale. Here the Olmec had a wide variety of meats, including the usual favorites such as chicken, deer, wild pig, and shellfish, but also (brace your-self) dog, turtle, monkey, alligator, and various insects. Happily you won't find these latter ingredients in modern Mexican cuisine (usu-ally).

Highways and Byways

The Great King of Persia had a lot of stuff to keep track of: east to west, from India to Greece, the Persian empire spanned three thou-sand miles. To keep the empire locked down—including the rebel-lious Ionian Greek colonies on the west coast of Anatolia—Darius I decided to build the world's first superhighway: a paved road run-ning about sixteen hundred miles, from the imperial capital in Susa to the provincial capital of Sardis, near the west coast of Anatolia.

The project was a mind-boggling feat of engineering. As the Royal Road resembled other ancient paving projects, it probably called for a layer of clay, a layer of sand, a layer of gravel, and then a surface layer of large cobblestones. In many places it was just a matter of connect-ing existing local roads together—but then the old roads were re-paved, too.

The road described by the Greek historian Herodotus included 111 lodges (roughly one every 15 miles) with free food, water, and bed-ding for travelers. The safety of travelers was personally guaranteed by the Great King, with Herodotus noting that "throughout ... it is free from danger." According to Herodotus, it took about three months to traverse the 1,600-mile distance—an incredibly short jour-ney at that time.

The Royal Road encouraged east-west trade contacts, and also allowed the establishment of a lightning-fast postal service for the Persian rulers. The kings of Persia could send messages—and armies—to far-flung regions of their empire at a moment's notice.

> "Nothing mortal travels so fast as these Persian messengers . . . These men will not be hindered from accomplishing at their best speed the distance which they have to go, either by snow, or rain, or heat, or by the darkness of night. The first rider delivers his dispatch to the second, and the second passes it to the third; and so it is borne from hand to hand along the whole line."
>
> —Herodotus, on the Persian postal service

Setting the Bar Really High for Valentine's Day

Although he's remembered in the Jewish Old Testament as a real SOB, King Nebuchadnezzar of Babylon was apparently a nice family man at home. In fact, he built one of the seven ancient wonders of the world just to keep his wife happy.

Nebuchadnezzar had a problem with his beautiful young queen Amyitis, and unfortunately this meant he had a political problem too. Amyitis was a princess from Medea (in modern-day Iran), and the Babylonian king had married her to cement an alliance with the Medes. But Amyitis complained that the Mesopotamian desert was depressing; she missed the greenery and mountain streams of her homeland. So Nebuchadnezzar brought the mountains to her.

Most of what we know about the Hanging Gardens of Babylon is based on sketchy descriptions in ancient sources—including its distinctive name, which sounds a bit weird to modern ears (from a distance, the gardens probably appeared to be suspended or "hanging" in midair).

The gardens were built to an impressive height, resembling a mountain; in fact, that was the whole point. The Greek historian and geographer Strabo described the structure in the following way: "It consists of vaulted terraces raised one above another, and resting upon cube-shaped pillars. These are hollow and filled with earth to allow trees of the largest size to be planted. The pillars, the vaults, and terraces are constructed of baked brick and asphalt." Another Greek writer, Diodorus

Siculus, added that "it was planted with all sorts of trees, which both for greatness and beauty might delight the spectators."

So how big were the gardens? Diodorus Siculus claimed they were four hundred feet on a side and eighty feet tall, making them one of the tallest structures in the ancient world. Small streams and waterfalls snaked everywhere, watering the greenery and providing the pleasant sound of running water. According to Strabo, getting the water to the top was a rather labor-intensive process: "The ascent to the highest story is by stairs, and at their side are water engines, by means of which persons, appointed expressly for the purpose, are continually employed in raising water from the Euphrates into the garden."

Let's hope Amyitis was happy.

Iron, Man!

Bronze ruled from around 3200 BCE to 1200 BCE, when it was replaced by an even stronger metal, iron. It took longer for people to make iron tools because, unlike copper, iron nuggets don't exist in nature. Iron sources were limited mostly to meteorites with high iron content, making the element very rare.

The Indo-European invaders who settled Europe, the Middle East, and India seemed to know the secret of smelting iron ore to create iron weapons. They created the Hittite empire in the Middle East around 1600 BCE and the Vedic civilization of India shortly afterward. A second round of Indo-European invaders, the Dorians, appeared in Greece with iron implements around 1200 BCE.

But it took a technological breakthrough to make large-scale iron production possible in the Mediterranean world. Beginning around 1300 BCE, special ovens called "bloomeries" allowed ironmongers to remove contaminants and produce relatively pure iron. Once it became widely available, iron allowed for the creation of stronger weapons and tools, such as scythes, plows, hammers, and axes.

Non–Indo-European civilizations such as Egypt and Assyria began using iron implements around this time. Iron-working technology may have developed independently in sub-Saharan Africa around

ALL THAT GLITTERS

At one time iron was considered more valuable than gold. Iron daggers were among the crown jewels buried with the dead pharaoh Tutankhamen, and the ancient Egyptians called the metal "black gold from heaven," in reference to its meteoritic origins.

1000 BCE, beginning with the Nok civilization of West Africa. The spread of iron working coincided with the rise of the Bantu people, who fanned out from their homeland in modern Nigeria and conquered sub-Saharan Africa in the first millennium BCE.

·········AND THANKS, BUT NO THANKS, FOR . . . ···

Hemorrhoids from Hell (or Heaven, Actually)
The variety of punishments inflicted on the enemies of the Jews (and on the Jews themselves) by the Old Testament God is kind of mind-boggling. Here's a good one: hemorrhoids! If hemorrhoids seem unpleasant today, just remember the ancients had neither explanation nor treatment for the burning anal affliction. Like many other areas of ancient medicine, the best doctors could do was advise prayer and a good attitude until you died.

Foreigners who arrived in Palestine around 1200 BCE, the Philistines weren't the Hebrews' favorite people to begin with. So when they defeated the Israelites during the reign of the Hebrew judge Eli and made off with the Ark—an ornate wooden case in which Moses (supposedly) had placed the stone tablets containing the Ten Commandments—they incurred God's wrath big time. The Ark was kind of like a security blanket for the Hebrews: it was really important for them to have it at all times, no matter what. When the ninety-eight-year-old judge Eli heard the news, he fell down and broke his neck—it was that serious.

But the Ark carried a special curse for the heathens who insulted it: God gave the Philistines a case of mass hemorrhoids. If you think an anal plague sounds improbable, you're right: there's no other case of a mass hemorrhoid attack in recorded history, and no transmissible virus or bacteria that spreads hemorrhoids, which are typically due to chronic disorders. But the Bible is very, very specific on this point. How specific? Well, more specific than contemporary commercials for Preparation H: "He smote the men of the city, both small and great, and they had emerods in their secret parts."

These were clearly no ordinary hemorrhoids: some of the Philistines actually died. And of course, when it rains, it pours: the Philistine cities were also overrun by mice, which ate all the food supplies and were generally unsanitary. After seven months of anal/mouse tag-team misery, the Philistines consulted their priests, who advised them to return the Ark to the Israelites with a "trespass" offering, to apologize for the whole misunderstanding. The offering was five golden mice and . . . wait for it . . . five golden hemorrhoids.

The Philistines "laid the ark of the LORD upon the cart, and the coffer with the mice of gold and the images of their emerods," and said good-bye to the Ark of the Covenant. Their mass hemorrhoids disappeared—but now the Hebrews got in trouble. Seeing the oxen pulling the unmanned cart from the Philistines, the simple Jewish farmers of Beth-Shamesh thought, "Free lunch!" and cooked the oxen up, using the cart as firewood. Worse, they looked at the golden hemorrhoids and mice, which involved opening the Ark of the Covenant, and that is Against the Rules According to God. So God wiped out the whole town, which actually makes hemorrhoids sound not that bad.

Pedophilia

The Greeks were a kinky lot by modern standards. Although modern critics point to them as an ancient civilization that accepted homosexuality, that's not quite right. They didn't identify "homosexuality" as a lifestyle pursued by a specific group of people called "homosexuals"; rather, it was a universal phenomenon that most upper-class males passed through and then left behind at a certain point in life. What's more, the Greeks approved of male-male sexual contact only if it involved an adult—typically a man over the age of eighteen—and an adolescent boy. We said it was kinky!

While the ancient Greeks would have found the idea of two grown men in a sexual relationship odd and undignified, man-boy love was something to be proud of—in fact, something to be publicly displayed. The older male suitor would declare his love for a boy openly, then court him with gifts. Once he won the boy over, he would take him on dates in public places, such as the agora or the gymnasium, where they would exercise together in the nude, slathered in olive oil. In private, sexual intercourse could range from kissing, to heavy petting, to "intercrural" (between the boy's thighs), to the "whole nine yards," as it were.

Homosexual relationships between men and boys served important social functions, with the older man introducing his young boyfriend to the adult world of politics and instructing him on his civic duties. In most cases, the older man would ask the boy's father for permission before beginning the relationship, and would later be responsible for the boy's education. The boy could also serve as the older man's shield bearer in battle—sort of like a modern-day golf caddy.

Some Greek observers did express concern about the detrimental effects of these pedophilic relationships—but not for the boys! Instead, they warned that the passions excited by the love of boys could lead to immoderate, irrational behavior among the adult men. The Greeks also disapproved of men who visited boy prostitutes or forced themselves on young male slaves, who had no say in the matter. Unlike Greek girls during this time, boys were allowed to reject the advances of suitors who didn't tickle their fancy.

Handsome boys could have a number of lovers through their teenage years. However, ancient scolds warned them against becoming conceited because of their good looks. The Greek legend of Narcissus tells of a beautiful young boy who spends all his time looking at his own reflection in a river, and gets turned into a flower (still called Narcissus today) as punishment for his arrogance.

On this subject, in Plato's *Dialogues* the philosopher Socrates talks to his friend about the best way to seduce a "good-looking boy" named Lysis. His friend is head over heels in love with Lysis, to the point that he is boring his friends with tedious poems praising the boy and his ancestors. Socrates advises his friend to drop the flattery, which makes boys "swell-headed" and arrogant. Instead, Socrates says his friend should cut out the compliments and engage Lysis in a philosophical dialogue but really, how much fun would that have been?

·················· **BY THE NUMBERS** ··················

269,000	size, in square feet, of palace built for Assyrian king Ashurnasirpal
69,574	number of guests invited to the opening of the palace
2 million	blocks of limestone used in an aqueduct built to serve Nineveh, an Assyrian city
100,000	number of civil servants in the Assyrian bureaucracy
2.9 million	size of Persian empire, in square miles
16 million	number of subjects in Persian empire under King Darius
1,600	length of the Persian Royal Road, in miles
111	number of free lodges for travelers along the Royal Road
47	number of kingdoms incorporated into the Persian empire
14,560	annual revenue of Persian empire under King Darius, according to Herodotus, in Euboean silver talents
366,912	the same amount of silver, in kilograms

404.5	the same amount of silver, in tons
200,000	number of helots working under Spartan domination
10,000	number of Spartan citizens they worked for
35,000	number of Athenian male citizens
19,000	miles sailed by Phoenician fleet to circumnavigate Africa in 600 BCE

3

ATHENS, ALEXANDER, AND ALL THAT

(500 BCE–0 BCE)

Out of the ashes of the ancient "Dark Ages," a shining new world emerged between the years 500 BCE and 0: legendary leaders created huge empires that have never been equaled since. These mega-states were ruled from capitals that were the biggest cities the world had ever seen. It all began with a major shift in the balance of power, as the world's first global empire, Persia, declined and new contenders arose in Europe.

Persia's decay began with the stunning defeat of King Xerxes by the Greeks, who were able to triumph against overwhelming odds by trying something new: working together. But their victory didn't mean smooth sailing. At the moment of their greatest triumph, they threw it all away in an incredibly destructive civil war that brought their Golden Age crashing to a close.

It took new management under a young king from north of Greece, Alexander of Macedon, to unite the Greeks again in a common purpose. And what purpose was that? Revenge (of course)! The Persians may have tried to forget Greece, but the Greeks weren't going to forget them. And Alexander the Great was just the leader they needed to settle the score.

Alexander did a bit more than settle the score: he conquered the whole Persian Empire. But like all rock stars, he was fated to die young, and his empire didn't outlast him. Nonetheless, by spreading Greek culture, he created a new international community, and paved the way for the most successful empire in history: Rome (perhaps you've heard of it).

Rome was truly remarkable, but it had some stiff competition half a world away, in Asia, where a similar process of consolidation created the first Chinese empire: the Han Dynasty. Like the West, China had a couple of false starts, including an insanely ambitious conqueror named Qin Shi Huang who grabbed it all—and lost it all—with breathtaking speed.

Meanwhile, an Indian prince named Chandragupta Maurya took advantage of regional instability to create his own huge empire.

Covering most of India and modern-day Pakistan, the empire took his family name, Maurya.

And a few letters away, the Maya hit fast-forward in Central America, leaping ahead of their Olmec ancestors as they built societies of unprecedented complexity in what is now Guatemala and Mexico.

All in all, this period was an incredible recovery from the chaos that went before, and with its orderly empires, grand cities, cultural achievements, and rampant conquering, it is still considered one of the high points of human civilization.

 ·············· **WHAT HAPPENED WHEN**··············

509 BCE Roman republic founded.

492 BCE Greek colonies in the Persian Empire rebel but are defeated.

490 BCE Darius invades Greece.

480 BCE Darius's successor, Xerxes, invades Greece.

479 BCE United Greeks defeat Persians at Platea.

475 BCE "Warring States" period begins in China.

433 BCE Athens and Sparta go to war against each other.

415 BCE Alcibiades leads Athenian invasion of Sicily.

405 BCE Sparta defeats Athens.

399 BCE Socrates is forced to commit suicide for corrupting Athenian youth.

359 BCE Philip II becomes king of Macedon.

334 BCE-326 BCE Philip's son Alexander the Great conquers Persian Empire.

300 BCE Chandragupta unites India, founds Maurya Dynasty.

221 BCE Qin Shi Huang unites China in short-lived Qin Dynasty.

218 BCE Hannibal attacks Rome.

206 BCE Chinese peasant general Liu Bang founds Han Dynasty.

202 BCE Hannibal is defeated.

146 BCE Romans destroy Carthage.

88 BCE First Roman civil war.

58 BCE Julius Caesar invades Gaul.

44 BCE Julius Caesar is elected dictator for life, but is then assassinated.

31 BCE Caesar's adopted son, Octavian, defeats Antony and Cleopatra.

27 BCE Octavian becomes first emperor of Rome.

··················· **SPINNING THE GLOBE** ············

China Takes It on the Qin
(Then Gets Everything in Han)

China's Zhou Dynasty didn't so much collapse as fade away, with the kings of Zhou drifting off into secluded irrelevance as the rest of the country descended into civil war. The chaos that followed from 475 to 221 BCE is known as the "Warring States" period, and the name pretty much sums it up: six main contenders and a bunch of smaller also-rans duked it out in bloody wars until a surprise late entry—a "barbarian" kingdom in northwest China called Qin (pronounced Chin)—suddenly rose to power.

Like Alexander the Great, the leader of Qin, Qin Shi Huang, was a talented outsider who conquered a huge amount of territory in the "civilized" world. And as with Alexander, Qin Shi Huang's empire didn't last, but it did lay the groundwork for the Han Dynasty, which united China around the same time Rome united the Mediterranean world. The English word *China* comes from "Qin."

Qin Shi Huang was incredibly

SOMETIMES YOU CAN TAKE IT WITH YOU . . .

Qin Shi Huang's burial included an army of 8,099 life-size clay soldiers, horses, and chariots, which would fight for him in the afterlife. Still on display near his capital city, Xi'an, his "terra-cotta army" was assumed to be legendary until 1974, when Chinese farmers digging a well discovered it. The soldiers range in height from five feet, eight inches to six-two. Every face was sculpted individually, possibly using real soldiers as models. The clay soldiers were probably symbolic substitutes for human sacrifices common during earlier periods.

brutal. He had thousands of prisoners of war executed, burned most of China's books, and worked to death hundreds of thousands of peasants in giant projects. Some of these projects were good for China—its first national road system, for example—but the Great Wall proved fairly useless, and his extravagant tomb was pure vanity.

Qin Shi Huang's most lasting accomplishment was abolishing China's feudal system. Helped by his prime minister, Li Si, he broke the power of the independent nobility who brought down the Zhou Dynasty. Qin Shi Huang replaced them with civilian administrators and military commanders, separating responsibilities so no official could become too powerful. Although the feudal system slowly returned, the central administration allowed later Chinese emperors to reestablish order even after bloody civil wars.

Happily, the first bloody civil war wasn't long in coming. After Qin Shi Huang died, in 210 BCE, his incompetent son Huhai survived only four years on the throne before his own prime minister forced him to commit suicide. But thanks to Qin Shi Huang, this period of disorder didn't last long. In 206 BCE, a charismatic general from Jiangsu province, Liu Bang, reunited Qin Shi Huang's empire. Even though he was born a peasant, Liu Bang proclaimed a new dynasty, called the Han.

The Han Dynasty is considered a golden age when China enjoyed peace and prosperity. Part of this was a shift in the judicial system, moderating the harsh "legalism" of Qin Shi Huang with the more moderate ideals of both Taoism and Confucius.

THE QUOTABLE LAO TZU

"In governing, don't try to control. In work, do what you enjoy. In family life, be completely present. When you are content to simply be yourself and don't compare or compete, everybody will respect you."

"When the Master governs, the people are hardly aware that he exists."

"Governing a large country is like frying a small fish. You spoil it with too much poking."
(from the Tao Te Ching, trans. by Stephen Mitchell)

Under "legalism," draconian laws were supposed to inspire obedience through fear of terrible punishments; there were so many laws, in fact, that everyone could be found guilty of *something*. By contrast, Taoist and Confucian legal theorists said that fewer laws were needed, as long as leaders enforced them consistently and taught the common people the reasons behind them: preventing injustice and maintaining order. With popular understanding came respect for the law and a "harmonious" society.

The Maurya Empire:
Size Does Matter

Like Alexander and Qin Shi Huang, Chandragupta Maurya was a great unifier. Maurya, born around 340 BCE, overthrew the ruling Nanda Dynasty of eastern India and kicked Alexander's governors out of western India before he reached the age of twenty. In 305 BCE he defeated Seleucus, the general whom Alexander put in charge of Persia, adding the modern territory of Afghanistan and Pakistan to his realm. Then he turned south to conquer southern India. In all, he conquered about 1.6 million square miles in two decades—a close second to Alexander's empire of 2.0 million square miles.

And Maurya was actually more successful than Alexander—because his empire survived. In fact, the Maurya Empire peaked under Chandragupta's grandson Ashoka. Ruling more than forty years, from 273 to 232 BCE, Ashoka consolidated control of southern India, established a centralized administration, and guaranteed the rule of law.

Ashoka was a spiritual leader as well, who embraced Buddhism and spread it throughout India after witnessing the terrible slaughter caused by one of his conquests. He also banned slavery, renounced further territorial expansion, and sent diplomats to open friendly relations with neighboring states. He built a huge system of roads, bridges, and canals to connect the different parts of his empire, and lodges, hospitals, and temples to improve the lives of his subjects. Agriculture and commerce flourished, as Indian merchants traveled thousands of miles to trade luxury goods, including ivory, silk, spices, and gems.

DEVIATED SEPTUM, I SWEAR . . .

Indian surgeons invented plastic surgery around 600 BCE, beginning with the reconstruction of noses, which were often cut off as punishment for adultery. (Why cut something off just to put it back on? We have no idea.) The first text on plastic surgery was the *Sushruta Samhita*, by a renowned surgeon and teacher named Sushruta, who is called "the father of plastic surgery." Practicing in Banaras (Varanasi), Sushruta invented a nose-reconstruction technique that involved slicing off a patch of skin from the cheek, reattaching it to the area of the severed nose, molding it into a new nose, and creating new nostrils with two small pipes. Another Indian technique for nose reconstruction called for taking a skin graft from the buttock. The techniques were perfected by the fourth century BCE, according to Vaghbat, a contemporary scholar who described them in two books.

The reign of Ashoka is considered an Indian golden age. But make no mistake: the stability was based on overwhelming military power.

Ashoka guaranteed peace in south Asia with a huge army of six hundred thousand foot soldiers, thirty thousand cavalry, and nine thousand war elephants.

Maya:
Taking It Higha

The boundary between Olmec civilization and the Maya is fuzzy, but the Maya definitely got rolling by 300 BCE, when their first cities emerged in the lowlands of Guatemala and the Yucatan Peninsula. Much of the space for these settlements, and the farms supporting them, was hacked out of Central American rain forests.

Thousands of years after they were abandoned, these early Mayan cities stand out from the jungle (literally) because of the giant pyramids the Maya built. The Maya took this Olmec tradition to the "next level" by constructing stepped pyramids, some over a hundred feet tall, at cities such as Calakmul, Cival, and Nakbe. These cities had as many as ten thousand inhabitants.

The growth of these cities was closely related to the rise of an aristocratic elite, including kings who doubled as high priests. According to the Mayan creation myth, the world was created by the children of the maize (corn) god, who ruled as an all-powerful king at the center of the cosmos. The Mayan kings linked their authority to his divine rule, symbolized by elaborate headdress made of maize leaves and priceless ornaments, including jade breastplates and jewelry made of jade, shell, bone, and pearl, which were buried with them when they died. Mayan kings assumed ceremonial names with religious meaning, such as K'ahk 'Yipyaj Chan K'awiil (Fire Is the Strength of the Sky God) and K'Inich Yax K'uk Mo' (Sun Green Quetzal Macaw).

WITH GREAT POWER COMES GREAT RESPONSIBILITY . . .

It wasn't all wine and roses for Mayan kings. In one of their more painful responsibilities, the kings had to pierce their foreskins with a stingray spine. The blood from the wound symbolized procreation, specifically the gods' creation of the universe. Meanwhile, piercing the ears allowed the kings to hear divine wisdom, and piercing the tongue meant they could speak with divine authority.

The kings and nobles carried out important ceremonial duties, and their doings were recorded with an elaborate pictorial writing similar to ancient Egyptian hieroglyphs, often on the long staircases leading to the temples atop the pyramids. As priests, the king and nobility would fast and possibly ingest hallucinogenic plants to enter divine trances that would reveal the will of the gods. They also honored the gods through human sacrifices (always of some other poor bastard, never themselves).

~ Special Report: Mediterranean Fight League ~

Round 1: Greeks vs. Persians. Fight!

In 500 BCE, the Persians ran most of the known world, and it was an article of faith that they would rule forever. Meanwhile, the Greeks figured that they themselves were divinely favored over the "barbarians"—all those dirty, immoral, illiterate people who lived outside of Greece. So the two cultures were bound to clash when they came into contact.

Unfortunately, that's exactly what happened in Ionia, on the west coast of Asia Minor (Turkey). Picking up the disunited Greek colonies was child's play for Cyrus the Great in the 540s BCE. The Athenians couldn't accept Persian oppression of their Ionian "brothers" in Asia Minor, so they encouraged the colonies to rebel ... then acted surprised when the Persians took their encouragement seriously. Darius the Great invaded Greece in 490 BCE to punish Athens for stirring up trouble, but the plucky Athenians defeated him at Marathon. (The Spartans had skipped out to observe a religious festival, which always seemed to happen when the Athenians needed help.) But it wasn't over ... not even close.

Round 2: Greeks vs. Persians

Athens—and the rest of Greece—got off easy the first time. But Darius's son Xerxes (pronounced ZURK-sees) wasn't kidding around. Two hundred and fifty thousand strong, his mammoth invasion force included troops from all over the Persian Empire. The cream of the

AN UNWELCOME DINNER GUEST ...

Being a Persian vassal was relatively easy until the king of kings showed up in your territory and, in the words of Herodotus, you "had to entertain the Persian army and provide a dinner for the king." On the march, Xerxes dined with fifteen thousand officers, family members, and an entourage (who got fancy food), plus another couple hundred thousand rank and file. Feeding all these people supposedly cost 400 silver talents, or about $100 million. While incredible, the price tag makes more sense when you consider it included gold and silver cups and bowls made especially for the occasion, as well as a giant pavilion where the king relaxed. The icing on the cake: when they moved on the next day, the Persians took it all with them!

crop were the "Immortals," the elite Persian cavalry who, despite their name, would rather die than be defeated. There were ten thousand of these highly trained fanatics.

Xerxes loved big engineering projects, and why not? With slave labor, they were free—although, not problem-free: Xerxes first wanted his engineers to build a giant floating bridge across the Hellespont, a sea channel almost a mile across separating Europe from Asia. When the first bridge was destroyed by a freak storm, Xerxes had the designers beheaded and the sea whipped for its insolence (standard procedure). Inspired by their predecessors' fates, the second engineering team produced not one but two much sturdier bridges, each composed of about three hundred ships bound together with ropes a foot wide.

Now the Greeks really started freaking out. Athens, the main target, sent envoys to Sparta begging for an alliance, but the Spartans were split on what to do. One side, led by King Leonidas, wanted to send an army to help Athens immediately. But the more conservative faction argued that Sparta was safe (finding yet another religious festival as an excuse).

To shame the conservative Spartans into doing something, Leonidas bent the rules a little (okay . . . a lot) by recruiting three hundred like-minded men as a "bodyguard" and heading to a narrow strategic pass in northern Greece called Thermopylae. Incredibly, the Spartans managed to hold off a quarter million Persian soldiers for three whole days. Ultimately the Spartans vowed to stay and give their lives for the cause of freedom; their suicidal "last stand" inspired the rest of Greece to unite against the Persians.

Of course, getting the Greeks to agree on anything was almost impossible. Luckily, they had a wily politician from Athens (where else?) to bring them together. One of history's most gifted political leaders, Themistocles (pronounced "Thuh-MIST-oh-klees") knew Sparta would never help Athens unless the Spartans were in charge. So he persuaded the Athenians to give the Spartans overall command of the allied forces, including the Athenian fleet—even though everyone, including the Spartans, knew they were clueless about sea warfare. Then Themistocles privately persuaded the Spartans to let him do the naval planning. To help things along, he wasn't above distributing huge bribes and having a few opponents kicked out of Athens.

Themistocles's most impressive accomplishment was getting the Athenians to evacuate their city. Although they had fortified part of the city on his advice, Athens was still largely defenseless. Now a brilliant speech persuaded them to recognize realities, pack up their belongings, and move to an island just off the coast. Typically for Themistocles, this was a bit devious. Xerxes knew he had to capture the people of Athens to truly subdue the city, and by moving them to an island, Themistocles was using the Athenians as bait for the Persian fleet. If he could lure the Persian fleet into the narrow channel between Athens and the island, the Athenian fleet could trap and destroy it.

On the day of the battle, Xerxes watched the whole thing from the top of a nearby hill, where he relaxed on a golden throne, clearly expecting an easy victory. He was bitterly disappointed. The first great Greek victory, at Salamis, swept the Persian navy from the sea, eliminating half the invasion force. The second victory, on land, came two years later, outside the city of Plataea. Here the Greek army, united around ten thousand Spartan warriors, annihilated the Persian land army. (The Spartans could probably have done it alone, but it was nice that everyone came.)

Round 3: Greeks vs. Greeks

Now that the Greeks had pulled together in a common cause, you might think they'd at least agree to stop fighting each other—but no such luck. After the Persian Wars ended in 479 BCE, Athens formed the Delian League, supposedly an "alliance" against Persia (named after Delos, the island where the alliance was "agreed" upon), which quickly turned into an Athenian Empire covering the Aegean Sea. The Athenian navy collected tribute payments from the "allies," money that paid for the navy that was used to collect the tribute, which paid for the navy, and so on. Wising up after the Persian attack, the Athenians also built huge stone walls around their city and its port, effectively canceling out Spartan combat skill.

To counter Athens, the Spartans reformed their own club, the Peloponnesian League, which had no navy, but claimed total superiority on the ground. Basically, one side owned the sea, the other the land—a recipe for a bloody stalemate.

Naturally suspicious of each other, in 433 BCE the Athenians and Spartans allowed a small dispute to spiral out of control. Ironically, it began with events totally unrelated to either city. Corinth, a traditional ally of Sparta, got into a slap fest with one of its own colonies, Corcyra (Corfu), Corcyra went to Athens for help, Corinth went to Sparta, and the war was on.

BONUS ROUND: ATHENS VS. THE PLAGUE

When the Peloponnesian War began, the Athenians had no way of knowing that their strategy of waiting out the Spartan siege was placing them at risk for an epidemic. But the close quarters proved to be perfect breeding grounds for a mysterious, deadly disease. According to the Greek historian Thucydides, in the first stage "the throat and tongue became bloody and emitted an unnatural and fetid odor." After this came "sneezing, hoarseness, and a hard cough. Diarrhea and vomiting ensued, accompanied by terrible pain." At this point, "the burning sensation was so terrible that the patient could not bear to wear clothing, and many went stark naked." Most died after a few days, while survivors often lost their fingers, toes, eyes, or genitals. Some escaped physical harm—but lost their memories entirely, unable to recognize friends or family.

This plague struck Athens for the first time in 430 BCE, the second year of the war, and killed about one third of the total population, including refugees from the countryside—fifty thousand to eighty thousand people. According to Thucydides, the constant burning of bodies on funeral pyres so frightened the Spartan army outside the walls that they fled, convinced that a divine curse was at work. (When the Spartans are scared, you know

The whole thing is too long and tedious to describe here, but the short version goes like this: safe behind their city walls, the Athenians watched the Spartans burn their fields and farmhouses year after year, knowing they could survive off the Athenian Empire. Meanwhile, the Athenian navy blockaded the Peloponnesian peninsula, the center of Spartan power, which was still able to produce everything it needed to continue fighting. There was no resolution in sight . . . until Athens fell under the sway of a young aristocrat named Alcibiades (pronounced Al-sih-BUY-uh-deez).

Young, rich, and handsome, Alcibiades was far too ambitious for his own good, or for the good of his country. Nonetheless, his eloquent speeches persuaded the Athenian assembly to mount a major invasion of the island of Sicily, which was largely allied with Sparta. This plan was a long shot at best, and just plain crazy at worst: at almost ten thousand square miles, Sicily was larger than the entire Athenian Empire! There were also hostile natives there living in isolated hill towns . . . perfect terrain for guerrilla warfare. To top it off, the Athenians probably weren't aware of any of this; Six hundred miles away, Sicily might as well have been on the moon.

The defeat was total. With the loss of half its troops and navy,

Athens was doomed. Its fate was sealed when the Spartans finally built a fleet that could challenge Athenian control of the seas. After Sparta's decisive naval victory over Athens at Aegospotami in 405 BCE, the Spartans were effectively bosses of Greece.

But in the end, the Peloponnesian War had no real winners. Sparta's victory was hollow, as its core territories on the Peloponnesian peninsula had been impoverished by the twenty-seven-year war, and Athens was a wasteland. Greece's not-very-long golden age was over, and power was shifting to a small northern kingdom called Macedonia.

it's serious.) The second round picked off the great Athenian leader Pericles, who'd planned the city's grand strategy and kept its various political factions united during the early part of the war.

But Athens not only survived—it fought on for another twenty-three years, almost defeating Sparta on several occasions. Overall, it's inspiring evidence that if they hate them enough, people can triumph over adversity to go on killing other people indefinitely.

So what caused the Athenian plague? Nobody knows. But contemporary medical experts have named a number of diseases as possible culprits, including the bubonic plague, Typhus, and typhoid fever.

Round 4: Alexander vs. Everyone

Alexander of Macedon may have been the greatest military genius of all time, but his father, Philip II, was the one who got the ball rolling. After the Peloponnesian War, Philip took advantage of Greek weakness to build Macedonia into a major player. He reorganized the Macedonian phalanx to include cavalry, a deadly new formation, armed with spears fourteen feet long, and crushed regional competitors. Then he headed south, annihilating the Greek armies at Chaeronea in 338 BCE.

> . . . not only no Greek, nor related to the Greeks, nor even a barbarian from any place that can be named with honors, but a pestilent knave from Macedonia, where you can't even buy a decent slave.
>
> —Demosthenes, an Athenian politician, on Philip II of Macedonia

Knowing the Greeks dismissed Macedonia as an ignorant Hicksville (it was), Philip invited famous Greek scholars to the royal court. That's how his son Alexander got Aristotle as his personal tutor. Aristotle was

ON THE IMPORTANCE OF THANK-YOU NOTES

Alexander's first tutor was Leonidas (no relation to the Spartan king), a gruff old man hired to toughen him up. One day, when making a sacrifice to the gods, Alexander threw too much incense into the fire, and Leonidas scolded him, reminding him that incense was expensive: "When you conquer the lands where spice grows, you can use as much as you like, but until then, don't waste it!" Alexander never forgot this minor reprimand. Fifteen years later, when he conquered Giza (the spice warehouse of the ancient world), he sent Leonidas eighteen tons of frankincense and myrrh, worth its weight in gold, with a note thanking his old tutor for inspiring him as a boy . . . and advising him not to be such a cheapskate.

a perfect teacher for the teenage prince. Just as Philip planned, Alexander grew up assuming two things: a right to rule Greece, and an obligation to punish Persia.

While Alexander felt Greek enough, the Greeks themselves weren't so sure. After Philip died, the Greeks rebelled in 335 BCE, giving Alexander the first test of his reign. He passed with honors, or horrors, depending on your perspective. He captured Thebes, the ringleader of the conspiracy, and burned it to the ground, shocking the rest of Greece into submission. But Alexander was just getting started. The real enemy, Persia, still had to be dealt with.

First up, Asia Minor (modern-day Turkey). Here Alexander liberated the Ionian Greek colonies on the west coast, then headed east to defeat a huge Persian army at Issus in 333 BCE. Along the way he dealt with a famous puzzle called the Gordian Knot. According to legend, any man who wanted to conquer Asia had first to untangle this incredibly complicated tangle of rope kept at the city of Gordium. Alexander's solution was simple: he cut the knot in half with his sword. Next question?

The next question was Tyre, an impenetrable island fortress off the coast of what is now Lebanon that had been founded by the Phoenicians. Alexander had an equally simple answer to this problem: his army built a kilometer-long causeway connecting the island to the shore. This seven-month project brought his siege engines within range of the city walls. Furious at the delay caused by Tyre's stubbornness, once the walls were breached Alexander ordered the city burned to ground—sensing a trend?

Next came Egypt, the bread basket of the ancient world. In addition to the country's fabulous wealth, Alexander (who was fast developing a god complex) liked the sound of the word *pharaoh*, the ancient title of Egyptian god kings.

After Egypt, Alexander chased Darius III into modern-day Iran and Afghanistan. The chase ended in Iran when Darius was finally betrayed by one of his own satraps, Bessus, who assassinated the Persian king, figuring it would please Alexander. But Bessus figured wrong. Alexander—a king himself, after all—was horrified to see royal blood spilled. A classy guy, he covered the Persian king's body in his own cloak, handed Bessus over to Darius's family for execution, and ordered a lavish funeral for the king. He also married a few persian Princesses to cement his control.

But Alexander was about to learn even his power was limited, in the only defeat he ever suffered, ironically delivered by his own troops.

When his Macedonians arrived in northern India in 326 BCE, they had been away from home for eight years. They were entering a place the Greeks considered the edge of the world, where diseases such as malaria began to take a toll. After defeating an Indian army (including war elephants!) by the Indus River, they simply refused to follow Alexander any farther. He reluctantly led the army on the fifteen-hundred-mile trek back to Babylon, his new imperial capital.

The mutiny was a discouraging setback for Alexander, who was also bored by the administrative duties of imperial government; he

SPIN CITY

In addition to conquering the world and everything, Alexander the Great was an amateur city planner, and not a bad one at that. His pet project in northern Egypt, Alexandria, became one of the great cities of the ancient world—and indeed the modern world as well.

Alexander chose as the location for the city a place with symbolic significance on the western branch of the Nile Delta, on an isthmus shaped like a Macedonian military cloak. Walking around the site, he personally laid out the defensive fortifications with chalk. He also chose the locations of the central market, the docks and harbor, and a slew of temples to both Greek and Egyptian gods, including the goddess Isis. To connect the city to an offshore island called Pharos, he ordered the construction of a stone causeway about 450 feet long. Later the Great Lighthouse, one of the seven wonders of the ancient world, would be constructed on Pharos.

By midday the young conqueror ran out of chalk, but he refused to take a break. So his entourage provided him with barley flour (originally intended to feed their servants) to finish laying out the city walls. Of course, seagulls immediately descended on the free meal, and Alexander freaked out, interpreting this as a bad omen. But his clever Greek soothsayer, Aristander, put a good spin on it: just as it fed the gulls, the city would provide "abundant and helpful resources, feeding men of every nation."

just wasn't made to stay in one place. Surveying a swamp-draining project in southern Mesopotamia in 323 BCE, he contracted a fever (probably malaria) and a few weeks later, the conqueror of the known world was dead. He was just thirty-three years old.

········· **WHO'S UP, WHO'S DOWN** ················

Rome: **WAY UP**

Alexander's empire didn't last, but it laid the groundwork for the most successful empire in history: Rome.

Culturally and militarily, Rome was a notch below Macedonia through most of this period; Alexander didn't even think to send an ambassador to the little town on seven hills in central Italy. But the Romans were descended from heroes (they were pretty sure) and were bound for greatness.

According to Roman legend, the city was founded by refugees from Troy, the city besieged by Mycenaean Greeks in Homer's epic poem *The Iliad*. After Troy burned, around 1200 BCE, a Trojan hero, Aeneas, supposedly left western Turkey and settled in central Italy. Genetic evidence (from cows!) supports the ancient Roman founding myth, suggesting that Trojan refugees may indeed have settled there, bringing their livestock with them.

ETRUSCANS/SNACSURTE

The Etruscans are one of history's more mysterious peoples. Unlike almost any other culture in the world, they wrote "back and forth" across the page—from left to right for the first line, and right to left for the second. Weirder yet, the "backward" lines were literally written in reverse, with letters appearing as if reflected in a mirror.

Several groups occupied central Italy, including the Etruscans, distant cousins of the Romans. Like extended families everywhere, the Romans and Etruscans weren't friendly. In the early days the Etruscans had the upper hand, and Etruscan kings ruled Rome for almost two hundred years. But when the Romans gave the Etruscans the Italian boot in 509 BCE, the tables began to turn.

The changes began at home, with the establishment of a republican political system based on elections. It consisted of the three-hundred-man Senate, chosen from the city's "patrician" aristocracy, and popular assemblies open to members of any social class. Each year the Senate chose two consuls, responsible for military affairs. While more democratic than most governments of the day, Rome's voting system—like any good voting system—was rigged so the lower classes got fewer votes than the well-to-do.

Already feeling imperial, the Roman Republic turned to its neighbors: first neighbors in Italy, then the islands of Corsica, Sardinia, and Sicily. But it wasn't easy, especially after Roman involvement in Sicily brought them into direct confrontation with Carthage, a powerful rival to the south.

Since its founding by Phoenician sea merchants in 814 BCE, Carthage had come to control a powerful maritime empire covering much of the western Mediterranean, including the north coast of Africa, Spain, and Sicily. When the first "Punic War" between Rome and Carthage began, in 264 BCE, Carthage was larger and more powerful than Rome. But the famed Roman legion helped Rome prevail.

During the Second Punic War beginning in 218 BCE (yes, the one with the elephants in the Alps), the Carthaginian general Hannibal set out to avenge his city's earlier defeat, and he wasn't screwing around. When he annihilated fifty thousand Roman troops at the battle of Cannae in 216 BCE, it became clear this was the most serious threat Rome had ever faced. But the Romans refused to give in, and by 202 BCE they had pushed Hannibal back to Africa, where the consul Scipio defeated him in what is now Tunisia.

> *Carthago delenda est! (Carthage must be destroyed!)*
> —Cato the Elder

At this point, the Roman Empire was officially the dominant power in the western Mediterranean, and was quickly drawn into the complex wheelings and dealings of the eastern Mediterranean political scene. Here Alexander the Great's death in 323 BCE had left a rather confusing situation, which only worsened in the following century. Figuring it was too big for one man to rule—and hoping to avoid a civil war—Alexander's generals had divided his empire into three main parts: Seleucus got Mesopotamia and Persia (the "Seleucid" kingdom), Ptolemy got Egypt (the "Ptolemaic" kingdom), and a third general, Antigonus, got the rest. But these kingdoms were soon feuding with one another anyway (no surprise).

Ironically, Roman expansion was fueled in part by the Roman Senate's desire to maintain a balance of power in different parts of the Mediterranean—always, of course, on Roman terms. Sometimes this involved switching sides when local allies got too strong. Other times the locals asked for it: in 89 BCE, for example, Mithridates of Pontus ordered the massacre of 80,000 Roman citizens in Asia Minor. This was, of course, the last mistake Mithridates ever made.

In sharp contrast to the three kingdoms fighting in the eastern Mediterranean, the areas to the west, what are now Spain and France, were politically and technologically primitive—in a word, "barbaric." Dealing with backward Celtic tribesmen, the Romans weren't afraid to crack the whip (burn villages, lay waste to the countryside, crucify a couple thousand people...whatever) to establish their authority.

EVEN THE ROMANS DIDN'T SPEAK LATIN . . .

As Rome expanded, its job was made easier by one of Alexander's key legacies: the common Greek language and culture of the ruling classes. In fact, the Romans adopted Greek as their official language in the eastern Mediterranean and employed the Greek elite to keep things running smoothly.

Enter Julius Caesar, a precocious Roman senator who got himself elected consul in 59 BCE and invaded Gaul (modern France) a year later. Caesar's amazing conquests made him amazingly rich; under Roman law, successful generals got to keep most of the loot from foreign wars. Caesar used his incredible cash haul to buy political influence and gain control of the Senate. (Democracy and political corruption: two great tastes that taste great together.)

In fact, Caesar's mind-boggling wealth allowed him to transform Rome from a worn-out republic into a one-man party. (Literally: free banquets, games, and public festivals were central to his strat-

THE QUOTABLE JULIUS CAESAR

"I came, I saw, I conquered."

"I would rather be first in a village than second in Rome."

"If you must break the law, do it to seize power: in all other cases observe it."

"Men are quick to believe what they wish were true."

egy.) With the Roman public solidly behind him, his political opponents feared he would next declare himself king, Rome's big no-no. And the rest, as they say, is history: Caesar was stabbed to death on the floor of the Senate in 44 BCE, in a scene immortalized by Shakespeare and a number of so-so movies.

Ironically, the assassination led to the thing the pro-republican conspirators feared most: the establishment of a true dictatorship under Caesar's adopted son, Octavian, who was later voted the superhero title of Caesar Augustus by a brown-nosing Senate. In the Pax Romana, or Roman Peace, the entire Mediterranean world was united under Roman rule. But the Roman Republic was dead; from now on, one man would rule the Roman Empire.

Slaves: BRIEFLY UP, THEN RIGHT BACK DOWN

Spartacus, who was born north of Greece, in Thrace, received training in the Roman army as a barbarian "auxiliary" (ally) before becoming a slave in 73 BCE. It's not clear why he was enslaved after serving Rome. However, his combat skills made him a natural candidate for the gladiator school at Capua, about one hundred miles from Rome.

Here Spartacus and his fellow slaves learned how to entertain a Roman audience with dramatic hand-to-hand combat. Knowing they were going to their certain deaths, however, about eighty gladiators followed Spartacus into rebellion—using kitchen utensils as weapons.

Before long they armed themselves with real weapons, slaughtering Roman soldiers who tried to stop them. Then they escaped to the countryside, where Spartacus incited a general slave uprising, attracting thousands of field workers to his cause. He led the rebel slaves to a mountaintop, where they built a fortified encampment.

At first the Roman Senate viewed the uprising as a minor threat, but they soon learned better, and dispatched two commanders (praetors) to besiege the mountain and starve the slave army into submission. Spartacus launched a daring counterattack, ordering his soldiers to use vines to rappel down the side of the mountain.

Of course the Roman Senate couldn't allow the slave rebellion to succeed, as the Roman economy was increasingly based on slavery. So they dispatched a new commander, Crassus, with twelve legions—a huge force—only to have the advance force of two legions annihilated by the slave army.

Spartacus now led the rebels south, to Sicily, where he planned to rendezvous with pirates he'd hired to take them to safety. But the pirates never showed, and the slaves found themselves trapped on a narrow peninsula. (Lesson: never trust pirates.) Desperate, Spartacus decided he had no choice but to fight the Romans head on. Here the Romans finally defeated the rebel army, showing no mercy as they butchered sixty thousand runaway slaves, including women and children. Sixty-six hundred survivors were crucified along the Appian Way connecting Capua to Rome. However, the body of Spartacus was never found.

Overthinking: UP—But What Does That *Mean?*

Concurrent with the golden age of Athens, Greek thinkers produced thoughts so profound we call 'em classics. Here's a quick run-down of the Classics Club.

Heraclitus, 535–475 BCE. "*The only constant is change,*" said Heraclitus, who also observed "*you can never step in the same river twice.*" A native of Ephesus, an Ionian Greek city in Asia Minor, Heraclitus is considered by some the founder of the Western philosophical tradition. His major contribution was the notion that the universe is always in motion—not static and unchanging, as in most traditional worldviews. Its motion isn't chaotic, but is structured by laws and relationships that human beings can understand using reason. Heraclitus was a mystical thinker who said that as part of the universe, we can comprehend its profound harmony if we look deep inside ourselves.

Anaxagoras, 500–428 BCE. "*No matter how small the object, it is composed of something smaller. And no matter how large, it is part of something larger.*" Also an Ionian Greek, Anaxagoras agreed with Heraclitus that the universe functions according to natural laws, adding that everything is made up of smaller constituents, which themselves are made up of even smaller things, etc., down to infinitesimally small essential units, which he called "seeds." For example, because it helps us grow, food must contain the "seeds" of skin, bones, hair, and so on. Anaxagoras studied natural phenomena such as stars, meteors, storms, and rainbows to understand the rules governing them.

Democritus, 460–370 BCE. "*Nothing exists except atoms and empty space; everything else is opinion.*" With his teacher Leucippus,

Democritus invented the theory of "atoms," tiny, spherical particles that can't be further subdivided, resembling the "seeds" of Anaxagoras. Democritus said atoms are always in motion, even in apparently solid objects; their interactions produce the physical properties we perceive with our senses. For example, a grape's "flavor" is simply the result of its constituent atoms interacting with the atoms that make up our taste buds and saliva.

Zeno, 490–430 BCE. "*The goal of life is living in agreement with nature.*" Leave it to Zeno to sum up the meaning of life with a paradox. After all, he proved that nature was a lot more complicated then we think . . . because it's actually much simpler than it looks. Confused? *Exactly!* Zeno's most famous paradox is the story of a race between Achilles and a tortoise. Achilles, who can run one thousand feet a minute, lets the one-foot-a-minute tortoise get a head start of one thousand feet. In his first minute, Achilles almost catches up with the tortoise, but in that time, the tortoise has moved forward another foot. In the next one-one thousandth of a minute, Achilles again arrives where the tortoise used to be—but the tortoise has again moved forward a tiny amount. Even though it makes no sense, it looks as if Achilles can never catch the tortoise. Why did Zeno pose this scenario, knowing its implications were false? Think about it.

Socrates, 470–399 BCE. "*All I know is that I know nothing.*" Socrates doubted that anybody can know the truth with absolute certainty. He focused on rhetoric, a sophisticated technique of verbal persuasion that Athenian orators used to convince their audiences of statements that weren't always true. Ironically, Socrates used the same rhetorical tricks in his critique (a sort of complicated philosophical joke, which most people didn't get). Even more ironically, he considered his skepticism a patriotic duty—even though it infuriated his fellow Athenians, since he was attacking the Athenian democracy. When Athens was defeated by Sparta in the Peloponnesian War, his criticisms made him an attractive scapegoat, and in 399 BCE, he was put on trial on the vague charge of "corrupting the youth" with strange ideas. He was forced to commit suicide by drinking hemlock.

So what exactly is the "music of the spheres"? Does it refer to actual music? And what the hell are the spheres, anyway? We're not promising this explanation will make sense, but here goes . . .

Beginning with the Greek mathematician Pythagoras, ancient philosophers said that the cosmos was made up of crystal spheres of increasing size, with the bigger ones enclosing the smaller ones like Russian nesting dolls. The sun, the moon, the planets, and the stars were all mounted on different rotating spheres, nearer or farther from the Earth. There were twenty-two spheres in all, including the nine spheres of the solar system.

The Greeks said that the proportions of the spheres reflected divine ideals. Pythagoras studied triangles and circles because he believed that these perfect shapes (later called "Platonic forms," after Plato picked up the idea) had mystical importance. The same mystical proportions applied to every aspect of reality, including music and space.

According to the ancient Greeks, "harmony" was closely linked to geometry, as both are ultimately based on combinations of whole numbers. Because the cosmic spheres were mathematically perfect, the Greeks believed their movement created musical harmony—even if humans couldn't hear it. Aristotle described the Pythagorean theory in these terms: "The whole universe is constructed according to a musical scale . . . because it is both composed of numbers and organized numerically and musically." Aristotle himself was skeptical, but Pythagoras practiced what he preached: at mystical ceremonies he used real musical performance to "heal" his students from being out of sync with the universe—whatever that means.

· · · · · · · · **SO LONG, AND THANKS FOR ALL THE . . .** · · · · · · · ·

Better Ways to Kill
Incontrovertible proof of Chinese badass-ness at least as early as 341 BCE, crossbows are also an important contribution to humanity's repertoire of ways to kill people. Thanks, China!

Crossbows are indeed a feat of simple genius. In the sixth or fifth century BCE, a Chinese military engineer realized that the traditional bow and arrow was terribly inefficient, because it relied on individual physical strength, which varies hugely from person to person. Drawing an arrow and aiming it accurately was more than many a peasant conscript could manage: while some muscular heroes might send their arrows a hundred yards on target, more puny archers . . . well, not so far.

Enter the crossbow, which fixes the bowstring on a notched trigger mechanism, allowing the soldier to draw the bowstring, load the arrow, and aim in three separate motions. The first crossbows were composed of a metal loading and trigger mechanism set in a wooden stock (like a gun barrel) attached to a wooden bow.

Early hints from Chinese literature, including the *Art of War,* by the Chinese master strategist Sun Tzu, suggests that crossbows were in use sometime in the sixth century BCE. The first definite reference to a crossbow used in battle comes from China in 341 BCE, at the battle of Ma-Ling. Models of the weapon were included in the ceremonial burial of the first Chinese emperor, Qin Shi Huang. But the earliest actual crossbow artifact is a bronze lock mechanism dating to 228 BCE, discovered in the tomb of the Han emperor Yu Wang.

The weapon may have been developed independently in the West. It first appeared in the Mediterranean during the campaigns of Alexander the Great, when the Macedonian army used crossbows in the siege of Tyre, in 332 BCE. Alexander's crossbows were called *gastrophetes,* with the root *gastro* referring to the human stomach: soldiers supposedly rested the stock of the crossbow on their bellies (*gaster*) to cock the bowstring behind the arrow.

The Romans later supersized the Macedonian *gastrophete* into the ballista, an extremely powerful siege weapon that could penetrate stone walls and also devastate armies in the field during pitched battles. The ballista was used to shoot sharpened iron darts or round stone balls.

Tabloid Power Couple "Cleopantony"

As queen of the richest state in the Mediterranean, Cleopatra provided most of the glamour in this power couple. Born in 69 BCE, Cleopatra VII—her full regnal name—ruled as the tenth generation of the Ptolemaic Dynasty, and was a direct descendant of Alexander the Great's general Ptolemy, who received Egypt as his inheritance from the Macedonian conqueror three hundred years before. Although Greek, she ruled the ancient realm of Egypt as an absolute monarch in the tradition of the pharaohs.

For his part, Marc Antony was an accomplished Roman politician who almost attained absolute power—but was outmaneuvered by Octavian, an even more ambitious opponent. Born in 83 BCE, Marc Antony joined the Roman army as a young cavalry officer and distinguished himself in combat in Syria, but he was always dogged by his early reputation as a party animal.

Antony eventually served under Julius Caesar in the conquest of Gaul. He also helped Caesar defeat his arch rival Pompey. When Caesar was assassinated in 44 BCE, Antony partnered with Caesar's adopted son, Octavian, to defeat two of Caesar's assassins, Brutus and Cassius, at the battle of Philippi in Macedonia.

Although they were allies, by this point Antony and Octavian were clearly rivals in pursuit of absolute power. After their victory they parted ways, with Octavian returning to Rome and Antony sailing to Egypt to begin a partnership (and romance) with Cleopatra. Cleopatra, who had once visited Julius Caesar in Rome and even bore him a son, was more than willing to partner with another Roman politician to secure her throne.

But the wily Octavian took advantage of Rome's traditional fear of Egypt to turn the Roman people against Antony and Cleopatra, accusing Antony of plotting with Cleopatra to bring Egyptian-style absolute monarchy to Rome (ironically, in the end it would be Octavian who set up a dictatorship).

In 31 BCE, the dispute between Octavian and Antony exploded into full-scale civil war when Antony and Cleopatra proclaimed Caesarion, Cleopatra's son by Caesar, his rightful political heir—an attempt to cut Octavian out of his fortune and political support.

Octavian was no general (he usually pretended to be sick during important battles), but his chief general, Marcus Agrippa, defeated Antony and Cleopatra at Actium, off the coast of Greece. Then he pursued them to Egypt, where he defeated their army outside Alexandria. Antony killed himself by falling on his sword, and when Cleopatra heard the news a few days later, she killed herself by allowing a poisonous snake called an asp to bite her forearm.

Inner Peace

If you've never felt as if the material world were basically an illusion, it's probably time to hear about Siddhartha, aka the Buddha.

Siddhartha was an Indian prince from a minor kingdom in northern India (now Nepal) called Sakya, born sometime around 500 BCE. For the first twenty-nine years of his life, he lived in seclusion in the royal palace, where his parents sheltered him from the daily suffering of the commoners. By chance, however, Siddhartha happened to wander outside the royal cocoon and saw poor and sick beggars in the streets. He also saw a meditating monk, who sparked his interest in meditation.

Disillusioned with his comfortable existence, he gave up all his possessions and spent six years fasting, and meditating in utter poverty—but nothing happened. Siddhartha concluded that it was pointless to punish himself further. Instead, he began advocating "the middle way," meaning moderation in all things, including meditation and fasting.

> Do not dwell in the past, do not dream of the future; concentrate the mind on the present moment.
> —Buddha

Returning to some more relaxed meditation under a sacred fig tree in Bodh Gaya in what is now the modern Indian state of Bihar, Siddhartha comprehended the universe and humanity's place in it, becoming "Buddha," or "the Knower." The essential message: you must free yourself from desire. The Buddha explained that all human suffering is caused by desire—for comfort, possessions, power, sex, love, or life itself. Tranquility is within reach of all human beings, according to the Buddha, but we must free ourselves from all desire by acquiring true self-knowledge.

Knowledge of ourselves comes from contemplating three basic facts. First, nothing in the universe is lost. Even though you will die, your constituent parts are part of the universe forever. Second, change is constant, so any happiness based on things outside ourselves is an illusion. Third, every action has a consequence—a reminder that everything we do affects others. If you understand these principles, you will naturally try to perfect yourself in speech, action, and thought.

Once we achieve tranquility in our own lives, Buddha said that we can also help others to free themselves from suffering, through our words and deeds. And indeed his preaching in northern India proved contagious. Within two months of achieving enlightenment, he had attracted a thousand disciples. His father, the king, now sent nine delegations asking Buddha to come meet him, but on hearing the Buddha's teaching, all the ambassadors became disciples and stayed with him. When Buddha finally visited his home again, the entire royal family converted.

Although spiritual, Buddha was something of an agnostic. Traditional Hindu gods such as Brahma and Indra do appear in Buddhist teachings, but none of them is an all-powerful creator. Buddha also admits the origin of the universe is shrouded in mystery. He did preach the doctrine of reincarnation, but not as commonly understood—e.g., a "bad" person is reborn as, say, slime mold as punishment for his "bad" behavior. Instead, Buddha taught that human souls are aggregations of energy that leaves the body at death. This energy goes into the creation of new beings, including inanimate objects and lower forms of life. Buddha taught that the only way to leave the endless cycle is to attain spiritual perfection, or Nirvana, thus becoming a "Buddha" (he wasn't the only Buddha).

···· AND THANKS, BUT NO THANKS, FOR ... ········

Drunken Orgies
(Okay, So We're on the Fence About Where to File This One)

So did the Romans really have orgies? You betcha! In the early days of the Roman republic, orgies began as simple banquets that got out of hand. The banquets could last twenty-four hours, beginning in the late afternoon. Plenty of wine was served, and by the next morning/afternoon-ish, anything could happen. As the Roman republic declined, morals apparently got looser ... much looser. Public figures led the way with bisexual affairs and generally scandalous behavior. A contemporary accused Julius Caesar, for example, of being "every woman's husband, and every man's wife."

According to the historian Suetonius, the first emperor, Caesar Augustus (originally Octavian), exiled his daughter Julia because she held drunken all-night orgies in the Roman Forum. Augustus also exiled the poet Ovid, whom he blamed for corrupting Julia with dirty poems. Her male consorts weren't so lucky: Augustus had them executed.

Later, the emperor Tiberius supposedly staged shocking sexual events on his island retreat of Capri involving men, women, prepubescent children, and animals. By comparison, his adopted son, Caligula, was a responsible sort: he hosted adult-only orgies (again in the Roman Forum), to raise money for the bankrupt imperial treasury.

The naughty Romans could always claim that their all-night sex fests were just a continuation of Greek ceremonies in honor of Dionysius. But this was a bit lame, as they focused on the fun part—group sex—while forgetting about the more gruesome aspects of Dionysian festivals, where, for example, participants tore wild animals apart with their teeth.

The Original Blue Man Group

Designers of athletic undergarments have long groped (heh) for answers to the difficult question: how to combine freedom of movement with the right measure of "support" and protection? The ancient Celts, of northern England and Scotland, however, being practical and primitive people, dispensed with garments altogether, favoring armor that was "barely there": blue war paint. And nothing else.

Julius Caesar, who briefly invaded Britain in 55 BCE, recalled: "All the Britons paint themselves with *vitrum*, which gives their skin a bluish color and makes them look very dreadful in battle." To complete the portrait, the Roman historian Tacitus added that the Celts went to battle "ranged in order, with their hands uplifted, invoking gods and pouring forth horrible imprecations."

The sight of blue buck-naked Celtic warriors approaching across the fields of France, Spain, and Britain was apparently a pretty terrifying spectacle for the more civilized Romans, who at least wore a skirtlike armored garment (the "cingulum") to protect their nether regions. In addition to body painting, the Celtic warriors also spiked their hair with lime and clay, which turned it blood red, and covered themselves with tattoos. In fact, the Romans called one group of Celts Picts, because they covered their bodies with "pictures."

— Iron Chef, BCE Edition: Romans vs. Chinese —

Rome:
Milk-fed Snails Fried in Oil with Boiled Tree Fungi

Roman banquets are a thing of legend, but that's kind of the problem—what exactly is fact versus fiction in the ancient reports about these insane parties? Actually, most banquets probably weren't that extravagant. But if he *really* wanted to show off, a powerful Roman demonstrated his wealth and generosity by serving dishes with exotic ingredients from all over the world, including a number of items that strike us as positively bizarre.

For an appetizer, try milk-fed snails or sea urchins fried in oil with boiled tree fungi, served with pepper and fish sauce. If that doesn't tickle your fancy, you might like dormice—yes, mice—fattened in clay jars that basically kept them immobile (think "mouse veal"). Or how about jellyfish stuffed with eggs? If all else fails, you'll surely go for pig uterus, ovaries, and udder with leeks, pepper, and cumin. Thus endeth the appetizers.

For an over-the-top first course, you might have chicken drowned in red wine, crane, boiled ostrich with sweet sauce, roast parrot,

Did the Romans really make themselves vomit between meals so they could eat more? Short answer: yup, but it was considered decadent. The Roman philosopher Seneca condemned the practice, recalling that at one feast "while we recline at a banquet, one slave wipes up the spittle, as another, beneath the table, collects the leavings of the drunks." The Roman orator Cicero attacked Julius Caesar for expressing "a desire to vomit after dinner." However, the notion that the Romans had a dedicated room for this purpose, a *vomitorium*, is a myth. There were in fact structures called *vomitoria*, but they were simply lobbies where the audience exited a theater (the words *vomit* and *vomitorium* both come from *vomere*, a Latin verb meaning "to disgorge").

peacock, pig kidneys and testicles, puppies, rabbit fetuses, seahorse, swan, or boiled flamingo served with spiced date sauce. To honor the goddess Minerva, one Roman emperor served a concoction made of pike liver, pheasant brains, peacock brains, flamingo tongues, and lamprey roe. Uh . . . yum?

Overall, the goal was to amaze your guests with the sheer variety and exotic nature of the foods. In fact, one of the most famous Roman chefs, Apicus, boasted that if a host followed his recipes, "No one at the table will know what he is eating." To spice things up, the food sometimes concealed non-edible party favors such as gold, pearls, amber, and jewels.

China:
Domesticated Leopard Fetus

Not to be outdone, the Chinese have a long history of holding equally expensive and extravagantly weird banquets to celebrate . . . well, just being really rich. Like the Romans, elite Chinese divided their meals into several courses, including at least an appetizer, a first course, a main course, and dessert. They also organized banquets by rank, with the most important people receiving the more exotic dishes.

So what would the fancy folk eat at these high-class banquets? For the soup course they might enjoy a thick soup of flattened dog meat, or bird's nest soup in clear broth. And yes, the latter dish (still served today) involves real bird's nest. These prized delicacies are constructed by a bird called the cave swift, with salivary secretions that turn gelatinous in hot water.

As always, the meat is where things got weird, including a couple of live specimens. The real delicacies, served at the emperor's table, included bear paw, domesticated leopard fetus, elephant, frog, horse, live baby mice, lizard, sparrow, turtle, snake, shark, and wolf. Contemporary Chinese chefs reconstructing Han Dynasty banquets suggest dishes such as "Golden Toads and Jade Abalone," live soft-shell turtles, and "Camel Hoof Thick Soup."

As in ancient Rome, extravagant Chinese banquets were an excuse for all kinds of naughty behavior, which contemporary Chinese moralists condemned (or maybe envied?). The general tone was set during the Shang Dynasty when a poet described an imperial banquet in these words: "With a pool of wine and a forest of hanging meats, men and women chased each other naked, drinking all night." Good times!

···················· **BY THE NUMBERS** ····················

29   length, in years, of the Peloponnesian War

4,500   weight, in pounds, of golden goblets captured by Alexander the Great from the Persian king Darius III after the Battle of Issus

329   number of Persian concubines captured by Alexander after the same battle

277   number of Persian caterers captured

17   number of Persian bartenders captured

40,000   number of silver talents captured by Alexander from the Persian capital at Susa

1,111   weight, in tons, of this amount of silver

6,600   number of rebels crucified by the Romans along the Appian Way after the failed slave revolt led by Spartacus

52,000   miles of roads built by the Romans

46,837   total length, in miles, of U.S. Interstate Highway system in 2004

9,000   number of war elephants employed by the Indian emperor Ashoka

120,000   number of Chinese nobles moved by Qin Shi Huang to Xi'an, his capital, so he could keep an eye on them

6,000   miles of roads built by order of Qin Shi Huang

1,000   miles of canals built by his order

2,500   length, in miles, of the Great Wall built at his order

25   height, in feet, of the wall in most places

14   depth, in feet, of the wall at the top

1,000,000   number of Chinese peasants said to have died building the wall

22   area, in square miles, of Qin Shi Huang's tomb

4

THERE'S NO PLACE LIKE ROME (EXCEPT CHINA, PERSIA, INDIA, MEXICO, AND PERU)

(1 CE–500 CE)

Human sacrifice. Socially sanctioned infanticide. The invention of algebra.

This was mankind at his most classical.

Or at least, it was the last five hundred years of a period often considered the Classical Age.

For the first time, most people were the subjects, citizens, or slaves of large governmental entities. In fact, about half of the world's estimated population of 250 million lived under the auspices of just three empires: Rome, Parthian/Sassanid Persia, and Han China.

These empires were put together and defended by massive armies. They were organized and operated by massive bureaucracies, paid for by massive tax systems and fed by massive groups of forced laborers.

In addition to the Big Three, other empires and city-states grew, flourished, and, in most cases, collapsed. By the middle of this period, Berber traders were using camels to establish trade routes across North Africa.

One of the largest cities in the world was at Teotihuacán, in what is now Mexico. On the nearby Yucatan Peninsula, Mayans were becoming the first fully literate culture in the Americas. Several city-states developed distinctive cultures in what is now Peru.

The period also saw the birth and growth of Christianity. It was just one of scores of novel belief systems and curious religions that sprang up and faded out of fashion—only, this one hung on, and profoundly changed not only the way hundreds of millions of people worshipped, but how entire nations were governed.

There were individual and group achievements that would be enviable in any era. In China, they came up with paper. The Romans' use of the arch, borrowed from the earlier Etruscan culture, enabled engineers to construct huge buildings and other structures. In medicine, physicians in several countries increasingly began looking inside the human body for links among various organs, common maladies, and possible cures. And in the Egyptian city of Alexandria, a Greek named Diophantus was writing thirteen books on variable equations that became key to the development of modern algebra.

Of course there were also other myriad examples of human behavior at its weirdest and most wicked (beyond "solving for x.") In Rome, as in other cultures, it was routine to kill infants born with defects. In the mid-fifth century, the Huns, led by Attila, so devastated the Balkan city of Naissus that the stench from the carnage was said to have made the area uninhabitable for several years after the battle.

But, the biggest development of the period was the contemporaneous growth of large-scale cultures. As nation-states strove to push outward, they brought with them their customs and beliefs. War was a common result when two or more of these states pushed up against one another. But exchanges of ideas—and new religious beliefs—also resulted, aided greatly by the widespread use of two languages: Greek and Latin.

There were more commercial benefits as well. The development of the Silk Road, a network of routes between China and the Mediterranean, and the use of Monsoon winds on the Indian Ocean, which switched direction with the seasons, greatly increased trade between East and West. Silk, spices, and bronze moved from China, while coins, ivory, gems, and glassware made their way east.

············ **WHAT HAPPENED WHEN**··············

14 Caesar Augustus, Rome's first true emperor, dies at the end of a forty-one-year reign.

~30 Jesus of Nazareth is crucified by Roman soldiers at Jerusalem.

70 Roman soldiers burn the Temple at Jerusalem and largely destroy the city, after a nine-month siege.

79 Mount Vesuvius erupts, destroying Pompeii and the resort town of Herculaneum.

91 The Han Empire defeats the neighboring Xiongu, or "Mongols," forcing them to move west into Central Asia.

100 The first Chinese dictionary is published.

117 The Roman Empire reaches its greatest geographic extent.

~200 The Bantu tribes migrate into Central and South Africa and begin to dominate much of the area.

220 After four hundred years, China's Han Dynasty collapses.

224 The Sassanid Dynasty in Persia is founded by Ardashir I, who overthrows the Parthian Empire.

320 The Gupta Empire begins with the accession of Chandra Gupta I to the throne of a small northern Indian kingdom.

350 The Huns invade Persia.

391 A North African named Augustine becomes a Christian priest, in the city of Hippo, in what is now Algeria.

391 The Roman emperor Theodosius I makes Christianity the official religion of the empire.

395 The Eastern and Western Roman empires are formally split by a codicil in the will of Theodosius I.

400 What is now Afghanistan is invaded and its Buddhist culture destroyed by the Hephthalites, or "White Huns."

410 The Visigoths, under Alaric I, enter Rome and help themselves to the city's goodies.

439 The North African city of Carthage falls to the Vandals.

476 The Western Roman Empire formally ends.

480 The Hephthalites begin overrunning the Gupta Dynasty in India.

· · · · · · · · · · · · · · · · · · SPINNING THE GLOBE · · · · · · · · · · · ·

Rome (the City):
You May Have Heard of It . . .

The Silk Road was a good example that despite the old saying, all roads did not lead to Rome. But a whole lot of them not only led there, but were also built by subjects of the Roman Empire.

As imperial capitals go, Rome was pretty impressive. For the most part, the Romans were borrowers rather than innovators. But they made the most of what they appropriated from other cultures. While their architecture was heavily influenced by Greece, for

TOASTY UNDER THE TOGA

During the first century CE, some of the classier homes in Rome were built with terracotta tubes embedded in the walls. The tubes carried warm air from fires in the basement: the first central heating systems.

example, the Romans added their own distinctive flourishes. As with most Roman cities, Rome was generally well laid out, and relatively clean by contemporary standards, even if the most popular way of disposing of bodily waste was basically throwing it out the window.

But there was plenty of water to go around from a dozen aqueducts, and free heated public baths. And boy, were the Romans conspicuous consumers! The Mons Testaceus, a one-hundred- foot-high hill of broken pottery containers built up from nearby warehouses along the Tiber River during Rome's heyday, is still evident today.

> Will anybody compare the Pyramids, or those useless though renowned works of the Greeks, with these aqueducts?
> —Sextus Julius Frontinius, the city of Rome's water commissioner, 97 CE

The people who ruled over the city—and the sprawling empire it dominated—were a decidedly mixed lot. There were some great leaders, such as the much-traveled Hadrian, who in his twenty-one years as emperor visited much of the empire and consolidated Rome's control over it; or Constantine the Great, who was the first emperor to embrace Christianity and who founded the immodestly named city of Constantinople, which became one of the world's great metropolises.

THESE BOOTS ARE MADE FOR BOSSES . . .

The Roman emperor Gaius Caesar Germanicus was nicknamed "Little Boots" because he was brought up in army camps and sometimes dressed like a miniature soldier. The nickname stuck, and the world remembers him by its Latin version: Caligula.

And there were some real bozos, such as Vitellius the Glutton, who hosted three or four banquets a day, feasted on chow such as flamingo tongues and pike liver, then used a peacock feather to induce vomiting so he could make room for more.

As the Roman Empire began to unravel from within and without, the capital city began to feel the pinch. Once comprising the foundation of the state's agrarian economy, many Roman farmers gave up competing with cheaper crops from outlying provinces and moved to the city. As early as 6 CE, Rome was importing 14 million bushels of grain per year, mostly from North Africa, and the city swelled to a population of more than 1.5 million by the third century.

But by the second century CE, the city of Rome was essentially a welfare state. Free food was handed out daily, and mammoth specta-cles were staged to keep the natives from getting too restless.

PUCKER UP

Roman husbands kissed their wives on the mouth at the end of the day, but their motive was not at all romantic. They were checking their spouses' breath to see if they had been sitting around drinking wine all day.

In 395 CE, the empire permanently split into two pieces. The Eastern half transmuted into the Byzantine Empire and lasted until the mid-fifteenth century. But in the West, invading Huns ravaged Italy in the middle part of the fifth century, and in 410 CE, the Visigoths sacked Rome itself.

ROME BURNS: WHO DUNNIT?

During the night of July 18, 64 CE, a fire broke out in the shops near the Circus Maximus, the city's mammoth stadium. It spread quickly and lasted more than a week. Ten of the city's fourteen districts, covering more than 70 percent of Rome, were destroyed.

As soon as the smoke cleared, the shocked citizenry began pointing fingers at the emperor Nero. After all, this was a guy who had murdered both his mother and his wife in his climb to the top.

Rumors were Nero wanted to build a glittery new palace in the heart of the city, and the Senate had balked at tearing down buildings already on the site. The fire would remove the Senate's objections. Armed thugs were said to have stopped efforts to fight the fire. Another rumor was that the emperor, who fancied himself a talented musician, had strummed his lyre and sung songs while Rome burned.

Actually, Nero wasn't even in Rome when the fire started, and rushed back when he heard about it, throwing open public buildings and providing food to those fleeing the fire.

But the mutterings continued, so Nero looked around for someone else to blame. He decided on a small, shadowy religious cult rumored to engage in sordid rites such as cannibalism and orgies. They were called "Christians."

Nero had some Christians tortured. They pointed fingers at other Christians, giving Nero the excuse to order general persecution. Hundreds were executed in grisly fashion: burned alive, crucified, or torn apart by wild animals in the arena.

Although it's most likely the fire started accidentally, some historians believe it's possible that Nero may have ordered the conflagration. It's also possible, according to others, that Christian zealots trying to fulfill biblical prophecies actually did start it.

Whatever the truth, it would be more than two centuries before Christians got a respite from systematic persecution. Nero had far less time left. Within four years of the fire, he was ousted from office by the Senate and army, and killed himself.

China:
Bureaucracy at Its Finest

While the Roman Empire was definitely the big dog during the first five hundred years of this millennium, it was by no means alone.

In China, the Han Dynasty was midway through its 426-year run. Also at its height in the second century, it was as widespread and dominant in the East as Rome was in the (relative) West, extending over most of what is now China and reaching into Korea and Southeast Asia.

The Han Dynasty, which rose to power in 206 BCE, was based on ideals espoused by the government-organization expert/philosopher Confucius (551–479 BCE). Those ideals embraced good behavior, manners, education, and duty. And while Han emperors and officials certainly didn't live up to those ideals all the time, they did run a pretty efficient government.

At its peak, Han China probably had a population of more than 60 million, with the largest city of Luoyang serving as home to about 240,000. The empire, which was divided into 80 provinces, and subdivided into about 1,600 prefectures, was administered by a herd of 130,000 civil servants, who got their jobs only after taking competency exams.

HAN MAN

As something of a tribute to the most enduring of China's dynasties, the modern Chinese word that denotes someone who is from China translates as "man of Han."

KEEP YOUR MOUTH SHUT AND YOUR PEN IN YOUR POCKET

It was a capital offense to write the name of the Han emperor or speak directly to him.

PAPER WORK

Han-era Chinese weren't all politicians, bureaucrats, and artists. There were also a lot of busy scientists and inventors, coming up with, or improving on, things such as ships' rudders, accurate maps, and the wheelbarrow.

Even the bureaucrats came up with good ideas from time to time. In 105 CE, an imperial Court administrator named Cai Lun is credited with taking scraps of bark, bamboo, and hemp, chopping them up, and boiling them with wood ash. The result was paper. (Of course, being a eunuch, the guy had a lot of free time.)

The invention of paper helped officials compile voluminous records and solidify the use of a single written language in an empire with myriad spoken languages. By the end of the second century, the Han were using wooden blocks of type to print entire books.

And castrated bureaucrats could immerse themselves in paperwork.

Along with bureaucrats, the arts and sciences flourished in the Han Dynasty. Han Chinese were great workers in bronze, and Han porcelain and lacquer ware were not only beautiful, but were durable enough to survive centuries in leaky tombs.

The Han army was endowed with crossbows, the bronze trigger mechanisms of which could not be duplicated by their foes. When it came to armies, the dynasty's military leaders ran a pretty tight ship. And unlike earlier Chinese leaders, the Han emphasized offense rather than defense, invading the territory of their chief adversaries, the Mongols, in 91 CE.

Han China was far less dependent on trade than the Roman Empire, although the Chinese did trade widely, and sent diplomatic and trade commissions to both Rome and Parthia. Its economy was based not on slavery, but on a system sort of like sharecropping. Land was the chief object of taxation. Big landowners, in turn, exacted taxes and shares of crops from the peasant population.

Like the Roman Empire, Han China was increasingly plagued by government corruption, internal

HAN, INTERRUPTED

In 9 CE, Han rule was interrupted by a reform-minded usurper named Wang Ming. Over a fourteen-year run, he instituted a series of changes that ranged from offering low-cost loans to peasants for funerals, to outlawing slave trading. The reforms, however, angered the upper classes and confused the lower. Wang Ming ended up having his head chopped off by rebel members of the army in 23 CE, and the Han dynasty was restored for another two hundred years.

struggles for power and the complexities of running a vast governmental entity. Unlike Rome, however, the Han Dynasty sank quickly. In 220 CE, it collapsed, to be replaced at first by three kingdoms: the Wei, Shu, and Wu. The empire was briefly unified by the Jin Dynasty, but in the main, for the next three hundred years China was to be dominated by warlords and torn apart by civil war.

The Middle East:
Empire to the Left, Empire to the Right

Sandwiched in between the Roman and Han empires during the Late Classical Period were a couple of descendants of the ancient Persian dynasties.

The first of these were the Parthians, Iranian nomads who rebelled against the rule of the Seleucid Empire in 240 BCE. They really came into their own about a century later, under the leadership of Mithradates II, also known as "Mithradates the Great." Under the rule of Mithradates and his successors, the Parthians conquered a total of eighteen separate small kingdoms, centered on what is now known as Iran, and stretching from Syria to what is now Afghanistan. Parthian rulers thus became known as "the kings of kings."

The Parthians were skilled horsemen who relied on spiffy cavalry tactics in battle. After conquering a territory, they tended to leave local rulers and administrators in charge, and thus lacked the central governmental core that marked the Han and Roman empires. They also did not keep the same meticulous records as did their two rivals, so relatively little is known about the Parthians' internal affairs.

MAKING THEIR POINT

One of the tricks used by the Parthian armies was to send mounted archers into the enemy's ranks, fire a fusillade, and then retreat. But pursuers often got a nasty surprise: The Parthians would turn in their saddles, reload, and fire off another volley. Then it was "a Parthian shot." Today we call it "a parting shot."

Parthia and Rome had traded victories in battles over Middle Eastern territory in the half century before 1 CE, and the fights continued well into the new millennium.

In addition to invading Roman armies to the west and marauding Huns to the north, Parthia was subject to a hefty amount of immigration of Arabs from the south. Jews, who had been dispersed after Rome sacked Jerusalem, joined the Arabs after 70 CE.

Besieged on all sides, the Parthians were defeated and supplanted in the area around 224 CE by the Sassanians, under a guy named Aradashir I. Unlike the Parthians, the Sassanians used a more centralized, four-tiered governmental system and put their own administrators and tax collectors in place.

Like the Parthians, however, they also were almost continually at war with Rome. And like the Romans, the Sassanians eventually got around to embracing an official state religion: Zoroastrianism. Based on the teachings of the prophet Zoroaster, and perhaps the world's first monotheistic religion, Zoroastrianism did not seek converts. That meant the Sassanians tended to be fairly tolerant of other religions.

That changed, however, when Rome formally adopted Christianity in 391. After that, Christians came to be looked at as potential traitors, and were enthusiastically persecuted.

The Sassanid Empire eventually stretched from Syria into what is now northern India. Of the Big Three empires of the Late Classical Age, it was the only one to last past 500 CE. In fact, it lasted almost 150 more years, before it was done in by Arab forces unified under the banner of a new religion, Islam.

India:
Let the Good Times Roll

If there were a sea of tranquility among the storm-tossed oceans of empires during this period, it might have been in India, where the Gupta Empire dominated from about 320 to 550 CE.

From about 365 BCE to about 180 BCE, the Maurya Empire had dominated much of the Indian subcontinent. With the demise of the Mauryans, however, India became a vast collection of regional

LIKE FATHER, LIKE SON

Legend has it that as Chandra Gupta lay dying in about 330 CE, he told his son Samundra to "rule the whole world."

The kid took a pretty good whack at it. After defeating attempts by his older brothers to usurp him, he began a series of wars on rival kingdoms along the Ganges River Plain. Samundra wasn't shy about getting into battle himself: one account says that in old age, he displayed the marks of more than one hundred wounds received in fighting.

At the height of his fifty-year run, Samundra's empire, which was centered near what is now the city of Delhi, controlled most of the Ganges River Valley. He is credited with ending the monarchies of nine rival kingdoms and subjugating a dozen others.

Samundra was survived by his sons, who expanded the Gupta Empire even further, until its ultimate demise in about 550 CE.

powers that periodically shifted alliances and waged war with one another. The biggest of these was the Kushan Empire, which was centered in what is now Afghanistan and which extended over northern India and into Central Asia from about 80 to 180 CE.

The Kushan gave way in about 320 CE to the Gupta, who were led by a succession of five strong rulers, starting with Chandra Gupta I.

The Gupta Empire, which at its height extended over most of the northern and central Indian subcontinent, was run with a laissez-faire attitude: Defeated local rulers could stay in power, provided they behaved themselves and paid proper deference, and taxes, to the empire.

The Gupta Empire period is often referred to as India's "Golden Age." Politically, things were pretty peaceable. Trade with Rome (India provided exotic eastern goods; Rome provided gold) was so good that at least one Roman historian complained that the empire's bullion reserves were drained not by wars but by Indian merchants.

Although Hindus, the Gupta emperors were tolerant, and even supportive of, Buddhism and Jainism. The rules of grammar for the written language of Sanskrit were established, and literature and other arts prospered.

The Gupta Empire's cultural influences, in fact, reached beyond its geopolitical power, and left its imprint on civilizations in Southeast Asia, much as Greece had done in the West.

Unfortunately, a group of Huns called the Hephthalites were unimpressed. After several decades of fighting, the Gupta Empire fell to the Hephthalites about 550 CE, and India returned to a collection of small, and usually squabbling, kingdoms.

Africa:
Where Axum Is the Place to Be

Unlike Europe and Asia, the African continent was relatively devoid of mega-powers during this period. Most of North Africa, including what had been the mighty Egyptian empire, was under Roman control.

But that's not to say there weren't some significant things going on. The cultural influence of the Bantu, who had long used their mastery of iron forging to enhance their agricultural skills, spread both east and west from what is now Nigeria. The Bantu language and customs came to dominate other groups who were more hunters and gatherers than farmers.

At some point, the Berbers of North Africa came up with the idea of using domesticated camels to transport goods such as gold, ostrich feathers, and ivory from areas in West Africa, such as the kingdom of Ghana to ports on the Mediterranean.

But the happening place on the continent was in Northeast Africa, on the site of modern-day Ethiopia. It was Axum, a city-empire right smack on the trade routes between India, Arabia, and Africa. In addition to easy access from the land routes of Africa, Axum also enjoyed the advantage of the Indian Ocean's monsoon winds, which shifted directions with the seasons. That meant a ship could go back and forth within a year and sail downwind all the way.

Also known as Aksum, the city exported gold, ivory, rhinoceros horn, hippopotamus hides, slaves, imported textiles, metal goods, raw metals, and luxury goods.

The Greeks heavily influenced Axum. Its coins bore inscriptions in both Greek and the Axumite written language, Ge'ez. And starting in about 350 CE, the city was the only Christian state in Africa outside the areas still controlled by Rome.

The Americas:
Doing Their Own Thing

While not as impressive in size and scope as their Old World counterparts, several cultures in the Americas nonetheless had some accomplishments worth noting in the first five hundred years CE.

Chief among them were two groups in what is now Mexico. On the Yucatan Peninsula, the Maya were building a collection of city-states, literally carved out of the jungle. Although they lacked metal tools, plows, or wheels, the Maya developed a written language, an advanced calendar, some pretty solid astronomy, and architecture rivaling that of ancient Egypt.

In 455, they founded Chichen-Itza, a city covering six square miles, which included pyramids, temples, a ball field, and housing. Unlike their European and Asian counterparts, however, the Maya did not form a centralized government, and spent much of their time fighting among themselves.

On the Mexican mainland, a bit north of what is now Mexico City, a group of fierce warriors called the Teotihuacános established a vast metropolis about 1 CE. By 500 CE the population of the city of Teotihuacán may have reached two hundred thousand. The city's Pyramid of the Sun was the largest structure in the pre-Columbian Americas.

Farther south, in southwest Peru, the Nazca culture was carving 780 miles of lines in the desert floor. With mathematical precision, they created lines forming figures of spiders, killer whales, and

If you can name the largest city in the world around 500 CE that had an economy based on a volcanic by-product, well, you could've been an Aztec—even though the city had nothing to do with the Aztecs.

In fact, Teotihuacán rose and fell hundreds of years before the Aztecs came along. But they're the ones who gave the metropolis its name, which in English means "City of the Gods." We don't know what the actual inhabitants called it.

The city was situated about 30 miles northeast of what is now Mexico City. It covered about eight square miles at its peak, and was laid out along a precise grid, with a 2.5-mile-long main street.

The city was dominated by the Pyramid of the Sun. It loomed 216 feet tall, covered 547,000 square feet at its base and required a million cubic yards of building material, mostly volcanic rock.

Speaking of which, the economy was based on obsidian, which craftsmen turned into spearheads, knives, scrapers, figurines, and masks, as well as incense burners, pottery, and other goods that were traded all over Central Mexico.

By the mid-eighth century, however, the place was pretty much a ghost town. A huge fire, possibly sparked by raids from outside cultures such as the Toltecs, destroyed much of the city, and the population dispersed.

geometric shapes that could only be discerned from the air above. The Nazca also developed an efficient subterranean irrigation system and were masters at ceramics.

In Northern Peru, a people called the Moche used millions of adobe bricks to build huge tiered pyramids. Like the Nazca, they were masters at pottery work.

And in what is now the central United States, the Adena and the Hopewell were building flourishing trading cultures. They also built elaborate burial mounds, at least one of which stood seventy feet high.

SLICE OR DICE?

Judging by the records left behind in the form of various artwork, the Nazca preferred to cut the heads off their captives, while the Moche liked to slit their throats.

Like most of their European, Asian, and African counterparts, the Teotihuacános, Nazca, Moche, Adena, and Hopewell were all but dim memories by the end of the sixth century.

But while much of what would be considered "civilization" had yet to occur in the Americas, the rest of the world was approaching the early stages of Middle Age.

Or at least the early Middle Ages.

The Romans: SLOWLY DOWN

Unlike many empires whose destruction was often swift and could be attributed to a single cause (drought, plague, fast food), the Roman Empire saw its fall brought about by a number of factors, which actually took a few hundred years to occur.

Chief among the reasons may have been its sheer size. A big empire means long borders to defend, especially in a world full of envious neighboring empires and restless nations of have-nots. The Roman Empire was pressured, often simultaneously, from lots of different directions—the mounted nomadic tribes of the Asian Steppe, the Germanic tribes in what is now Northern and Central Europe, the Berber peoples in North Africa.

That meant having either to pay a big army to keep out invaders, or bribe potential invaders not to invade. Coupled with an economy that relied heavily on imports while producing relatively little in the way of goods themselves, the continual drain of maintaining a massive defense system meant high inflation. In 98 CE, the Roman denarius was 93.0 percent silver; in 270 it was 0.02 percent silver.

> Now that no one buys our votes, the public has long since cast off its cares; the people that once bestowed commands, consulships, legions and all else, now meddles no more and longs eagerly for just two things—bread and circuses.
>
> —Juvenal, a second-century Roman satirist writing about Rome's transition from republic to empire.

Political instability was another problem: in 68 CE, there were four different emperors; in 238 CE, eight different men either held or shared the title. The Roman Army became the single biggest influence on who was in charge, and the army itself was often fragmented into warring camps. It's something of a tribute to the Roman bureaucracy that the government continued to sputter along, given the turnover at the top.

From time to time emperors tried to make the empire a little less unwieldy by sharing control. In 293 CE, the emperor Diocletian appointed himself and one of his generals as emperors of the Eastern and Western halves of the empire, respectively. Each had the title "Augustus," and each had a vice-ruler with the title "Caesar." (Luckily for Diocletian, his rule occurred after 253 CE, so he wasn't murdered or killed in battle—he retired after passing rule on to his successors, and died peacefully.)

Being emperor of Rome wasn't all toga parties and throwing out the first Christian on Opening Day at the Colosseum.

For one thing, there was no actual title of "emperor" attached to the job during the period 1–500 CE. Instead, the guys we think of today as emperors held titles such as "princeps senatus" ("lead senator") or "pontifex maximus" ("greatest bridge-maker," or "chief priest of the Roman religion"), or "pater patriate" ("father of the fatherland"). Emperors were known as "imperators," designating them as commanders of the army, and "augustus," which basically meant "majestic" or "venerable."

Moreover, there were no specific powers inherent in the job beyond what the emperor could assert on his own. A strong leader with good political sense, firm control of the army, and intimate knowledge of his enemies and potential enemies could make it a pretty good job, with a lot of fringe benefits. But a weak, lazy, or timid emperor was almost always in for a very short reign.

Getting the job wasn't easy. Some emperors took office because their dads or granddads named them as successors. Some were adopted by the incumbent and groomed to take over. Some were elected by the Senate or whichever part of the army they commanded. Some were forced to take the job as puppets for various factions. More than a few got it by killing a relative or two.

However the job was secured, the pension plan was generally lousy, mainly because your chances of living to collect a pension were about the same as being hit by lightning. (Actually, the emperor Carus was found dead in his tent in 283 CE, reportedly the result of his tent being hit by lightning, but more likely the result of poisoning.)

Consider this: Of the nineteen guys who served either as emperor or co-emperor between 218 and 253 CE, all but one were either murdered or died in battle. The one guy who wasn't? He died of plague.

This "tetrarchy" lasted until 324 CE, when one of Diocletian's successors, Constantine, decided he could handle things on his own. When Constantine died in 337 CE, co-ruling was tried on and off until 395 CE, when the empire was formally divided in two.

By then it was too late. Various groups of "barbarians" had been invading and sacking various parts of the empire for a century, and in 410 CE, the city of Rome itself was sacked. Alliances between the remnants of the Western Roman Empire and some of the invaders postponed the inevitable until 476 CE.

In that year, however, a mutiny of Germanic troops under Roman employ—who felt they had been cheated out of a land deal with the empire—took place. They forced the last Western Roman emperor to quit and turn over the reins to the Germanic leader Odoacer.

Irony lovers will revel in the fact that the last emperor was Romulus Augustus—named after both the legendary founder of Rome, and its first and possibly greatest emperor.

And sentimentalists will be happy to know that Romulus Augustus, who was probably no more than a teenager, was allowed to retire to Naples with an annual pension of six thousand gold pieces.

The last Roman emperor wasn't even important enough to execute.

The Barbarians: MOVING ON UP

The popular image of the different groups of people who fought on and off with the Roman Empire is of a bunch of giant hairy lunatics who lived for nothing but looting, raping, and pillaging, followed by heavy drinking.

Actually, such life goals aside, most of these groups, such as the Ostrogoths, Visigoths, Franks, and Vandals, had very different motives for clashing with Rome. Originating in Northern Europe, the Germanic tribes were pushed west and south by overpopulation, the need for new food sources—and fear of the Huns, who in turn had been pushed west out of Central Asia.

They were stuck with the common label "barbarian," which is a word the Greeks came up with because the Europeans' language sounded to them like nothing but a repetitive "bar-bar-bar."

The Romans actually began prodding the Germanic tribes first, seeking to conquer areas of present-day Germany that had been settled by some of the other groups. The Roman army won most of the key battles, but the Germanic tribes kept coming back for more.

Eventually, the empire began to enlist different tribes as confederates, or *foederati*, to help Rome fight the Huns, or other "barbarians." In return, the tribes enjoyed the protection of the empire and were sometimes granted territory to call their own.

> ## TWO MEN AND A LADY
>
> The wedding customs of having a "best man" and of carrying the bride across the threshold probably date from the third-century practice of Germanic men abducting brides from neighboring villages and carrying them home, with the aide of a loyal companion.

Things came to a head, however, in the late fourth century, when a group of as many as eighty thousand Visigoths pushed across the Danube River into the empire to seek refuge from marauding Huns. The

Roman emperor Valens allowed the immigration, but reneged on promises of food and land, and tried to disarm the Visigoths.

Bad idea. Valens was killed and the Roman army defeated. The defeat sparked the beginning of the end for the Roman Empire. In 410 CE, the Visigoths sacked Rome. (While they stole a lot of stuff, they burned relatively few buildings and generally treated the city's inhabitants humanely.) In 439 CE, the Vandals took Carthage and cut off the empire's Northern Africa breadbasket. In 452 CE, the Huns swept through Italy and would have sacked Rome again except for the personal plea to their leader, Attila, from Pope Leo I. No matter—the Vandals sacked it three years later.

By the beginning of the sixth century, various Germanic tribes had carved up the Western Roman Empire into kingdoms that roughly paralleled the nations in modern Europe: the Vandals in North Africa; the Visigoths in Spain; the Franks and Burgundians in France, and the Ostrogoths in Italy, Germany, and Austria.

Not bad for a lot of people limited to "bar-bar-bar."

The Huns: UP, DOWN, WHO CARES? (As Long as We Can Break Something)

Okay, there was at least one group in the Late Classic Age that fits anyone's definition of "barbarians."

The Huns were a nomadic people who originated in north central Asia and generally received bad press wherever they went. As early as the third century BCE, they made the Chinese nervous enough to erect a big section of the Great Wall.

Ferocious warriors, the Huns basically lived in the saddle. They didn't farm; they didn't trade. They just rode around and terrorized people.

IF AT FIRST YOU DON'T SUCCEED . . .

One thing you could say about Alaric: He didn't give up easily. Alaric was a Visigoth leader born around 370 CE in what is now Romania. In 395 CE he led an assault on the Eastern Empire and plundered his way through Greece before being defeated by a Roman force and forced to retreat.

In 401, he invaded Italy, lost a few battles, and retreated again. In 408, after Roman soldiers had killed thousands of "barbarian" wives and children, Alaric led a confederation of tribes and besieged the city of Rome itself.

He made it clear he didn't want to bring down the Empire, but would settle for a guarantee of peace and a chunk of land for the Visigoths.

But the deal fell apart, and in 410, Alaric laid siege to Rome again. This time, his troops burst into the city itself—and for the first time in eight hundred years, the heart of the Roman Empire had fallen.

After some internal feuding and a defeat at the hands of a Chinese army, the Huns gradually began moving west in the decades before 1 CE. By the time they got to Europe in the last half of the fourth century, they had developed an effective infantry to go with a killer cavalry.

The Huns were the scourge of the continent. They were fast, ferocious, and merciless. They didn't fight to conquer territory; they kicked booty to win booty. The Huns literally triggered a mass migration of Germanic tribes up to and into the Roman Empire.

In 434, command of the Huns passed jointly to a man named Bleda and his brother, a man named Attila, who quickly earned the nickname "Scourge of God." By then, the Huns were sometimes extracting huge sums of money simply for not attacking.

The power might have gone to Attila's head. He killed his brother, set up a headquarters city (in what is now, naturally, Hungary), and invaded Italy. In 453, however, Attila died. On his wedding night. Of a nosebleed. Really.

THEY MILK HORSES, DON'T THEY?

The Huns weren't big produce eaters. They avoided scurvy by drinking large amounts of mare's milk, which has four times as much ascorbic acid as cow's milk.

After Attila's death, his many sons quarreled among themselves. In 455, they were defeated by an alliance of Germanic tribes, and the Huns' run as world terrors was over.

The Jews: DOWN. So What Else Is New?

There have been very few times in recorded history when it was easy being Jewish, and the Late Classic Period wasn't one of them.

In the first century or so after Judea was taken over by the Roman Empire in 63 BCE, the state's Jewish population got along relatively well with their conquerors.

In 66 CE, however, increasing poverty and a Roman decision to confiscate money from the newly re-built Jewish temple at Jerusalem led to a revolt. Roman garrisons in the city were wiped out. Extremists known as "Sicarii" ("dagger men") went around stabbing people

"JUST KEEP DIGGING . . ."

According to legend, the Huns were pretty secretive about where they laid their main man Attila after he passed on. They reportedly put him in a triple-layered iron, silver, and gold coffin and buried him in an unmarked grave. Then they killed all the members of the burial party, so they couldn't reveal the grave's location.

Which leads one to wonder how they kept quiet the guys who killed the guys who did the digging.

faithful to Rome. A Jewish sect known as the Zealots seized the mountain fortress of Masada in what is now southeastern Israel.

Not surprisingly, the Romans reacted negatively. A few years of internal political struggles in Rome delayed the inevitable, but in 70, the Romans laid siege to Jerusalem. After nine months they had destroyed the new temple and most of the rest of the city. In addition to about one hundred thousand Jews killed, another hundred thousand were taken prisoner and variously crucified, burned alive, forced into slave labor, or turned into gladiators.

Four years after the fall of Jerusalem, Roman legions attacked the fortress at Masada, still held by Jewish rebels. The place was so formidable that it took fifteen thousand Roman soldiers almost two years to subdue Masada's one thousand inhabitants, including women and children. Only seven of the defenders survived; many killed themselves rather than surrender.

There were two more rebellions, one in 115 CE and the second in 132. The latter flap started in part because the Romans decided to build a pagan temple at the site of the destroyed Jewish temple, and because the emperor Hadrian outlawed circumcision, an important ritual of Judaism.

Led by a messianic man named Simon Bar Kochba ("Son of the Star"), the Jews successfully waged a hit-and-run war for about three years. Eventually, however, Roman military might—coupled with some really disturbing atrocities against the civilian populace—prevailed. As many as six hundred thousand Jews were killed, and Simon's head was delivered to Hadrian at the end of 135 CE.

To ensure against future rebellions, Hadrian ordered Jewish temples destroyed. Jews were banned from entering the rebuilt Jerusalem, which was renamed Aelia Capitolina, and Judea was renamed Syrian Palestine. Jews were dispersed throughout the empire, and there would be no official Jewish state for another eighteen hundred years, give or take a decade.

Roads: UP

One of the most remarkable accomplishments of the Roman Empire was its road system, which at its peak consisted of more than fifty thousand miles of hard-surfaced highways and thoroughfares, stretching from Great Britain to North Africa.

Specially trained army units built the roads. Actual construction varied according to the materials available at the site, but most of the main roads were admirably put together. They were sloped from the middle to facilitate drainage, built on multilayered foundations, and paved with thick, tightly fitting stones, and then concrete.

Along each side were unpaved paths for pedestrians and for horseback riders who wanted to save their horses' feet from the wear and tear of the paved roads. The excellence of the construction is evidenced by the continued existence today of many of these Roman roadways.

Markers placed alongside the main roads to indicate distance traveled, called *mila passum,* were about 4,800 feet apart, or a little short of a mile.

Two kinds of overnight accommodation existed along many roads, usually about fifteen miles apart. Pretty nice villas were available for those on official business—or with money and connections. Less prosperous travelers had to make do in often seedy inns/hostels called *cauponae.*

The road system also accommodated two kinds of mail service. The *cursus publicus* was for official business. Urgent mail was carried by riders using relays of horses—a Roman pony express—and it was said a letter could travel as far as five hundred miles in twenty-four hours. Private mail could be sent through a sort of UPS-type service that used slaves.

ROME'S BELLY BUTTON

Loving order and tidiness, the emperor Augustus had a "Golden Milestone" constructed in the city of Rome, on which were listed the distances to all the major cities in the empire. The emperor Constantine later referred to this as the Umbilicus Urbus Romae—or "navel of Rome."

Despite the great road system, most large shipments of goods and food still traveled by ship. This was because as smart as the Romans were in many things, they failed to develop a well-designed wagon or cart.

Religions: ALL OVER THE PLACE

Aided by improved transportation systems, common languages such as Greek and Latin, and increasing trade among nations, religions began to move beyond the borders behind which they'd originated.

Buddhism moved out from its original base in northern India across China and Central Asia. Hinduism spread throughout the Indian subcontinent.

But no religion benefited more from the confluence of empires than

Christianity. The new faith took advantage of the empire's reliable postal system and spread along the extensive network of Roman-built roads; it even organized itself like the empire. Dioceses were like Roman administrative districts, reporting to broader divisions, with central power shared at Rome, Antioch, and Alexandria. From an obscure and sometimes persecuted cult in the Middle East, by 391 CE Christianity had become the official religion of the Roman Empire.

While Christianity was taking advantage of the Roman road system to spread itself around the empire, followers of Buddha took a different path: they used the Silk Road. By the beginning of the millennium Buddhism had gained a firm foothold in the Kushan Em-

HERE COMES THE SON

Whatever one's personal religious beliefs, it's pretty hard to argue against the proposition that Jesus of Nazareth was one of the most important figures in world history.

What's more difficult to determine is just who Jesus was and what he did. The only historical documents we have with much detail of his life are the Gospels of the New Testament, along with letters by St. Paul and a few references in first-century Roman and Jewish documents.

Scholars generally agree that Jesus was born between 4 BCE and 6 CE in the town of Bethlehem in what is now Israel, to a Galilean woman named Mary, and raised in the town of Nazareth by Mary and Joseph, a carpenter.

Very little is known of Jesus's youth and early adulthood. When he was about thirty, he apparently began a public preaching career that lasted about three years. His sermons sometimes drew huge crowds, and his basic message—nonjudgmental love of God and one's fellow humans—was coupled with a warning that the world would end without notice and that people would be judged on their behavior.

About a week before his death, probably around 30 CE, Jesus and his followers went to Jerusalem for the observance of Passover. At some point he ran afoul of Caiaphas, the local Jewish high priest. Accused of blasphemy, Jesus was turned over to the Roman governor Pontius Pilate.

Although Pilate almost certainly didn't care about Jewish religious disputes, he also probably saw Jesus as a possible troublemaker, and ordered his execution. Following his crucifixion, several of Jesus's followers claimed to have seen him alive and well.

A whole lot of people eventually believed them, and the impact of that historical fact has been felt in most of the world ever since.

pire of northern India and modern-day Afghanistan, and reports of it had reached the Han Empire court in China.

According to contemporary Chinese historical accounts, around 68 CE the emperor Ming had a dream about a golden figure, and was advised by his ministers that the figure was the "god of the West." Ming sent an official named Cai Yin to India to investigate. Three years later, Cai Yin returned, accompanied by two Buddhist monks. Eventually a Buddhist community grew in the Han capital of Luoyang.

In 148, a Buddhist temple was opened in Luoyang, and translations began of Buddhist texts into Chinese dialects. Chinese pilgrims began to visit India as well, to study on what had been Buddha's home turf. By the end of the fifth century, there were an estimated two million Buddhists in China, and Buddhist missionaries were pushing into Japan.

The spread of Islam in the seventh century helped begin the decline of Buddhism along the Silk Road. But its impact lived on throughout Central Asia in art and architecture.

········ **SO LONG, AND THANKS FOR ALL THE** ··········

Cold Cream

Quick: What do your wrinkled aunt Suzie and gladiators have in common? Right. Cold cream.

And Galen of Pergamum, the second-century Greek physician, anatomist, and self-promoter whose work dominated much of the medical world for a millennium.

After studying medicine for more than a decade, Galen began practice at a gladiator school in what is now Bergama, Turkey. Looking for ways to soothe tired sword arms, he mixed olive oil, beeswax, and rose petals. The resulting glop's water content evaporated on the skin, which left a cool, soothing feeling. Galen called it *ceratum humidum*. We call it cold cream.

Galen eventually left the gladiatorial gig for a practice in Rome. There he became famous as a doctor to emperors. Insatiably curious, he dissected hundreds of animals, particularly Barbary apes, in an effort to understand more about the human body. One of his conclusions was that arteries were used to circulate blood and not air, as had been previously believed. Score one for science! Of course, he also believed his research supported the theory of the four humors—good health required a balance of four bodily fluids: blood, yellow bile, black bile, and phlegm.

A prolific writer, Galen cranked out about three hundred works, about half of which survive today. And he must have known something about health: he lived until the then-almost-unheard-of ripe old age of eighty-seven.

Saddle Sores

It seemed like kind of a no-brainer once it had been invented, but the humble stirrup made a huge difference in warfare during and after the Late Classic Period. Men had been riding horses into battle for a long time, but not always to great effect. For one thing, it was hard to hang on the horse and wield a weapon at the same time, since the rider had to use his thigh muscles to keep his seat, and couldn't rise off the saddle. Sometimes it was hard even getting to the battle: a Persian king named Cambyses was reported to have stabbed himself to death with his spear while getting on his horse.

But by the middle of the fourth century, someone in China had figured out that putting two rigid loops on the sides of the horse for the rider's feet to rest in would make it a lot easier for him to shoot bows, swing swords, and so on. It also allowed riders to carry bigger weapons and wear more armor, and still maintain their balance.

This use of "heavy cavalry" greatly diminished the impact of slow-moving infantry and greatly changed battlefield tactics. Small nomadic groups could practice hit-and-run warfare on larger but less mobile armies.

At least one historian even maintains that the development of the stirrup led to the development of the feudal system, since armored knights on horseback became much more important than a bunch of peasants with battle-axes.

All that horseflesh and armor cost money, and kings paid off the knights with huge tracts of land and special privileges. Everyone else became serfs. Interesting theory.

Preserving Pompeii

Sure, their houses were on the side of a volcano, Mount Vesuvius, but it hadn't erupted in hundreds of years. True, there had been some violent earthquakes in 63 CE, but the inhabitants of Pompeii and Herculaneum, about twenty miles southeast of the site of modern-day Naples, weren't worried—until about noon on August 24, 79 CE.

A huge eruption of ash and pumice fell on Pompeii, quickly covering the city in almost ten feet of debris. Herculaneum was barely touched at first. But the eruption continued throughout the night. Sometime early on the morning of the twenty-fifth, a swirling cloud of super-heated gases and ash poured down on that city. Scientists estimate that the "pyroclastic flow" may have reached speeds of sixty miles per hour and temperatures of seven hundred degrees Fahrenheit. Any living thing in its path was instantly killed. Deaths totaled more than twenty-five thousand.

The Roman writer Pliny the Younger was an eyewitness to the blast from a nearby town, and wrote two vividly descriptive letters about it to the Roman historian Tacitus. Pliny's uncle, the naturalist Pliny the Elder, was also commander of the Roman Navy in the Bay of Naples, and led an unsuccessful rescue mission to Pompeii. The elder Pliny was killed, after calmly bathing, dining, and taking a nap as the sky rained fire.

> . . . A darkness came that was not like a moonless or cloudy night, but more like the black of closed and unlighted rooms. You could hear women lamenting, children crying, men shouting . . . we stood up and shook the ash off again and again, otherwise we would have been covered with it and crushed by the weight
> —Pliny the Younger, describing the eruption of Mount Vesuvius

Herculaneum was eventually buried in a layer of volcanic mud that in some areas was fifty feet thick. Pompeii was under a layer of pumice stones and ash about half that thick. Except for looters, both cities were essentially forgotten until the mid-nineteenth century, when a systematic excavation was begun. Nowadays, the site is visited annually by thousands of tourists, who are treated to what life was like in Roman times—just before it ended.

Sex Laws

It has inspired more X-rated websites than just about anything, but there's a lot more to the *Kama Sutra* than kinky sexual positions. The work, whose title translates loosely as *Aphorisms of Desire,* was written sometime between the first and sixth centuries in India, probably during the reign of the Gupta Empire, and is attributed to a religious student named Vatsyayana.

It's organized into thirty-five chapters: four chapters on love in general; ten chapters on sexual topics ranging from kissing to anal sex; five chapters on how to get a wife; two chapters on how to treat a wife; six chapters on how to seduce someone else's wife; six chapters on courtesans, or mistresses, and two chapters on how to attract people in general.

Despite the *Kama Sutra*'s reputation, only one portion of one of its chapters deals with sexual positions, listing sixty-four, including "the curving knot," "the tigress," and "the sporting of the sparrow."

Women in the Sciences

She was a leading Egyptian female philosopher and mathematician, which in the fifth century could get you killed as a witch.

The daughter of a noted scholar named Theon, Hypatia was born sometime between 350 and 370 (historians differ). After attaining adulthood, she became the leader of the Neoplatonist school of thought in the Egyptian city of Alexandria, attracting a sizeable following of students. She was also apparently an accomplished mathematician and astronomer, although any works directly attributable to her have been lost.

It's believed that Hypatia helped develop early versions of a hydrometer, used to measure densities of liquids; a hydroscope, used to look underwater; and a plane astrolabe, used to measure the positions of heavenly bodies. She also made extensive revisions in the work of the mathematician Diophantus, particularly in the field of algebra.

> *Fables should be taught as fables, myths as myths, and miracles as poetic fancies. To teach superstitions as truths is a most terrible thing.*
> —Hypatia of Alexandria

Being a Neoplatonist meant Hypatia believed humans could attain perfection and happiness without the help of a deity. This was a dangerous belief in the early fifth century, since the Roman emperor Theodosius I had declared open season on non-Christians.

In fact, it was fatal. A mob of Christian zealots who believed Hypatia to be a pagan witch attacked her in 415, beating her to death. The mob then hacked her body to pieces and burned the various parts.

Nonetheless, Hypatia will doubtless be remembered in coming centuries as a pioneer for a woman's right to think for herself—and solve for x.

A Really Big Tombstone

Nintoku Tenno was the sixteenth-century imperial ruler of Japan, according to tradition. Not much is known about him, except that he lived around the middle of the fifth century and apparently sent emissaries to China twice during his reign. There is also a legend that he suspended forced labor for three years and sacrificed his own comforts until prosperity returned to his empire.

Whatever. What we remember him for today is his tomb. The keyhole-shaped tomb of pushed-up earth is 1,600 feet long and 115 feet high, and covers 1.5 million square feet. Located near the city of

Osaka, it is alternately surrounded by three moats and two green-belts, and is one of the three largest tombs in the world. (The others are the tomb of Shihuang-di, the first emperor of the Chinese Qin Dynasty, and the Great Pyramid of the Egyptian pharaoh Khufu.)

Nintoku's tomb was thought to have been covered by more than twenty thousand haniwa, clay sculptures. The tomb may have taken twenty years to complete. So much for no forced labor.

········· AND THANKS, BUT NO THANKS, FOR . . . ····

Sore Losers

While we don't know as much about Pok-a-tok—the popular ball game played by the ancient Maya and other Meso-American people—as we do, say, baseball, it's highly likely that the players were too nervous to eat before the big game.

Just how it was played is unclear, but archaeologists have figured out it involved a rubber ball, which could vary in size from that of a baseball to that of a beach ball. Its composition also varied, from solid rubber to hollow, to containing a human skull.

Pok-a-tok was played on large walled fields that could be longer than modern football fields, although narrower. Side walls sported stone rings as much as twenty feet above the ground, and the object of the game was to touch the ring with the ball, or pass the ball through the ring. Players, who could number from one to four per side, couldn't use their hands to accomplish this feat, which meant matches could take a really long time to complete.

Which is just as well if you were on the losing side. Often, although not always, the losers were decapitated and their blood drained as an offering to the gods. And you thought the sports fans in Philadelphia were tough.

Zorobuddhachristianism

Not much is known for sure about the founder of Manichaeism—including his real name. It is known that "Mani" (actually a title of respect) was Persian by birth, the son of a woman with ties to Persian royalty. He began preaching at an early age, after the first of two visions he claimed to have had.

Somewhere around 240, Mani revealed a new religion that attempted to combine elements of Christianity, Buddhism, and Zoroastrianism. Manichaeism contended that the spirit was good and the flesh was bad, and that salvation came through self-knowledge and identifying with the soul rather than the body.

Mani took his new religion to India, and then returned to Persia, where he won permission from the ruling family to preach—at least until about 276. When a ruler named Bahram I ascended to the throne, Zoroastrian priests persuaded him to have Mani executed. After a trial that lasted nearly a month, he was—apparently in a fairly gruesome fashion: one version of the tale is that he was flayed alive; another, that he was crucified, then flayed, with his skin stuffed and hung on the city gate as a warning to his followers.

AUGUSTINE OF HIPPO

As a theologian and writer, this North African–born guy was, well, a saint. In fact, he is generally regarded as one of the early Christian Church's most important and influential theologians.

Augustine was born in a small Roman community called Tagaste, not far from the city of Carthage, in 354. His mother was a Christian, his father a pagan. Augustine was well educated, and became a teacher in Carthage before leaving for Rome at the age of twenty-eight.

In Rome, and later Milan, Augustine taught rhetoric and began building a reputation as an accomplished speaker and writer. He also dabbled in religion, mostly adhering to the precepts of Manichaeism. According to his own account, Augustine converted to Christianity in 386 and returned to Africa, where he eventually, and somewhat reluctantly, became a priest and then bishop of the city of Hippo. (He's known to have had at least two concubines before he gave up sex to join the priesthood.)

He also became a prolific and widely known writer, the bulk of whose works—more than five million words—have survived to the present, and played a key role in bridging the transition of Christianity from its beginnings to the Middle Ages. The most important—the twenty-two-book *City of God*, and the thirteen-book *Confessions*—laid out not only details of his life, but also the foundations for orthodox Christianity.

Augustine attacked pagan beliefs and the numerous variations on Christianity that sprang up in the first few hundred years after Christ's death. He described a vision of life that saw this world as doomed to disarray and disappointment, and counseled that man should instead focus on getting ready for life in the next world.

Augustine died in 430, at the age of seventy-six, while the city of Hippo was under siege by the Vandals. His writings have since influenced not only theology, but also philosophy, sociology, and other areas of Western thought—including the concept of a "just war," or a war that is fought after peaceful options are exhausted and the potential for civilian loss of life is accounted for.

Following his death, Mani's religion spread quickly, both east and west from Persia, into Rome, Egypt, and the Eastern Roman Empire, and even reached into Tang Dynasty China. Its followers included St. Augustine, for the eight or nine years before he became a Christian.

As with any good religion, its followers were fiercely persecuted just about everywhere. Although it enjoyed sporadic success for several centuries, Manichaeism never reached the levels of influence of the religions from which it was distilled.

· · · · · · · · · · · · · · · · · · · BY THE NUMBERS · · · · · · · · · · · · · · · · · ·

0   number of women who ruled Rome from 1 CE to 500 CE

0   number of women who ruled China during the same period

3   average length, in years, of a Roman emperor's reign in the third century

40   average life expectancy, in years, of citizens of the Roman Empire

41   reign, in years, of Octavian Augustus Caesar

7   number of years between 1 CE and 500 CE that the doors of the temple of Janus were closed, signifying that the city of Rome was at peace

26   number of contemporary nations absorbed into the Roman Empire

122   height, in feet, of Colossus Neronis, the bronze statue of himself that the emperor Nero erected in Rome in the first century CE

123   number of days the celebration lasted for a Roman military victory in 107 CE

11,000   number of exotic animals killed in the arena as part of the celebration

177   number of annual official Roman holidays by the fourth century

1,000,000   estimated population of Rome at the time of Christ

250,000   seating capacity of Rome's Circus Maximus arena by the fifth century

50,000   estimated population of Rome after final sack by Visigoths in 476 CE

547,000   area, in square feet, of the base of the Pyramid of the Sun in Teotihuacán

5,500   number of pounds of gold paid by Roman citizens to the Visigoths in 410 CE to prevent destruction of the city

3,000   number of pounds of pepper paid in same ransom

6,000   number of men in a Roman legion

4,000   length, in miles, of the Silk Road, linking China to the West

5

THE NOT-REALLY-THAT-DARK (UNLESS YOU LIVED IN EUROPE) AGES

(500–1000)

The decline and eventual collapse of the Roman Empire in the West during the fifth century CE plunged the world into centuries of doom and gloom, wherein humanity became a collection of dull-witted, superstition-ridden dolts who accomplished next to nothing and waited around for the Renaissance to begin.

Or not.

Actually, the "Dark Ages"—the term used to describe the first half of what is traditionally described as the "Middle Ages"—is something of a misnomer. So is the "Middle Ages" for that matter. The idea that there was a thousand-year period between the end of the Roman Empire and the beginnings of the Renaissance where nothing much happened was fostered mainly by intellectuals starting in the fifteenth century, especially in Italy. These bright lights wanted to believe—and wanted others to believe—that they had much more in common with the Classical Age than they did with the centuries that had just preceded them. By creating, and then denigrating, the Dark, or Middle, Ages, the "humanists" also sought to separate themselves from the very real decline in the quality of life in most of the European continent after the Roman system fell apart.

It was a pretty Eurocentric view of things. In reality, there were a lot of places in the world where mankind was making strides. Centered on what is now Turkey, the Byzantine Empire was a direct link to the culture and learning of ancient Greece and Rome. In the deserts of what is now Saudi Arabia, an empire centered on the new religion of Islam was spreading with lightning speed, and carrying with it not only new beliefs but also new ways of looking at medicine, math, and the stars. In the North Atlantic, Scandinavian ships were exploring the fringes of a New World, while in the Pacific, the Polynesians were pushing across even more vast aquatic distances to settle in virtually every inhabitable island they could find.

In the jungles of Central America, the Maya were reaching the peak of a fairly impressive civilization. In the jungles of Southeast Asia, the Khmer were setting up an equally impressive cultural and trade center. Even in Europe, which admittedly was pretty much a mess, devoted monks were doing their best to keep the flame of learning burning.

As in every age of man, there were great individuals. At six-foot-four, the Frankish king Charlemagne literally towered over his contemporaries. Sometimes referred to as the father of modern Europe, he was a success at war and politics, and also a great patron of education.

And there were those capable of horrific acts by the standards of any age, such as the Tang Dynasty empress Wu, who killed her own infant daughter in order to gain power by framing a rival with the murder. (It worked.)

There were astounding feats of human endeavor, such as the construction of the Grand Canal in China, which stretched more than 1,200 miles and connected the farmlands of the Yangtze Valley with the markets of Luoyang and Chang-an. There were astounding feats of human barbarity, such as the blinding of more than fourteen thousand prisoners by the Byzantine emperor Basil II. And there were equally astounding feats of individual endeavor, such as the founding of a major world religion by a comfortably fixed middle-aged Arab trader who became known as the Prophet Muhammad.

As Christianity had done in the late Classical Age, the rise of a new religion set in motion a hurricane of political and military clashes that would stir things up far beyond the Not-So-Dark Ages. But the storm also precipitated a mixing of cultures and ideas that would reap benefits for the various affected groups.

·············· **WHAT HAPPENED WHEN**··············

527 Justinian begins a thirty-eight-year reign over Byzantine Empire.

538 Buddhism reaches Japan from Korea via Chinese missionaries.

570 Muhammad is born.

637 Islamic armies capture Jerusalem.

661 The assassination of Muhammad's cousin Ali widens schism among Muslims that results in Shiite and Sunni sects within the religion.

664 Christianity replaced pagan religions in Britain after Synod of Whitby. Almost simultaneously, British Isles are ravaged by plague.

695 The first Arab coins are minted.

~700 Polynesian voyagers reach New Zealand.

~750 Mayan civilization nears its peak.

762 Baghdad becomes the center of the Islamic Empire.

768 Charlemagne begins a forty-six-year rule, briefly (more or less) uniting Europe.

793 Vikings attack the village of Lindisfarne, their first raid on the British Isles.

~800 Tribes in Mississippi Valley of North America begin using bows and arrows.

~825 Irish monks reach Iceland.

~900 The Khmer Empire establishes its capital at Angkor.

~900 The Anasazi have established cliffside adobe settlements in what is now the southwestern United States.

907 The Tang Dynasty collapses after nearly three centuries ruling China.

954 All English kingdoms are united under the Saxons.

~1000 Leif Ericsson, son of Eric the Red, reaches North America from Greenland.

1066 William, the Duke of Normandy, defeats the Saxon king Harold at the Battle of Hastings and takes over England as William I.

················· **SPINNING THE GLOBE** ·············

The Middle East:
Islam Rising

At the time of Muhammad's birth in 570, the Arab people were a relatively obscure group of desert dwellers, best known by other cultures as traders. Like their Semitic cousins, the Jews, Arabs claimed the biblical patriarch Abraham as one of their key ancestors. But their religious beliefs tended toward the polytheistic, and they generally weren't big on thoughts about the afterlife.

Muhammad changed all that. Orphaned at an early age, he was raised by an uncle and became a trader and merchant. At the age of twenty-five, he married an older widow and was financially set for life. But when he turned forty, he said he experienced the first of a set of revelations from the angel Gabriel and began preaching a new religion called Islam, or "submission to God."

The religion initially didn't go over well in Muhammad's hometown of Mecca, and in 622 he and his relatively few followers were forced to flee to the more hospitable town of Medina. But Islam—and its promises of paradise for the faithful believer and hell for the infidel—proved very attractive to both poor and rich, especially poor. Over the next decade, Muhammad put together an impressive army, and by the time of his death in 632, Islamic warriors had conquered most of the Arabian Peninsula.

> As for the unbelievers, their works are like a mirage in a desert. The thirsty traveler thinks it is water, but when he comes near he finds that it is nothing. He finds Allah there, who pays him back in full. Swift is Allah's reckoning.
> —From the Koran

After Muhammad's death, his followers found themselves embroiled twice in civil wars within the culture that sprang up around their religion. In 661, the victorious Umayyad Dynasty began an eighty-nine-year run, taking charge of things. That dynasty was overturned in 750, by the Abbasid Dynasty, which moved the Arab capital from Damascus, in what is now Syria, to Baghdad, in present-day Iraq. The Abbasids were to stay in charge through the middle of the thirteenth century, when they were overthrown by another Muslim culture run by the Turks.

Despite the infighting, Muslim armies rapidly swept over a huge section of real estate like ants over a picnic, taking advantage of the internal squabbling going on in the various empires around them. By the middle of the eighth century, Arab armies dominated from the Iberian Peninsula in the west to the borders of China in the east, and from North Africa in the south to Russia in the north.

The Arab conquerors were fairly tolerant, and for a very practical

The army of the caliph Al-Mu'tasim, like that of many Arab rulers, was made up in large part by soldier-slaves who had been, uh, "drafted" from other countries, such as Turkey and Armenia. The soldiers sometimes didn't get along particularly well with the locals, and by 836, relations between Al-Mu'tasim's army and Baghdad's residents were so tense that the caliph decided it would be politically smart to relocate his capital.

He chose Samarra, a site about seventy-five miles north of Baghdad, near the Tigris River. Al-Mu'tasim and the several caliphs who followed him built some pretty impressive palaces, which stretched for eighteen miles along the river, as well as barracks for the army that were kept on the outskirts of town. The city was the heart of the expanding Muslim empire.

There were three—count 'em—three racetracks, two of them out-and-back courses six miles long, and the other an oval track. There was also a huge game preserve. The city was laid out along seven parallel avenues. But the coolest local attraction was the Great Friday Mosque, the largest mosque of its time. Its construction begun in 852, the mosque compound covered almost 500,000 square feet and featured a spiral minaret that was about 150 feet high and 100 feet in circumference.

By 892, however, things had calmed down enough in Baghdad that the capital was relocated there. Samarra's importance, save as a pilgrimage center for Shiite Muslims, pretty much dried up after that.

economic reason: Under Islamic rule, Jews and Christians were allowed to practice their own religions—as long as they paid a tax on it. The fewer converts to Islam, the more money there was to run the empire.

The Arabs brought more than just a pay-to-pray tax system. Muhammad had been a big fan of learning and scholarship, and literacy rates in Arab-dominated areas were quite high for the time. Arab scientists excelled in taking the building blocks of classical Greek learning and improving on them, especially in math, astronomy, and medicine.

They also left their imprint on architecture and the arts, with intricate geometric designs, pointed arches, and gilded domes. Because they spread out in all directions at once, Arabs brought together heretofore-unknown types of food to other areas of the world, most significantly sugar, rice, and coffee.

Eventually, infighting among factions and a lack of strong leaders led to the weakening of the Arab empire. By the middle of the tenth century, much of the power of Arab caliphs had transited to military commanders who used the title "sultan." Many of these were not

Despite their impressive record in terms of empire-expanding, Muslim armies didn't always win. Sometimes this was due to underestimating the enemy. At least that's what happened near Tours, France, in 732.

Muslim armies under Emir Abdul Abd-ar-Rahman had just trounced a Frankish force, and were feeling pretty frisky as they got ready to take on another Frankish army, under the command of a guy named Charles. Charles lacked a formal title, but was the de facto ruler of much of what is now northern France.

Without a real cavalry, Charles had taught his infantry to fight in a phalanx-like formation that resembled a large square. He also carefully picked his place to fight: a wooded area uphill from the enemy, which made it tough for the latter to maneuver on horseback.

After six days of feeling out the Frank defenses—which historians figure were probably significantly outnumbered—Abd-ar-Rahman attacked. Bad move. The Arab cavalry could not penetrate the Franks' square; Abd-ar-Rahman was killed, and the Muslim army retreated during the night.

One of the significant impacts of the battle was that—coupled with an uprising by the Berbers, former North African allies of the Arabs—it halted Muslim expansion into Europe. The second important effect was that it cemented Charles's hold on the region and paved the way for his son, Pepin the Short, and his grandson, Charlemagne, to follow him.

And the coolest result? After the battle, folks began calling the Frankish leader "Charles Martel," or "Charles the Hammer."

Arab, but Turk. But they were Muslim, and therefore the political, cultural, and military influence of Islam would continue well into the middle of the next millennium, even as the Arab Empire faded.

China:
Tang-y and Delicious!

While the Arab Empire basically started from scratch, the two dynasties that ran things in China during most of the Not-So-Dark Ages actually did their best work in reestablishing governmental and cultural structures that had been lost after the collapse of the Han Dynasty in 220.

For more than three centuries after the Hans cashed in their chips, China was pretty much a cluster of petty warring kingdoms and badly run territories. Around 550, however, the Chinese formed a temporary alliance with the Turks and drove out a barbarian group known as the Juan-juan. In 581, a Chinese general named Yang Chien became the emperor Wen Ti, the first of two emperors of the short-lived Sui Dynasty.

The two Sui leaders employed—surprise—pretty brutal methods to get things done. They got the country's Grand Canal dug, which was a good thing for the farmers of the Yangtze Valley and consumers elsewhere in China. But the cost was the lives of more than one million people who worked on the project. The Sui also resurrected the notion of a strong centralized government.

But high taxes and forced labor led to a peasant revolt in 618, and the beginning of the Tang Dynasty. For just about the next three centuries, Tang rulers would steer China through a most decidedly un-Dark Age. Roads and canals effectively linked the country together. The Silk Road was reestablished, bringing China's highly coveted goods, such as silk, porcelain, and spices, to the West in return for gold. The city of Chang'an (now called Xian) was one of the world's most massive metropolises.

The Tang raised the standards of both the military and the bureaucracy, while allowing commoners a chance to succeed and rise in both areas. The introduction of tea from Southeast Asia helped raised health standards, since boiling the water eliminated a lot of sickness-inducing germs. Artisans devised a kind of three-color glazed porcelain that their

BUT THEY DON'T TAKE AMERICAN EXPRESS

Trade grew so rapidly in Tang China, they had a coin shortage. To make up for it, they used paper money and letters of credit. The letters were called "flying cash."

JAYWALKING NOT RECOMMENDED

Chang'an, city on the plains of the Wei River, southwest of Beijing, was probably the largest in the world in the middle of the eighth century, with more than one million inhabitants in a metropolis that covered thirty square miles.

We're talking about a city whose main thoroughfare was as wide as a modern forty-five-lane highway—if we had forty-five-lane highways. There were striking temples and pagodas (including the Big Goose Pagoda, which is 331 feet high) and a statue of Buddha that was one of the largest in the world.

In addition to being a major trade hub, Chang'an was also a spiritual and artistic center. It was so admired that the Japanese modeled their own capital of Kyoto after it in 794.

The firecracker's origin is somewhat short on details, and further confused by the invention of gunpowder. Historians believe that as early as the third century, the Chinese were roasting bamboo to enjoy the pop it made when heated. One version of the invention of gunpowder is that an alchemist searching for a formula for eternal life concocted the substance. But the most often-repeated explanation for gunpowder's invention is that a Chinese cook inadvertently mixed up the right proportions of three ingredients—sulfur, saltpeter, and charcoal—sometime in the tenth century. All three items would have been found in a Chinese kitchen of the time: the sulfur for intensifying the heat of a cooking fire, the saltpeter as a preservative, and the charcoal as fuel.

The idea of confining the powdery substance to a hollowed piece of bamboo is generally credited to a monk named Li Tian, who used them to drive away evil spirits from the city of Liu Yang. Whether it's true or not, the fact is that the city is today one of the world's biggest producers of fireworks.

European counterparts wouldn't match for several hundred years. And someone invented gunpowder.

When it came to matters of the soul, the adaptable Chinese took morality direction from old-school Confucianism and spiritual solace from Buddhism. And the Tang Dynasty's political influence extended far beyond its borders: Korea, what is now Vietnam, and Japan were all heavily swayed in their way of doing things by the Chinese. Japan, in fact, began largely to model its government structures after the Tang model. In fact, Tang China was considered so cool by the rest of the world that large Chinese cities of the time were truly cosmopolitan, sporting communities of expatriate Arabs, Greeks, Romans, Asians, Turks, and other assorted groups.

Internal power struggles and external sniping by barbarian groups and the Turks, however, gradually led to the disintegration of the Tang Dynasty, which disappeared in 907. What reappeared was another century of governmental and cultural chaos in China.

The Byzantine Empire
(aka the Eastern Half of the Empire Previously Known as Rome)

If the Arabs were inventing themselves and the Chinese reinventing themselves, empire-ically speaking, the Byzantine Empire was basically trying to hang on to and preserve the status quo during this period.

What had originally been the eastern half of the Roman Empire kept a lot of what was good about that entity (e.g., a well-organized government structure), while harking back to the Greeks for some stuff (such as a common language).

Centered on its capital of Constantinople, the Byzantine Empire was well situated to act as the world's middleman when it came to trade between East and West. The empire's bezant replaced the Roman denarius as the world's most widely accepted currency, and Byzantine merchants took a little taste of the action in goods that flowed through the empire in both directions.

While it had able leaders at the beginning and end of the Not-So-Dark Era (Justinian at the front and Basil II at the end), the Byzantine Empire did occasionally have a bozo in control. Nonetheless, it did okay even during those periods, mostly because the Roman way of doing things still lingered in the bureaucracy.

It also didn't hurt that most of the time farmers doubled as soldiers, which kept down the expense of standing armies, which in turn helped keep taxes low. In addition, the codification of Roman law in 534 by Justinian helped reinforce the legal system and served as a model for Western legal thought for centuries to come.

Although it spent a good deal of time fighting off the attentions of Rome's old rivals, the Persians, the Byzantine Empire generally chugged along during this period. In the sixth century, Justinian's armies expanded the empire nearly to the limits of the old Roman Empire. In the tenth century, Basil II took back a lot of land that had been lost to the Arabs, and claimed new territory in Eastern Europe. As the millennium ended, the Byzantines were still hanging in there, although somewhat withered by age and attrition. They would continue to hang for a few hundred years more.

GOT SILK?

For centuries, the Chinese jealously guarded the secret that silk was produced from the cocoons of the mulberry silk moth. Their secret eventually reached India in the fourth century CE, but the West still had to pay dearly for it.

Sometime around the middle of the sixth century, however, according to the Byzantine historian Procopius, two Indian monks came up with a way to smuggle the insects' eggs out China to Constantinople, by covering them in dung to keep them alive and secreting them in their hollowed-out walking sticks.

However the eggs actually got there, by the middle of the next century, sericulture (the process of silk production) had become a thriving industry in the West.

Basil II was only five when his dad, the Byzantine emperor Romanos II died, so he had to wait quite awhile to succeed his pop. While he was waiting, he honed his military skills.

It proved to be time well spent. Once he took over the empire, he beat back uprisings by powerful landowners in Asia Minor, in part by marrying off his sister to a Russian prince. In return, Prince Vladimir I of Kiev allied his armies with Basil's and converted to the Orthodox Christian Church. Then he whupped the Arabs and restored much of Syria to Byzantine rule.

Basil followed this up by beating the Bulgarians. After crushing the Bulgarian army at the Battle of Kleidion, he had 99 percent of the fifteen thousand captured enemy soldiers blinded. The remaining 1 percent had only one of their eyes put out, so they could lead the rest back to the Bulgarian leader, who subsequently died of a stroke.

By the time of Basil's death in 1025, the Byzantine Empire was at its greatest height in several centuries. When he died at the age of sixty-seven, he was buried near the cavalry field, reportedly so that he could forever hear his troops training for battle.

The Roman Empire
(aka the Western Half of the Larger Empire Previously Also and Somewhat Confusingly Known as Rome)

The western half of the old Roman Empire (which covered most of what we now call Europe), however, was another story. The collapse of the empire left Europe with no central government and no military protection. The population of urban areas rapidly dwindled, since cities were prime targets for marauding hordes. (This turned out to have something of a silver lining, since more people on the farms meant more production, and famine generally lessened.)

> O Christ . . . if you accord me the victory . . . I will believe in you and be baptized in your name. I have called on my gods, but I have found from experience that they are far from my aid . . . it is you whom I believe able to defeat my enemies.
> —A contemporary account of the prayer offered by the Frankish ruler Clovis before a battle in 496 with a Germanic tribe. Clovis won and not only converted to Christianity, but forced his entire army to convert as well.

The transportation system fell apart, and since Europe's main exports were heavy things such as timber and metals that were hard to transport, trade with the rest of the world withered. People rarely traveled far from home, which meant the exchange of ideas ceased.

Even here, however, where the "Dark Ages" appellation could arguably be applied, there was progress. Stone and wooden tools were replaced with metal implements. The water-powered mill became commonplace. Farmers learned to rotate their crops in order to rejuvenate soil. And the harness was redesigned so that it fell across a horse's shoulders rather than its throat, thus increasing its proficiency in pulling a plow.

Charlemagne managed to put together a respectable empire in the second half of the eighth century, and even got crowned Holy Roman emperor in 800 by the pope after helping his holiness out of a jam in northern Italy with a Germanic group called the Lombards. But things soon fell apart again after Charlemagne's death, and Europe reverted to a collection of futilely feuding feudal states.

If there was a unifying element for Europeans during this period, it was their fear and hatred of their northernmost brethren, the Vikings (more to come on these guys).

The Americas:
Huari and Chimu and Toltecs . . . Oh My!

In what is now Peru, the Huari culture conquered a five-hundred-mile-long strip on the coastal side of the Andes and supplanted the Moche.

LACKLUSTER LEADERS, SUPERIOR SOBRIQUETS

They didn't get to vote for their leaders, but that didn't stop folks in the Not-So-Dark Ages from giving their rulers some pretty descriptive nicknames. Such as: Basil the Macedonian, Basil the Bulgar Slayer, Charles the Bald, Charles the Fat, Charles the Simple, Edred Weak-in-the-feet, Edward the Martyr, Louis the Pious, Louis the German, Louis the Sluggard, and Louis the Stammerer.

The roots of most nicknames were pretty self-explanatory. Pepin the Short, for example, was, at a reported three-foot-six, decidedly height-challenged. (Conversely, one of Pepin's sons, Charles the Great, aka Charlemagne, was a really big guy, described as being seven times as tall as the length of his foot, or about six-foot-four.)

But the nicknames weren't always straightforward. Take Ethelred the Unready. Historians say the name wasn't due to his not being prepared. Instead, the language of the time meant that he was "without counsel," or lacked good advice. That made it sort of a pun, since *Ethelred* meant "well-advised."

Another Peruvian group settled around a town called Tiahuanaco, in the Bolivian highlands, which eventually grew to a population of thirty-five thousand, or much bigger than London or Paris at the time. In northern Peru, a group called the Chimu was making its presence felt. All three were predecessors to an even greater culture to come: the Inca.

In Central America, the Mayan civilization on the Yucatan Peninsula had peaked and was on its way down. A new group, the Toltec, had traded its meandering ways for militaristic ones, and was taking over much of central Mexico.

And in the Southwest of North America, several tribes were developing irrigation systems and creating high-quality ceramics, while tribes in the Mississippi Valley were mastering the bow and arrow and settling in true towns.

But all of this was just a warm-up for the advent of civilizations in the Americas that in terms of architecture, sophistication, science, and really sick bloodthirsty gore would rival any of those in Europe and Asia.

··········· **WHO'S UP, WHO'S DOWN** ···············

Monks: UP

Monasteries, which had existed since the days of the early Egyptians, were originally collectives of hermits who didn't want to be alone but who didn't want much to do with the outside world, either.

But in the Not-So-Dark Ages, they played an entirely different, and virtually indispensable, role, particularly in Europe. Monasteries became repositories and preservers of the learning of the Classical Age. They were virtually the only providers of education.

They also provided health care and social welfare programs, and even encouraged agricultural innovations by experimenting with new farming methods. And they became launching pads for missionaries, who spread the Christian religion throughout the "barbarian" lands.

Medieval monasteries were given an organizational boost in the mid-sixth century when an Italian monk named Benedict came up with a set of operating regulations for monks. The Benedictine Rule covered virtually every area of life, from what should be eaten and how many hours one should sleep (not many), to how often to pray (a lot!) and how to prevent impure thoughts (this involved bleeding).

MEANWHILE, BACK AT THE VATICAN . . .

One of the other things monks did was set a good example, at least in comparison to what sometimes was going on at church headquarters in Rome.

Take the case of popes Formosus and Stephen VI. An Italian, Formosus was born around 816. He became archbishop of Bulgaria, but ran afoul of Pope John VIII because of political differences and was excommunicated. He was eventually pardoned, and in 891 became pope. While pontiff, Formosus had a bitter feud with a powerful family led by a guy called Guido of Spoleto. (We are not making this up.)

When Formosus died at the advanced age of eighty, in April 896, he was replaced as pope by a guy named Boniface VI. But Boniface either died of gout or was deposed (it's not clear) after two weeks in the papacy. Stephen VI, who was an ally of the Spoletos, replaced Boniface.

Stephen VI may well have been the craziest pontiff in the long history of the Church. He was so vindictive that in January 897 he ordered the decomposing body of Formosus exhumed, dressed up in papal vestments, propped up in a chair, and put on trial for perjury and other crimes.

The late pope was found guilty. His body was stripped of its robes. The three fingers on his right hand with which he used to bless people were cut off. Then the body was thrown in a grave in a cemetery for transients. Then it was removed and thrown in the Tiber River. A sympathetic monk retrieved it, and Formosus was eventually re-interred with appropriate papal pomp.

As for Stephen, he was soon thrown into prison after an insurrection. While in jail, friends of the late Formosus managed to sneak in and strangle him.

So important was the role of the monastery in this period that in 1964, Pope Paul VI named Benedict the patron saint of Europe (which was not a bad turn of events for him, considering the monks at his first monastery had tried to poison him because his rules were so strict).

Although monks took a vow of poverty, along with ones of obedience and chastity, monasteries could actually be comparatively comfortable. Wealthy nobles found it convenient to dump second sons into them, where they wouldn't be likely to cause a fuss when the eldest son inherited everything.

CREATURE PREACHER

In 565, the Irish monk and missionary St. Columba reported seeing an unknown creature in a Scottish lake. It was history's first recorded sighting of the Loch Ness Monster.

Convents, which often were located near monasteries, likewise drew a fair share of unmarriageable daughters from rich families.

The result was that monasteries often received handsome contributions. By the turn of the millennium, in fact, much of the wealth of Europe was concentrated in monasteries. By the end of the thirteenth century, however, the influence of monasteries had declined, as secular institutions took over many of the roles the monasteries had earlier played.

Vikings: UP, DOWN, ALL OVER THE PLACE

Not everyone who lived in the Scandinavian countries during the eighth through eleventh centuries was a Viking. In fact, the word *Viking* was actually a verb, which loosely translates to "go voyaging" or "go raiding." The Viking part of the population, in fact, usually did its "Viking-ing" as a sideline: They'd farm in the spring and early fall, and then pillage and plunder in the summer and late fall. Winters, they'd party.

Even though it wasn't their full-time job, Vikings struck absolute terror in the hearts of most inhabitants of Western Europe. Their use of swift narrow-hulled ships with true keels and shallow drafts meant

BARE-NAKED BERSERKERS

When the going got tough among the Vikings of yore, the tough got . . . well, certifiably nuts. As in *berserk*, which has been translated as either "bare of shirt" or "bear-skinned." Both descriptions may have been applicable to a group of Viking warriors who became known as "Berserkers." These guys often went into battle without armor, and sometimes even without clothes, but also so pumped with murderous rage that they were said to take on the spirit of a bear or wolf and to have superhuman strength—a trait noted by some folklorists as the origin of the werewolf legend.

Berserkers were the Vikings' shock troops, so caught up in the battle that they were impervious to pain and often kept fighting after receiving really nasty wounds. How they got that way is something of a mystery. Some historians attribute their rage to a pre-fight ritual, others to a hallucinogen mixed with mead, and still others to psychedelic mushrooms.

Like Frankenstein's monster, however, the Berserkers eventually got out of hand. Off the battlefield, they were portrayed in Norse sagas as murdering, raping brutes who often terrorized their own villages. Sometimes they would challenge rich countrymen to duels, and then claim their lands—and their widows—after slaying them. In 1015, Berserkers were outlawed, and by 1123, "going berserk" could result in being banished for three years.

that they could penetrate upriver, so their raids often came without warning. Since they weren't Christians, they saw no reason to declare churches and monasteries off-limits to ravaging. This struck the pre-Crusade Europeans as *really* barbaric—and the Vikings as sound business, since that's where Europeans kept a lot of the stuff they had that was worth stealing.

Mostly, however, Viking society was pretty egalitarian for the time, especially in areas such as the legal system, government and the status of women. What's more, Vikings actually bathed fairly regularly, which couldn't be said of most other Europeans.

Starting in about the mid-eighth century, Vikings raided the British Isles and what is now France on a fairly regular basis. They also pushed as far south and east as North Africa and the Byzantine capital of Constantinople. At one point they controlled much of what is now Great Britain and Ireland.

They also moved west, although voyages in this direction were more land than booty. They leapfrogged from the British Isles to the Shetlands to the Faroe Islands, arriving in Iceland toward the end of the ninth century. Toward the end of the tenth century, a murderous Viking chief named Eric the Red was kicked out of Iceland and led a group of Vikings to a settlement in what became known as Greenland.

Around the year 1000, Eric's son, "Leif the Lucky," landed somewhere around what is now Labrador, in northeastern Canada. Mistaking some seasonal berries for grapes, he called the place Vinland. Subsequent expeditions took a stab at settling the place, but the locals weren't friendly, supply lines home were long, and the area wasn't brimming with easily exploitable natural resources. By 1020, the Vikings had bagged their incursion into the New World.

And by the middle of the eleventh century, the Vikings were pretty much out of the picture: some had been Christianized, some absorbed into the local populations

ALONG CAME POLY

As intrepid seafarers as the Vikings were, they paled in comparison to the Polynesians. Probably originating from what is now New Guinea, by 1000 CE, the Polynesians had settled on every large inhabitable island in the Pacific Ocean, by sailing thousands of miles across open water in small craft, which they steered by the stars. They carried with them crops such as yams and taro, which became staples in the islands.

where they had once plundered, and an increasingly powerful Danish empire absorbed the freelance fighters into a more governable fighting force.

By the way: Except possibly during some religious ceremonies, the Vikings didn't wear helmets with horns on them. Think about it. Would you want to go into hand-to-hand combat wearing a helmet with two ready-made handles for your foe to grab? The horned-helmet thing was popularized by nineteenth-century romanticists who probably rarely engaged in hand-to-hand combat.

The Mayans:
We're Not Exactly Sure Why, but DEFINITELY DOWN

Unlike the Roman or Byzantine empires, the Maya had never been collectively under a single overreaching governmental structure. Instead, they were subjects of a collection of individual kingdoms that shared common cultural traits.

By 750, what we will refer to anyway as the Mayan Empire had

MAYA BORROW YOUR CALENDAR?

Although the Maya have become famous for having developed an incredibly accurate calendar, they should be thrice as famous: They actually developed three calendars.

One was the "Long Count," which started when they believed this version of the world began, on August 13, 3114 BCE. The Long Count calendar is slated to end on December 21, 2012. More on that in a bit.

The Tzolkin calendar was based on thirteen twenty-day periods called *kals*, which represented the time it took to prepare a cornfield or plant and harvest it. (The Maya might have used twenty as a base rather than ten because they counted fingers and toes, rather than just fingers, in setting up their counting system. Really.)

Since neither of these calendars squared with the time the Maya knew it took for the earth to complete its yearly cycle around the sun, they came up with the Haab calendar, which was eighteen months of twenty days each, plus a five-day period called the *uayeb* tacked on at the end.

The calendars were used for different things: the Long Count for historical purposes, the Tzolkin for religious and farming purposes, and the Haab for civil functions. All of them were coordinated with each other and were amazingly accurate.

Incidentally, various alarmists and people with not enough to worry about often cite the date December 21, 2012, the end of the Long Count calendar, as the date of the end of the world. Most Mayan scholars disagree as to whether that was what the Mayans were predicting, but it's still a great fact for terrorizing any of your more gullible friends.

reached what probably was its peak population of about thirteen million. It also was at the top of a steep slide—most of the civilization disappeared into the jungle within a few hundred years. It began going downhill in the cities of the southern lowlands, in what is now Guatemala. New construction halted in mid-building. Entire metropolises were abandoned, with their buildings left intact and seemingly inhabitable.

It was a gradual, but inexorable, process, and its causes remain a subject of debate among archaeologists. One theory is the Maya succumbed to "agricultural exhaustion," meaning that repeated burning and clearing of jungle to plant more corn simply wore out the soil. Other theories include peasant uprisings, unsustainable population increases, earthquakes, epidemics, extensive malnutrition, and a climactic change that triggered a horrific drought. Actually, many factors may have combined to tip over what had become a teetering civilization. It's quite possible, for example, that a drought caused a famine that caused civic unrest.

Although the collapse of the cities in the southern part of the empire marked the decline of Mayan civilization, cities in the north—in what are now the Mexican states of Campeche, Yucatan, and Quintana Roo—continued to exist, if not flourish.

The northern cities were possibly sustained by an infusion of culture from invaders from Central Mexico, called the Toltecs, who were moving on up, culturally speaking, at the beginning of the millennium. By the time Spanish invaders got there at the beginning of the fifteenth century, the glories of the Mayan Empire were distant memories.

Justinian: UP, Until His Plans Were Plagued

Justinian I was one of the most important figures of the Not-So-Dark Ages, and might have been even more important if so many people hadn't come down sick during his reign.

A peasant born in Illyria, on what is now the Balkan Peninsula, Justinian was lucky enough to have an uncle in Constantinople who was a big-shot military commander and, later, Byzantine emperor. Uncle Justin took his nephew under his wing, and Justinian succeeded him as emperor when Justin died in 527.

One of the first, and most important, things Justinian did as boss was order the collection and revision of all Roman law. When finally completed in 534, the *Corpus Juris Civilis* (more popularly, "the Justinian

Code") codified both civil and ecclesiastical law for the empire, and became a source of laws for many nations and cultures in succeeding centuries.

Of course it wasn't all beer and skittles for Justinian. In 532, a riot broke out in Constantinople, led by (get this) chariot-racing fan clubs called the "Blues" and the "Greens," shouting "Nika!" ("Conquer!") The fracas had Justinian and his court ready to flee the capital, only to be talked into staying to fight by Justinian's wife, Theodora.

Justinian dispatched a trusted general named Belisarius to restore order. Belisarius, who was just back from fighting the Persians and had a seasoned army at the ready, accomplished this by trapping the rioters inside the Hippodrome and massacring about thirty thousand of them. Efficient, if not quite merciful.

The Nika Revolt and its aftermath cemented Justinian's hold on the throne, and he began formulating big plans for a comeback for the Old Roman Empire. His armies retook North Africa and most of the Italian peninsula, including the city of Rome from various Germanic tribes.

FROM HOOKER TO HOLY HELPER

It seems only fitting that if Justinian the peasant could become an emperor, Theodora the prostitute could become his empress. The daughter of a bear trainer, Theodora grew up around entertainers at what was the Constantinople version of *The Ed Sullivan Show*: the Hippodrome, where horse races, stage productions, and vaudeville-type performances were held.

Theodora became an actress in lowbrow productions and picked up money on the side as a prostitute. She eventually embraced a variation of Christianity called Monophysitism, gave up show business, and became a wool-spinner.

Somewhere along the way, she caught the eye of the emperor-in-waiting Justinian and became his mistress, and then his wife. When Justinian became emperor, Theodora became the de facto co-ruler, although her status as such was never formalized.

As a leader, Theodora was generally credited with helping her hubby build or rebuild a lot of cool things in Constantinople, including twenty-five churches. She's also credited with many reforms that benefited women, including expanding the rights of divorced women, protecting and sheltering ex-prostitutes, and ending the legal killing of women who committed adultery.

But the emperor's plans were derailed by the onset of bubonic plague.

It's highly possible the plague originated in North Africa and migrated to the Byzantine Empire on the backs of flea-infested rats, who hitched rides on the massive grain shipments that helped keep the empire fed. However it happened, the disease reached its peak in 542, killing as many as five thousand people per day in Constantinople alone. By the time it was over, historians estimate the plague killed as many as twenty-five million people, or one third the population of Eastern Europe.

It was the first known pandemic (i.e., a disease occurring over a widespread geographic area and affecting a large proportion of the people therein). Justinian's goal of reviving the Roman Empire was stopped in its tracks. (And as a dubious consolation prize for the emperor, the pandemic would forever be referred to as the "Plague of Justinian.")

The plague's long-term effects were just as important. The depopulation of Eastern Europe made it more difficult for the area to withstand the armed Islamic onslaught that came in the middle of the next century.

Sects: UP

There's nothing like the subject of religion to start an argument (except for maybe politics or baseball), so it may be unsurprising that two of the world's major religions experienced severe sect-ual tension during this era.

In the case of Islam, the religion was barely out of its infancy when trouble started. After the death of Muhammad in 632, a committee of prominent Muslim leaders decided that his successor to the caliphate—that is, their secular leader—should be a fellow named Abu Bakr, who was one of the Prophet's fathers-in-law. (Muhammad had a number of wives.)

But followers of Muhammad's son-in-law and cousin Ali Ibn Abi Talib claimed that Muhammad had designated Ali to succeed him. Ali eventually became caliph in 656, after the guy then in charge was assassinated. A powerful family called the Umayyads, however, revolted and established their own caliphate. Ali was assassinated in 661 and succeeded by his son. But when Ali's grandson, Hussein Ibn Ali, and his entire force were wiped out at the Battle of Karbala in 680, the Umayyads basically took over, and their branch of Islam eventually became known as Sunni.

But the "Shi'a Ali," or "followers of Ali," refused to recognize anyone who wasn't a lineal descendant of the Prophet. They came up with their own leader, and their own title for him—imam—and eventually became known as Shi'ites.

The Umayyad dynasty remained in control of things until 750, when they were overthrown by the Abbasids. By 1000 CE, the Islamic Empire had spread so far so fast that secular control by just one group proved impossible. While Islam would continue to expand and remain united in areas such as language, customs, and culture, political control would be fragmented.

Speaking of fragmented, the Christian religion had also endured its share of sects and experienced its share of divisions in its youth. But its first big split had its roots in the formal breakup of the Roman Empire into East and West in 330. Differences began to pop up between the branches of the Church in each empire. In 726, for example, the Byzantine emperor Leo III issued an edict of iconoclasm, which banned the veneration of religious images. This angered the pope, who condemned Leo's action.

In 787, a Church council restored the veneration of icons, but another Byzantine emperor, Theopolius, restored the ban in 832. By the turn of the millennium, the East and West were fighting over theological issues such as whether the Holy Spirit came from just the Father or from both the Father and the Son, and more earthly issues such as whether priests could get married and whether the pope was really the head of the whole church.

In 1054, Eastern patriarch Michael Cerularius and Western pope Leo XI excommunicated each other. Despite at least two attempts to reconcile, the Eastern Orthodox and Roman Catholic branches of Christianity would remain divorced.

Sex: DOWN (At Least for Roman Catholics)

The Roman Catholic Church dominated the rules and mores concerning sex in Europe during the Not-So-Dark Ages. Jesus Christ had been fairly quiet on the subject, at least judging by the New Testament, and early Christian theologians had mixed opinions. But by the sixth century, the Church had come up with some pretty strict rules when it came to sex. What they basically amounted to was "Don't Do It." All sex outside marriage was considered a sin, and so was most sex inside marriage. The act was prohibited on Sundays, fast days, feast days, during menstruation or pregnancy, while a woman was breast-feeding, and for at least seven weeks after she gave birth. Married couples were also not supposed to go at it during the daytime or while completely naked. Sort of makes you wonder how Europe repopulated itself after all those plagues.

> **DREAM DATES**
>
> Medieval people had to worry about not having sex not only while they were awake, but when they were asleep, too. That's because there was a widespread belief in incubi and succubi. These were demons (male and female, respectively) who visited sleeping people and had sex with them. It was thought that repeated visits could cause ill health, and even death.

.... **SO LONG, AND THANKS FOR ALL THE ...** ......

Representative Government

By 930 CE, Norwegian immigrants had been hanging out in Iceland for about sixty years, and it was starting to get crowded. The Irish monks who had been there when the Norwegians showed up had long since departed, but as more people arrived from what is now Norway, rivalries and disputes began to arise between the various chieftains who led the island's extended families.

So the bosses got together and decided to form a central authority. They called it the *Althing*, or "Assembly of All Things". They decided to hold it in a field about twenty-seven miles east of what would someday be the country's capital city. The way it worked was the clan leaders got together once a year to decide on laws and adjudicate them. Then all of the island's free men could make themselves heard on certain matters. The *Althing* became the main social event of the year, with parties, fairs, and the equivalent of trade shows occurring around it.

The *Althing* continued even after Iceland was taken over by Norway in 1262. It was dissolved temporarily around 1800, but was restored in 1844. Some historians consider it the first example of representative government, and it is often hailed as the world's oldest surviving legislative body and "the grandmother of parliaments."

The Ol' Battle Axe

She was the illegitimate daughter of Eric the Red, half-sister of Leif the Lucky—and a world-class butt-kicker.

Although Viking women generally enjoyed greater status and more rights than their counterparts in most other contemporary cultures, Freydis Eiriksdottir was unusually assertive. She participated in at least two of the voyages to Vinland (modern-day Newfoundland) that her half-brother Leif took in the early eleventh century.

One Norse saga credits her on the first expedition with giving birth to the first European born on North American soil. It also credits her with thwarting an Indian attack by ripping open her bodice, baring her swollen breasts, and slapping a sword on them, much to the consternation and confusion of the natives, who subsequently retreated.

On the second trip, Freydis apparently was actually a co-sponsor of the expedition. A falling-out with her partners led to the establishment of separate settlements in the New World. She further strained relations when she told her husband that the men at the rival settlement had raped her. He and his men dutifully killed all the men at the rival camp, but drew the line at killing their women. Freydis then reportedly picked up an axe and did the job herself.

After a three-year try, the Viking settlement was abandoned and Freydis returned to Greenland. It's possible, though unconfirmed, that she and her spouse were exiled for their activities in Vinland.

A Beautiful Mind

Abu Ali al-Husain ibn Abdallah ibn Sina was, quite simply, one of the brightest guys in history. Known in the Western world by his Latinized name Avicenna, he was the son of a local government official whose home, in what is now Iran, was a gathering place for the area's learned men.

Avicenna was a precocious, and largely self-taught, child. By the age of ten, he had memorized the Koran and volumes of Arabic poetry. By the time he was sixteen, he had completed extensive studies in physics, math, and logic, and by the age of twenty-one he was an accomplished and practicing physician.

He is believed to have written about 450 works, about a third of them dealing with philosophy. One effort—called the *Kitab al-shifa'* (or Book of Healing)—was a compendium of math, logic, and the natural sciences and is considered by some scholars as the single largest work of its kind written by one man. He also authored *Al-Qanun fi'l-tibb* (The Canon of Medicine), which for centuries was one of the most authoritative medical texts in the world.

> *I prefer a short life with width to a narrow one with length.*
> —Avicenna, to friends who had asked him to take things easier

In addition to his scientific smarts, Avicenna was also such a gifted bureaucrat that he was sought out by various political leaders for help in running civil matters.

Somewhat unfortunately for the brilliant scholar/doctor/administrator, the part of Persia in which he lived was politically unstable for much of his life. For a fair part of his adult life, he wandered from village to town, practicing medicine or working as a civil servant by day and churning out treatises on everything from music to mechanics to metaphysics by night.

And he did it all despite being intermittently ill during the last few years of his life, which ended at the age of fifty-eight.

The АБBs

Here's something they didn't teach you on *Sesame Street*. In 862, a guy named Prince Rostislav of Great Moravia (modern day Czech Republic) asked the Byzantine emperor Michael III to send him some missionaries to help Christianize the Slavs. The emperor looked around and chose two brothers from the Macedonian province of Thessalonica, named Constantine and Methodius.

The brothers were noted scholars (both of whom eventually were canonized) who had an affinity for languages. They also decided it would be easier to teach the Scriptures in the Slavs' native language, and invented, or helped invent, an alphabet to use in the translation. The alphabet was called the Glagolitic, which later morphed into the Cyrillic alphabet.

The Cyrillic alphabet, with some slight modification over the years, became the national script for all kinds of Slavic peoples, including the Russians, Serbs, Bulgarians, and Ukrainians. It also became a source of controversy in the Christian Church, because some Church leaders objected to the use of anything but Latin when it came to liturgical matters.

And where did *Cyrillic* come from? From *Cyril*, which is what, for unknown reasons, people started calling Constantine shortly before his death.

A Fishy Fairy Tale

Have you heard the one about the young girl who had a wicked stepmother and an ugly stepsister, was forced to wear rags and do all the chores, and in the end got to marry a dream guy?

Sure, everyone knows the story of Yeh-Shen. "Who?" you ask. Ah, you're forgiven for thinking it was Cinderella. After all, the story line has shown up in folktales from Africa to England to the Algonquin of North America.

The earliest-known version of the tale was first recorded by a Chinese author and folktale collector named Tuan Ch'eng-Shih, who put it down on paper about 850 CE. In his version, the heroine's only friend is a ten-foot-long magical fish, which lives in a nearby river. Yeh-Shen's evil stepmother finds out about the fish and kills it. An old man advises the girl to collect the fish bones and make a wish. Her wish is to attend a festival, and her rags are turned into a gorgeous outfit. Fleeing the affair after bumping into her stepmother, Yeh-Shen loses a slipper.

The slipper winds up in the hands of the richest merchant in the district, who launches a search and . . . yada yada yada. In the end, the girl marries the merchant, and the stepmother and stepsister are killed in a rockslide. No singing mice, no pumpkin coach, no bibbidy-bobbidy-boo. But still a pretty good story.

Salty Goodness

It's hard to believe, but mankind has not always had the pretzel as part of its larder. It appears that we have some well-behaved children and a kind-hearted monk in seventh-century Europe to thank for its creation.

In 610, a monk-baker in what is now northern Italy was baking unleavened bread for Lent when he hit upon an idea to reward local children who had learned their prayers. He twisted the dough so it looked like arms crossing the breast in supplication. Then he baked it and named the creation *pretiola*, Latin for "little reward."

Judging by their appearance in numerous works of art and literature, pretzels were pretty popular in the Not-So-Dark Ages, and were soon thought of as symbols of good luck and long life. One contemporary illustration of St. Bartholomew, for example, shows him surrounded by pretzels.

Pretzels also helped save the city of Vienna in the early sixteenth century from invading Turks. It seems the Turkish army was secretly digging tunnels under the city's walls late at night. Viennese pretzel makers who were working

NO SUGAR? NO FRYING? YOU CALL THAT A DIET?

Sugar was so rare in the Medieval European diet that it was kept under lock and key. Animal fat was usually reserved for making soap and candles, and for greasing wagon axles. As a result, most food was boiled rather than fried.

the midnight shift to ensure their product's freshness heard the digging and thwarted the attack. A grateful king awarded the bakers with their own coat of arms, featuring a pretzel, which many Viennese bakers still display outside their shops.

Great Divides

An undated Tang Dynasty document unearthed in a Dunhuang cave in China's Gansu Province in about 1900 indicates that the people of the age were pretty darned civilized when it came to divorce.

AND TO GO WITH THOSE PRETZELS . . .

Around 850, monks in the Kaffa region of Ethiopia apparently begin using a drink brewed from the red berries of a local bush to help them stay alert. According to a popular story, they learned of the berries from a local goatherd, who had observed how frisky his animals got after eating the "berries"—which eventually became known as coffee.

The document, entitled "Agreement on Letting the Wife Go," says that when a couple become antagonistic toward each other, "it'd be better for them to meet their respective relatives and return to their respective original way of life.

"The man said: 'I wish that you, my wife, after divorce, would comb your beautiful hair again and paint your pretty eyebrows, and thus present your gracefulness and marry a man of high social status. Then we put an end to our enmity, refrain from resenting each other. Henceforth, we will feel relaxed after separation and will enjoy happiness.'"

Plus, if she got married again, it would likely let him off the alimony hook.

· · · · · · · · **AND THANKS, BUT NO THANKS, FOR** · · · · · · · ·

One Hot Weapon

Tired of five years of blockades and attacks on their capital of Constantinople by Arab forces, the Byzantine navy came up with a new—and definitely secret—weapon in 677 for the Battle of Syllaeum, which was fought in the inland Sea of Marmara in what is now Turkey.

The weapon was . . . well, we're not exactly sure what it was. We're pretty sure it was invented by a Greek-speaking mathematician and engineer named Kallinikios. He was either a Christian or a Jew, and he fled his native Syria after the Arabs invaded it. His invention was a highly incendiary liquid that was pumped onto enemy ships and troops through large siphons mounted on the Byzantine ships' prows. The liquid apparently would ignite on contact with seawater, and was extremely difficult to extinguish. The ingredients of what eventually would become known as "Greek Fire" were a closely guarded secret, shared only by the Byzantine emperor and members of Kallinikios's family. Historians think it was some unholy mixture of naphtha, pitch, sulfur, lithium, potassium, metallic sodium, calcium phosphide, and a petroleum base.

The substance was first used a few years before the Battle of Syllaeum, but it was in that fight that it came into its own as a terrifying weapon. The Arab fleet was defeated, and coupled with a subsequent land victory, the Byzantine win resulted in peace in the region for almost three decades.

Other nations eventually came up with their versions of the stuff. The Arabs even used it themselves during the Crusades. But its instability often made it as dangerous to its users as to its victims, and it went out of military fashion by the mid-fifteenth century.

Serfs Without Turf

The term *feudalism* is usually used to describe what passed for a system of government in the Europe of the "Middle Ages." Like the term *Middle Ages,* however, feudalism has become a subject of intense debate among historians, some of whom say the system it describes was not widespread, or that it existed in way too many variations to warrant using it as a blanket description of the way things worked back then.

With that caveat in mind, here's a blanket description of feudalism:

Rulers such as Charlemagne needed the support of the various powerful nobles. The kings, therefore, traded to the nobles some of the land they controlled, in return for economic, political, and military support. The nobles then swapped some of that land to lesser nobles in return for their support. The lesser nobles contracted with the peasantry to work the land in return for a place to live and food to eat.

The serfs also got the protection of the lords of the manors when Vikings or Magyars or other raiding groups showed up. Everyone did okay in this system, except of course the peasants, who were virtual slaves, and whose labor kept everyone up the ladder in munchies.

Feudalism also didn't do much to establish a more centralized government, because as time passed, the nobles came to look on the land as their own and therefore felt less allegiance to any old king.

And as the pandemic plagues of the sixth, seventh, and eighth centuries ran their courses and agricultural production methods improved, Europeans produced more food, and reproduced with enthusiasm. By 1000 CE, the continent's population had reached about thirty-five million, and towns and cities began to get bigger and more numerous.

Markets for surplus products appeared. Landowners found it was cheaper to hire labor than support a laborer and his family as tenants.

Gradually, the feudal system gave way to a system based on exchanging money for labor or services. Nowadays we call it capitalism, even though it still frequently makes us feel like serfs.

.... BY THE NUMBERS ....

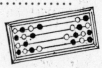

    0   useful number whose utility was described by mathematicians in India between 500 and 900; borrowed by Arab scholars and eventually shared with Europeans

    1   number of women who ruled as empress of Tang Dynasty China

 2–10   estimated percentage of candidates who successfully passed civil service exams in Tang Dynasty China

    5   number of times each day faithful Muslims were supposed to pray

   15   number of years older than the Prophet Muhammad his wife was

  114   number of chapters, or suras, in the Koran

    6   number of years it took to build the Hagia Sophia cathedral in Constantinople. (It was completed in 537. It dome was 180 feet high.)

    6   number of lashes recommended by St. Columba in the early seventh century for monks who sang out of tune

   24   number, in years, of the reign of Leo III, the Byzantine emperor who protected Eastern Europe from Arab invaders

   34   number, in years, of the reign of Constantine V, the son of Leo III

  260   number of days in the Mayan ceremonial year

  289   number of years the Tang Dynasty lasted in China

48,900   number of poems included in the *Quan Tang Shi* (*Complete Tang Poems*), written by about 2,300 authors

 3,000   number of people thought to be capable of writing poetry who were executed by Tang Dynasty ruler Huang Chan, after Chan was offended by an anonymous satirical verse about his methods of governing

   70   number of libraries in the eighth century in the Moorish city of Cordoba

50,000   estimated population of Mayan city of Tikal around 800

30,000   estimated population of London around 1200

42 height, in inches, of the Frankish ruler Pepin the Short

76 height, in inches, of his son Charlemagne

387,204 area, in square feet, of the Great Mosque of Al-Mutawakkil, built at Samarra between 848 and 852. (For centuries, it was the largest mosque in the world.)

3,000,000 estimated number of workers who labored on construction of the Grand Canal from 605 to 610 in Sui Dynasty China

1,000,000 estimated number of workers who died working on the canal from various causes, such as disease and malnutrition

6

THE FAIR-TO-MIDDLIN' AGES (EVEN IF YOU LIVED IN EUROPE)

(1000–1300)

For many people, the term "olden days" conjures images of knights, castles and the Round Table. And yeah, it had plenty of the King Arthur stuff (although no real King Arthur). But there was a lot more to the age than just jousts, jesters, and pulling swords out of stones.

In reality, the late Middle Ages was a roughly three-to-four-hundred-year period that bridged the end of the after-Rome confusion known popularly (if a bit inaccurately) as the Dark Ages, and the beginning of the Renaissance and the Modern World. The period saw the beginnings of some pretty impressive empires, the end of others, and the beginning and the end of still others.

Among this last group were the Mongols, the nomadic group that rose early in the thirteenth century under Genghis Khan, and then Kublai Khan, to establish one of the largest empires ever, encompassing most of Russia, Central Asia, and China—only to begin disintegrating by the middle of the fourteenth century.

The once-mighty Byzantine Empire shrank until it was little more than the city of Constantinople. When that city fell to the rising tide of Ottoman Turks in 1453, it marked the end of the last vestige of the glory that had once been the Roman Empire.

Meanwhile, the Muslim way of life continued to dominate over much of the Middle East, Arabia, and North Africa, although it was by no means a unified force. Seljuk Turks, Egyptian Mamelukes, and Syrians under the command of the great leader Saladin all vied for power over parts or all of the Muslim-dominated territories.

Much of the subcontinent of India was a collection of small warring states until the sultanate of Delhi came to dominate in the mid-fourteenth century. In Africa, flourishing kingdoms existed among the Mali, and in Ghana and Zimbabwe. And in the New World, the Chimu in Peru, Toltecs in Mexico, and Mississippians and Anasazi in North America flourished, while even more powerful groups known as Incas and Aztecs waited in the wings.

In addition to war, virtually all of the Old World shared one other thing in common during this period: epidemics of plague that periodically swept from east to west and left populations decimated in their wake.

Ironically, the plagues' rapid spread was made possible by improvements in communication and transportation among countries. Those changes, in turn, had been made possible by the military successes of nomadic groups—most specifically the Mongols.

These nomads conquered areas that overlapped traditional national boundaries, bringing different groups together, albeit sometimes unwillingly. The result was increased trade and the sharing of ideas between groups of people who heretofore stuck to themselves. The spread of innovations such as the magnetic compass helped fire people's imaginations and jump-start the age of exploration that was just around the corner, historically speaking.

The earlier widespread establishment of religions such as Christianity, Buddhism, and Islam also served to create bonds among people in different geographic areas. And even the clash of major religions, such as between Christians and Muslims during the Crusades, increased more contact between the cultures and more familiarity with what each had to offer.

Despite man's seemingly best efforts to kill his neighbors rather than get to know them, the world was getting smaller.

· · · · · · · · · · · **WHAT HAPPENED WHEN** · · · · · · · · · · · · · ·

~1000 Tula, capital of the Toltec Empire, is sacked and burned.

1015 Japanese baroness named Shikibu Murasaki writes *The Tale of Genji*.

1016 England, Norway, and Denmark are united under King Canute.

1055 The Seljuk Turks conquer Baghdad and cement their dominance of the Muslim world.

1099 Christian crusaders from Europe capture Jerusalem.

1120 An Anglo-Saxon scientist named Walcher of Malvern pioneers the measurement of latitude and longitude in degrees, minutes, and seconds.

1150 The Hindu temple of Angkor Wat is completed in the capital of the Khmer Empire (now Cambodia).

1154 Henry II ascends to the throne of England and rules both it and much of France.

1163 Building begins on the Cathedral of Notre Dame in Paris.

1187 Muslim forces under the leadership of the Egyptian ruler Saladin retake Jerusalem.

~1200 A heretofore-nomadic people called the Aztecs enter the central valley of Mexico.

~1200 The Shona Empire in South Central Africa begins mining gold and copper.

1211 The Mongol leader Genghis Khan invades China, adding chunks of the country to his expanding empire.

1215 English nobles force King John Lackland to sign a document known as the Magna Carta, which reaffirms individual rights and puts limits on royal power.

1231 The Japanese shogun Yoritsune bans the practice of parents selling their own children into slavery.

1259 Armies of the Song Empire in China use bullets fired from bamboo tubes to help beat back a Mongol invasion—the first use of small firearms.

1274 The Chinese emperor Kublai Khan sends a massive invasion force against Japan, but a typhoon wipes out much of the invading fleet.

1291 The Christian-held city of Acre, in the Holy Land, falls to invading Muslims, effectively ending the Crusades.

~1300 The Chimu begin conquering more than 600 miles of Peruvian coast.

Europe:

A Case of the Plagues

The Middle Ages were full of good news and bad news for Europe, although, to be honest, the bad was a lot nastier than the good was good. The worst of the bad came in the thirteenth and fourteenth centuries, when a rather sudden climactic change created a succession of colder-than-average years. This led to a series of famines. And just when it looked like things had hit rock bottom, a string of plague epidemics occurred, wiping out huge chunks of the population and generally depressing everyone to the point that survivors got either almost giddy or totally hopeless.

The good news, sort of, was that the precipitous drop in the population meant there was more stuff for the survivors: more food, more land, more building materials. It also meant there were fewer people to compete for work, which made labor more valuable. This contributed to more independence for anyone with a marketable skill.

It also helped lead to the rise of trade associations, where merchants or craftsmen of various types could band together to set rules and conditions among themselves and present a united front politically.

Speaking of politics, there was good news on that front, too. While Europe had been mainly a collection of small feudal entities in the years after the collapse of the Roman Empire, governments began to coalesce and embrace larger groups of people. This added more stability to civic life and provided greater security from outside threats.

THE REAL MCCOY

In 1040, a Scottish lord murdered the incumbent king and assumed the throne. He held it until 1057, when the dead king's son avenged his pop. The usurper's name was Macbeth. Someone eventually wrote a play about him.

The Holy Roman Empire (which as the eighteenth-century French philosopher Voltaire pointed out "was neither holy, nor Roman, nor an empire") pulled together Germany, Austria, northern Italy, and eastern France. Its leaders were selected by a council of nobles rather than through accident of birth, which led to a generally better class of rulers. It also served as both a check on the power of the Christian Church and as the Church's protector.

France, as the second millennium began, was pretty much centered on the three cities of Paris, Orleans, and Leon. Expanded in the early thirteenth century by Phillip II Augustus, it came into its own as a nation in the mid-fifteenth century, when it finally defeated England in the Hundred Years' War.

In northwest Russia, a leader named Yaroslav I put together a kingdom centered on the city of Kiev. The city, which boasted some four hundred churches, became a major trading center between Europe and the Byzantine Empire. By the end of the twelfth century, however, the kingdom had all but disappeared, a victim of internal power struggles between Yaroslav's successors.

Midway through the eleventh century, England was conquered by the Norman ruler William I. Normans, followed by the French-speaking Angevins, ruled the country until 1399.

TAXABLE . . . ASSETS

Leofric, who was the Earl of Mercia in England, apparently was a sport. So in 1040, he agreed to remit a heavy tax if his wife rode naked through the streets of Coventry. The Lady Godoifv, aka Godiva, agreed. And the earl kept his word.

China:
From the Song to the Yuan to the Ming

The Song Dynasty, which started under the warlord Chao K'uang in 960, revived the use of Confucian principles of government, with tough civil-service exams required to obtain government posts. This inspired confidence in the government and prompted civil servants to take pride in their jobs. And that, at least for a while, made for a more efficient government.

JUST THE TYPE

Around 1045, a Chinese alchemist named Pi Sheng carved blocks of clay into characters, fire-hardened them, fixed them to an iron plate, and gave the world moveable type.

The Song Dynasty fostered a strong business and trade climate. Song ships were the masters of sea routes all over Asia and into the Persian Gulf. The population soared to 110 million by 1100 CE, and the country had several cities that were huge even by today's standards. Song art and culture were the envy of much of the world.

But good times bred complacency and corruption, which led to incompetence and weakness. Continually threatened by nomadic forces from the north and west, which gradually nibbled away at the country, the southern Song Dynasty fell to Kublai Khan and the Mongols in 1279.

Kublai immediately established the Yuan Dynasty, which lasted

While the Chinese had been known for hundreds of years for their artistic accomplishments, many art scholars believe their porcelain-making skills reached their zenith during the Song Dynasty (960–1279 CE).

Song porcelain was known for its complexity and inventiveness, and for its restraint in the use of color. It was often painted over after it had been glazed, which added a new wrinkle. While thousands of kilns and porcelain factories sprang up all over the empire, there were five dominant brands: Ru, Guan, Ge, Ding, and Jun.

So popular was Song porcelain in other countries that many factories began using assembly lines and other mass-production techniques. And you thought that Henry Ford invented all of that.

until 1368, when it fell to the Ming. Under the Ming, the entire country was reunified under a native-run government for the first time in several hundred years.

Japan:
Shogun-ing for Power

Japan was heavily influenced by China during what is called the Heian Period, from 794 to 1185, and like early medieval Europe, it was pretty much just a bunch of small quarreling states stuck together.

By the late eleventh century, however, two powerful aristocratic clans—the Minamoto and the Taira—had developed enough influence to thwart the ambitions of all the other groups. The two settled things in the usual way, by fighting, and the Minamoto clan came out on top.

Instead of abolishing the highly symbolic but generally impotent position of emperor, the Minamoto clan instead chose to rule "in the emperor's name." The clan leader became Shogun, or military governor. For most of the next four hundred years, a Shogun of the Minamoto clan would rule Japan.

A KNIGHT BY ANY OTHER NAME . . .

Instead of knights, medieval Japan had Samurai, professional warriors who served as policemen (or enforcers) for provincial lords. So if our Eurocentric view of history had been Japan-centric, whenever we thought of the Middle Ages we might think of Bushido ("the way of the warrior") instead of chivalry, and seppuku (ritual suicide) instead of the search for the Holy Grail.

The Muslim World:
Controlling Trade, Crushing Crusades

By 1000 CE, the part of the world dominated by Islamic governments stretched from the Iberian Peninsula (Spain and Portugal) to the Malay Peninsula (Southeast Asia).

But the sheer distances from one part to another led to a continual struggle for dominance among various Muslim groups: the Berbers in North Africa, the Mamelukes in Egypt, the Seljuk Turks and later the Ottoman Turks in Asia Minor.

Despite the spate of spats among different Muslim factions, the faithful of Allah continued to spread their influence. They gradually ate away the Byzantine Empire, and by the mid-fourteenth century they dominated most of the subcontinent of India. In Africa, Islamic forces controlled most of the northern part of the continent, including the vital trans-Saharan trade routes for gold and slaves. And they still had time to win most of the battles they fought with Christian Europeans during the Crusades.

LION TAMER

Salah-al-din Yusuf ibn Ayyub was an iconic Arab civil and military leader and arguably the most famous Muslim warrior of the Crusades. He was known in the West by the name Saladin, which means "righteousness of faith" in Arabic.

In July 1187, Saladin's forces destroyed most of the Crusader forces at the Battle of Hattin, in Palestine. The Muslim army took back all but one or two Holy Land cities that had been conquered by the Crusaders. In October, Saladin's armies capped a three-month siege of Jerusalem by capturing the city and ending eighty-eight years of Christian control.

Saladin's successes stunned Christendom, which decided to launch a Third Crusade, led by King Richard I of England, known as "the Lionhearted." Both men were personally brave and were able military leaders, and each had a deep mutual respect for the other.

According to contemporary accounts, Saladin once offered Richard the use of his personal physician when Richard was wounded, and gave him a horse after the English king had lost his mount.

In 1192, after the Crusaders had taken back some territory but failed to retake Jerusalem, Saladin and Richard agreed to an armistice. Under it, the city remained in Muslim hands, but Christian pilgrims were free to visit.

Saladin died in Damascus in March 1193, not long after Richard returned to Europe.

The Byzantine Empire:
We'll Always Have Constantinople . . .

The inhabitants of the Byzantine Empire generally started the eleventh century in pretty good shape. A succession of emperors from Macedonia had provided stability, beaten down challenges from the Bulgarians and other Slavic neighbors, and actually expanded the borders of what once was the eastern half of the Roman Empire.

It remained a center of arts, culture, and learning, even during tough times. It also enjoyed a robust economy as the crossroads of trade between East and West and the manufacturer of many goods on its own. Its gold coin, the bezant, was standard currency for the Mediterranean basin.

But like its Roman forebear, Byzantium suffered from a combination of internal weaknesses and external threats. After the death of the last Macedonian ruler, Basil II, in 1025, the Byzantines had thirteen emperors over the next fifty-six years.

In the West, Norman forces took the last Byzantine strongholds in Italy. In the East, the Seljuk Turks, the dominant force of the Muslim world, were a constant threat. Because of the split between the Church of Rome and the Eastern Orthodox Church of Constantinople, Byzantium could expect little help against the Muslims from its fellow Christians in Europe.

> ### — CAE WHAT?
>
> The dominant political ideology of the Byzantine Empire favored the consolidation of authority over both the Church and the State. It was called caesaropapism. Really.

In fact, the Crusaders were generally bad news for the Byzantines, since the Western armies were covetous of the empire's wealth. By the time of the Fourth Crusade, the Crusaders proved to be as interested in conquering Constantinople (which they did, in 1204) as they were in "freeing" the Holy Land. Western-backed emperors then ruled the city until 1261.

By that time, the empire had devolved into a collection of independent city-states. The Black Death decimated Constantinople in 1347; the city began paying tribute to the Turks around 1370, and finally fell on May 29, 1453.

Many historians think the fall of Constantinople severed the world's last active link with the Classical Era. It may also have marked the end of the Middle Ages and the beginning of modern times.

The Americas:
Empire-of-the-Month Club

As in the Old World, the Americas saw an ebb and flow of dominant cultures, although there were fewer of them competing simultaneously.

In South America, the Chimu used advanced irrigation techniques to build an impressive empire along the coast of Peru. By the end of the fourteenth century, however, they would give way to an even more impressive group known as the Inca.

In Mexico, the Toltec nation built an imposing capital at Tula, near the Central Valley of Mexico. The Toltec empire was based on stealing or extorting loot from neighboring groups, which is not a particularly sound basis for an economy. By the beginning of the thirteenth century, the Toltecs were out of business and being replaced by the new kids on the block, the Aztecs. The Aztecs parlayed their success as mercenaries for other groups into a formidable society that came to dominate Central Mexico until the coming of the Europeans in the early sixteenth century.

In North America, a group known as the Mississippians took advantage of fertile lands and good location in what is now the American Midwest to become proficient farmers and traders. They did well until the mid-thirteenth century, when environmental stresses caused

GOODBYE, CAHOKIA

The Mississippians' ability to grow maize let them settle down in a city at the confluence of the Mississippi, Missouri, and Illinois rivers, on a fertile floodplain called the American Bottom. Called Cahokia, the city probably covered about six square miles and had a population of as much as thirty thousand people at its peak.

It featured a fifty-acre earthen plaza, surrounded by a wooden stockade with a series of watchtowers. More than one hundred earthen mounds dotted the city, on top of which were various domiciles, religious centers, and astronomical sites. The largest, later dubbed Monk's Mound, was a thousand feet long, seven hundred to eight hundred feet wide, and a hundred feet high.

Cahokia's trading routes extended as far west as the Rockies and as far east as the Atlantic. At its peak, the city was probably the largest in North America (until it was surpassed by Philadelphia in about 1800).

By 1300, however, Cahokia was abandoned. Scholars are not completely certain why, although theories range from political instability to the depletion and/or pollution of the area's natural resources such as woodlands and waterways.

by rapacious land practices may have caught up with them and ended their run.

In the less hospitable Southwest, a group known as the Anasazi built incredible edifices into the sides of cliffs. They also adopted clever methods of farming and irrigation that enabled them to support populations in excess of what the local environment could ultimately support. As in the case of the Mississippians, the local environment won, and the Anasazi pretty much faded away in the 1200s.

– Royalty Watch –

He Came, He Saw, He Conquered England

When Edward the Confessor cashed in his chips in January 1066, after twenty-three years as king of England, he left no obvious heir. But that didn't mean there were no candidates for the post. In fact, there were at least three: Harold Godwinson, Edward's brother-in-law; William, Duke of Normandy; and Harald Hardrada, the king of Norway.

The trio of claimants quickly embraced the generally accepted eleventh-century way of settling such disputes: they went to war. Hardrada and Harold slugged it out first, at the Battle of Stamford Bridge, near York. Harold won, slaughtered most of Hardrada's troops, and paused to catch his breath.

WEAVING A TALE

The history of William the Conqueror's fight for the crown was recorded in a novel way: a 230-foot-long, 20-inch-wide embroidery called the Bayeux Tapestry. The tapestry is made up of hundreds of scenes joined in a linear sequence, and is believed to have been commissioned by William's half-brother. And since the winners generally write history, the account is heavily slanted toward William's version of things.

As it turned out, he didn't have long to rest. A couple of days after the fight at Stamford Bridge, William, Duke of Normandy, landed his army on the southern end of England, near the town of Hastings. Harold rushed south, and on October 14, the two armies collided.

It was a tough all-day battle, but in the end William's archers and cavalry prevailed. Harold was killed, and William continued his trek toward London. He was crowned king of England on Christmas Day in 1066.

The Queen Machine

She was one of the most powerful women of the twelfth century—and she lasted about four fifths of it. Eleanor of Aquitaine was the queen consort of France, and then of England. Three of her sons (Richard I, John Lackland, and Henry III) became kings of England, and two daughters married and/or bore kings and emperors. She went on a Crusade, and helped encourage good manners and troubadours.

Plus, she lived to be eighty-two, which was pretty remarkable for anyone in the twelfth century, let alone someone as busy as she was.

Eleanor was the eldest daughter of the Duke of Aquitaine, a large and independent duchy in southwestern France. This made her a very eligible fifteen-year-old when her dad died and left her as his heir. And that explains why she was married to the French king Louis VII in 1137.

Four years later, Eleanor volunteered about a thousand of her vassals to fight in the Second Crusade—and threw in herself and three hundred women to go along. Although the women didn't do any actual fighting, Eleanor did get to Constantinople and Antioch, and discomfited the Crusade's male leaders enough to get women officially banned from future efforts. (In fact, there were rumors that Eleanor had a dalliance in Antioch with her uncle Raymond, who was a prince there.)

In 1152, Eleanor and Louis wheedled their way out of their loveless marriage by persuading Church officials to dissolve it on the grounds they were distant cousins. But Eleanor wasn't alone long. Less than two months later, she married King Henry II of England, giving the two of them control of all of England and much of France.

> *How could anything fortunate, I ask, emerge from their copulations?*
>
> —Twelfth-century writer Gerald of Wales, raising a rhetorical query about the union of Eleanor and Henry II, since she was rumored to have slept with her father-in-law, too

When not having kids by Henry (eight of them), Eleanor pretty much ran her own kingdom in Aquitaine. Her court at Poitiers became a haven for troubadours and poets and a fountain of etiquette and courtly manners.

But when her sons rebelled against Henry and she sided with her progeny, Henry had her placed under house arrest—for sixteen years. In 1189, Henry died; Richard ascended to the throne, freed his mother, and put her in charge of England while he went off on the Third Crusade.

When Richard was held for ransom, Eleanor raised the dough. And when Richard died, she helped her second son, John, hold on to the throne. She also arranged the marriage of a granddaughter to a grandson of her first husband, Louis VII. All in all, she was one busy mom until she retired to an abbey in France, where she died in 1204 and was buried. And even at that, she outlived all but two of her children.

·········· **WHO'S UP, WHO'S DOWN** ···············

Chimu: UP

One of the more successful of the pre-Colombian societies in South America, the Chimu often go unmentioned in history books because they had already fallen when Europeans got to the New World. But for most of the Middle Ages, they were definitely up.

An agricultural society, the Chimu rose to prominence in the Moche River Valley in Northern Peru. Their major asset in putting together an empire was a knack for irrigation in an area that was and basically still is a desert. The Chimu linked rivers and built canals as long as fifty miles. Their water system allowed them to grow enough food to sustain a sizeable population. The Chimu capital city was Chan Chan, on the northern coast of Peru. At its peak, the forty-square-mile city had a population of more than fifty thousand, ensconced behind adobe and brick walls that were as much as ten feet thick at their base and thirty feet high.

While the social structure was strictly divided along class lines, the Chimu did extend equal legal rights to females and treated their elderly fairly well: If you could make it to the age of sixty, you didn't have to pay taxes or serve in the military. Of course, if you committed a crime, a common punishment was to be burned alive.

Beginning in about 1000 CE, the Chimu began expanding their sphere of influence up and down the Peruvian coast. By 1400, they controlled as much as six hundred miles of the coast. But their biggest asset—their irrigation system—was also a liability when the rival Inca nation attacked the Chimu in the 1460s. The Inca disrupted the water supply enough to bring down the Chimu, and inherit their mantle as the area's top dog.

Mongols: UP AND ALL OVER

If the Mongols had a motto, it might have been "Have weapon, will travel."

They started out as a nomadic group of, well, nomads in the eastern part of Central Asia. The Mongols were loyal almost exclusively to their close relatives, so it was difficult for them to organize themselves on a larger scale, despite their prowess in battle.

> *The greatest pleasure is to vanquish your enemies and chase them before you, to rob them of their wealth and see those dear to them bathed in tears, to ride their horses and clasp to your bosom their wives and daughters.*
> —Genghis Khan

That all began to change in the last half of the twelfth century, with the rise of a man named Temujin. Pushed around and poor as a youth, Temujin rose to power by combining extraordinary courage in battle with an uncanny knack for Mongol-style diplomacy. This consisted mainly of forming alliances and then betraying them if something better came along.

A "DIVINE WIND" TODAY KEEPS MONGOLS AWAY

Although the Mongols had conquered a big piece of Europe and Asia by 1274, they still had a yen for more, and turned their attention to the island nation of Japan.

In the fall of 1274, Kublai Khan packed up a force of about forty thousand Mongol and Korean fighters on nine hundred ships to invade. After initial success, a fierce storm blew in and destroyed part of the fleet. Demoralized, Kublai's forces withdrew.

They tried again in 1281. This time Kublai put together two armies totaling 140,000 men in more than 4,000 ships. Once again, the invaders did pretty well against the outnumbered defenders. And once again, a major typhoon blew in, smashing much of the Mongol-Korean fleet over a two-day period. The storm forced the biggest part of the invading army to beat a hasty retreat, and the part that was left behind was either slaughtered or captured.

Although Kublai wanted to try yet again, he died before he could get a third invasion off the ground, and the Japanese would remain unconquered until the middle of the twentieth century, at the end of World War II.

And the typhoons that proved so valuable in fighting off Kublai's armies? They were called kamikazes ("divine winds"), and they helped convince the Japanese people that they were protected by the gods.

By 1206, Temujin had united the Mongol tribes into a single confederation, and they had designated him "Genghis Kahn," or "universal ruler." Genghis quickly put together a relatively small but lightning-quick army of superbly skilled mounted archers who could travel up to sixty miles a day to surprise opposing armies.

The Mongols had a pretty simple game plan: They were magnanimous to those who surrendered without a fight, and slaughtered those who chose battle. Under Genghis, they conquered Central Asia, Northern China, and Persia.

Nor did they slow down after his death in 1227, adding most of modern-day Russia and the rest of China. The Mongol Empire got so big, in fact, that it was divided into four regional empires, each with its own khan.

The Mongols weren't great administrators, but they were smart enough to absorb bright bureaucrats from the people they conquered. They were also savvy enough to do the same with skilled artisans, even transferring them around to various parts of the empire where they were needed. They were relatively tolerant when it came to religion, and encouraged trade.

By the mid-fourteenth century, the Mongol empire had pretty much run out of steam, plagued by a lack of great leaders—and by the plague. The empire's last big gasp came in the form of a nomadic Turk named Tamerlane, who molded himself after the great Genghis. In the last half of the century, Tamerlane's armies conquered much of Afghanistan, Persia, and India. He died in 1405, and not long afterward, the Mongol Empire (actually empires) collapsed for good.

Crusaders: DOWN

The eighteenth-century Scottish historian-philosopher David Hume called the Crusades "the most signal and most durable monument of human folly that has yet appeared in any age or nation." That's a tough statement to argue with.

From a medieval Christian's perspective, Pope Urban II launched the Crusades in 1095 with a noble cause: to liberate the Holy Land from pilgrim-harassing Seljuk Turks.

European Christians responded with enthusiasm, and the First Crusaders actually succeeded in taking Jerusalem in 1099. They celebrated with a wholesale slaughter of the city's occupants. While most of the Crusaders went home, the ones who stayed behind built massive castles and set up mini-kingdoms around the area.

In 1146, several European leaders launched the Second Crusade, ostensibly designed to reverse the losses of several Christian cities in the Holy Land. The Crusaders burned and looted their way to Constantinople, stumbled across Asia Minor, and then made it to Damascus, where they were routed and lost most of their army.

FOUR GOOFY THINGS ABOUT THE CRUSADES

1. **Peter the Hermit.** A French priest who got harassed when he tried to visit the Holy Land and helped recruit volunteers for "the Peasants' Crusade," part of the First Crusade in 1096, Peter the Hermit lost 25 percent of his force on the way. Most of the rest were killed or captured by the Turks while he was elsewhere. Peter tried to desert when he and his Crusaders were caught in a Muslim siege of the city of Antioch, then talked the besieged Crusaders into attacking the besiegers, who promptly slaughtered them. After the Crusaders took Jerusalem, Peter went back to Europe.

2. **Walter the Penniless.** A French knight who wasn't actually broke, Walter got his name when later historians mistook his French surname Sans Avoir, as "without means" instead of as a reference to the Avoir Valley. Anyway, he co-led the Peasants' Crusade with Peter, and was in charge when most of the Crusaders got wiped out. That included Walter.

3. **The Goose Crusade.** According to Jewish historians, a fanatical group of German peasants decided in 1096 that a goose had been "blessed by God." They followed it around for a while, and along the way attacked and killed any Jews they encountered.

4. **The Children's Crusade.** Sometime in 1212, large groups of poor people wandered around France and Germany, and the word got around that thousands of children were marching to the Holy Land. It was probably more aimless shuffling of homeless people than a crusade, but a bunch of kids apparently did show up in Marseille to seek passage to the Holy Land. Most of then ended up being sold into slavery in North Africa.

In 1187, the Muslim armies under Saladin retook Jerusalem, which triggered the Third Crusade. This one was notable for pitting Saladin against the English king Richard I, the Lionhearted. The battle basically ended in a draw, with the Muslims agreeing to reopen the Holy City to Christian pilgrims.

Not content with a record of 1-1-1, Pope Innocent III launched a Fourth Crusade in 1198. It was a disgraceful event, marked mainly by the mass slaughter of thousands of innocent Jews along the way and the sacking of Constantinople, which wasn't even Muslim but, rather, Eastern Orthodox.

A few more halfhearted or imbecilic tries were made, but by 1291, the last Christian stronghold in the region had fallen, and the Great Crusades, which had cost hundreds of thousands of lives, finally fizzled out.

White bread was the most desirable of medieval breads because it was the most finely ground and the least likely to have dirt and other stuff in it.

London: MOVING ON UP

All world-class cities have a setback or two from time to time. One of London's came in 1348–1349, when the Black Death may have taken more than 25 percent of the city's population.

But the city made a lot of progress during the Middle Ages. First, William the Conqueror made it the capital for Norman kings and built the first version of the Tower of London. Between 1050 and 1300, quays were built along the Thames River to expand the waterfront and increase the city's importance as a trading center. In 1176, construction of a stone bridge over the Thames began and was completed just thirty years later. An impressive building called Westminster Abbey was rebuilt between 1245 and 1269.

In 1085, the city had a population of about ten thousand. By 1200, it was up to thirty thousand and just one hundred years later it was up to eighty thousand. The city grew up in two parts: Westminster, where the government stuff was, and the City of London, which was the center of commerce. The parts gradually grew together.

Naturally there were a few problems besides the plague. In 1087, a major fire burned down a big part of the city. In its aftermath, some of the wooden buildings were replaced by stone walls and tile roofs instead of straw. But the city's narrow, twisting streets and crowded conditions made fire a constant threat. And there was something of an air pollution problem because of the burning of a whole bunch of low-grade coal.

But business opportunities abounded, fueled by the one hundred trade guilds that were important political contributors, and which therefore had a lot of clout when it came to running the city. And as of the twenty-first century, the city is still one of the world's greatest.

Church-State Relations: DOWN

One of the most dominant aspects of medieval politics, particularly in Europe, was the touchy relationship between Church and State. As political systems and nation-states became more sophisticated, their rulers became more openly secular in their political dealings.

This put a strain on what was still a symbiotic partnership between the secular politicians and the Church: The lay rulers needed the Church's imprimatur to legitimize their activities, and the Church needed the lay rulers' military resources to back their ecclesiastical activities.

A classic clash of the two interests came in the late eleventh century, when Pope Gregory VII told Henry IV, emperor of the Holy Roman Empire (which was basically Germany, Austria, and part of northern Italy), to stop appointing bishops and other Church officials on his own. These appointments were an important tool for Henry and other rulers, since they helped them ensure local religious leaders' support when they wanted to do stuff.

Henry retaliated by getting his bishops to call for the pope to step down; and Gregory retaliated by excommunicating Henry in 1077. When subordinate princes threatened to revolt, the emperor was forced to apologize to the pontiff—by kneeling in the snow outside the castle where the pope was staying and kissing the papal toe.

That's pretty humiliating for an emperor, and Henry eventually withdrew his apology—and was excommunicated again. This time, he marched on Rome and seized the city; Gregory hired a Norman leader named Robert "the Resourceful" Guiscard to drive Henry out, and Guiscard and an army comprised mainly of Saracen fighters did so.

Then Guiscard's forces spent a few days sacking the city before escorting the pope back in.

The dispute over Church appointments lasted beyond the lives of both Gregory and Henry. In 1122, an agreement called the Concordat of Worms (yes, really) basically called it a draw, and the issue was allowed to die.

But the uneasy relationship between Church and State continued to be, well, uneasy. By the end of the thirteenth century, a council of princes, and not the pope, was choosing the emperor. By the end of the fourteenth century, the Church itself had become so divided that in 1378 two popes were elected, one in France and one in Rome. Not until 1417 did the two factions reunite.

> *Let another assume the seat of St. Peter, one who will not practice violence under the cloak of religion, but will teach St. Peter's wholesome doctrine. I, Henry, king by the grace of God, together with all our bishops, say unto thee "come down, come down, to be damned throughout all eternity!"*
>
> —Emperor Henry IV, in a 1077 letter to Pope Gregory VII, after Gregory ordered the emperor to stop appointing church officials on his own

Poetry: *Taking a Stanza*

It's some of the best-known poetry in the world and perhaps the Eastern verse that is most appreciated in the West: comprising more than one thousand four-line poems, or quatrains, that have rhyming first, second, and fourth lines.

They're known as the *Rubiyat* (Arabic for "quatrain") *of Omar Khayyam*. And for most of the time during and after his life, Omar Khayyam himself was known as perhaps the most accomplished scientist of medieval Turkey—not as a poet.

Born in Persia in 1044, Khayyam was the kind of guy who spent his time doing stuff like designing calendars, calculating the exact length of the solar year, and coming up with geometric methods to solve cubic equations. He died in 1132.

In 1859, a British historian named Edward Fitzgerald translated and published some of what was believed to be poetry written by the famous scientist. The verses became famous around the world. An example:

> *A book of verses underneath the bough,*
> *A jug of wine, a loaf of bread—and thou*
> *Beside me singing in the wilderness—*
> *Oh, Wilderness were paradise enow!*

Since Fitzgerald's day, however, there has been considerable controversy as to whether the poems were correctly translated and whether Khayyam wrote all—or even any—of the quatrains, particularly since there are no contemporary accounts of the scientist ever picking up a quill and placating his muse.

But you have to admit, it sounds cooler than calling them *The Rubiyat of Anonymous.*

Prose: *Never Letter Go*

She was young, beautiful and intelligent. He was charismatic, brilliant—and twenty years her senior. And their love was passionate, tragic—and made for some pretty hot reading. Like this:

> God is my witness that if Augustus, emperor of the
> whole world, thought fit to honor me with marriage
> and conferred all the earth upon me to possess

forever, it would be dearer and more honorable to me
to be called not his empress but your whore.

Pierre Abelard was the son of a noble Breton family. Born in 1079,
he had started his own school in Paris by the time he was twenty-two.
At thirty-six, he was named master of the prestigious cathedral
school at Notre Dame.

Heloise, who was born in about
1100, caught Abelard's eye, and he
finagled an appointment as her tutor. He also persuaded her uncle
and guardian, a church official
named Fulbert, to allow him to
move into the house to better teach
the girl.

So Abelard moved in, and yada
yada yada. When Uncle Fulbert
found out, he evicted Abelard, but
the couple kept meeting secretly.
Heloise got pregnant, and the couple ran away. Then they got married, much against Heloise's desires, to appease her uncle.

LOVE CHILD

Heloise named their son (who was
eventually adopted by Heloise's sister) Astrolabe, after the ancient astronomical device that's sort of like a
computer for solving time/sun/star
problems. Nowadays, it would be sort
of like naming your kid "GPS."

But when Heloise took a break in a convent, Uncle Fulbert thought
Abelard had deserted her. In revenge, Fulbert and a couple of bud-
dies broke into Abelard's room and castrated him.

Then things really went downhill. Heloise spent the rest of her life
in convents. Abelard eventually went back to writing and teaching.
But he had made a lot of enemies, was accused of treason, and had to
burn a book he had written. Then he was found guilty of heresy, and
had to take refuge in a friendly monastery. He died a few years later.

While their active love life was relatively short, Heloise and Abelard became immortalized in the annals of romance because of letters between the two, particularly those written by Heloise. Another
example:

> I have endeavoured to please you even at the expense
> of my virtue, and therefore deserve the pains I feel. As
> soon as I was persuaded of your love I delayed scarce a
> moment in yielding to your protestations; to be
> beloved by Abelard was in my esteem so great a glory,
> and I so impatiently desired it, not to believe in it
> immediately. I aimed at nothing but convincing you

of my utmost passion. I made no use of those defences
of disdain and honour; those enemies of pleasure
which tyrannise over our sex made in me but a weak
and unprofitable resistance. I sacrificed all to my love.

A little wordy maybe, but still pretty hot stuff.

. . . . **SO LONG, AND THANKS FOR ALL THE** . . . .

Starry Sky Surprise

"It's a bird! It's a plane! It's supernova!" Okay, maybe
that's not exactly what people all over the world yelled
the morning of July 5, 1054, but it's pretty certain a whole lot of them
yelled something as they witnessed the death of a giant star, six times
brighter than Venus, in the morning sky. The Chinese called it "the
guest star," and described it as being reddish-white in color and surrounded by pointed rays in all directions.

The explosion from the star, which had burned up its energy, collapsed in on itself, and finally burst from the pressure, was so bright
it could be seen all over the world. It was also bright enough to be seen
with the naked eye in the daytime for as much as a month after it was
first observed, and for up to two years at night.

In addition to Chinese astronomical records, the phenomenon
shows up in Japanese and Arab documents. It apparently was also
noted by Anasazi Indians in what is now New Mexico and Arizona,
and commemorated in petroglyphs. While Europeans almost certainly saw the supernova, they either were too scared or too unimpressed to write about it. There may be a vague reference to it in
records kept by Irish monks, but that appears to be it.

More than six hundred years later, scientists using the recently
invented telescope began observing the star's remnants—a cloudy
mass of gas and dust about seven thousand light years from Earth. In
1774, it was named the Crab Nebula, because someone thought it
looked like a crustacean—proving the adage that it's all in the eye of
the beholder.

Flying Buttresses

It seemed like a pretty good place for a cathedral. After all, there
had been two earlier churches on the site, and a temple dedicated to

the Roman god Jupiter. So, in 1163, Pope Alexander III laid the foundation stone for the Notre Dame de Paris ("Our Lady of Paris") Cathedral.

The edifice was one of the first cathedrals to embrace the Gothic style of architecture, and its construction took up much of the Gothic period. It was one of the first buildings to use "flying buttresses," external supports that allow designers to include giant windows and openings while not weakening the walls.

The cathedral, which covers an area a little bigger than an American football field, was built in stages: The apse, or section behind the altar, and choir area were finished in 1182; the nave, or central approach to the altar, in 1196; and the two big towers at the front of the church, in 1250. Of course there were also the finishing touches—which took until 1345.

MAKING A WITHDRAWAL

In 1307, the French king Philip IV charged the Knights Templar, a military and chivalric order, with witchcraft. The head of the order was eventually executed and the order disbanded. Philip seized most of the assets of the knights' sizeable banking operation. (By the way, Philip's nickname was "the Fair.")

Once it was done, the cathedral went through some pretty hard times in the following four or five centuries, and was smashed up pretty badly during the French Revolution. Napoleon, who used the site to crown himself emperor in 1804, is credited with saving it from destruction. In 1939, the cathedral's fabulous stained-glass windows were removed to protect them from German bombers. They were put back after the war.

Poetic Inspiration

Countless schoolkids have had to learn stanzas from the nineteenth-century poem by Samuel Taylor Coleridge called "Kubla Khan." You know, the one that starts:

> In Xanadu did Kubla Khan
> A stately pleasure-dome decree:
> Where Alph, the sacred river, ran
> Through caverns measureless to man
> Down to a sunless sea.

Learning the lines probably would have been more bearable if students had been given background on who the heck Coleridge was writing about: Kublai Khan, who completed the conquest of China for the Mongols, founded a dynasty, and befriended a European adventurer.

Born in 1215, Kublai Khan was a grandson of the legendary conqueror Genghis Khan. In his thirties, he succeeded his older brother Mangu as khan after Mangu died—and after Kublai won a three-year civil war with another brother.

By 1279, Khan had defeated the Song Dynasty in China, conquered all of the country, and begun what would become the Yuan Dynasty.

As ruler, Khan relied on both Mongol and Chinese advisers. His administration developed regular mail service, improved irrigation systems, expanded the empire's highways, nationalized currency, welcomed foreign trade, and was religiously tolerant.

ONE LONG BUSINESS TRIP

The Italian adventurers-traders the Polos left Venice for Mongol-ruled China in 1271, and didn't get back to Venice until 1295. Legend has it that their surviving relatives didn't recognize them.

But he also divided the populace into a strict class system according to ethnic background and forbade marriage between the different groups. The economic benefits of his government's policies were concentrated in the hands of a relative few, and his largely unsuccessful military adventures in Japan and Southeast Asia were a huge drain on the economy.

Fortunately for his popular historic image, Kublai did befriend a family of travelers from Vienna named Polo, who reached his court in 1271. One of the visitors, a young man named Marco, became a close friend of the khan and served for years as Kublai's personal emissary to various parts of the empire.

When Marco Polo returned to Europe and wrote about his experiences, his highly flattering portrayal of Kublai cemented the Eastern potentate's place in the Western imagination.

Kublai's last years were problem-plagued. His wife, who had sort of nagged him into many of his successes, died in 1281, and he suffered greatly from gout. He died in 1294, at the age of seventy-eight, the last of the great Mongol khans.

Sweet Dreams

Early Arab documents allude to the inhalation of various substances to sedate patients for surgery. But the idea was introduced to Western medicine in the late twelfth century by a Bolognese army surgeon named Hugh of Lucca. Hugh also found that wine made an effective wound cleanser.

Hugh's son Theodoric was an even bigger promoter of the use of "soporific sponges" as an anesthetic. The sponge was soaked in a combination of opium, mandragora, hemlock juice, and other elements.

Theodoric was also big on keeping wounds clean and free of pus. He must have kept his own wounds pus-free. He lived to be about ninety.

Clearing Things Up

The idea of using a device to see better certainly didn't originate in the Middle Ages. The Chinese had used flat pieces of glass to reduce glare, although these didn't serve to correct vision. The Roman emperor Nero is said to have used an emerald to view gladiatorial games, although he probably did it for the novelty of the color and not to see better.

Arabic scientists did a lot of early work in optical studies, and European monks developed "reading stones" made of thin pieces of transparent beryl or quartz. But prior to the late thirteenth century, reading aids were one-eye-at-a-time affairs.

Sometime in the 1280s, in the Italian town of Pisa, a glassblower or glassblowers came up with the idea of using a curved lens for each eye to enhance reading and close work. Historians have identified at least two likely candidates—Alessandro Spina and/or Salvino Armato—as possible inventors of spectacles.

Whoever was responsible for them, glasses caught on quickly. In 1289, an Italian writer named Sandro of Popozo noted that the recent invention was "for the benefit of poor aged people (including himself) whose sight has become weak." By 1326, they were widely available. Italians called them "lentils," because they sort of looked like the seed—hence the English word *lens*.

Early glasses were held on with cords or straps, since the idea of rigid metal arms that hooked over the ears didn't come along until the eighteenth century. They also weren't of much help to the nearsighted, since lenses to correct myopia didn't come along until the fifteenth century, and were pretty expensive.

Still, the use of spectacles to correct farsightedness was a big boon to reading—which in turn was a big boon to writing and book production, which of course encouraged more reading, which . . . well, you get the idea.

Forks!

While there's some evidence that people in the Middle East were using forks around the beginning of the eleventh century, they may have used them more for pinning down meat so they could cut it than for conveying the bite-size chunks to their mouths. But by the eleventh century, the fork was being used as a food purveyor in the Byzantine Empire.

A Byzantine princess reportedly introduced a two-tine model in Tuscany, where the clergy roundly condemned it: God-provided food should enter the mouth only via God-provided fingers. Despite the Church's opposition, the fork caught on pretty quickly in Italy. But it was slow going elsewhere in Europe. In England, for example, a 1307 inventory of the royal cutlery tallied thousands of knives, hundreds of spoons—but only seven forks, six of them silver and one of them gold.

In fact, using forks didn't become common in much of Europe until the eighteenth century—and even then they were sometimes used to spear food, shake off the excess sauce, and then steer the food past the lips with the fingers.

Maybe that means all those ten-month-old kids who eat with their hands aren't being childish—they're just emulating Europeans of the Middle Ages.

> Refrain from falling upon the dish like a swine while eating, snorting disgustingly and smacking the lips.
> —From a thirteenth-century Italian text on etiquette

The Ace of Polo Sticks

Like so many of man's most important inventions, the precise origin of playing cards is uncertain. And like so many inventions—whether their origins are certain or uncertain—many historians think the inventors of playing cards were the Chinese.

There are a number of theories on how cards spread from China. One theory has Marco Polo bringing them back to Europe in the late thirteenth century from the court of Kublai Khan. Others claim they were imported from India or the Middle East by returning Crusaders and/or Gypsies. But the best bet is they came from the Islamic dynasty of the Mamelukes of Egypt in the 1370s.

Early decks were hand-painted and very expensive. But advances in woodcut techniques allowed mass production in the fourteenth century. While the Mamelukes' fifty-two-card deck had suits of swords, polo sticks, cups, and coins, it was the French who gave us the modern quartet of spades, hearts, clubs, and diamonds, in the fifteenth century.

And the joker? Americans added him to the deck, in the eighteenth century.

········ **AND THANKS, BUT NO THANKS, FOR** ... ·····

Black Death

The bacteria were on the flea, which was on the rat, which was on the ship or in the wagon.

At least that's the prevailing theory on how an epidemic disease swept through much of the world in the mid-fourteenth century. Popularized in Western literature as "the Black Death," the disease is widely believed to have been either a combination of various forms of plague—bubonic, pneumonic, and septicemic—or a close relative of them.

Whatever it was, it was pretty nasty stuff. It's safe to reckon that as many as twenty-five million of the European population of about eighty million were killed by the disease between 1347 and 1351, and it's entirely plausible that the death rate was even higher. In many regions, as much as two thirds of the populace was wiped out. Worldwide, the death toll might have topped seventy-five million.

The disease was not only horrifically proficient, but persistent. In England, for example, there were thirty-one outbreaks between 1348 and 1485.

Although reports of plague epidemics first popped up in China and the East in the 1330s, it probably didn't reach Europe until 1347, when a virtual ghost fleet of Genovese trading ships reached the Italian port of Messina with most of their crew dead or dying. The plague got to England by 1348 and Russia and Scandinavia by 1351.

There was no cure, although the usual methods of leeches, bleeding, sweating, and herbs were tried.

It not only spread quickly across populations, but also progressed with frightening speed in individuals: a sudden high fever was followed within days by terrifying, painful black swellings in the armpits and groin (lymph nodes overwhelmed by the bacteria) that sometimes burst, emitting a mixture of blood and foul-smelling pus. Death usually came within five days, and sometimes less than one; the Italian writer Boccaccio claims that some victims "ate lunch with their friends and dinner with their ancestors in paradise."

> *Dead bodies filled every corner. Most of them were treated in the same manner by the survivors, who were more concerned to get rid of their rotting bodies than moved by charity towards the dead. With the aid of porters, if they could get them, they carted the bodies out of the houses and laid them at the door; where every morning quantities of the dead might be seen.*
>
> —Giovanni Boccaccio, the famous Italian writer who lived through the Black Death as it ravaged the city of Florence in 1348

The Black Death had ramifications on European—and world—history far beyond its staggering death toll. The plummeting population meant there was more stuff for fewer people, which made for generally greater wealth. Fewer workers meant that labor was more valuable, and some historians point to that factor as leading to the demise of feudalism and the beginnings of capitalism. It also may have contributed to increased interest in developing labor-saving technology.

Human nature being what it is, survivors looked for scapegoats. The most popular target was the Jews. They had already been periodically expelled from various European countries so their possessions could be confiscated. The plague gave their persecutors another excuse.

One of the hardest-hit segments of the population was the clergy, since they were often called to the sides of the dead and dying. This weakened the Church's influence, as did the Church's inability to do anything to thwart the spread of the disease.

In fact, there was probably no aspect of the human condition not affected by the Black Death. That included fighting: In 1346, Tartars who had besieged the Christian-held city of Caffa in the Crimea loaded their catapults with the bodies of plague victims and lobbed them into the city.

It worked. Panicked Italian merchants inside Caffa abandoned the city and fled—on rat-infested ships—to Europe.

Lethal Efficiency

Although most battles in the Middle Ages were still the hand-to-hand variety, military types were always looking for ways to kill effectively from a safe distance (safe for their side, anyway).

One such weapon was the longbow, which was usually as long as the archer was tall and was made of yew. A trained longbowman could loose as many as nine arrows a minute, and the weapon had an effective range of as much as two hundred yards.

The longbow became particularly associated with English archers, who could release almost continuous volleys of arrows at an enemy and inflict a lot of damage before the infantries or cavalries engaged.

One trouble with the longbow, however, was that there was a fairly long learning curve. That's probably the biggest reason it was superseded in popularity by the crossbow.

Although versions of the crossbow had been used in East Asia as early as 2000 BCE, it started showing up in Europe about the tenth century. It was pretty simple to operate, so it was a favorite among military leaders fighting with conscripted or raw armies.

The crossbow remained the most ubiquitous missile-firing weapon of most armies well into the fifteenth century, when the firearm gradually replaced it. And we all know where that led.

Deal or Ordeal

The justice system in much of Europe during the Middle Ages was a curious mix of silly and stupid. A member of the upper classes who was charged with a crime could stand "trial by oath," which consisted of the accused swearing he didn't do it, and getting other people to say he didn't do it.

Lesser citizens weren't so lucky: They faced a trial by ordeal. The idea was that God would intervene in cases where the defendant was innocent. So the accused might be forced to carry a piece of red-hot metal in his hand for a specified distance, or lift a stone out of a pot of boiling water. If his hand became infected within three days, he was declared guilty, and usually executed.

> If anyone shall have stolen 5 shillings, or its equivalent, he shall be hung with a rope; if less, he shall be flayed with whips, and his hair pulled out by a pincers.
> —One of the laws promulgated by Frederick I, emperor of the Holy Roman Empire, between 1152 and 1157

Another method was to tie up the defendant and throw him into a lake, pond, or river. If he floated, he was guilty. If he sank, he was innocent. Of course he also sometimes drowned.

In some cases, especially in civil disputes, the matter could be settled through combat between the disputants. The winner was, well, the winner. But money talked even in trials by combat, because participants could hire a champion to fight for them.

Perhaps ironically, the Church wasn't crazy about a justice system based on divine intervention. By the mid-thirteenth century, members of the clergy were forbidden to take part in trials by ordeal. The Church's stand helped push trials by ordeal into disrepute, and they all but died out by the beginning of the fourteenth century.

Joust for Fun

Nothing captures the popular image of the Middle Ages more than the joust: two knights in full armor galloping full bore at each other with long wooden poles. Sort of like hockey, only with horses.

While events similar to medieval jousting probably began not long after someone first climbed on a horse's back, the first rules for jousting that we know of were written down in 1066, by a French knight named Geoffroi de Purelli. Whether they were enforced is unclear, since de Purelli was killed in the very tournament for which he had written the rules.

> ## DOES THIS MAKE ME LOOK HEAVY?
>
> A full suit of combat armor in the early Middle Ages could weigh between forty-five and eighty pounds.

Early jousts were often held in lieu of actual battles. Combatants would get together, joust to the death, and the winners could be home by dark. By the twelfth century, those battles had evolved into "melees," in which a group of knights would charge into each other all at once, with the winner being the last guy still on his horse.

Melees, in turn, more often became one-on-one contests. By 1292, a Statute of Arms for Tournaments set rules to limit bloodshed. The contests became more tests of skill and less of brute force.

Although condemned by the Church and frowned on by some royalty, jousting remained a popular spectator sport through the mid-sixteenth century. It began to lose steam in 1559, however, after King Henry II of France was killed in a joust. It seems a lance splinter got through the viewing slot in his helmet and penetrated his brain.

Belts and Bridles

It's a common scene in many ribald tales of the Middle Ages: The macho Crusader, off on his way to a few years in the Holy Land, has his wife, daughters, or any other women he feels protective toward (or possessive of) fitted with a chastity belt. You know, those things that sort of look like metal underwear, only with a lock on them to prevent hanky panky.

Trouble is, it didn't happen, at least not among medieval knights. The earliest such devices that have been found date from the sixteenth century, well after the Crusades and the Age of Chivalry. It appears that linking chastity belts to knights and Crusaders was dreamed up by nineteenth-century writers who loved to romanticize about courtly love during the Middle Ages.

Far more common, and somewhat less romantic, was the brank, also known as the scold's bridle. It was sort of an iron cage with a tongue depressor. Women who were deemed nags or gossips were forced to wear the thing as punishment. Fortunately for radio talk show hosts, use of the device faded out in the seventeenth century.

· · · · · · · · · · · · · · · · · · **BY THE NUMBERS** · · · · · · · · · · · · · · · ·

3   number of books in Dante's *The Divine Comedy* (*Inferno, Purgatorio,* and *Paradiso*)

7   number of oxen considered equal in value to one pound of nutmeg, according to a 1393 German table of prices

10   estimated percentage of the population of Nuremberg, Germany, killed by the Black Death (believed by some historians to be the lowest death rate from plague of any major European city)

12   period of apprenticeship, in years, that a medieval European craftsman might have to serve before being considered a master

13   number of years it took to build Westminster Abbey, which was finished in 1065

17   number of years the Venetian trader and explorer Marco Polo spent at the court of Kublai Khan

21   minimum age for being a knight

23   number of years in the thirteenth century when the Holy Roman Empire had no emperor (a period, between 1250 and 1273, known as "The Great Interregnum")

30   approximate number of Mongol tribes united by Genghis Khan into a unified fighting force

100   number of cantos, or divisions, in *The Divine Comedy*

116   length in years of the Hundred Years' War between France and England, from 1337 to 1453

400   number of years spent building the spectacular royal palace of Great Zimbabwe in southeastern Africa

2,000   number of Jews hanged simultaneously at Strasbourg, Germany, in 1348 because they were held responsible for the Black Death

5,000 number of flour mills in England in 1086, according to the Domesday Book, a census of the country's assets ordered by William I

30,000 number of Scotsmen under the command of Robert Bruce VIII, who defeated an English force of one hundred thousand and took the last English-held castle in Scotland at the Battle of Bannockburn in 1314

100,000 estimated number of men and women who volunteered for the First Crusade in 1095

110,000 approximate maximum size of Genghis Khan's army, which was pretty small by medieval standards

500,000 approximate population of Kyoto, Japan, in 1185

1,000,000 approximate population of the Song Chinese city of Hangzhou in the late 1200s

7

RENAISSANCE, ANYONE?

(AND HOW ABOUT GENOCIDE AND SLAVERY?)

(1300–1575)

To be honest, the Renaissance was one bizarre era: incredible violence was everywhere, as great thinkers made huge advances in art and philosophy—by returning to the ancient past. In fact, it was a sort of "Great Leap Backward" in human civilization. During this period, educated people in southern Europe reconnected with Roman and Greek culture from the Classical Age, laying the foundations for modern society. Yet the themes of the movement—reason, harmony, and humanism—were totally at odds with what was going on in Europe at the time. Even more strangely, the Renaissance arguably resulted from one of the worst disasters in human history: the Black Death.

In northern Europe, the Hundred Years' War and endless struggles between kings and powerful nobles convinced the kings that it was time to subdue the nobles once and for all. Chipping away at the nobles' territory and power, the English and French kings created something entirely new: nation-states, whose citizens were bonded to each other by shared identities and history, instead of by loyalty to noble lords.

Other European kingdoms were sharpening their claws in preparation for a devastating period of global expansion. The first wave of exploration, colonization, and genocide was led by Spain, a new hyper-Catholic nation created by Ferdinand and Isabella from the ashes of a Muslim empire. They not only helped Europe map out the globe, but also destroyed the largest and most powerful empires in the history of the Americas, the Aztecs in Mexico and the Inca in Peru (with a little help from those empires' respective rivals).

Meanwhile, in 1376, angry Chinese peasants, led by a charismatic commoner named Zhu Yuanzhang, threw out the last Mongol rulers of the Yuan Dynasty. The native Ming Dynasty he established was one of the most powerful in Chinese history.

But it wasn't all bad news for the Mongols. They had one last hurrah, in India, well after the Chinese chucked them out. Unlike their cousins who conquered China, the Moghuls (a corruption of *Mongol*) of eastern Persia kept their nomadic ways, thus remaining effective warriors. In 1527 they left Afghanistan to conquer the broad fertile floodplains of Pakistan and India.

Nearby, another set of nomadic horsemen from Central Asia—the Ottoman Turks—established a very powerful empire encompassing most of the Mediterranean Basin and Eastern Europe. The Muslim Ottomans had the kings of Western Europe shaking in their ermine-lined boots for a good two centuries. Their arrival also doomed the wealthy medieval trading republic of Venice, in northern Italy, which lost control of Mediterranean trade routes.

As Venice declined, other Italian city-states launched an intellectual, economic, and cultural revolution—the whole Renaissance thing. The ideas and cultural creations of the Italians were so compelling they soon spread across Europe, making the Renaissance a continent-wide affair. Europe was awakening from its long medieval slumber, and the world would never be the same.

············ **WHAT HAPPENED WHEN**··············

1305 Papal Schism begins.

1348 Bubonic plague strikes Europe, eventually killing one third of the population.

1376 Ming Dynasty established in China.

1378 First attempt to end the Papal Schism fails.

1402 Florence defeats Milanese tyrant Gian Galeazzo.

1405 Tamerlane dies.

1415 Henry V of England invades France, claiming throne.

1453 Ottomans seize Constantinople, ending Byzantine Empire.

1492 Ferdinand and Isabella take back Spain from the Moors; Columbus "discovers" America.

1509 Hernando Cortés begins Spanish conquest of Aztecs.

1517 Martin Luther posts his "95 Theses" in Wittenberg.

1519 Ottomans besiege Vienna.

1527 Moghul Dynasty founded in India.

1532 Francisco Pizarro begins Spanish conquest of Inca.

1558 Elizabeth I becomes queen of England.

1584 Second Ottoman siege of Vienna.

— In Case You Haven't Heard of that —
"Renaissance" Thing . . .

While it's hard to say that something like the Black Plague was a good thing, it may actually have provided the jolt that ended the medieval period and started the Renaissance. This movement—literally, a "rebirth"—had an economic and an intellectual component. With a third of the labor force gone, surviving workers had much more leverage when bargaining for employment; it was in the wake of the Black Death that "free cities" dominated by merchants prospered, and peasant farming collectives became more common. On the intellectual side, the decimation of the population—while devaluing life in the short term—actually made people more thoughtful about what it meant to be human.

The Renaissance was a mostly European endeavor, but it wouldn't have been possible without contributions from Arab scholars and Greeks fleeing the collapsing Byzantine Empire. In the medieval period, Arab scholars in Spain amassed huge collections of manuscripts from Greek and Roman poets and philosophers that were unavailable in Europe. Meanwhile, Greek scholars fleeing the Ottomans in the old Byzantine territories also carried copies of ancient manuscripts to Italy, where they found work as teachers and translators (a step down, but at least they weren't disemboweled and burned alive).

This "Renaissance" was actually firmly rooted in the Catholic tradition. As a matter of fact, most Renaissance scholars were devout Catholics who felt that their movement was perfectly compatible with the teachings of the Church. But the basic method behind it—throwing out existing interpretations of ancient texts and thinking about what they meant from one's own perspective—opened a huge can of theological worms, because it implied that the teachings of the Catholic Church about the Bible were open to debate. (This provided the basis for Protestantism, which proved to be a bit of a problem.)

Renaissance scholars shared two things above all: their respect for ancient Rome and Greece, and their desire to emulate ancient Greek and Roman ideals. These ideals—education, reason, and personal virtue—provided a complete program for life: a program that has come to be called "humanism" because it prizes the independence and potential of individual human beings over other values such as authority and tradition.

One of the first Renaissance thinkers was a poet and essayist named Petrarch (1304–1374), whose Italian family moved to Avignon, France, when he was young. Petrarch spent a good part of his life sitting around thinking and writing about why it was so important to sit around thinking and writing, as well as mooning over a long-term crush named Laura, who was married to someone else (long-term, as in four decades; and of course, it never went anywhere). This description makes Petrarch sound kind of self-absorbed and annoying, which he may have been, but with his beautiful poetry and essays he was a one-man literary revolution. He's also credited as the inventor of mountain climbing—yup, you heard right. Petrarch turned his ascent of Mount Ventoux into an engaging mini-adventure story that is still read today.

> *Books have led some to learning and others to madness.*
> —Petrarch

Another early Renaissance great was Dante Alighieri (1265–1321) who wrote a hilarious—if somewhat petty—book called *Inferno,* in which he imagined all the people from history he hated being punished in Hell in various twisted ways. Although perhaps slightly creepy, Dante was innovative because he wrote in his native Italian so that ordinary people could read his books. In fact, his books became so influential that many standard spellings and grammar for modern Italian are traced back to them.

For the most part, Renaissance thinkers were literary types who stayed away from contemporary politics, but later Renaissance scholars were not afraid to take it on, sometimes at personal risk. The great political movement of the Italian Renaissance, civic humanism, was born in the northern Italian city of Florence, in the face of terrible oppression.

In the medieval period, Florence and its big cousin to the north, Milan, had generally gotten along. But all this changed in 1386, when Milan came under the tyrannical rule of a military strongman named Gian (pronounced "John") Galeazzo. In 1394 the powerful Galeazzo attacked Florence, and everyone was sure the tiny city-state was a goner. But under the leadership of a great Renaissance humanist Coluccio Salutati, the Florentines pulled together and withstood the Milanese enemy.

Salutati helped formulate an ideology called civic humanism, which still permeates modern democratic society. Civic humanism applies humanist ideals to the political world, encouraging leadership, self-sacrifice, and integrity in the people who wield power. Like earlier strains of Renaissance thought, it was built on classical sources, and

PRINCE OF PRAGMATISM

As far as political theory goes, Coluccio Salutati was the "nice" side of the Italian Renaissance. The much more interesting, "bad" side was depicted by another Florentine, named Niccolò Machiavelli, who grew up in a very different city a century after Salutati.

Florence fended off the Milanese bully Gian Galeazzo only to become prey to much larger bullies: France and Spain, which fought for control of Italy throughout the fifteenth and sixteenth centuries. Born in 1469, Machiavelli grew up in an Italy devastated by foreigners—often with the help of local princes, also vying for power.

This situation disgusted Machiavelli, and he began studying the classical world, including ancient Greece and Rome, to understand what made rulers successful. He summed up his controversial conclusions in *The Prince*, a book of advice he sent to the Medici family, who ruled Florence.

"Politics have no relation to morals," wrote Machiavelli, who also observed, "Of mankind we may say in general they are fickle, hypocritical, and greedy." Power came from the ability to inflict violence and terrorize people, and Machiavelli advised: "Before all else, be armed." In an ideal situation, the ruler will enjoy the affection of his people, but when the chips are down, "It is better to be feared than loved, if you cannot be both."

Contrary to accepted Christian morality, Machiavelli openly advocated lying ("A prince never lacks legitimate reasons to break his promise") and murder ("If an injury has to be done to a man, it should be so severe that his vengeance need not be feared"). He made no exception for "innocent" people who opposed the ruler, reasoning that there was a greater good: the well-being of the general population.

Ironically, the amoral (many said immoral) philosophy depicted in *The Prince* had one goal: protecting the common people from foreign invaders such as the French and Spanish, who were terrorizing Italy. By defeating his foreign and domestic enemies, Machiavelli wrote, the ruler guaranteed the peace and tranquility of his realm, and the safety of his people. So, ultimately, he had humanitarian aims.

placed the greater good above individual concerns. Armed with this ideology, against all odds the Florentine republic outlasted Gian Galeazzo, who died in 1402.

— And Then There's That Other R — the Reformation

The Protestant Reformation that swept northern Europe is a lovely example of people at their best and their worst. During the fifteenth and sixteenth centuries, religious reformers dissatisfied with the Catholic Church displayed remarkable idealism and self-sacrifice. But their movement also became a tool for opportunistic princes who resented Rome's meddling in their affairs and would stop at nothing to throw off the "yoke of Rome." In the long run, this led to the deaths of millions (and we mean *millions*).

Like a bad quiche, the first rumblings of dissent came in the fourteenth century, when the growing power of the French kings allowed them to sponsor their own popes in Avignon, beginning in 1305. The result was the so-called Great Schism in the Catholic Church—a period when the involvement of the various competing popes in politics led to widespread disillusionment among common people. It's not hard to see why, with first two, then three, then four (!) popes vying for power.

What happened? In 1409, the French and pro-"Italian" faction agreed to withdraw their claimants to the papal throne and elect just one pope, who would return to Rome and end the Great Schism—but the whole plan fell apart. The two sides did indeed elect a new pope, Alexander V, who was supposed to replace the two current popes, Gregory XII and Benedict III. But Gregory and Benedict backed out at the last minute, so now there were three popes. This situation continued until 1417, when a new council of the Catholic Church elected yet another pope, Martin V, to replace the three popes currently holding office. Before the three deposed popes voluntarily abdicated, there were technically four popes ruling the Catholic Church. If TV had existed, this could have been a great reality show: "This is the story of four popes, all of whom claim to be infallible . . ."

With management a mess, it's not surprising many early "Protestant" critiques actually came from inside the Church. Several Protestant revolutionaries began as Catholic scholars. These early dissenters included an English professor at Oxford University named John Wycliffe and a Bohemian activist named Jan Huss, who was inspired by Wycliffe.

From 1376 to 1379, Wycliffe wrote a series of essays arguing that corrupt Catholic priests forfeited all their spiritual authority. This was controversial, as it denied the effectiveness of the Catholic Mass, absolution, and penance, which allowed ordinary people to atone for their sins. Wycliffe also said that Christians should be able to read the Bible in their native language, rather than listen to a priest read it in Latin, a language meaningless to commoners. Wycliffe was almost imprisoned for uttering these revolutionary ideas and might have been burned alive, but thanks to powerful protectors in England, he escaped. His successful defiance was a sign of things to come.

Jan Huss wasn't so lucky. Like Wycliffe, Huss believed that preachers should speak to ordinary people in their native language—in his case, Czech. Beginning in 1402, Huss ruled the roost in Prague, preaching dissent against corrupt priests, bishops, and the pope. But the Church brought the hammer down in 1414, calling Huss to a Church council to have him "explain" his views. The Holy Roman emperor, Sigismund, promised Huss his safety, but reneged on the deal, and Huss was burned at the stake in 1415.

Much to the dismay of the Church hierarchy, the trouble was just beginning. The next century brought a firestorm of dissent stoked by two more maverick theologians: Martin Luther and John Calvin.

Like Wycliffe and Huss, Martin Luther began a devout Catholic but ended in radical opposition—and also like them, his opposition sprang from fundamental contradictions in the Church's teachings. A Catholic monk in Wittenberg, Germany, Luther objected to the Church's entanglement with political authority, its ownership of property, and especially the sale of "indulgences," which promised the absolution of sin for a fee—basically "Get out of Hell Free" cards, which he considered totally worthless. Luther staked out his basic position in his famous "95 Theses," which he nailed to the door of the cathedral in Wittenberg in 1517. Luther also advocated "justification by faith"—meaning Christians were redeemed by faith alone, with no need for sacraments or absolution by a priest.

When I am angry I can pray well and preach well.
—Martin Luther

Though Pope Leo X would probably have liked to burn Luther at the stake for this impudence, Luther got away with it because powerful

German princes found his ideas a useful justification for their own defiance.

John Calvin took a different route. Born in France in 1509, Calvin studied theology all over Europe. Unlike Luther, he had a vision for Protestant society sketched out in his head. Calvin made his major contributions to Protestant thought in Geneva, Switzerland, after its inhabitants rebelled against their northern Italian rulers and established an independent city-state in 1536. The city invited him to establish a Protestant church, which he did in 1540. In keeping with his strict ideas, "immoral" activities such as dancing and drinking were soon made illegal. Fun town.

> *A dog barks when his master is attacked. I would be a coward if I saw that God's truth is attacked and yet would remain silent.*
> —John Calvin

IT'S A GOOD THING PAPAL INFALLIBILITY COVERS PROSTITUTION AND SODOMY

If you're still wondering why the authority of the Catholic Church collapsed in the fifteenth and sixteenth centuries, just consider the "Ballet of the Chestnuts," an uber-depraved party thrown by the son of Pope Alexander VI in 1501. This bizarre and deeply naughty celebration was attended by fifty prostitutes, and got its name from the after-dinner, ahem, "activities." The prostitutes had their clothes auctioned, and were then made to crawl around on the floor to pick up chestnuts—a rather thin excuse to get them on all fours. An orgy-game ensued in which the "players" (the super-rich male attendees) had their orgasms tallied by a servant, with each in pursuit of the highest score; this particular "rule" was ordered by the pope himself, who was also in attendance.

Aside from these occasional blowouts, the popes probably got away with most of their debauchery...but there were times it just couldn't be covered up: specifically, when they died "in the act." In 939, Pope Leo VII died of a heart attack in bed with his mistress; in 964, an enraged husband found his wife in bed with Pope John XII, then bludgeoned him to death, naked in bed (a great way to go); incredibly, the exact same thing happened to John XIII in 972; and then in 1471, Pope Paul II died of a heart attack...while being sodomized by a page boy.

France:
Growing Pains

French kings began centralizing administration in the late 1200s, but it wasn't until the fifteenth century that they finally consolidated the new French state. In the end, most of the feudal fiefdoms were welded into a single royal domain by Louis XI. Coming to power in 1461, Louis XI had his work cut out for him, and cut he did: long-standing family ties, limbs, heads—whatever needed cutting.

The back story: in 1415, the English king Henry V took advantage of a civil war between two French noble families, the Burgundians and the Armagnacs, to invade a weakened France and reclaim the French throne, which he believed he had inherited. Eventually the English were sent packing, but the destructive war made it clear to the future King Louis XI that he could never again allow his noble relatives to gain so much power. Feuding and rebellion could weaken the country and open it to foreign rule. Thus he set out to break the power of the nobles once and for all—with some rather dirty tricks.

> If you can't lie, you can't govern.
> —Louis XI

For example, in the case of the aged Duke of Burgundy, Louis waited until the man was senile, then seized his lands in Picardy (northern France) by pressuring him to rewrite his will. Of course this subterfuge infuriated the duke's rightful heir, his son Charles the Rash, who soon earned his nickname by organizing a revolt of the French nobility against the king.

As Burgundy's rebellion drifted along, Louis XI was working to form his own powerful standing army. To secure funding for a new army of professional soldiers, Louis called a meeting of the rarely used French general parliament (called the Estates-General) in 1468. He didn't really have a choice: as fighting rebellious nobles cost more and more money, the loyal nobles, clergy, and wealthy merchants who were lending him money and paying taxes demanded a say in how the money was spent.

It all came to a head when the Swiss towns that belonged to the Duke of Burgundy rebelled in 1475. All the duke's old enemies (with a name like "the Rash," he had a lot) sprang out of the woodwork to ally themselves with Louis XI. The most powerful, the Duke of Lorraine, killed the Duke of Burgundy at the Battle of Nancy in 1477. Louis conquered Burgundy for himself—a giant increase in his power—and from there it was all gravy. When the Duke of Anjou died without a male heir, Louis picked up his territory in southern France, too, increasing his power even more. In fact, over his reign, French royal territory almost doubled.

England:
Bow Down or Get Out

The English kings began welding England into a single nation shortly after French kings centralized rule in their own kingdom, with similar results. But England, unlike France, had a wild card: a popular Protestant movement that undermined the Catholic Church. The two trends—royal centralization and Protestant Reformation—converged in a uniquely English "compromise."

In England the final push to centralization was provided by the long, bloody War of the Roses—which was not nearly as pleasant as it sounds. After a good number of peasant dwellings were burned (no surprise; the little guys always got the worst of it) the last man standing after the War of the Roses was Henry Tudor, who took the name Henry VII after defeating his rival, Richard III, in 1485. When Henry died in 1509, rule passed to his son Henry VIII—who had some, ah, issues with his wives and the Catholic Church.

Building on his father's achievements, Henry VIII wielded unprecedented control over England. Because the pope wouldn't allow him to divorce his wife—or his second wife, or his third—in his endless quest to produce a male heir, Henry simply established a new church, independent of Rome, called the Anglican Church. He also enriched the royal treasury by looting Catholic monasteries and established a special court with its own secret police, the Star Chamber, to dispose of uncooperative nobles. Thus Henry VIII paved the way for the greatest monarch in English history: his daughter Elizabeth.

Before coming to power in 1558, Elizabeth's attitudes were shaped by the reign of her half-sister, Mary, a devout Catholic who rejected their father's attempt to establish a separate English church and earned the nickname Bloody Mary for her execution of hundreds of English Protestants. Elizabeth herself was nominally a Protestant, but concluded that religion should take a backseat to politics—period. As a result, her policies angered Protestants and Catholics alike.

> There is only one Christ, Jesus, one faith. All else is a dispute over trifles.
> —Queen Elizabeth I

Elizabeth dealt with the religious problem first, issuing a revised "Book of Common Prayer" in 1559, a text that basically papered over religious conflicts between Catholics and Protestants by being very, very vague. No one was happy with the Book of Common Prayer—especially a fanatical Protestant group called the Puritans—but that was sort of the point: religion was great and all, but obedience to the English monarch came first. Indeed, dissenters from both the Catholic and Protestant camps soon found out what it meant to cross Elizabeth.

Catholic opposition to Elizabeth was led by Thomas, Duke of Norfolk, whose conspiracy provided the queen with a perfect opportunity to crush Catholics and nobles in one big bloodbath. She allowed Thomas to enter into a conspiracy with the pope, then produced evidence of his treason (possibly manufactured), and had him executed in 1571.

But Elizabeth also subdued Protestants who opposed her religious reforms. She paid special attention to crushing the Puritans and Presbyterians, Protestant sects who believed (correctly) that Elizabeth was trying to shift political control of the church from the pope to herself.

Spain:
Spreading the Love

In Spain, although Ferdinand and Isabella were extremely powerful, they operated almost entirely through the old feudal system. And their grandson, Charles V, ruled in the same way. These monarchs wanted above all to gather land and subjects—even if they didn't fit neatly into their existing empire. By distributing massive bribes (gold looted from the New World), Charles V got himself elected Holy Roman Emperor, a big boost in prestige. But his European empire was a crazy quilt, including Spain, Austria, the Netherlands, parts of Italy, Sicily, Sardinia, and chunks of Germany.

Of course, Ferdinand, Isabella, and Charles V did have one thing going for them: religion. To kick off the empire, Ferdy and Izzy

A BAD HAIR CENTURY

Hoping to cement his scattered European empire with truly "cosmetic" changes, Holy Roman Emperor Charles V ordered his entourage to cut their hair, because it was the current fashion in northern Europe. Although they obeyed, they wept as they cut their waist-length locks. In southern Europe, the length of one's hair, like the length of one's beard, was a sign of one's age—and therefore of authority. Unfortunately, Charles V was never able to grow a beard, and his followers were also forced to trim their beards to imitate their girlish leader.

summoned their Spanish subjects to a common cause by proclaiming a new Crusade against the Muslims of southern Spain. By the mid-1400s, Muslim Spain had been whittled down to a "rump kingdom" (seriously, that's what they called it) in the southern peninsula called Al-Andalus. Ferdinand and Isabella finished it off with the capture of Granada in 1492, followed by the expulsion of all Jews in Spain, for good measure.

Around this same time, Ferdinand and Isabella were presented with a great opportunity to continue their "crusade" when a little

> I speak Spanish to God, Italian to women, French to men and German to my horse.
> —Charles V

side venture involving a Genoese sailor named Christopher Columbus produced unexpected results. In 1492, they had funded a small expedition by Columbus to find an ocean route to Asia. Columbus returned in 1494 with reports of islands he thought were modern Japan and Indonesia (actually Haiti and Cuba).

The royal couple agreed to fund return expeditions, and soon out-of-work European thugs and petty nobility calling themselves "conquerors" (conquistadores) realized that there were two wealthy native empires—the Aztec and Inca—located across the ocean. These kingdoms were technologically primitive but socially advanced, with large, complex urban centers—in other words, wealthy targets ripe for the picking.

> These people are very unskilled in arms . . . with 50 men they could all be subjected and made to do all that one wished.
> —Christopher Columbus

The Aztecs:
Running an Empire on Blood and Chocolate

The Aztecs were into blood—human blood, baby. In fact, they believed their gods required human blood to live. So, as their power grew in Mexico in the fourteenth and fifteenth centuries, they sacrificed ever greater numbers of captives from the neighboring tribes and cities.

They were probably offing somewhere in the neighborhood of twenty thousand people a year by the time of the arrival of Hernando Cortés in 1509. Even better was the preferred means of sacrifice: cutting open the rib cage and offering the victim's still-beating heart to heaven in a brazier filled with burning coals. Nice.

Aside from this incredibly brutal aspect of their religion, the Aztecs achieved a level of social complexity and urban organization exceeding any other Native American state in history. With about two hundred thousand inhabitants, the capital Tenochtitlan, located on an island in the middle of Lake Texcoco, ruled an empire with millions of subjects.

The Aztecs began building their empire in the late fourteenth century, driven by the ambition of their warrior caste and the orderly organization of Aztec society in general. Beneath the warrior caste of Eagle and Jaguar knights, most Aztecs were farmers, tending giant floating gardens on Lake Texcoco, where they grew corn, cotton, and vegetables. Meanwhile, Aztec merchants traveled the length of Mexico looking for luxury goods such as gems, precious metals, dyes, and plumage from exotic birds.

In some ways, the Aztec religious pantheon resembled the divine households of the Olmecs, Toltecs, and Mayans. But Aztec gods had a mean streak a mile wide. There was Coatlicue, a clawed

YES, OUR MONEY GROWS ON TREES

From at least the fourteenth century, the Aztecs used cocoa beans as coins, valuing them because they were both rare and delicious. Indeed, if they felt like splurging, they weren't afraid to down their tasty money, drinking it in a thick beverage called *chocolatl*, which probably tasted more like our modern coffee than it did hot chocolate. Calling cocoa beans "the food of the gods," the Aztecs also offered them to divinities alongside human sacrifices that could claim hundreds of victims from neighboring tribes. Taxes from neighboring tribes were also collected in the form of cocoa beans. Hernando de Ovieda Valdez, a historian who accompanied Hernando Cortés in his conquest of the Aztecs, recorded the prices of different goods and services in cocoa beans: a rabbit cost four beans; a slave, one hundred. A visit to a prostitute would cost you ten beans.

goddess representing pain, who wore a skirt made out of snakes and a necklace of human hearts. Xipe Totec was the god of spring and rebirth, but also of suffering, requiring priests to skin a sacrificial victim alive and then don the skin to symbolize the cycle of life.

To be fair, not all Aztec gods were cruel. The sun god, Huitzilpochtli, protected the Aztecs and granted victory in battle. Xochipilli, the "good times" god, embodied dawn, dancing, and love. And Quetzalcoatl, the "feathered serpent," represented wisdom and creation. In fact, in the fifteenth century, Quetzalcoatl became the object of a popular cult that forecasted his return in physical form to free the Aztecs from the burden of human sacrifice. Unluckily for them, the last Aztec emperor, Montezuma (or Moctezuma) II, may have mistaken the Spanish conquistador Hernando Cortés for the returning messiah Quetzalcoatl—with disastrous results.

The Inca:
Another Golden Target

Like the Aztecs, the Inca Empire was relatively young, and the neighboring tribes they conquered were not terribly fond of them.

When the Spanish showed up in 1532, the Inca Empire was a fairly recent construction, less than a hundred years old. It was founded in 1438 by a dynamic military leader named Pachacuti, who subdued the central mountain valleys of modern Peru. His successors added modern Ecuador, Bolivia, and northern Chile. Geographically the Inca Empire was far larger than that of the Aztecs, measuring 2,500 miles from north to south.

The Inca developed a sophisticated urban society with large cities supported by productive agricultural hinterlands. Again, like the Aztecs, they demonstrated both impressive engineering skill and an ability to mobilize mass labor for big projects by constructing huge ceremonial structures. The chief Inca ceremonial centers, Cuzco, the capital, and Machu Picchu, a mystical mountain redoubt, required tens of thousands of laborers to move stone blocks weighing up to fifty tons to positions high in the Andes Mountains.

The Inca also constructed fourteen thousand miles of roads that rivaled Roman roads in their durability; in fact, some Inca roads are still used today. Deep ravines in the Andes were spanned with rope bridges. Like the Romans, the Inca used their elaborate system of roads to facilitate trade and the movement of armies.

The empire was blessed with enormous mineral wealth, including silver and gold deposits, and Spanish conquistadores' eyewitness descriptions of Incan cities, while mind-boggling, are likely accurate. It seems the walls of the Court of Gold in Cuzco—an astronomical observatory housing about four thousand Inca priests—were hung with thin sheets of gold; a solid gold disc representing the Sun God reflected sunlight on the sheets to illuminate the building's interior.

Of course this incredible wealth made the Inca Empire a prime target for Spanish conquest, as with the Aztecs in Mexico. In 1532, shortly after Hernando Cortés conquered the Aztecs, a Spanish adventurer named Francisco Pizarro attacked the Inca and—wait for it—looted the empire. The Spanish melted down priceless Inca objects into gold bars, which they shipped back to Spain, and enslaved the Native American population to mine rich ore deposits at places such as Potosí, Bolivia.

China:
On the Money

Any comparison of Western Europe and China at this time has to look at the numbers—the number of people, for starters. In 1300, China probably held upward of one hundred million people. And these were all subjects of one emperor. Compare this to Europe, which had about fifty million people. It's no surprise that the Mongols of the Yuan Dynasty found themselves hopelessly outnumbered. But the Mongols weren't doing themselves any favors. In 1348, the last Mongol emperor, Togan Timur, appointed a particularly nasty SOB named Bayan as his prime minister, who suggested the best way to end Chinese dissent was to exterminate nine tenths of the population. Shockingly, the Chinese did not like Bayan, or his boss Togan, and 1348 saw the beginning of a twenty-year rebellion, led by a charismatic commoner named Yuanzhang.

So who was Yuanzhang, who took the imperial name Hongwu, and founded the new Ming Dynasty? As with earlier dynasties, he founded a new administration that mirrored the structure of previous ones—but unlike most self-made emperors, he was a peasant. In fact, he was able to succeed in part because the old aristocracy had been sidelined by the Mongols. As emperor, Hongwu was deeply insecure about his humble background, and ruthlessly suppressed his enemies—real and imagined. But he also passed agrarian and tax reforms to make life easier for peasants. To keep the Mongols out, Hongwu undertook the reconstruction of the

Great Wall, which was supposed to seal off northern China from Mongolia. Previous Chinese dynasties had built long walls along the route of the Great Wall, but the modern structure of that name is mostly a Ming construction.

China was broke when the Mongols left, and it was about to get broker. After taking over the reins of power, Hongwu gave almost all the copper coins in circulation to the Mongols, basically as "protection money," so they wouldn't invade China again. The Mongols would have laughed at paper money, which they considered worthless—and how right they were. To make up for the shortfall in copper coins, Hongwu introduced paper money in the late fourteenth century, leading to a boom in trade. But he soon discovered the great thing about paper money: you can print as much of it as you want! There was just one small problem: it became worthless, falling to one seventieth of its previous value, and in 1425 the Mandarin bureaucrats were forced to reintroduce copper coinage. Despite the mixed results, China still deserves credit as the first state in history to try using paper money on a large scale. It was an example that would be followed by Europe in the seventeenth century, often with a similar outcome (a lot of useless paper stuff).

India:
Babar's Shop

In the early sixteenth century a Mongol prince named Babar (yes, the cartoon elephant is probably named after him) founded the powerful Moghul (Mongol) dynasty.

Babar came from the same stock as the earlier warlord Tamerlane, who claimed to be a descendant of Genghis Khan and certainly slaughtered and conquered with similar flair. Around 1500, Babar decided to follow the example of his illustrious predecessors by saddling up and kicking some serious ass. But Babar was actually a just, evenhanded administrator as well as a capable military commander. With a reputation for delivering both serious smack-downs and good government, he was soon in control of a large amount of northern India.

Still, it would fall to Babar's weird, charismatic grandson Akbar to consolidate the empire. Akbar (who sadly does not have a cartoon elephant named after him) assumed the throne in 1561, at the age of thirteen, and immediately began expanding his territory to cover all of northern India as well as Pakistan and even Afghanistan. Governing from the central city of Delhi, Akbar developed a sophisticated

GOOD KHAN, BAD KHAN

Babar and the Moghuls were nice guys compared to their distant cousin Tamerlane, who ranks as one of the meanest bastards in history, hands down, no contest.
Also known as Timur ("iron" in Turkic), he learned the ways of horse-mounted
warfare early on from his father, chief of a small nomadic tribe. Timur was lame in one
leg from a battlefield injury acquired as a young man (Timur+lame=Tumerlane),
but this didn't impair his skill in cavalry combat. In 1369 he eliminated his chief
rival for the throne of Samarkand, then led his motley collection of followers on a
series of lightning campaigns against Persia, Iraq, Syria, Russia, India, and China.

Some essential numbers: Timur ordered the death of seventy thousand inhabitants of the Persian city of Isfahan in 1387. At Delhi, in northern India, in 1398,
his army slaughtered one hundred thousand unarmed captive Indians. In 1400, he
buried alive four thousand Armenian prisoners. His soldiers massacred twenty
thousand civilians in Baghdad, where Timur ordered each soldier to return with at
least two human heads. Last but not least, after his soldiers allegedly killed eighty
thousand people in Aleppo and twenty thousand in Damascus, he built twenty
pyramids of skulls around the devastated cities.

One account recorded conditions in Delhi after Timur's visit: "The city of Delhi
was depopulated and ruined ... followed by a pestilence caused by the pollution
of the air and water by thousands of uncared-for dead bodies."

Although he left behind plenty of skeletons, Timur made no bones about being
evil. Before burning Damascus to the ground and killing most of its inhabitants, he
gathered the leading citizens for a little lecture, saying, "I am the scourge of God
appointed to chastise you, since no one knows the remedy for your iniquity except
me. You are wicked, but I am more wicked than you, so be silent!"

Timur was planning an invasion of China to reunify the empire of Genghis
Khan when he died at the age of seventy.

administration to rule his vast empire. He appointed military governors who were held responsible for any government misdoings in their
province, including corruption—sometimes on penalty of death.

The most remarkable thing about Akbar was his extreme religious
tolerance. To get on the majority Hindus' good side, Akbar took the
wise step of repealing the *jizya*, or Muslim tax on all non-Muslims;
repealed a tax on visits to Hindu pilgrimage destinations; and allowed
legal cases to be tried in Hindu courts.

These were all smart steps. But his descendant Aurangzeb, who
ruled three generations later, was a Muslim zealot who persecuted

> *I love my own religion. Is there anything that I will not do for my*
> *religion? . . . The Hindu Minister also loves his religion. Does he not*
> *have the right to love the thing that is his very own?*
> —Akbar the Great

Hindus and alienated the Hindu majority. This kind of cruelty paved the way for the British conquest of India in the eighteenth and nineteenth centuries, when the Brits benefited from Hindu resentment toward their Muslim rulers.

Ottomans
(No, the Plural Is Not Ottomen)

The Ottomans were originally employed by the Byzantine emperors as border guards holding off fierce Mongol incursions into Asia Minor—modern-day eastern Turkey—on the theory that "it takes a nomad to fight a nomad." Later the Ottomans were almost "out-nomaded" by Tamerlane, who killed Sultan Bajazet I, "The Thunderbolt," in 1403. But Tamerlane died, and the Ottomans continued their climb to power. They turned on their weak Byzantine masters (never hire Central Asian nomads as your security detail) conquering Constantinople in 1453.

The city's massive triple walls had protected it for centuries, but the Ottoman sultan Mehmed II ordered a Hungarian metallurgist to build him a twenty-seven-foot monster cannon nicknamed the "Basilic" ("King"), which could hurl a twelve-hundred-pound cannonball as far as a mile—the most powerful gun in history up to that point. Meanwhile, Ottoman naval commanders figured out how to get around the giant underwater chains protecting Constantinople's harbors: they drafted local peasants to carry their ships overland around the barriers.

On the morning of May 29, 1453, the bloody final battle began with human-wave assaults by poorly armed Ottoman Bashi-bazouk fanatics. The exhausted Byzantines were able to fend off another attack by Turkish regulars on the northeastern walls, and even stopped a third assault by the sultan's elite shock troops, the Janissaries. Ironically, this fateful battle was decided by a slight oversight: the Byzantine defenders forgot to lock one of the small gates in the northeastern wall, and the Janissaries poured into the city. The last emperor, Constantine XI, probably died fighting in the streets. Because no one saw him die, there was an enduring myth that he would one day return to save the Greeks from Ottoman rule. (Didn't happen.)

> *In the early dawn, as the Turks poured into the City and the citizens took flight, some of the fleeing Romans managed to reach their homes and rescue their children and wives. As they moved, blood-stained, across the Forum of the Bull and passed the Column of the Cross, their wives asked, "What is to become of us?" When they heard the fearful cry, "The Turks are slaughtering Romans within the City's walls," they did not believe it at first . . . But behind him came a second, and then a third, and all were covered with blood, and they knew that the cup of the Lord's wrath had touched their lips. Monks and nuns, therefore, and men and women, carrying their infants in their arms and abandoning their homes to anyone who wished to break in, ran to the Great Church. The thoroughfare, overflowing with people, was a sight to behold!*
>
> —Eyewitness account of the Greek historian Doukas on the fall of Constantinople

Ottoman power peaked under Suleiman the Magnificent (one of history's best names). Coming to power in 1520, he is known in the Muslim world as "the Lawgiver" because of the code of law he issued in 1501, which is an amalgam of Islamic Shari'a and good old-fashioned Turkish tribal law.

Suleiman also dispensed a substantial amount of whup-ass. He laid siege to the great Christian city of Vienna, Austria, in 1519, forcing the Holy Roman emperor Charles V to summon troops from all over Christendom to defend the city. The siege failed, but Suleiman picked up the Balkan Peninsula as a consolation prize. He also conquered Iraq, Armenia, Libya, and Algeria.

Unfortunately many of Suleiman's successors sucked. In fact, his son Selim II is remembered as "the Drunk"—a nickname that speaks for itself. Meanwhile, newcomers called the Portuguese were already scheming against one of the Ottomans' main sources of revenue: customs duties on spices from Asia.

· · · · · · · · · · · · · · · **WHO'S UP, WHO'S DOWN** · · · · · · · · · · ·

Explorers: **UP**

Spain wasn't actually the first European power out of the gate in the race to explore and brutally conquer the rest of the world. That dubious honor goes to Spain's smaller neighbor Portugal.

The pioneering king who launched Portugal's empire was Prince Henry, fittingly called "The Navigator." Born in 1394, Henry (at the tender age of nineteen) led the Portuguese conquest of Ceuta, in modern-day Morocco, where he saw the incredible riches of Africa and Asia on display in the markets, including spices, Oriental rugs, gold, and silver. It occurred to him that Portuguese sailors could reach the sources of these luxury goods directly via sea, cutting out the numerous middlemen who dominated the land routes.

Henry showed an early interest in seafaring and recruited cartographers from all over Europe to help him at his headquarters in Sagres, Portugal. Around the same time, Portuguese merchants were perfecting a new type of ship, the caravel, which became the workhorse of global exploration. They also invented important navigational tools, such as the quadrant, and filled books with ways to calculate lines of latitude (distance north or south of the equator) through observations of the sun.

Beginning in 1420, Henry supported Portuguese colonization of the Canary Islands, the Madeira Islands, and the mid-Atlantic Azores. He also sponsored voyages of discovery down the west coast of Africa. He also gets credit for initiating one of history's most barbaric types of commerce. In 1444, Portuguese traders bought slaves from native African princes who were later sold back in Lagos, Portugal. After Portugal settled Brazil, Portuguese slave traders transported millions of African slaves to work on rubber, sugar, and tobacco plantations. The success of slavery in Brazil set the precedent for the importation of slaves by other colonial powers such as Spain and England.

The exploration of Asia was driven by lust for black pepper from India. Why go to all that trouble? Because the Ottoman Turks had a monopoly over all the overland and maritime trade routes between India and Europe, and made

THIS AIN'T THE SAME OL' SHIP

As England competed with Spain and Portugal for control of the seas in the sixteenth century, one of the main English advantages was the sleeker, more aerodynamic hull that English shipwrights introduced sometime around the middle of the century. The old-fashioned Spanish galleons, with large wooden "superstructures" housing officers' quarters and storage rooms fore and aft, didn't stand a chance against new English ships, called "razed" or "race-built" galleons, which basically chopped off the luxury housing for officers, thus decreasing drag—an all-important consideration when wind was the sole source of power. These faster ships would allow England to gain control of trade routes, and also allowed English privateers to outfit Spanish ships again and again.

a fortune charging customs duties on all the goods crossing their territory. To get to the source and cut the Ottomans out of the equation, Christopher Columbus, sponsored by Ferdinand and Isabella of Spain, tried to find a new ocean route linking Europe to Asia across the Atlantic Ocean to the west—but bumped into America on the way.

Meanwhile Portuguese navigator Vasco de Gama tried another route, heading east around the southern tip of Africa, and made it to India in 1498. When de Gama returned to Portugal with a hold full of black pepper, his expedition earned a profit margin of 6,000 percent! Over the next twenty years, 95 percent of all cargo from India unloaded in Portugal was black pepper—an indication of the incredible demand for the stuff.

The vast profits earned by Portugal gave other European kings ideas, and before long, explorers of all nationalities were fanning out over the globe in pursuit of fame, adventure, and most of all, money, money, money. Of course, it was still plenty hazardous for the second wave. Spain hired Ferdinand Magellan, a Portuguese sailor, whose crew circled the globe for the first time—though Magellan himself didn't make it, as he was eaten by natives in the Philippines in 1572. The English roster included Henry Hudson, who explored the East Coast of North America, until his men mutinied in 1611. Francis Drake, the first Englishman to circumnavigate the globe, began his voyage with six ships in 1577 but returned with just one in 1580, having lost the majority of his crew.

Ivan the Great: UP (And Legitimately Pretty Great)

As too many Russian princes learned, those who defied the Mongols usually met grim, early deaths. But in 1480, Ivan the Great struck boldly (kind of) by making camp for a couple months across a frozen river from the Mongols. (Both armies actually may just have been waiting for the ice on the river to melt to have an excuse to go home.) Nonetheless, in a brilliant show of "soft power," Ivan intimidated the Mongols by displaying his army of 150,000, including cannon and cavalry, before returning to Moscow to think about death.

Yes, Ivan was obsessed with his own mortality, and left his army facing the Mongols across the frozen river to ask advice from monks, bishops, and his mother about whether to fight. Ivan was also under intense pressure from the Russian commoners, who would suffer the most from Mongol retaliation. Archbishop Vassian urged Ivan to fight, asking, "Is it the part of mortals to fear death?"

> *He has overtaxed us, and refused to pay tribute to the Horde, and now that he has irritated the Khan, he declines to fight!*
> —An old Muscovite woman on Ivan

Eventually Ivan returned to the scene of the battle, but moped for several weeks in his tent while the armies traded insults across the river. Then, for reasons that are still unclear, both armies simultaneously panicked and withdrew. The Mongols' withdrawal became a headlong retreat as soldiers fled toward Central Asia. This bloodless defeat signaled the end of Mongol power in Europe.

"Witches": DOWN

Comically ignorant and frighteningly hateful, medieval Christians blamed women for basically everything that went wrong, which not coincidentally was a great excuse to kill them and steal their property. As a "vessel of the Devil," the first woman, Eve, caused the downfall of man by tempting Adam with the fruit of the Tree of Knowledge. Eve was the eternal archetype for all women, whose greed and lust led to sin and corruption.

So considering their evil origins, it's no surprise that women were frequently accused of being witches in medieval Europe. Of course there was no way to determine the truth of these accusations, but that didn't stop "experts" from issuing a big book of rules for investigating and prosecuting witchcraft. The *Malleus Maleficarum,* or *Hammer of Witches,* was a well-intentioned but fanciful work of fiction written in 1486 by two German Dominicans who were also Inquisitors.

According to the *Malleus,* "all witchcraft comes from carnal lust, which is in women insatiable." Unsuspecting women can be corrupted by demons that assume the form of handsome men, but they can also be recruited by other witches, who prey on them when something goes wrong, offering an easy fix through witchcraft. Witches can cast spells, fly, transform themselves into animals known as "familiars" (such as bats or black cats), and magically move objects from far away, including stealing men's penises: "There is no doubt that certain witches can do marvelous things with regard to male organs." They also practice cannibalism and infanticide and have sex with the Devil. Not good stuff.

But how to tell if someone was a witch? The *Malleus* instructed readers how to carry out a "legal" process that basically always ended with the woman dead, regardless of her guilt. There should be more than two witnesses willing to testify that the accused is a witch. Paradoxically, one of the key proofs of being a witch was denying that witches existed. Meanwhile, the judge might not be able to listen to the testimony of a witch, because she could use her words to enchant him. The proof? Sometimes judges released the accused women after talking to them! Of course, a woman could be so corrupted by the Devil that she was unable to confess to being a witch—meaning she was an extra-bad witch. And it goes without saying that any woman who didn't cry during her trial was automatically guilty of being a witch.

D'ARC TRIUMPHS

In 1425, at the age of thirteen, Jeanne d'Arc, an illiterate peasant girl, began hearing voices that she believed to be God and Catholic saints instructing her. According to Jeanne, the voices were later accompanied by a blazing light, and she was eventually able to see whichever saint was speaking to her. One theory holds that the progressive character of the visions may have been symptoms of mounting schizophrenia or bipolar disorder.

In any event, the voices explained Jeanne's mission to her by 1428 at the latest, when she decided she had to help the embattled king of France, Charles VII, free the land from English domination. At that time, the English were about to capture Orleans, sealing the fate of France. Although Jeanne protested that "I am a poor girl; I do not know how to ride or fight," the voices insisted that she take command of the French armies and destroy the English. By this time, the French situation was so desperate that Charles VII was willing to try anything, including putting a seventeen-year-old peasant girl in charge of his armies. However, he wisely first sent her to be examined by French doctors and bishops in the nearby city of Poitiers to determine if she was a fraud.

Returning to Orleans, Jeanne immediately scored a brilliant victory over the English by leading the king's troops on a lightning dash into the city to reinforce it. The sudden arrival of help cheered the defenders, who went on to throw off the English siege before routing them in a series of battles that ended with Charles VII being crowned as French king in the holy city of Rheims in 1429. Jeanne's success saved France, but not her. She was captured by John of Luxembourg in a later battle, who handed her over to his English allies. Charles VII did nothing to help the teenage girl who had saved his crown and his kingdom, remaining silent as English church officials tried and convicted Jeanne of witchcraft and heresy—in part because she wore men's clothing on the field of battle and in prison—and burned her alive on May 30, 1431. She was nineteen years old.

Ultimately, the guilt of witches can be "proved" by physical "trials" using a red-hot iron or dunking them underwater. In the first trial, if the accused woman can carry a red-hot iron three paces without getting burned, she's a witch. If she gets burned, she's not a witch, although she is mutilated for life. In the second, the accused woman is bound with stones and thrown into a pond. If she survives, she's a witch, and if she drowns, she's innocent. (And dead!)

If the accused woman lived long enough to be convicted of witchcraft, she would be burned alive. In the end, fifty thousand to one hundred thousand women—and a few men—were burned as witches in Europe in the medieval and Renaissance periods. Many of the women were probably accused of witchcraft because they were rude or eccentric (exhibiting behaviors that today would be classified as signs of mental illness), were too independent, questioned the authority of male officials or the Catholic Church, or owned property. In cases where the witch owned property, upon her death the land would be divided three ways, among the Catholic Church, the Inquisitors, and the royal treasury— thus giving all three entities a good incentive to find her guilty.

Jews: DOWN. AGAIN.

Comically ignorant and frighteningly hateful, medieval Christians blamed Jews for basically everything that went wrong, which not coincidentally was a great excuse to kill them and steal their property.

Blackmailing Jews was also a favorite tactic of bankrupt kings looking for new sources of income. In 1290, Edward I ordered the expulsion of all England's Jews. (In one story, a sea captain "helping" some of the English Jews to flee left his cargo of refugees—to drown—on a sandbar in the English Channel at low tide.) French nobles expelled the Jews several times, confiscating all their property, but always invited them back when commerce began to suffer. Later, Jews were said to be poisoning wells during the first wave of the Black Death, 1348–1349, and were killed en masse; in Basel the entire Jewish population was moved to a wooden building on an island in the Rhine River, where they were burned alive.

As usual, not the best era to be Jewish.

Mali (and Western Africa): DOWN

Although it had been one of the most powerful empires of medieval times, Mali completely collapsed during this period. The demise of this wealthy West African state had nothing to do with European meddling (which was just getting started) and everything to do with a classic African phenomenon: the overthrow of established powers by nomads from the Sahara desert.

The Tuareg and Songhai were familiar troublemakers who launched rebellions during the reign of Mansa Musa II in the early 1370s. Unfortunately, Mansa Musa II wasn't much of a king: his prime minister, Mari Djata, assumed responsibility for crushing the rebels and took care of the Tuareg (temporarily). But he couldn't defeat the Songhai rebellion. From there, it was all downhill for Mali.

In fact the Songhai would go on to form West Africa's next great state, covering even more territory than Mali. Like the Malinese before them, the first Songhai kings grew wealthy off the trans-Saharan trade in salt and gold. But Portuguese merchants exploring the west coast of Africa did an end run around the kings of Songhai, going straight to the source. West Africa's economy then entered a long downward spiral from which it has never recovered.

········ **SO LONG, AND THANKS FOR ALL THE . . .** ········

Words

It's strange to think of a time before phrases such as "c'est la vie" and "ménage à trois" were common, but in the medieval period, the people of France spoke a variety of dialects, some of which were so different that they were basically different languages. In the north they spoke the *langues d'oïl*—different combinations of Roman Latin and Celtic dialects of the pre-medieval period. There were five major dialects in this group. Meanwhile, in the south of France, people spoke the *langue d'oc,* a dialect more closely related to Latin and Spanish languages such as Catalan. Finally, in the west of France, the inhabitants of the Brittany peninsula spoke an old Celtic language, *Breton.*

Beginning in the late thirteenth century, however, the kings of France employed a new lingua Franca, or "French language," that would serve as the language of administration, and the model of correct pronunciation and spelling. Because royal power was concentrated in Paris, this "official French" was strongly influenced by the Parisian dialect. In 1539 it was proclaimed the official language of France by Francis I, replacing Latin.

Like France, the new English national identity also required linguistic conformity.

After the conquest of England in 1066 by William the Conqueror, a "Norman" descendant of Vikings, Norman French was the language of the English royal court. Meanwhile, the regular people of England spoke a hodgepodge language descended from all the previous conquerors of the British Isles, including the ancient Celts,

Romans, Anglo-Saxons, and Vikings. Over time, the "Old English" of the regular people fused with the Norman French of the kings to produce "Middle English" (Geoffrey Chaucer used this version of English in writing *The Canterbury Tales*). Just like French, the new English language was based closely on the dialect of the royal capital—in this case, London. It was adopted as the official language of Parliament in 1362, and was also used by the Protestant reformer Wycliffe for his "vernacular" (common language) English Bible in 1382.

The Printing Press:
The Most Important Invention Between the Wheel (c. 4000 BCE) and Sliced Bread (1928)

The standardization of national languages such as French and English was possible only because of a world-changing invention: the printing press. The mass production of texts encouraged authors, printers, and readers to agree on standard spellings and rules of grammar. This process was accelerated by the mass printing of dictionaries, which codified national languages.

The first printing presses were actually just blocks of wood that had been meticulously carved with a single page of text. Chinese printers used these primitive presses from at least the ninth century CE to print religious texts for wide distribution. The first European printers used them for similar purposes, including "Pauper's Bibles" (generally heavy on pictures and light on text).

The Chinese nobleman Bi Sheng invented the first moveable-type printing press in 1041 CE. But it was another leap to mass printing, as the individual characters or letters were still carved by hand in Europe and China. In the 1450s the German goldsmith Johann Gutenberg began mass-producing metal type by casting large numbers of metal letters with reusable molds. This made moveable-type ("typeset") printing far more economical.

Gutenberg's first major publications were beautiful "Gutenberg Bibles," which incorporated much of the fine artistry of monastic calligraphy—including gold leaf and other precious materials—without the need for the tedious and sometimes inaccurate hand-copying that belabored the old process. Gutenberg's printing technique soon spread throughout Europe, and was quickly adapted to myriad nonreligious uses, including technical manuals for mining and manufacturing and—of course—propaganda!

From the end of the 1400s onward, printing presses were central to the propaganda struggle waged by Protestant sects against the Catholic Church, and to the furious counterattacks waged by the pope in

Rome. In one famous example, a pro-Protestant cartoon depicts the pope issuing a "Papal Bull" . . . in the form of a giant, gassy fart.

Hash Browns, Home Fries, and Latkes

It might seem like a weird thing to get excited about, but after its discovery in the New World in the sixteenth century, the potato took Europe by storm. (Don't laugh.) The tuber grew well in dry, sandy soil, and was a perfect staple to feed the poor peasants of Europe. Potato cultivation began as a top-secret enterprise, with a cloak-and-dagger operation started by Sir Walter Raleigh, who received a couple of potatoes from his buddy and sometime rival Sir Francis Drake, who had just sailed around the world and picked up some potatoes in Peru or Colombia.

Once Raleigh had perfected the cultivation of the potato, the story goes, he informed Queen Elizabeth, but her royal cooks—who were unfamiliar with the tuber—cooked the green "eyes" growing on the potato rather than the potato itself. This made everyone in the royal family sick, and put Raleigh firmly in the royal doghouse.

Elizabeth outlawed potatoes for a hundred years, but their growing popularity in Spain, France, and Italy (where the Spanish introduced them after the discovery of the Americas) paved the way for their large-scale cultivation in the British Isles. Cultivation was particularly widespread in Ireland, where it expanded to the exclusion of other staple crops—setting the stage for disaster in the 1800s, when blight on the potato crop caused the horrendous Irish Potato Famine.

Nutritious, Delicious Beer

The medieval period and Renaissance have reputations for being rather drunken times, but ironically Public Enemy No. 1—good ol' beer—was usually consumed for its nutritional value, not to get drunk. Indeed, in the early medieval period, beer was probably more like porridge, but by the Renaissance it had more or less acquired its modern form, especially with the addition, in the early sixteenth century, of hops—a grain that helps preserve the beverage for longer periods of time and also gives it its bitter taste.

People used all kinds of ingredients to flavor beer, from yummy things (blackberries) to weird items (garlic and tree bark) to positively bizarre stuff (chicken . . . yes, chicken). These ingredients probably reflected beer's continued status as a meal in itself in the late medieval and Renaissance period. Beer was also considerably safer to drink than water, because the fermentation process "cooked" the bacteria that caused diseases such as cholera and dysentery.

In fact, beer was so important as a source of nutrition and recreation that it became one of the very first areas where the German states of the Holy Roman Empire decided to cooperate and institute a uniform legal code: in 1516, the Bavarian Beer Purity Law became the first "consumer protection" regulation by legislating the required alcohol content, fermentation process, and appropriate ingredients for German beer. According to one anonymous monk, beer actually helped drinkers be better Christians: "He who drinks beer sleeps well. He who sleeps well cannot sin. He who does not sin goes to heaven. Amen."

Amen.

A Vodka You Can't Refuse . . .

First things first: the story that "vodka" comes from the Russian word for "water" is not true, though modern Russians (and many college students) may treat it that way. Vodka was first distilled from rye, and early forms of the drink probably existed by the fourteenth century, though large-scale production didn't begin until the 1600s.

Vodka has long been intertwined with Russian politics. In the later fifteenth century, Ivan III made vodka production and sale a state monopoly: from 1533, vodka was sold exclusively by small taverns called *kabaks*, which provided one of Ivan's main sources of revenue. Food wasn't served, but customers could drink and play dice as much as they liked—leading to endless fights. In the seventeenth century there were a series of *kabak* revolts by angry customers who thought the tavern-keepers were cheating them by diluting the vodka. (They were.)

Vodka even played a role in foreign policy: in the late sixteenth century, the rulers of Moscow tried to convince the Nogai Tartar tribe to join a military alliance by sending them a vodka still. And of course, vodka was an important part of official functions (another Russian tradition that continues today), though the early revels sound more like frat parties than diplomatic ceremonies: it seems one governor of Moscow trained a large bear to serve pepper vodka to his guests and—if they refused—to remove their clothes, piece by piece.

····· AND THANKS, BUT NO THANKS, FOR . . . ········

Toxic Makeup

Of all the substances you'd want to grind into a powder, mix into a paste, and spread all over your body, lead is probably pretty low on the list. Lead's toxicity is well established now. In children it causes retarded mental development and, in extreme cases, death; adults with lead poisoning suffer from fatigue, depression, heart failure, gout, and kidney failure. But none of this was known in the sixteenth century, when Queen Elizabeth I of England wanted to look fabulous, so her ladies-in-waiting thought nothing of painting her skin with a compound of white lead. Following an attack of smallpox in 1562, Elizabeth coated her face with vinegar and white lead to cover up her smallpox scars. She also stuffed her cheeks with rags to combat the facial wasting associated with age and disease. Anything for beauty, darling!

Syphilis

Nothing typifies this time period better than syphilis. That's right, an entire historical epoch is probably best summarized by a venereal disease. Why? Because syphilis spread around the world on European sailing ships, just as Europeans ventured far from their home continent for the first time in centuries.

There is still a great deal of debate as to whether syphilis originated in the Old World or the New, but Europeans considered the deadly venereal disease, which drove people bonkers, an American import.

The Spanish claimed they got it from Native Americans, and soon gave it to Italian women during a long series of wars between Charles V, the Holy Roman emperor, and Francis I, the king of France. Thus, the Italians called syphilis "the Spanish disease." But when French soldiers brought the disease home from Italy, the French came to know it as "the Italian disease." It should come as no surprise, then, that English gentlemen visiting prostitutes in France dubbed it "the French disease," and—in a final twist—British colonial subjects abroad called it "the English disease." Talk about playing the blame game.

Family Jewels

It turns out feminism is nothing new: the Thais were practicing a radical form of female empowerment five centuries ago. We know this because of testimony from Chinese sailors who sailed around Asia and the Indian Ocean basin. The patriarchal Chinese were shocked by what they saw in Thailand (then the kingdom of Siam).

For starters, women enjoyed unusual power in Siamese society: They directed the affairs of great agricultural estates, merchant families, and ordinary households. Worse still, Siamese society seemed to have reversed the "natural" roles of men and women. Women of the upper class were straightforward, businesslike, and went about unadorned, while their husbands grew their hair and nails long, wore luxurious silk garments, and prided themselves on their makeup and elaborate jewelry.

The jewelry in particular took an interesting direction: when Zheng He's Chinese fleet visited Thailand in the mid-fifteenth century, it was common practice for men of the Siamese upper classes to insert small silver beads into their scrotums, between their skin and testes. When this cosmetic procedure was done correctly, the beads produced a jingling sound when the men walked.

Painted "Ladies"

Sixteenth-century England had some interesting thoughts on gender roles. Consider this: though homosexuality was viewed as an abomination, it was seen as perfectly normal—decent, in fact—to dress boys in women's clothing, paint them with makeup, and have them impersonate women in public places. Often this meant their having sex with adult men as prostitutes.

Of course, there was a good reason behind pressing boys into service as "actresses" and prostitutes: it was essential to protecting the virtue of real women. During the Elizabethan period, the English thought nothing of boys impersonating women for dramatic purposes; when William Shakespeare staged his plays at the Globe Theatre in London, it was far more respectable to have a boy playing a female role than a real woman.

And since actors were considered just a step above prostitutes, it wasn't a big leap to forcing boys into prostitution—again as female impersonators. The name of one notorious street, "Lad Lane," is self-explanatory. Boy prostitutes were also a common sight along the quays where English ships returned to port after years circling the globe. Apparently, sailors returning from long tours of duty weren't picky when they set foot on Ol' Blighty again—the origin of the tongue-in-cheek salutation "Hey, sailor!"

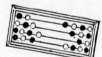 ········· **BY THE NUMBERS** ····················

83,000,000 estimated European population, 1345, pre-Black Death
57,000,000 European population in 1352, post-Black Death
81,000,000 European population in 1500

>300	number of autonomous territorial units in the Holy Roman Empire in 1500
6,000%	profit margin of Vasco de Gama's first trading expedition to India in 1498
95%	percentage of cargo from India unloaded in Lisbon, Portugal, that was black pepper, over next two decades
40,000,000	estimated native population of Americas pre-1492
10,000,000	estimated native population of Americas by mid-1500s
300,000	estimated native population of Hispaniola in 1492
60,000	estimated native population of Hispaniola in 1508
<500	estimated native population of Hispaniola in 1548
6,000,000	annual silver output, in ounces, of Spanish possessions by 1585
2,000,000,000	total silver output, in ounces, of the Potosi mine in Bolivia, to date
3,000	number of Spaniards in Potosi in 1611
76,000	number of Indian slaves in Potosi in 1611
60	tons of silver captured by Francis Drake from the Spanish in two raids, 1573 and 1579
7,000	number of soldiers in the last Byzantine army protecting Constantinople in 1453
100,000	estimated number of Ottoman soldiers besieging the city under Mehmet II
8,800,000	hectares of farmland devastated by Mongols reclaimed by the Ming Dynasty
40,987	number of water reservoirs repaired by the Ming
1,000,000,000	number of trees planted by the Ming to renew forests destroyed by Mongols
1,500	length, in miles, of Great Wall rebuilt by Ming Emperors to keep Mongols out
400	number of raids by one nomadic tribe, the T'u chije Turks, across the Great Wall

8

WAR AND SLAVERY
(AND, UH, ENLIGHTENMENT)

(1575 –1750)

In the two centuries following the Protestant Reformation, Europeans inflicted incredible violence on themselves and the rest of the world, all in the name of God. (Good old-fashioned greed was actually behind most of it.)

In Europe, the king of Spain, Philip II, was determined to seize control of the British Isles, destroy Protestantism, and force the English to embrace the Catholic Church again. He built a huge fleet, the Spanish Armada, but the English teamed up to defeat the Armada and save England.

Although the English beat Philip, fifty years later they were torn apart by an internal religious conflict between different groups of Protestants, which led to civil war and the execution of the English king, Charles I—an act that horrified Europe in an age of "absolute monarchs." Meanwhile, the dissatisfaction of one group of Protestant radicals called Puritans led them to leave England and settle in the New World.

Back on "the Continent," the early seventeenth century saw Germany torn apart by a bloody conflict between Catholics and Protestants—the Thirty Years' War. And a half century after Philip's Armada bit the big one, Louis XIV, the "Sun King" of France, dreamed up a similarly ambitious plan: basically, conquering Europe. Like Philip, Louis said he was protecting Catholicism. (Yet somehow this involved trying to conquer Catholic countries, too.)

To the east, the heirs of Ivan III of Moscow embarked on a series of conquests that created one of the largest empires in history. Styling themselves successors to the Roman emperors (*czars* and *czarinas*, from *Caesar*), they came to rule an empire that stretched from Poland to Alaska—an astonishing distance of 4,600 miles, encompassing 14 time zones and 130 million people.

The year 1644 also saw the overthrow of China's Ming Dynasty. The new rulers, Manchu barbarians from the forests of northern China, weren't quite as brutal as the Mongols, so their new dynasty, the "Q'ing," managed to control China. During the Q'ing Dynasty, China ruled more territory than at any other time in history—but soon discovered it had fallen far behind Europe in technology and governance.

Indeed, Europe was on the move in every arena, usually as violently as possible. The outlook for the non-European parts of the world was looking grim.

·················· **WHAT HAPPENED WHEN** ···············

1589 Spanish Armada is defeated.

1600 Tokugawa unites Japan, declares himself Shogun.

1607 Jamestown, Virginia, settlement founded by English colonists.

1618–1648 Thirty Years' War takes place.

1620 Salem, Massachusetts, settlement founded by English colonists.

1633 Galileo is forced to recant his heliocentric theory.

1642–1648 English Civil War takes place.

1643 Louis XIV becomes king of France.

1644 Ming Dynasty overthrown by Manchu invaders; Qing Dynasty established.

1649 King Charles I executed by English Parliament.

1664 Britain seizes New Amsterdam from the Dutch, renames it New York.

1676 Nathaniel Bacon leads a failed rebellion in Virginia.

1687 Isaac Newton publishes theory of gravity.

1689 Peter the Great becomes czar of Russia.

1702–1713 War of the Spanish Succession takes place.

One thing about the Spanish Armada: it was big, but probably not as big as most people imagine. The Armada contained 355 ships: 20 galleons and 44 merchantmen armed with cannons, eight galleys, and a large number of unarmed transports. It carried about 2,500 guns, 30,000 soldiers, and 14,000 support staff, including 19 justices and 50 administrators selected to govern England for King Philip II. One hundred and forty-six young Catholic noblemen from all over Europe also signed up for this fun excursion, with 728 servants to keep them fighting in comfort.

In 1588, King Philip II of Spain sent the badass *Armada Invencible* against England. But what was Philip's problem with our girl Queen Elizabeth? He had a couple, actually. For one thing, Elizabeth had turned down his marriage proposals—for good reason. Philip had been married to Elizabeth's sister, and after the death in 1558 of the lovely Queen "Bloody" Mary, Elizabeth came under a huge amount of pressure from her (male) advisors to marry someone— anyone, even Philip—thus placing a man on the throne of England. But Elizabeth preferred to rule herself, keeping England outside the Catholic Church and wielding enormous power as titular head of the Anglican Church. The last straw for Philip was Elizabeth's support of rebellious Protestants in one of Philip's prized possessions—the wealthy Netherlands.

But Philip's grand plan didn't survive the weather. He foolishly ordered the Armada to sail into a North Sea gale, explaining, "Since it is all for His cause, God will send good weather." Not so much. The Spanish broke formation and the disorganized (and suddenly *vencible*) Armada was blown by strong winds into the North Sea. The slow, clunky Spanish galleons now had to ride the currents wherever they went. This turned out to be Ireland, where the Spanish soon discovered that the Irish Catholics were not much friendlier than the English Protestants. Hundreds of shipwrecked Spanish sailors were killed by Irish natives, who kept everything that washed ashore.

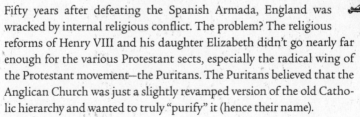

·················· **SPINNING THE GLOBE** ··············

England:
When Puritans Attack

Fifty years after defeating the Spanish Armada, England was wracked by internal religious conflict. The problem? The religious reforms of Henry VIII and his daughter Elizabeth didn't go nearly far enough for the various Protestant sects, especially the radical wing of the Protestant movement—the Puritans. The Puritans believed that the Anglican Church was just a slightly revamped version of the old Catholic hierarchy and wanted to truly "purify" it (hence their name).

Religion wasn't the only cause of conflict: the monarchy's finances were also a problem. When Charles I called Parliament to approve taxes for a war against Scotland in 1640, the delegates wanted to discuss the king's spending habits. Charles wasn't interested in a financial intervention and dismissed Parliament immediately (thus its historical name, the "Short Parliament"). In 1642, however, having run out of money again, he was forced to reconvene Parliament, and this time it was even less friendly (the "Long Parliament").

Charles and the Long Parliament weren't able to hammer out a compromise—so he tried to break the deadlock by arresting five leading members of Parliament. Parliament was understandably not thrilled by these bullying tactics. The result: civil war.

In the English Civil War, Parliament controlled London, the rich south, and the ports—bad news for Charles. In 1644, under Oliver Cromwell, the forces of Parliament triumphed over Charles' Royalists. After Cromwell's "New Model Army" defeated the Royalists again in 1645, Charles was captured—though he escaped and tried to make a deal with the Scots (yes, the same Scots he had just tried to conquer).

Plotting with "foreigners" against his own people turned out to be another bad idea. After they recaptured him in 1648, Parliament tried Charles for treason and executed him. Now Oliver Cromwell became the dominant force in English politics—turning himself into an iron-fisted "Lord Protector" who crushed dissent as ruthlessly as any king.

Cromwell was actually quite different from the radical Puritans who'd helped him gain power. He managed to contain the Puritans and steer England on a moderate religious path. But his role in the trial and execution of King Charles I made him a controversial figure until his death in 1658. Fundamentally conservative, most English were still more comfortable with a king than a "Lord Protector" whose only claim to power was armed force.

So when Cromwell died, Parliament bowed to popular opinion by placing on the throne the son of Charles I—the aptly named Charles II. Charles II turned out to be a bit of a loser, but that wasn't really the point; what was important was English monarchy was back for good (albeit with much less power).

North America:
Those Feisty Colonies

The English colonization of North America began in 1607 with the founding of Jamestown, Virginia. Soon England began using North

THE CASE OF THE MISSING COLONISTS

Roanoke, the first English attempt to colonize the New World, ended in failure—though no one can say why, when, or how it met its fate. Actually, this was Sir Walter Raleigh's second attempt to found a colony on Roanoke Island. Raleigh's first effort, in 1585, ended when the colonists—all men—abandoned the island and returned to England in 1586. Undeterred, in 1587 Raleigh founded a second colony on roughly the same spot, with about 150 new recruits. Unlike the earlier expedition, this group included women and children.

Unfortunately, it seems the leaders of the new colonists—without any proof—decided that local Native Americans were responsible for the demise of the first colony, and in 1587 they attacked the native town on Roanoke Island. They failed to realize these natives were from a different tribe than the ones encountered by the previous colony. Worse, these natives had powerful allies on the mainland, in the Croatoan tribe.

In 1590 another expedition visited the site of the second colony, where they found a European-style fort with wooden palisades and iron tools lying on the ground. Grass had grown up around the tools, indicating that they had been there for a long time. The search party found two more enigmatic clues before they left: the letters CRO carved on a tree outside the town, and the full word CROATOAN carved on a tree in town. Were the words a warning, a plea for help, or a forwarding address? This is one historical mystery that will likely never be solved.

America like a safety valve to rid itself of religious troublemakers, including the Pilgrims, radical Protestants who founded Plymouth, Massachusetts, in 1620, and the Puritans, who founded Salem, Massachusetts, in 1630.

Unsurprisingly, the colonies had rather different characters, depending who settled them. Up north, the Puritan Commonwealth of Massachusetts was a theocracy—and not the fun kind. Activities such as drinking and dancing were strictly forbidden, and were punishable with a day in the stocks (humiliating public imprisonment where passersby could insult you and pelt you with rotten fruit).

By contrast, the southern colonies tended to be looser, more freewheeling places. In fact the early success of the American colonies was driven by the Virginians' discovery of one of history's most popular vices: tobacco. Meanwhile, the colony of Georgia was founded by English debtors who couldn't pay up and had decided to risk it in the New World rather than go to jail. And Maryland (named after the Catholic Mary, Queen of Scots) welcomed not only Catholics but Jews as well—remarkable tolerance that drove the Puritans nuts.

Interestingly, one of England's prized possessions, New York, wasn't actually English at all. Originally named New Amsterdam, it began as a Dutch colony, founded during the first half of the seventeenth century, when Holland ruled the seas. As England made itself the dominant sea power during several "Wars of Navigation," it seized New Amsterdam and the rest of the Hudson River Valley from its sometime ally in 1664. The new English ruling class married into wealthy Dutch merchant families to form a new "Anglo-Dutch" aristocracy, the Knickerbockers (seriously), who ruled New York into the nineteenth century.

As the Colonial economy grew, so did tension with the kings of England, who held firm to a "mercantilist" policy—the colonies were allowed to trade only with England. Meanwhile, the Brits forbade poor colonists from moving across the Appalachian Mountains, to avoid antagonizing France and the Native American tribes there.

This led to a bloody rebellion exactly one hundred years before the Declaration of Independence. In 1676, accusing the English governor of "treason," a rabble-rouser named Nathaniel Bacon led an uprising in Jamestown, Virginia, during which poor whites seized the town for several months and murdered upper-class Brits and Native Americans wherever they found them. This reign of terror lasted until Bacon died from typhus brought on by a hellish infestation of body lice (yes, death by crabs).

France:
Bringing Home the Beavers

Louis XIV was called "the Sun King" because he was the center of European politics for his whole reign—an astonishing seventy-two years, from 1643 to 1715, far longer than the lifespan of an average European at the time. He lived in opulent luxury, commanded giant armies, and made every effort to conquer the continent.

Beginning in the 1660s, Louis tried to expand French power in four directions—Spain, Italy, Germany, and the Netherlands—not realizing that a major new ideological force, nationalism, had taken root in all four places. This new sense of community meant that they would never submit to French rule. Regardless, Louis XIV launched four bloody wars to subdue them, saving the best for last: the War of the Spanish Succession, 1702–1713, history's first real "world war." In every corner of the globe, from Germany to America to the high seas of the Indian Ocean, France faced off against England, Holland, the

Holy Roman Empire, Prussia, Denmark, Portugal, and a number of smaller European states. (For some reason, Spain was not involved in this war over the Spanish crown.) Louis was decisively defeated in August 1704 at the Battle of Blenheim—but still the war dragged on for another nine bloody years.

In the New World, France found England had beaten it to the punch, seizing the most desirable land and leaving France the chillier bits to the north (Quebec, in modern-day Canada) and the malarial bits to the south (Haiti and other Caribbean colonies such as Martinique). France picked up North America's fertile Midwest, which Louis modestly named "Louisiana"—but didn't really do much with the place. Still, the colonies weren't totally useless: Quebec and the Midwest were home to beavers, whose luxurious pelts fetched a high price in Europe, and the Caribbean colonies were perfect for growing sugar, a very lucrative crop.

Russia:
Bigger, Badder, and Drunker Than Everyone Else

Beginning in the late sixteenth century, Russia rose from an Eastern European backwater to become one of the most powerful empires in history. Although it remained socially backward, its huge population, natural wealth, and geographic size terrified Western Europeans. It also spelled bad news for its southern neighbors—the Ottoman Empire and Safavid Persia.

Russia's rise began slowly. For hundreds of years the Mongols of Central Asia had ruled European Russia. But when the Mongols got lazy and lost touch with their nomadic roots, the tables began to turn. In 1547, Ivan the Terrible became the first czar of Russia and conquered much of Siberia by 1581. At home, Ivan was a brutal autocrat who established a long-lived Russian institution—the secret police, or *oprichnina*, which kept tabs on his enemies (and made them disappear, if necessary).

In addition to being generally "Terrible," Ivan was Unstable too, suffering a complete mental breakdown in 1581, after killing his own son. He left Russia a medieval state with a backward economy and military. But all this changed one hundred years later, when a remarkable seventeen-year-old, Peter soon-to-be-called-the-Great Romanov, assumed the throne. Russia was about to be transformed.

Peter was obsessed with the sea; in fact, as a teenager he commanded mock naval battles, and as czar he traveled incognito to England to learn how to build ships. Above all he was determined to get access to the sea so Russia could trade with Europe and the Middle East.

Six years after assuming the throne in 1689, Peter declared war

In 1698, Peter traveled to England and lived anonymously in Deptford, where he studied shipbuilding for several months. With secret permission from His Majesty's government for this ruse, Peter took part in strenuous manual labor every day, disguised as a common peasant, because the signs of royal office—including ceremonial clothing, entourage, and bodyguard—would have made it impossible for him to see the "nuts and bolts" of shipbuilding up close. He also wanted to interact with his coworkers as equals.

Peter's desire to learn shipbuilding was sincere: before he left Russia, he had a special royal seal made that read, "I am a pupil; I need to be taught." While journeying to England through stormy seas aboard the H.M.S. *Yorke*, he insisted not only on staying on deck to see how the ship was handled, but also on climbing the main mast—amid lightning bolts—to look at the rigging.

Of course Peter didn't really abandon his privileges. Everyone at Deptford knew the real identity of this unusual foreigner, who was well over six feet tall and addressed by all as "His Royal Serfness." The czar also lived up to his reputation as a hard-drinking party animal. Sayes Court, where the Russian delegation stayed, was virtually destroyed by their carousing, with expensive antique carpets soiled beyond repair, crystal doorknobs stolen, windows broken, and valuable paintings used for target practice. Damage to the garden alone cost a then-astounding £350. After drinking huge quantities of vodka, the Russians apparently enjoyed sitting in wheelbarrows so their friends could send them crashing through carefully tended hedgerows—a seventeenth-century version of *Jackass*.

against the Ottoman Empire to gain access to the Black Sea. After capturing the port of Azov in 1696, he founded Russia's first naval base on the Black Sea at Taganrog, in 1698. Next he declared war against Sweden. At first the war went badly, but Peter was a determined commander, and he knew he had a special advantage: Russia's sheer size. He tricked the Swedish king, Charles XII, into chasing him into the Ukraine, five hundred miles from his supply base. Peter crushed Charles's army at the Battle of Poltava in 1709. (According to legend, Charles coined the word *hullabaloo* to describe this chaotic encounter.)

After his victory, Peter founded a great new port city on the Baltic Sea, which he deliberately gave a German name, to emphasize Russia's new connection with Western Europe: St. Petersburg.

India:
England Nibbles Away

America wasn't the only place where England and France competed for colonies: the two leading powers of Europe went head-to-head in India, too. Their conquest of the subcontinent was slow and subtle, beginning in the early 1600s with the establishment of small trading posts that doubled as military bases along the coast. Fueled by European commerce, these soon grew into large cities, including India's main ports: Bombay, Madras, and Calcutta.

Like the Portuguese and Dutch before them, English and French merchants made huge profits buying black pepper in India and selling it at a markup back home. In India they also discovered a powerful narcotic, opium, which they began cultivating and selling around the world—making the English some of history's first "drug runners."

The English began squeezing the French out in the mid-eighteenth century, when a dynamic new director took over management of the English East India Company. From 1751 to 1752, Robert Clive scored

> *The time now requires you to manage your general commerce with the sword in your hands.*
> —Gerald Ungier, chief trader for the English East India Company in Bombay

victories that spelled the end of France's empire in India. Then it was the Indians' turn, beginning with Bengal in 1757. Clive didn't conquer Bengal outright for Britain; instead, he cleverly supported a rival claimant to the throne who would do Britain's bidding. This would be the model for Britain's conquest of India, piece by piece, prince by prince, alliance by alliance.

China:
Meet the New Boss, Same as the Old Boss

For native Chinese, the revolution of 1644 was a terrible case of déjà vu, as northern barbarians poured into China and established an oppressive government, just like the Mongols had done a few hundred years before. But this time it was a different group of barbarians—the Manchu. Originally the Manchu were forest people, but Chinese immigrants taught them about farming and engineering, causing a population explosion, a technological revolution, and a newfound desire for power. Oops.

The Manchu likely killed millions of Chinese as they established the Q'ing (pronounced "ching," meaning "clear") Dynasty. The new emperors also enforced strict rules for social and economic life, as well as simple things such as appearance. Native Chinese couldn't occupy senior government positions, Manchu were forbidden to do manual labor, and intermarriage was illegal. The Manchu created an unusual dual bureaucracy in which Chinese clerks were responsible for keeping written records, while Manchu officials kept watch to ensure the clerks' "loyalty." The Q'ing also instituted a "literary inquisition" (*wenziyu*, or "imprisonment for unorthodox thought").

On the foreign-relations front, the Q'ing emperors adopted a policy of preemptive expansion, conquering Mongolia and other neighboring countries that might present a threat. But they were surprised when unwanted European merchants began showing up at China's seaports in greater and greater numbers throughout the seventeenth century, and by the eighteenth century the Q'ing emperors could no longer dismiss them as a nuisance. One group, the English, even insisted on recognition as China's equals—an idea that struck the Chinese emperor as absurd. Worse, the English were selling a highly addictive drug, opium, to the emperor's subjects. Trouble was brewing.

Japan:
Voting Everyone Off the Island

After a series of strong military commanders tried to unify Japan in the sixteenth century, in 1600 a lord (daimyo) named Tokugawa Ieyasu defeated all his rivals at the Battle of Sekigahara. Tokugawa won by adopting modern European weaponry, including muskets and cannons, but these would be the last European inventions Japan saw for a long, long time.

After making himself Shogun, Tokugawa ordered the country closed to prevent European merchants from contaminating Japanese culture with foreign influence, disarmed the Japanese peasants, and decreed that henceforth only the samurai warrior class would be allowed to carry swords. With the country locked down, in 1633, Tokugawa's successor, Iemitsu, forbade Japanese subjects from leaving the islands. Japanese ships could no longer leave Japanese waters, and any Japanese sailor caught working on a foreign ship would be executed.

Dutch merchants were still allowed to visit Japan to trade, but from 1641, the Dutch were confined to a small artificial island in Nagasaki Harbor that the Japanese had originally built to house the Portuguese (who never moved in).

The House of Hapsburg: DOWN

The defeat of the Spanish Armada was just one of several body blows suffered by the House of Hapsburg, a sprawling dynastic family, partly descended from Ferdinand and Isabella that ruled Spain, Austria, and the Holy Roman Empire. One hundred years after the glory days of Charles V, the Hapsburg Empire was torn apart by religious dissent and ambitious nobles.

The Thirty Years' War was actually a series of wars between the Hapsburgs on one side and basically all the other European states, including France, England, Sweden, Denmark, and Holland, on the other. As Protestant and Catholic nobles battled one another for control of the Holy Roman Empire, they ran rampant in Germany, killing an astonishing 20 percent of the population between 1618 and 1648—around seven million people!

The war began when Protestants in Bohemia (the modern Czech Republic) rebelled against the Holy Roman emperor Ferdinand II. The uprising began with some rough Bohemian justice, when two leading Catholic nobles were charged by Protestants with violating religious freedom, found guilty, and without further ado chucked out the windows of the castle (the famous "Defenestration of Prague"—actually the second famous event of this name, as chucking people out windows was apparently a popular punishment in Bohemia). The lucky nobles landed in a pile of horse manure and survived; meanwhile, Ferdinand II called on his wealthy Hapsburg relatives in Spain for assistance and soon crushed this uprising.

But the trouble was just beginning: now a Protestant rebellion against the Hapsburgs began in western Germany, with support from nearby Holland. Soon Denmark, England, and Sweden got involved, too. Ferdinand beat these alliances, but in 1634, France decided that the water was fine and it jumped in feet first. The last part of the Thirty Years' War (the "French" or "Catholic-vs.-Catholic" phase) was the longest and bloodiest, continuing for fourteen years, until the Peace of Westphalia in 1648.

When all was said and done, everything pretty much ended up back where it started. True, the Holy Roman emperor did lose authority in Germany—but this was a cosmetic change, as his had been mostly pretend power to begin with. The most significant result was the decline of Spanish influence in Germany and the bankrupting of the Spanish Empire. After the destruction of the Spanish Armada, defeat on mainland Europe spelled the beginning of the end. Spain, and the Hapsburgs, now entered a long, slow decline.

Tulips: UP, UP, UP! THEN DOWN, DOWN, DOWN

Sometimes sensible people (like the Dutch) do crazy things, such as obsess (and we mean *obsess*) over flowers. Yes, in the 1630s, Holland's economy was almost destroyed by irrational financial speculation in . . . tulip bulbs. How irrational? Consider this: in 1635, at the height of the tulip craze, one bulb was sold for a bed, four oxen, twelve sheep, four pigs, four tons of wheat, eight tons of rye, two tons of butter, a silver drinking cup, a suit of clothes, two barrels of wine, four tons of beer, and one thousand pounds of cheese! In 1635 another bulb sold for 6,000 florins—at a time when the average yearly income in Holland was about 150 florins. People sold houses, businesses, and large landed estates to raise money to buy tulip bulbs, which were traded on the Amsterdam stock exchange.

What was going on here? Had the Dutch all lost their minds? Well, kind of. Tulip bulbs were imported from the Ottoman Empire in 1559, and the flowers quickly became popular for their beauty. At first, tulip bulb prices rose because of demand from wealthy collectors who genuinely appreciated different breeds of tulip, including rare varieties with unusual coloration. But soon this growing demand caught the attention of speculators—businessmen who were in it just for a buck, buying up rare tulip bulbs on the assumption that prices would continue going up. For a while this was a safe bet, as increased demand pushed prices even higher, which drew more speculators to the market, which pushed prices even higher—and so on.

But at some point the bubble had to burst, and in 1636 it did. Eventually everyone seemed to realize, "Wait, I just sold my house to buy flowers! What the hell?!" and the bottom fell out of the market, with prices plummeting by 90 percent. Many of the wealthiest men in Holland, not to mention middle-class investors, were ruined by the tulip game.

Africans: DOWN

One of the worst crimes against humanity on record was entirely the product of human greed (shocking, we know). Indeed, African slavery was central to the colonial economies of North and South America. The first Africans were imported to work as slaves on Spanish and Portuguese plantations and in mines. Before this, Arabs had been taking large numbers of slaves from the east coast of Africa, facing the Indian Ocean, but there are few numbers documenting this trade.

The English expanded the market with their settling of North America, importing tens and then hundreds of thousands of slaves to work the tobacco and cotton plantations of the south.

The slave trade worked by kidnapping and splitting up families, erasing names and languages, and stealing any possessions that might indicate rank or achievement. In North America, slaves were forced to communicate in broken, pidgin English; those caught speaking their native languages were assumed to be conspiring and were hanged.

By 1680, England's Royal African Company was transporting five thousand African captives every year, a figure that rose to forty-five thousand in the eighteenth century. Conditions aboard slave ships were unspeakable, and once the captives arrived, masters could whip, rape, and murder them at will. Overall, Europeans probably imported about ten million slaves to North and South America. And the slaves who made it to the New World were the lucky ones, at least four million captives are believed to have died in transit. (Few merchants bothered to count dead slaves.)

Slavery's effects weren't limited to the kidnapped slaves themselves. Slave-taking was almost entirely an African enterprise, in which coastal princes raided inland tribes for prisoners to sell to the Europeans. There were two main areas where coastal princes denuded the inland population: the "Slave Coast" countries of West Africa, and Central Africa, from Cameroon to Angola. In both places the demand for slaves led to constant warfare, and the loss of labor probably impaired economic development in Africa for centuries to come.

Sultans: DOWN

The Ottoman Empire just managed to muddle along, for the most part suffering under lazy, incompetent sultans until their chief advisors, the viziers, took over. This fixed things for a while—but once the viziers became lazy and incompetent, too, there was only one direction to go (guess which one). Of course, there were still "good times." The last really dynamic Ottoman sultan was Mehmet IV, who ruled from 1648 to 1687. Mehmet IV gave Europe a run for its money in 1683, when he besieged Vienna with an army of 140,000 soldiers.

Except, he lost. After his catastrophic defeat, the Turkish rulers withdrew more and more from world affairs, isolated from the real world by self-interested courtiers with no higher goal than personal profit. The Ottoman Empire basically became a cash cow supporting a small and intensely disinterested ruling class. In fact, it was labeled "the sick man of Europe." Britain, France, and Russia decided they'd

Like the Ottoman sultans, the Persian shahs found themselves increasingly hemmed in by powerful European armies and navies on all sides. In the late seventeenth century, Peter the Great invaded northwestern Persia to conquer the Caucasus Mountains. The shahs of the Safavid Dynasty also faced internal opposition, led by Afghan tribesmen who rebelled in 1722. To the east, India came under British control, and the British ruled the seas with their mighty navy. The scheming Brits used their navy to put pressure on Persia and extract special trade privileges (standard practice).

let this sick man live, but only because chopping him up meant they'd have to fight each other over the pieces.

Pirates: UP. YAR!

Buccaneers, corsairs, pirates, privateers, swashbucklers—whatever you want to call 'em, the sixteenth to eighteenth centuries were the golden age of people who sailed the high seas stealing stuff, sometimes a lot of stuff.

In monetary terms, Sir Francis Drake was probably the most successful English privateer. After receiving a Letter of Marque (i.e., permission to plunder) from Elizabeth in 1577, he became the first English sailor to circumnavigate the globe, stealing a mind-boggling amount of Spanish treasure along the way: Elizabeth's take in 1580 exceeded all her other royal income *combined*. One of Drake's most lucrative captures, a Spanish treasure galleon nicknamed *Cacafuego* ("Shit Fire"), contained eighty pounds of gold bullion, thirteen chests of gold coins, a gold crucifix, jewels, and twenty-six tons of silver. No wonder Elizabeth knighted him!

Of course you don't really need anyone's consent to steal, and there were literally hundreds of straight-up pirates active during this period. Probably the most notorious English pirate was Blackbeard (1580–1618), born Edward Teach, who commanded a pirate fleet of four ships raiding the Caribbean and North Atlantic. To terrify his victims, Blackbeard stuck burning hemp and sticks into his beard and hat, so that "he looked like the Devil." His most famous act of piracy was blockading Charleston, South Carolina, in May 1718, while holding its leading citizens for ransom. He eventually received a royal pardon, but the governor of Virginia had him killed anyway, just to be sure.

—————— GET YOUR SHOVEL!

Historians estimate that $1–$2 billion in pirate treasure may still be buried on Cocos Island, a pirate hideout located three hundred miles south of Costa Rica in the Pacific Ocean.

On the opposite side of the world, in 1695 Henry Avery joined forces with a half-dozen other pirates to capture a fleet carrying wealthy Muslim pilgrims to Mecca for the annual Haj pilgrimage. One ship, owned by the

Moghul emperor of India, was said to be carrying between fifty and sixty thousand pounds of gold and silver, countless diamonds, and ivory elephant tusks worth their weight in gold. One witness said Avery—whose pirate career lasted less than a year—stole so much loot in that time he "was likely to be the Founder of a new Monarchy" (not that farfetched, since Avery also captured and married the daughter of the Moghul emperor). Sadly, he was cheated out of his ill-gotten goods by swindlers back home in England.

Bartholomew Roberts, aka "Black Bart," was a dilettante who became a pirate in 1719 "for the Love of Novelty and Change," which might strike some as insufficient motivation. But the Welshman was in fact a stunning success at it, capturing some four hundred ships in the Atlantic and Caribbean, including the *Sagrada Familia*, a Portuguese treasure ship, altogether worth about $1.6 billion in contemporary U.S. dollars.

In 1721, in the Indian Ocean, John Taylor captured the single biggest prize in history: the Portuguese frigate *Nostra Senora della Cabo*, carrying gold, diamonds, and other treasure from the Viceroy of Goa, in India. Each of Taylor's crew got forty-two large diamonds on top of what would today be a half-million dollars in gold, altogether valued at about two hundred million contemporary U.S. dollars. The other half, belonging to Taylor's partner, a French pirate named La Buse, is said to be buried on an island somewhere in the Indian Ocean. At his hanging, La Buse threw a sheaf of papers containing encrypted directions into the crowd, with the final words, "My treasure to he who can understand." Modern treasure hunters are still looking.

BETTER THAN AN HMO

Pirating and privateering could be a high-yield profession, but there's no question it was also a high-risk business. Crew members could expect to lose some body parts on the way—but like modern employers, really good pirate captains were conscientious about compensating them for hacked-off body parts. According to buccaneer Alexandre Exquemelin, who sailed under Captain Henry Morgan, Morgan ordered that "1,500 pieces of eight or fifteen slaves were to be granted for the loss of both legs, the choice being up to the injured man; 1,800 pieces of eight, or eighteen slaves were to be given for the loss of both hands; for the loss of a leg or a hand 600 pieces of eight or six slaves; and for the loss of an eye or a finger 100 pieces of eight or one slave. For the pain of a body wound that needed the insertion of a pipe, compensation was 500 pieces of eight or five slaves. For a permanently stiff arm, leg, or finger, the compensation was the same as for its actual loss."

Taylor actually shares the prize for the single biggest haul with Piet Heyn, a Dutch privateer. In 1628, Heyn commanded a Dutch fleet that captured sixteen Spanish treasure ships from Mexico carrying 11.5 million guilders, also worth about $200 million nowadays. This incredible sum paid the salaries of the entire Dutch army in the United Provinces of the Netherlands for eight months—enabling them to continue fighting the Spanish armies of their Hapsburg rulers (a delicious irony that wasn't lost on the Dutch, who still consider Heyn a national hero).

– The Enlightenment: A Cheat Sheet –

Like the Renaissance, the Enlightenment was a period when self-conscious intellectuals talked alot about what the world was all about. Here's a not-at-all comprehensive cheat sheet on ten of the most important.

On Space

Galileo Galilei (1564–1642) *"I do not feel obliged to believe that the same God who endowed us with sense, reason, and intellect intended us to forgo their use."* Credited as the inventor of modern science, Galileo perfected the telescope and used it to observe celestial bodies, including the larger moons of Jupiter (named in his honor). But his conclusion that the Earth moves around the sun clearly contradicted the Bible. When the Catholic Church attacked his theory in 1612, Galileo argued that studying nature actually brings people closer to God. But Pope Urban VIII was having none of it: under threat of death, Galileo recanted his theory in 1633, conceding that the Earth does not move around the sun. (Although as he turned to go, the proud astronomer muttered to himself, "Still, it moves.")

René Descartes (1596–1650) *"I think, therefore I am."* As Galileo is considered the "Father of Modern Science," Descartes is called the "Father of Modern Philosophy" and the "Father of Modern Mathematics" (by different mothers, of course). After grasping its essential tenets in a dream, in 1619 Descartes created a new discipline called analytic geometry, which allowed scientists to apply mathematical principles to the study of the physical world—laying the foundation for "physics." His interest in the relationship between mathematics and natural phenomena led him to deduce the law of the conservation of momentum, which governs (for example) the velocities of billiard balls striking one another. He also discovered the laws of reflection and refraction, which describe how light interacts with opaque and transparent objects.

Isaac Newton (1643–1727) *"To every action there is always opposed an equal reaction."* Building on the work of Galileo and Descartes, Isaac Newton made revolutionary contributions to mathematics, optics, and physics. His early studies included measuring the refraction of light with a glass prism and soap bubbles, from which he correctly deduced that light is made up of tiny particles. His book on the subject, *Opticks*, became the European standard after 1715. In geometry, Newton discovered simple formulae for calculating curvature and areas embraced by curves, helping invent calculus. Finally, his formula for gravity relates the "mass" (size) of any two objects and their positions in "space" (the distance between them) to determine the degree of attraction between them. This formula accurately predicted the elliptical orbits of Earth and the other planets around the sun.

On Grace

Baruch Spinoza (1632–1677) *"We feel and know that we are eternal."* A Dutch Portuguese Jew, Spinoza made contributions to ethics and theology that had a huge impact on Christian thinking as well. Drawing on classical Greek philosophers, Spinoza said that the entire universe represents a single substance governed by a single set of rules. This single substance is both God and Nature, meaning that we are part of a larger system, and therefore lack "free will." Spinoza also laid the groundwork for "biblical criticism," openly questioning the truth of the Bible for the first time. A moral relativist who said good and evil are in the eye of the beholder, he was labeled an atheist for his controversial ideas (actually, early atheists were called "Spinozists"), but Spinoza's belief was probably closer to pantheism, which sees God embodied in the universe.

> I believe in Spinoza's God who reveals himself in the orderly harmony of what exists, not in a God who concerns himself with the fates and actions of human beings.
> —Albert Einstein

Immanuel Kant (1724–1804) *"Live your life as though your every act were to become a universal law."* After Baruch Spinoza scandalized Europe's religious elite, turning many against the Enlightenment, Immanuel Kant helped resolve the conflict by creating a way for reason and logic to co-exist with God—or, more specifically, with morality. His philosophy was based on the belief that human beings are fundamentally unable to know whether God exists; nonetheless, they remain moral animals who try to use reason to understand the world. Kant appealed to reason to defend systems of morality because they are useful to mankind—not because "God said so." The "good" exists in and of itself, Kant believed, separate from and independent of God, and we must embrace our moral duties regardless of punishment or reward in the hereafter.

Georg Wilhelm Friedrich Hegel (1770–1831) *"The history of the world is none other than the progress of the consciousness of freedom."* Hegel believed that abstract concepts or "ideals" drive history, which is central to understanding philosophy, since what people consider "true" has changed over time. In fact, Hegel said that the course of history actually reveals the divine plan—God's purpose in creating the universe. According to Hegel, history unfolds as a "dialectic," or dialogue, between clashing ideals. In his model, a first idea (thesis) is challenged by a second idea (antithesis). The two sides reveal each other's contradictions, giving birth to a new idea combining them (synthesis). This synthesis eventually takes its place as a new thesis—the starting point for another round of debate and development.

On the Human Race

Thomas Hobbes (1588–1679) *"The condition of man . . . is a condition of war of everyone against everyone."* Still one of the most controversial political philosophers, Hobbes presented a "materialist" world-view stripped of religion and morality, arguing that law and order, peace and tranquility, all rely on armed force alone. Drawing on Machiavelli, in his book *Leviathan,* Hobbes said that mankind's natural state is disorder and conflict. This can be stopped only if everyone agrees through a "social contract" to give up their personal right to commit violence, yielding it to the state. Otherwise, crime, vigilantism, and even civil war will result. (Not coincidentally, Hobbes wrote during the English Civil War.) Although he claimed to believe in God, like Spinoza, Hobbes was accused of atheism, as God had almost no place in his philosophy.

John Locke (1632–1704) "*The end of law is not to abolish or restrain, but to preserve and enlarge freedom.*" Like Hobbes, Locke was also concerned with the "social contract," but he differed with Hobbes on several points. According to Locke, two related principles ruled humanity both in its natural state and in contemporary society: the right not to be harmed, and the obligation not to harm others. Unlike Hobbes, Locke believed that humans are essentially rational and benevolent beings, although of course they could be selfish, too. The primary purpose of government is to protect private property, which is accumulated through individual labor. When it functions properly, it allows men to engage in commerce, which increases the total wealth of society.

Jean-Jacques Rousseau (1712–1778) "*Man is born free, and everywhere he is in shackles.*" Also concerned with the "social contract," Rousseau took a rather different view from Hobbes and Locke. He believed that mankind's natural state, before exposure to culture or society, was fundamentally good—others called this ideal the "noble savage"—because he was self-sufficient. But society made men dependent on other men, introducing a corrupting influence; Rousseau condemned government for the same reason. As a remedy, he suggested a new social contract in which human beings renounced violence and hierarchy by common consent, forming a truly equal society. However, he opposed representative government, believing that laws should be made directly by the people, as in Athenian democracy.

On the Tax Base

Adam Smith (1723–1790) "*No society can surely be flourishing and happy, of which the far greater part of the members are poor and miserable.*" The inventor of the word *capitalism* and the founder of economics, Adam Smith said that labor, not land or gold, is the key to producing wealth. He also said that the laws of supply and demand regulate the prices for specific goods. When demand is high, prices rise, drawing more producers into the market; this leads to competition, which eventually causes prices to fall again. In the long run, he felt that a truly "free" market, without government interference in prices, would lead to the most efficient economy possible. Thus Smith was a pioneering advocate of free trade. This cut against the grain in England, which clung to a "mercantilist" policy imposing tariffs and other price constraints to protect domestic industry from foreign competition. But it proved very popular in the American colonies, which resented mercantilism (foreshadowing!).

········ **SO LONG, AND THANKS FOR ALL THE . . .** ········

Best Takeout Ever

China is one of the oldest civilizations on earth, so it may come as a surprise that the deliciously spicy Szechuan style of southwestern China is actually a pretty recent invention. That's because one of the most important ingredients, the chile pepper, didn't arrive in China until the seventeenth century.

Like potatoes, corn, tomatoes, and avocados, chile peppers hail from the Americas and were unknown in China before European colonization. Diego Alvarez Chanca, a physician who accompanied Columbus on his second expedition to the New World, brought chiles back to Spain in 1494. Chiles likely spread to Asia when the Spanish conquered the Philippines in 1521—perhaps bringing the spicy pepper along to cover the taste of food that spoiled during the long ocean voyage.

From the Philippines, it was a short hop to China via Asia's busy trade routes. Chiles probably arrived first in the southern province of Guangdong, before spreading inland to Hunan province. (Hunanese cuisine is also famously spicy.) Then migrating Hunanese peasants probably brought the pepper to Szechuan province with them.

To tell the truth, the Chinese of Szechuan province were already obsessed with spicy food: before the chile arrived, they were enjoying a native pepper with a citrus-y flavor, called the "numbing pepper." Still, the American chile revolutionized Szechuan cuisine—which became an American favorite hundreds of years later. In the

MAD ABOUT MUD

Tea and tulips weren't the only Asian imports that drove Europe wild. Chinese porcelain was another favorite, so valuable in fact that it was called "white gold." Porcelain is special because it uses a specific type of clay, kaolin, colored with rare pigments that are found in only a few places in China. Light pink or "rose" porcelain was invented during the reign of the powerful Qing emperor Kangxi, who ruled between 1662 and 1722. Of course, the Europeans tried to rip off the secrets of porcelain-making, and again, it was the clever (read: greedy) Dutch who led the way. Potters in the Dutch city of Delft produced a pretty good approximation of porcelain, though of course it wasn't the real thing. "Delftware" is still being made.

interest of drumming up business for Chinese restaurants, here's a short list of delicious Szechuan-style dishes that use chiles: Kung Pao Chicken, General Tso's Chicken, Twice-Cooked Pork, Ma-Po Tofu, Spicy Eggplant, Szechuan Beef, and of course "Bang Bang" Chicken.

Yes, you can go eat . . . the book will be here when you get back.

Tea Time

Through the medieval period and Renaissance, the English national beverage was beer. It wasn't until the seventeenth century, though, that they discovered the mildly stimulating effects of Chinese tea (though anyone who visits an English city between the hours of dusk and dawn can testify that beer is still going strong).

The Dutch were the first to bring tea back to Europe from China, and it quickly became popular among the upper classes in Holland, where the exiled heir to the English throne, Charles II, was hanging out. Charles got hooked, and when he became King of Great Britain, he married a Portuguese princess, Catherine of Braganza, who was also a tea fanatic. Between them the new royal couple made the drink all the rage back in England.

England's national tea addiction drove imports from forty thousand tons in 1699 to eleven million tons in 1785—and the government gave the companies who imported tea incredible powers to keep the magic herb flowing. Originally Parliament granted the tea monopoly to the John Company, allowing the corporation to coin its own money, pass laws, raise armies, make alliances, declare war, and conquer foreign territory. Then, in 1773, Parliament passed legislation incorporating the John Company into the East India Company— which became even more powerful.

By the mid-eighteenth century, the British were spending so much money on tea that it triggered a financial crisis, as all of Britain's silver was going to China to pay for the national addiction. So the British hit on a sensible solution: hooking the Chinese on an even worse addiction. From the 1750s on, the British promoted opium use in China, deliberately encouraging mass addiction among the Chinese. Soon the cases of silver flowing west for the opium balanced the cases of silver flowing east for the tea, and all was well again (except for Chinese society falling apart).

Location, Location, Location

Accurate sea navigation was impossible for most of human history because there was no way to know where, exactly, you were. It was easy enough to figure out one half of the equation: captains calculated what latitude they were on (i.e., how far north or south of the equator) by using an instrument called a quadrant to measure the distance between the sun and the equator at "high noon." But on the same line of latitude, the sun's path is identical wherever you go, meaning it's no help for determining longitude (how far east or west you've come).

The key to figuring longitude, it turns out, is time. Imagine you are traveling west from a certain point on the equator, with a reliable clock that you don't change as you travel: by the time you moved five "time zones" to the west, you would observe that "high noon" came at 5:00 p.m. according to the clock you brought with you (rather than 12:00 p.m.). Since the Earth measures twenty-five thousand miles at the equator and revolves once every twenty-four hours, you could determine that you had moved about five thousand miles to the west.

But it was impossible to tell time at sea with old-fashioned pendulum clocks, because the constant up-and-down motion threw off the pendulum's swing. It took a terrible tragedy to get a better way of telling time. On October 22, 1707, five British ships under the command of Admiral Sir Cloudesly Shovel (you can't make these names up) ran aground less than a day's journey from home port, killing almost two thousand men. In response, Parliament promised a reward of twenty thousand pounds to anyone who could build a reliable mechanical clock that worked at sea—*without* a pendulum.

The call was answered by an eccentric inventor and craftsman named John Harrison, who took twenty-one years to produce his first clock. The brass and wood timepiece, weighing seventy-two pounds, was a meticulous piece of work, amazing everyone with its accuracy and beauty. Harrison's key contributions were his obsessively fine crafting of gear wheels, and his hand-wound spring system for powering the clock.

But Harrison didn't claim the prize right away. A perfectionist, he took twenty more years to build progressively smaller and more accurate versions of it. The fourth timepiece, produced in 1759, was an easily transportable pocket watch. After sending it on a round trip to Barbados with his son William to test its accuracy, Harrison finally went to the Board of Longitude to claim his prize—but was refused!

It turned out that the Board of Longitude was under the control of a stubborn—okay, idiotic—royal astronomer named Nevil Maskelyne, who was convinced that longitude could be determined through astronomical observations. Parliament finally intervened, going over the royal astronomer's head to pay Harrison ten thousand pounds for the invention. Still, they owed John Harrison a lot more. So, in a brilliant PR move, his son William sent a clock to King George III, who was known to have an interest in astronomy and navigation. George asked Parliament to pay the rest of the prize money to Harrison. It's good to have the king on your side.

Gin and Juice

Believe it or not, gin began as medicine. It was invented in the early seventeenth century by Dr. Franciscus de la Boë, in the Dutch town of Leiden. The word *gin* comes from *genever*, the Dutch word for the juniper berry, which gives gin its distinctive taste.

Although it was a Dutch invention, gin was an even bigger hit in Britain (surprise, surprise). In 1660 the diarist Samuel Pepys wrote of curing a minor illness with some "strong water made with juniper," indicating that the beverage still had a medicinal use. But before long the Brits were drinking gin just get drunk. They've been doing it ever since.

Gin was to eighteenth-century London what opium was to China: a cheap, highly addictive drug that destroyed poor communities with astonishing speed. To get an idea of just how alcoholic London was during the gin craze, consider that by the 1720s about one out of every four households was involved in *making* gin. Gin was sold in bottles with rounded bottoms, so once you opened a bottle, you couldn't set it down; you had to finish it in one sitting (and they did).

The government tried to intervene in 1736 with the Gin Act, but this just drove production underground, to illegal stills that were dangerously unreliable: illegally made gin could cause blindness, and like modern meth labs, the stills had a nasty habit of exploding.

"English Riding Coats"

The seventeenth century saw the invention of one of history's all-time great prophylactics—the trusty condom, which was originally made from the intestines of sheep. Sheep intestines were elastic and durable enough to survive a great deal of wear, but also thin enough to allow sensation during sexual intercourse.

There had been an earlier version of the condom—a small cap of fine linen that fitted over the head of the penis, invented in 1564 by Italian physician Gabriello Fallopius (who also gave his name to a piece of well-known female reproductive anatomy). Fallopius thought up the linen proto-condom while looking for ways to prevent the spread of syphilis. Whether the condom worked to contain syphilis, let alone prevent conception, is anyone's guess. One nice touch: the cloth sheath was secured with a pink bow, to appeal to women.

But back to the classic sheep intestine condom: legend long held that if had been invented for King Charles II of Britain by a royal physician, the Earl of Condom, who was responding to Charles's fear of contracting syphilis from one of his many mistresses. Unfortunately, no record of an Earl of Condom has been found—though that doesn't mean the story's not true, as the king would have gone to great lengths to keep it quiet. A more likely derivation of the word *condom* traces it back to the Latin word *condon*, which means "receptacle."

Rumor has it the sheep intestine condom was popular with famous seventeenth-century "players" such as Giovanni Casanova, who referred to it as his "English Riding Coat." And it's likely the "armour" referred to by James Boswell in his *London Journal*, relating an encounter on May 10, 1763, in which he picked "up a strong young jolly damsel, led her to Westminster Bridge and there, in armour complete, did I enjoy her upon this noble edifice."

A gross final note: because they were so valuable and hard to make, men lucky enough to have a sheep-intestine condom in the first place would keep them and reuse them—usually without washing them. Thus the early condoms probably ended up causing as many hygiene problems as they prevented.

Big Guns

One easy way to make cannons more accurate was to understand how they actually worked. Up to 1638, European gunners believed that cannonballs moved in a straight line when fired from cannons, until they reached maximum altitude, at which point they entered a short downward curve of "mixed motion," after which they fell straight to the ground. But then Galileo Galilei (a busy guy, obviously) proved that if there were no air resistance, the trajectory would be a parabola; and in 1674, Isaac Newton came up with a formula explaining how cannonballs moved that also accounted for air resistance, explaining why the far side of that parabola was "smooshed" in.

The manufacture of cannons was also standardized and made more precise during this period. For one thing, the quality of iron used to make cannons improved with the construction of giant blast furnaces. The actual manufacturing process changed, too. Before 1747, all cannons were made by pouring molten metal over a cylindrical clay core, which was knocked out of the cannon's barrel when the metal cooled. This technique left imperfections on the inside of the barrel, which could change the spin of the cannonball in midair. Then the Dutch invented a new technique in which cannons were cast solid—with no clay mold—and then bored out by powerful drills. This resulted in smoother, more accurate barrels.

Little Guns

Cannons are great for blowing stuff up and killing people from far away, but what happens when you need to kill someone who's much closer? At one time, the best answer European armies could give was "blunderbuss!" The blunderbuss was a primitive barrel-loading gun that could shoot round metal balls or even gravel, if nothing else was available. The barrel of the blunderbuss (say that three times fast) widened out into a bell shape at the end to make it easier to load—this also made the gun inaccurate.

The next step for personal firearms was the musket, which had a straight barrel and an easier loading system. Gunpowder was wrapped up with the musket ball in a paper "cartridge" and driven home with a thin metal rod. Mass production of muskets became possible with the invention of metal-casting, which allowed gun makers to manufacture standardized gun components from 1700 on. Previously, each gun was its own customized piece of equipment, but now you could trade standard pieces back and forth between guns. This made maintenance a lot easier. The archetypal musket was the "Brown Bess" model issued to British soldiers beginning in 1722, which included a new flintlock trigger that made the gun safer and easier to reload.

Now Europe could arm itself to the teeth and conquer the rest of the world. Yea!

The Excessively Good Life

You think you know what the good life is? Well, you have no idea. Louis XIV, on the other hand, had some very specific ideas about living well. Requiring fifty years to build beginning in 1661, his crib at Versailles is without question the most splendid, luxurious, and extravagant palace complex in the history of the world.

All in all, the Palace of Versailles measures about 550,000 square feet in area, with 700 rooms incorporating construction materials such as marble, crystal, gold, silver, silk, satin, and exotic hardwoods. There are 2,000 windows, 1,250 fireplaces, 6,000 paintings, 2,100 sculptures, 50 fountains, 12 miles of roads, 20 miles of trellises, and a "Grand Canal" with a surface area of 55 acres—all set on about 2,000 acres of parkland and gardens.

Originally Versailles was just a small royal hunting lodge that Louis visited as a child—around the time he also witnessed a terrifying rebellion of power-hungry nobles in Paris. As an adult, Louis decided to leave Paris, which he associated with fear and insecurity, seeking the comfort and safety of the old hunting lodge outside of town. But knowing Louis, a small, dingy old castle wasn't going to cut it: it had to be nice. Ridiculously nice.

In 1682 Louis moved the French government to Versailles permanently, and expansion began in earnest. A local village and church were demolished to make room for more buildings, and Louis abandoned his old digs for the new Appartement du Roi, abutting his personal opera, which could seat more than seven hundred people around a mechanical stage that could be raised and lowered as needed to give the audience the perfect view; a single night in the opera consumed ten thousand handmade candles (a major extravagance).

Louis decided he liked to eat lunch in the countryside near a small neighboring village named Trianon, and so he bought the village and demolished it to build a marble "lunch palace," including a giant open pavilion and extensive gardens with statues, topiary sculptures, and fountains. Apparently the Trianon lunch palace was intended to allow Louis to relax, since life in Versailles had become too stressful (the main palace soon filled with aristocratic suck-ups seeking favor with the king).

But the sucking-up was actually all part of the king's master plan for maintaining absolute power. Versailles was supposed to be so comfortable that the French nobility would never want to leave—making it much easier for Louis to keep an eye on them. To keep them busy (and out of trouble), he hosted an endless series of banquets, balls, hunting trips, artistic performances, and the like.

Westerns

After an awkward period during the initial European colonization of the New World, Native Americans soon realized that horses could work to their advantage, if they could just get their hands on them. They recognized horses' obvious utility for hunting and warfare, and for carrying large loads long distances (before horses, their pack animals had been dogs, which obviously couldn't carry as much).

So native warriors stole horses from Spanish corrals, and also tamed wild horses—the descendants of runaways that wandered north from Mexico, roaming the plains in large herds. These were small colonial Spanish breeds, "Pinto" horses, then considered the best in Europe and remembered today as Native American "war ponies." These quick, sturdy horses spread to Nebraska by 1680, and to the upper reaches of the Missouri River by 1750.

Before the arrival of horses, native tribes such as the Sioux and Crow hunted bison on foot—a difficult and dangerous practice, considering that bison are equipped with horns and can run more than thirty miles per hour. Horses allowed hunters to approach their prey quickly and to outrun them, too, if things got ugly. This changed Native American society. Tribes such as the Sioux, Apache, and Comanche are actually fairly recent immigrants to the Midwestern Plains territory. Before the arrival of the horse, they all led more settled existences on the periphery of the plains.

But different tribes embraced horses for different reasons. In eastern areas, along the great Midwestern river valleys, tribes such as the Pawnee were more apt to use horses for agriculture. Over time, the nomadic and warlike tribes clashed with their more sedentary neighbors, raiding villages for food, horses, and women.

Ironically this breed of Spanish horses, still very much alive in North America, is now extinct in Spain, supplanted by more recent "Arabian" breeds. Similar horses can also still be found in Argentina, where runaways from the original colonial horses interbred with Portuguese runaways from Brazil, giving rise to herds of mixed-breed wild horses called *baguales*.

.... **AND THANKS, BUT NO THANKS, FOR** ....

A Plantation Nation

Tobacco was an indigenous plant used by Native American tribes in religious and diplomatic ceremonies—the famous "peace pipe"—rather than relaxation, which is how English colonists used it. Native Americans had cultivated tobacco in small quantities and used it sparingly, but the English, figuring you can never have too much of a bad thing, went whole hog.

At first only the wealthy could afford it, but mass cultivation of tobacco made it much more affordable, leading to widespread addiction in England. This endless demand for tobacco in turn drove the expansion of the Virginia colony, where plantation owners made a fortune on the new addictive plant. Poor colonists hoped to grab a piece of land to raise tobacco, too. In fact, tobacco became so important it was used as money: a man's wealth was estimated in the number of pounds of tobacco he grew per year, marriage certificates were bought with tobacco, and legal fines were paid the same way. People in other professions, including innkeepers and artisans, had to grow a small patch of tobacco on the side just to have spending money if times got hard.

Resenting Britain's mercantilist policy, which restricted colonial trade to the mother country, the American colonists weren't above cheating their customers: tobacco was routinely diluted with tree leaves, grass, and whatever substance maids swept up off the floor of plantation houses. To end the deception, in 1730 the British authorities passed the Inspection Act, which established warehouses and regulated tobacco preparation.

Tobacco cultivation had a number of ill effects beyond the obvious health risks (which the British already understood by 1604, when King James I issued a "Counterblaste Against Tobacco" calling it a "loathsome and hurtfull" "canker or venime" that is "hurtfull to the health of the whole bodie"). For one thing, tobacco leaches more minerals from the soil than virtually any other crop, resulting in barren fields that farmers have to let sit for years before they can be planted again. Worse, tobacco led to the importation of ever-greater numbers of African slaves to toil in tobacco fields in incredibly brutal conditions.

Passing the Poppy

As addictive as gin and tobacco are, they don't got nuthin' on opium, which ravaged all classes of Chinese society beginning in the seventeenth century.

Opium is derived from the poppy plant, which is native to South Asia and cultivated today in Iran (Persia), Afghanistan, India, and the "Golden Triangle"—a prime poppy-growing area that straddles Burma, Laos, and Thailand in Southeast Asia. To produce opium, poppy farmers make small slits in the bulb that grows just beneath the flower on the stalk of the poppy plant. Reacting to this injury, the poppy plant produces a white liquid that congeals into a thick, gummy substance on the outside of the bulb. The farmer scrapes this substance off and it's then refined into opium in a simple process involving boiling, filtering, and evaporation.

Although poppy cultivation has been with us for thousands of years, people didn't begin smoking opium to get high until the fifteenth century, when Persians and Indians recorded the first cases of opium addiction. Like vodka in Russia, by the late sixteenth century opium was a major source of revenue for the Moghul rulers of India, who set aside a large amount of land along the Ganges River and north of Bombay for poppy cultivation. When the British conquered India beginning in the eighteenth century, they were quick to realize the potential of this profitable and incredibly addictive drug.

The British paid close attention to pioneering Dutch operations in the mid-seventeenth century. The Dutch made a fortune selling opium to their Indonesian subjects, encouraging their customers to mix the opium with tobacco in clay tobacco pipes, which had just been introduced by the Portuguese.

The Dutch merchants paved the way for the British, who kicked the opium trade into high gear in the first half of the eighteenth century. By 1729, Chinese opium addiction had become such a huge problem that the emperor Yung Cheng banned the drug—but it was too late. In 1773, the British established a government monopoly over the sale of opium to counterbalance the flow of silver from Britain to China that paid for Britain's own national addiction to Chinese tea.

A Cooked Cook?

Captain James Cook achieved fame for his daring expeditions to map the South Pacific, some lasting for years, during which he cheated death again and again. But the great sailor's luck eventually ran out in 1779, when he ended his days hacked to bits and garnished with pineapple (maybe).

Cook began his life a simple farmhand, and ran away to sea as a boy. Before his untimely demise, he covered an amazing 150,000 miles, exploring Polynesia, the north and east coasts of Australia, and the more distant parts of the Pacific Ocean. These fantastic voyages took his crews to both the Arctic and the Antarctic, as well as to North America and Siberia. Cook was single-handedly responsible for filling in the details on approximately a third of the earth's surface—an unbeatable record.

These great accomplishments stand in terrible contrast to his awful death. While accounts of his death differ, it seems likely that the Hawai'ian king Terreeoboo, had been plotting to eliminate a man he perceived as a threat. Terreeoboo may have feared that Cook's expeditions would lead to European conquest and colonization. (And he was right.)

Fashion Police

A great way to demonstrate power is giving other people ridiculous haircuts and forcing them to wear clothing they don't like. During the seventeenth century, Russia and China were both ruled by fashion divas who gave their subjects a simple choice: "Put this on or we'll kill you."

In the case of China, the Manchus, who overthrew the Ming Dynasty in 1644, enforced a rather elaborate dress code on penalty of death. The most humiliating rule required Chinese men to shave their heads except for a small patch of hair at the back, which they had to grow long and braid into a waist-length ponytail. Supposedly the ponytail was just that—a reminder of the horses the Manchus had ridden to victory over the Chinese, thus symbolically making the Chinese subjects into pack animals. The Manchus also forced the

Chinese to wear robes with long sleeves and low-hanging skirts that impeded physical combat. The Manchu dress code was strictly enforced, under the slogan "Lose your hair or lose your head!" In 1646, after the last native Chinese contender for the throne was captured, scores of high officials from the old Ming Dynasty were executed for refusing to adopt the Manchu-imposed hairstyle. A lucky few managed to escape by shaving their whole heads and joining Buddhist monasteries.

In Russia, Peter the Great took it a step further, picking up the scissors himself if his subjects resisted. The involuntary salon visits and new clothes were part of Peter's big program to modernize Russia, which included economic and military reforms. Peter felt "the clothes make the man," and he gave Russia a European makeover that left old-timers in shock. Russian nobles had to shave their beards, and the traditional black robes worn by men in Moscow were banned, replaced by Western-style clothes including waistcoats and knee-length pants. When some nobles refused to shave their beards, he would brutally slice them off himself—sometimes taking a bit of skin too, to reinforce the point. Apparently Peter carried a pair of scissors around with him, and a good number of these royal shearings were conducted in the street on the spur of the moment.

Shouting at the Screen

William Shakespeare, the greatest playwright in the history of the English language, had to put up with audiences who would probably make a stripper walk off the stage nowadays. While his plays are now considered highbrow cultural experiences, back then they were popular entertainment for a rude, smelly, illiterate, spitting mob who if they didn't like the play—or even just one of the characters—felt quite at liberty to shout and throw things at the stage. After all, they'd paid a penny to get in!

The plays were performed at the Globe Theatre, a round three-story playhouse in London's "sporting," or red-light, district, owned by Shakespeare's theater company, the Lord Chamberlain's Men. In addition to prostitution, neighboring venues hosted cockfighting and bear-baiting, and pickpockets and scammers were everywhere. But the theater was usually filled to capacity for Shakespeare's plays, which drew more than three thousand people, including a large crowd of "groundlings," who had to stand through the entire performance.

Shakespeare's early successes at the playhouse included *Henry VI* in three parts (1590), the *Comedy of Errors*, (1592), *Richard III* (1592), and *Romeo and Juliet* (1594). When the first theater burned down during a performance of *Henry VIII* in 1614, another was built on the same spot. Amazingly, no one was injured in the fire, except for one man whose pants caught on fire; he doused them with ale.

> You say there are good examples to be learned in [plays]. Truly, so there are: if you will learn falsehood . . . if you will learn to become a bawd, unclean, and to devirginate maids, to deflower honest wives; if you will learn to murder, flay, kill . . . if you will learn to play the whoremaster, the glutton, drunkard, or incestuous person . . . and, finally, if you will learn to condemn God and all his laws . . .
> —Phillip Stubbes, a Puritan critic, on plays

While they might throw empty beer bottles and shout insults, the uncouth audiences also let know Shakespeare know what worked by cheering during performances of his plays. Watching *Romeo and Juliet*, they probably laughed at Mercutio's gags and the naughty nurse, and it's easy to imagine them shouting to Romeo to wait before drinking the poison in the end—to no avail! Unsurprisingly, educated people tended to have a rather different opinion of this popular entertainment. Contemporary critics found Shakespeare's plays bawdy, sensational, unedifying, and without merit. No wonder the Puritans closed the Globe permanently in 1642.

But we know who got the last laugh.

· · · · · · · · · · · · · · · · · · · BY THE NUMBERS · · · · · · · · · · · · · · ·

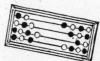

25	percentage of households in London involved in making illegal gin in the early eighteenth century
14,000	number of barrels of wine carried by the Spanish Armada
76,000	price paid, in modern-day dollars, for one rare tulip bulb in Holland during the period of Tulip Fever
40,000	amount, in tons, of British imports of tea in 1699
11,000,000	amount, in tons, of British imports of tea in 1785
30	amount, in tons, of English imports of American tobacco in 1622
10,000	amount, in tons, of English imports of American tobacco in 1700

1,357 amount, in pounds, of Indian opium sold by Dutch merchants to Indonesians in 1660

80 amount, in tons, of Indian opium sold by Dutch merchants to Indonesians in 1685

15 amount, in tons, of British exports of Indian opium to China in 1720

75 amount, in tons, of British exports of Indian opium to China in 1773

5,000 number of African slaves imported by English slave traders to North America in 1685

45,000 number of slaves imported annually a few decades later

50,000–60,000 amount, in pounds, of gold and silver captured by the pirate Henry Avery from one ship owned by the Moghul emperor in 1695

9

THE AGE OF LIBERATION, FRAGMENTATION, STAGNATION, AND PLAIN OL' NATIONS

(1750–1900)

In the second half of the eighteenth century, a wave of revolutions changed the world forever. It began in 1776 in North America, where the colonists kicked out the Brits and established a new, democratic nation with a framework—the Constitution—based on a crazy concept: simple reason.

Taking their cue from the uppity Americans, in 1789, French revolutionaries executed King Louis XVI and tried to establish a new republic on democratic principles—but instead they got a bloodbath known simply as the Terror.

It got even worse (or better, depending on your perspective). Terrified by the popular revolt, the crowned heads of Europe united against France. But the revolutionaries conquered all of continental Europe, for a time, thanks to the brilliance of an ambitious young artillery officer named Napoleon Bonaparte.

But it didn't last. After Napoleon's downfall, Europe's kings vowed to prevent revolution from ever happening again. It was time to stop fighting each other and cooperate against the real enemy: the poor masses embracing new, revolutionary ideologies such as "nationalism" and "communism." The kings formed a diplomatic club called the Concert of Europe to crush any new revolutionary movements.

They were galvanized by events in Latin America, where rebels led by Simon Bolivar threw off Spanish rule forever. And they were right to be worried: Bolivar's national revolutions in turn inspired European nationalists to create powerful new nation-states in Germany and Italy, disrupting their careful balance of power.

Meanwhile, well-established Asian empires that could have used a little revolution instead entered into steep declines. In the Middle East, the Ottoman Turks fell prey to the rising tide of nationalism, losing key territories in the Balkans and North Africa. In Persia, the Qajar Dynasty started off on the wrong foot and then discovered that the other foot wasn't much better, as Britain and Russia ganged up to kick it around. The Moghuls in India disappeared entirely, swallowed up by the British Empire, and Q'ing China saw tens of millions of its citizens addicted to opium by the clever and unscrupulous Brits. Japan under the shoguns stagnated with a backward military and clueless officials until a new upstart, the United States of America, delivered a very rude wake-up call.

That's not to say there weren't moments of badass-ness. Native Africans created two great empires in this period, with the Zulu and Ashanti terrorizing their neighbors and even holding off the Brits for a while. But like everyone else, they were about to be left in the dust by one more upheaval brewing in Great Britain: the Industrial Revolution.

 ··········· **WHAT HAPPENED WHEN** ················

1755–1760 French and Indian War takes place in North America.

1770 Royal governor dissolves General Assembly in Boston.

1776 American Revolution begins.

1783 Parliament acknowledges legitimacy of the United States.

1787 Alexander Hamilton organizes Constitutional Convention; French Revolution begins with "Revolt of the Nobles."

1793 The Terror begins in France, encouraged by Robespierre.

1794 Robespierre is toppled and executed.

1799 Napoleon declares himself Consul for Life.

1804 Napoleon crowns himself emperor of France.

1814 Napoleon is forced to abdicate; first steam-powered railroad invented in Britain.

1815 Napoleon makes "100 Days" comeback; is exiled to St. Helena.

1830 Giuseppe Mazzini imprisoned for advocating Italian unification.

1834	Giuseppe Garibaldi leads failed Italian nationalist rebellion, escapes.
1845–1849	Irish Potato Famine takes place.
1854	Commodore Perry "opens" Japan.
1857	Britain destroys Moghul Empire.
1861	Italy is united.
1861–1865	American Civil War takes place.
1868	United States buys Alaska from Russia.
1871	Germany is united.

– Revolution Watch: American Tax Dodgers –

It's fair to say the American Revolution was the work of tax dodgers who, in the time-honored American tradition, didn't want to pay up. But the truth is that it took a little more than just taxes to push the Founding Fathers into rebellion.

The countdown to the American Revolution began with the confusingly named French and Indian War (1755-1760), in which the French and some Indians fought the British and other Indians over beaver trapping rights. The Brits won, but went deeply into debt, and Parliament decided to make the colonists pay off the debt by taxing anything it could think of.

Each of the tax acts met with violent opposition, and when Parliament foolishly ordered the royal governors to dissolve the rebellious colonial assemblies, the colonists rose up to defend their already limited rights. To protest the dissolution of their General Assembly, in February 1770 Bostonians rioted against the Redcoats, leading to the infamous Boston Massacre in which six died.

Then, in 1773, came the Tea Act. This time, to prop up the failing East India Company, the Brits wanted to sell eighteen million pounds of unwanted tea at bargain prices. Local merchants feared the Brits' tea dump would drive them out of business, and ordinary Americans supported the merchants with a boycott, giving up one of their favorite vices (imagine giving up coffee today). Things were resolved peacefully in New York and Philadelphia—but in Boston they (once again) got totally out of hand. When the royal governor ordered the sailors to land their cargo, Samuel Adams led 150 drunken Bostonians (barely) disguised as Mohawk Indians in dumping the tea into Boston Harbor, with huge crowds cheering them on. As punishment for the "Boston Tea Party," the governor closed the port, putting working-class Bostonians out of work. He also forced them to open their homes as lodging for the hated Redcoats, who were sent to "keep the peace."

Enraged by these so-called "Coercive Acts," in September 1774, delegates from twelve colonies (Georgia couldn't make it) met in Philadelphia for the First Continental Congress. There, they created a "Continental Association" to enforce a total boycott of all British goods, and began to stockpile weapons and ammunition. Finally, on March 23, 1775 (the fifth anniversary of the Boston Massacre), when the royal governor of Virginia tried to dissolve Virginia's House of Burgesses, the Virginia patriot Patrick Henry delivered a fiery speech concluding, "Give me liberty, or give me death!"

It was on. Fighting started in April 1775, when the Brits sent seven hundred Redcoats to arrest Samuel Adams and John Hancock, an-

Nothing important happened today.
—King George III, diary entry, July 4, 1776

other leading patriot. The rebels already knew about the plan, and a metalsmith named Paul Revere rode north to spread the news. Adams and Hancock both got away, while rebels rallied on the Lexington town green for the first battle with the Brits.

The Revolution went well at first, with Ethan Allen's victory at Fort Ticonderoga and George Washington's capture of Boston. But at the same time the colonists were shocked by British brutality. So on July 4, 1776, the American colonists issued their Declaration of Independence, which concluded, "these united colonies are . . . free and independent states." And that was pretty much that.

But the hardest parts still lay ahead. During 1776 and 1777, Redcoats seized New York and Philadelphia. In the winter of 1777, with no cities to shelter his armies, George Washington's soldiers had to scrounge for essentials while camping out in frigid Valley Forge, Pennsylvania. Out of 11,000 men, 2,500 died—and many others deserted.

Luckily, America had a knight in shining armor: France. Still plenty angry about the French and Indian War, King Louis XVI of France was looking for ways to get back at Britain, and the American Revolution was just too good to pass up. The big payoff was help from the French fleet against the Royal Navy, and military advice from superb French generals.

In early 1781, a brilliant French general, Rochambeau, convinced Washington to make a surprise attack on the main British army, which had dug in on an isolated peninsula at Yorktown on Chesapeake Bay. The rebels easily cut the British off on the peninsula, while the French Navy blockaded them from the sea. With nine thousand Redcoats starving, the British prime minister resigned, and on September 3, 1783, Britain finally acknowledged the legitimacy of the United States.

Who's Your Daddy?
(The Founding Fathers in Four Minutes)

George Washington (1732–1799) "*I walk on untrodden ground. There is scarcely any part of my conduct which may not hereafter be drawn into precedent.*" As a young man Washington served in the British colonial militia during the French and Indian War (as a military commander, he was about a B). In 1759 he married a wealthy young widow, Martha Dandridge Custis, and through astute management of her estate became one of the richest men in the colonies. One of the few rebels with any military experience, he was a natural choice to lead the Continental Army in 1775. After the war, he retired to his plantation, but returned to preside over the Constitutional Convention in 1787. He then served as president for two four-year terms, from 1789 to 1797. He supported Alexander Hamilton's creation of a strong national government through assumption of the states' war debts and the formation of a national bank. In his Farewell Address, Washington warned against "foreign entanglements," especially with European powers.

Thomas Jefferson (1743–1826) "*I have sworn upon the altar of God, eternal hostility against every form of tyranny over the mind of man.*" Jefferson's father died when Thomas was fourteen, leaving his son five thousand acres of land. Like Washington, Jefferson also married a wealthy young widow named Martha (apparently a popular name) and was considered very well off. A practicing lawyer, he was elected to the Virginia House of Burgesses in 1768, where he became a spokesman for independence. He wrote the Declaration of Independence as well as laws protecting religious freedom (Jefferson himself rejected the divinity of Jesus Christ and the Bible). As president, 1801–1809, he tripled the size of the United States through the Louisiana Purchase, dispatching Meriwether Lewis and William Clark to explore the new territory. A prolific and ingenious inventor, Jefferson also founded the University of Virginia in 1819.

Benjamin Franklin (1706–1790) "*In this world nothing can be said to be certain, except death and taxes.*" The oldest of the Founding Fathers by several decades, Franklin was revered as the first advocate of independence. Born in Boston, Massachusetts, as a young man he moved to Philadelphia, where he became one of the leading printers in the thirteen colonies, giving the patriotic cause a public voice. His essays and cartoons helped rally public opinion in favor of unity and independence. In 1778, as ambassador to France, he negotiated the critical French alliance and the Treaty of Paris that ended the war in 1783. A polymath genius, in his spare time Franklin proved that lightning is electricity, invented bifocals, and founded the University of Pennsylvania in 1751.

Alexander Hamilton (1755–1804) "*The sacred rights of mankind are not to be rummaged for among old parchments or musty records. They are written, as with a sunbeam, in the whole volume of human nature.*" The illegitimate son of a Caribbean sugar baron (or maybe a sea captain), Hamilton was orphaned by the age of thirteen but worked hard to overcome his humble beginnings. Coming to America for school in 1772, he wrote essays attacking British colonial policy. His bravery in the disastrous Battle for New York impressed George Washington, who appointed him chief of staff in 1777. After the war, Hamilton organized a convention to draft a new Constitution for a strong federal government in 1787. With James Madison and John Jay he wrote *The Federalist Papers* in 1788, which argued for a strong central government. As the first secretary of the Treasury he accomplished this by convincing Congress to assume the war debts of the states and to form a national bank. Apparently a bit of a gossip, Hamilton was killed in a duel by his friend-turned-rival Aaron Burr, for spreading rumors about Burr during a political campaign.

James Madison (1751–1836) "*The essence of Government is power; and power, lodged as it must be in human hands, will ever be liable to abuse.*" The oldest son of a wealthy Virginia tobacco farmer, in 1776 Madison was elected to the Virginia legislature, where he was mentored by Thomas Jefferson. In 1787 he wrote most of the Constitution, based on discussions with the other Founding Fathers. To win over the Constitution's opponents, he also wrote the first ten amendments known as the Bill of Rights. Although he co-authored *The Federalist Papers* with Hamilton in 1788, Madison feared the United States might turn into a European-style state, with a bureaucracy and a standing army that could oppress the people. Paradoxically, as president from 1809 to 1817, he launched the War of 1812 against

Britain, which required an army, navy, and even more national debt. Madison prophetically warned against "factions" (lobbyists) who could corrupt the democratic process with their wealth.

John Adams (1735–1826) *"The only maxim of a free government ought to be to trust no man living with power to endanger the public liberty."* The son of a well-to-do farmer in Braintree, Massachusetts, Adams was a classic flinty New Englander who loved to argue. As a lawyer, he was driven to resistance by British use of warrant-less searches. Adams's *Thoughts on Government* became the model for many state constitutions, including bicameral legislatures with upper and lower houses. The second president of the United States, Adams was also the first one-term president, defeated by Jefferson in 1800. John Marshall, appointed by Adams as chief justice, helped create the strong government envisioned by the Federalists, and elevated the judicial branch to equality with the legislative and executive.

· · · · · · · · · · · · · · · · · SPINNING THE GLOBE · · · · · · · · · · · ·

Britain (at Home):
We Didn't Need That Stupid Colony Anyway

The loss of the American colonies didn't spell the end of Britain's empire. Just the opposite: after the American Revolution, the Brits went on to build the largest empire in history. It was powered by the Industrial Revolution, a period of unprecedented change in the technology of production—that is, making stuff. It began in Britain in the late eighteenth century then spread to France, Germany, and the United States.

The first step was the invention of new mechanical systems for the mass production of things such as textiles, including the spinning jenny, patented in 1770, and the power loom, patented in 1783. These allowed manufacturers to turn cotton into thread and to weave it into cloth hundreds of times faster than before. The new mechanical systems used power from waterwheels and windmills.

The second step was connecting the new mechanical systems to steam engines, replacing waterwheels and windmills with a more reliable source of energy. Steam engines had been around since 1698, when Thomas Savery patented a crude model based on a pressure cooker. In 1769, a self-taught Scottish engineer, Thomas Watt, added a separate condenser to cool steam, vastly increasing efficiency.

The third and final stage was the invention of machines for making other machines, which really kicked the Industrial Revolution into high

HOOKING 'EM YOUNG

During the Industrial Revolution, British women who went to work in factories often left their babies with seamstresses or women who took in washing—early daycare. But with one "baby-minder" for dozens of crying babies, the easiest thing to do was just knock the little nippers out. How? Opium, of course! Popular opium-based sedatives such as Godfrey's Cordial and Mrs. Winslow's Soothing Syrup sold thousands of pints a year.

gear. Now manufacturing power increased exponentially. The first systems for making "machine tools" emerged in Britain in the 1820s and 1830s. One example was a boring machine, for making perfectly round cylinders for steam engines, readapted from Dutch technology for boring cannons.

The Industrial Revolution also required large amounts of money to start new ventures, such as building factories. This influx of money fueled the growth of lending institutions, or banks, which could issue paper money and invest in new businesses. The practice of borrowing and lending money, or "capital," to create and expand businesses came to be called "capitalism," and its practitioners, "capitalists."

Working conditions and the standard of living were unbelievably awful during this period, but the Industrial Revolution made the upper classes of Britain the wealthiest group of people on the planet, and Britain its most powerful nation. Britain held on to its early lead by constantly conquering new territory, which provided raw materials and markets (customers) for more industrial development, enabling them to conquer even more territory, which . . . well, you get the idea. The Brits settled or conquered Australia (1788), South Africa (1814), western Canada (1840s), and Nigeria (1861). But the most important acquisitions by far were India and Pakistan.

WORST OF THE WORST

Australia was originally settled by Britain in 1788, as a penal colony for the dregs of its prisons. But if you were really bad, Australia had its own penal colony—that's right, a penal colony for a penal colony. Convicts who committed new crimes were sent to the Macquarie Harbor penal colony, established in 1820 on the west coast of Tasmania (aka the middle of friggin' nowhere).

Britain (Abroad):
India Will Do Nicely Instead . . .
Britain's involvement in India dated back to the seventeenth century, but "mopping-up" operations lasted until 1857, when the Brits crushed the Sepoy Mutiny. The Sepoy Mutiny was a last-ditch bid for freedom by 140,000 Indian officers

and soldiers, or sepoys, of the Army of Bengal. As the British annexed more and more territory, their Indian soldiers realized that they were helping foreigners conquer their own country, and sacrificed their lives to stop it.

By this point the Moghul Empire was pretty much a joke: Emperor Bahadur Shah's power didn't extend beyond the walls of his palace in Delhi. Nonetheless, needing a leader, the rebels proclaimed him emperor (again). But as usual, not everyone agreed, and the rebellion soon split apart.

When the Brits captured Delhi, Bahadur Shah was found hiding near the tombs of his ancestors and was arrested. His sons and grandson were beheaded and their heads thrown in his lap. Heartbroken, Bahadur was tried for treason, found guilty, and exiled to Rangoon, the capital of Burma, where he became an opium addict and died five years later.

India became the crown jewel of the British Empire, a key source of cheap cotton for British textile mills (replacing the lost American colonies), of indigo for dying fabrics, and of opium to keep the Chinese addicted. Meanwhile, hundreds of millions of Indians were avid consumers of British goods, including clothes made with the very textiles they grew cotton for. In typical fashion, the Brits got 'em coming and going, buying the cotton cheap and selling clothes at full price (of course the Indians weren't allowed to trade with anyone except Britain).

CRAZY TALK

Contrary to the official line, in private many British officials didn't think they had a God-given right to rule India. Sir Charles Napier, who conquered Sindh (Pakistan) in 1843, frankly admitted, "We have no right to seize Sind," while his subordinate Captain James Outram wrote letters "condemning the measures we are carrying out...as most tyrannical—positive robbery."

West Africa:
More British Fingers in the Pie

Colonial expansion was rarely a cakewalk for the Brits: all over the world, native powers tried to resist British expansion, with mixed results. One of the most successful, the Ashanti of West Africa, ran a well-organized empire centered on the modern country of Ghana. The Ashanti weren't exactly well loved by their subjects, but they didn't care, because they had two trump cards: gold and guns. One of the few African tribes to arm themselves with European firearms, they bought muskets from Dutch and English traders beginning in the seventeenth century. They used these to conquer all their neighbors by 1750, incorporating more than a dozen kingdoms into a powerful empire covering about one hundred thousand square miles, with three million inhabitants. Many of these were their slaves.

With a population of forty thousand in 1807, Dwaben, the largest city, was about the same size as New York. Meanwhile, at the royal capital, Kumase, nobles wore so much gold jewelry they needed attendants just to hold it up.

With all that gold, it wasn't long before the Brits tried to conquer the Ashanti (surprise). But with an army two hundred thousand strong, the Ashanti king wasn't about to knuckle under to a few hundred malarial Englishmen. The Ashanti annihilated the first invasion force in 1823, using British muskets and gunpowder (that familiar smell is irony) and besieged the British coastal fort in 1826, leading to a peace treaty in 1831. During the second "Anglo-Ashanti" war, in 1863, they were on the verge of wiping out the British settlement when both sides decided to call a draw in 1864.

In 1873, the Brits decided to settle things once and for all, sending overwhelming firepower to solve the "Ashanti problem." They even shipped in thousands of tons of iron rails to build a railroad to carry troops. This idea was a bit daft, as the Brits might say, since the path was completely blocked by jungles, rivers, and hills. But British industrial might was also evident in their weaponry, which included artillery, rockets, and modern rifles. The third Anglo-Ashanti war ended in humiliating defeat. But it still wasn't over: continued Ashanti resistance led to yet another war, in 1891–1894, before the Brits finally gained control of the Ashanti Empire.

Southern Africa:
A Mover and Shaka

In the early 1800s, southern Africa was rocked by a terrible upheaval caused by a fierce tribe, the Zulus, under the leadership of a great chief named Shaka, who came to be called the African Napoleon.

Shaka was born sometime around 1785. He was supposedly much larger than the average African, well over six feet tall, and blessed with unusual strength. He was born the illegitimate son of a Langeni chief, who chased him out of the tribe as a teenager.

In exile, Shaka undertook rigorous physical training. He was expert in hand-to-hand combat, but disliked the Zulu's traditional iron-tipped throwing spear and therefore replaced it with a longer swordlike blade attached to a short wooden haft, called an *iklwa*. Shaka was supposedly aided in his quest for power by an enchanted *iklwa* made by a witch doctor.

During his exile, Shaka joined the army of the neighboring Mthethwa tribe. He stood out because of his impressive physical attributes, and in 1812 the Mthethwa chief helped Shaka defeat his own brother to become ruler of the Langeni. This was a big victory for the boy who'd been run out of the same tribe more than a decade before. But Shaka was just getting started.

After the Mthethwa chief was killed by the head of rival tribe, Shaka went to war to avenge his death. During this period, Shaka began uniting various tribes under Zulu leadership with a clever combination of warfare and generous rewards. Their armies were absorbed into Shaka's force, which grew to tens of thousands of warriors.

Shaka revolutionized tribal warfare, training his followers in unorthodox fighting techniques he developed and deploying them in an innovative "buffalo" formation. In the Zulu "buffalo," two small divisions of younger, athletic warriors (the "horns") advanced on either side of the main army. These two rapid-strike forces could then perform flanking maneuvers on the enemy army—a surprising strategy for the Zulus, who usually clashed face-to-face in simple line formations. The main body of veteran warriors (the buffalo's "head") then advanced to finish the job, while older soldiers brought up the rear as reserves (the "loins"). Shaka trained his soldiers with endless drills, leading them on forced marches over fifty miles of rough terrain.

In all, Shaka's Zulu armies are said to have killed about two million people. Later, fierce Zulu warriors raised in Shaka's military traditions delivered one of the most humiliating defeats in the history of the British colonial empire. At Isandlwana in 1879, twelve thousand Zulus annihilated a British army of twelve hundred Redcoats and five hundred African allies.

Japan:
Maybe It's Time to Not Live Under a Rock

After two and a half centuries of isolation, the "hermit kingdom" of Japan was opened to outsiders in 1854, by an intrepid American naval officer who wouldn't take no for an answer.

Beginning in 1603, the first Shogun, Tokugawa, decided that European sailors and traders represented too much of a threat to the island kingdom's traditions. Foreigners were banned from the islands, and Japanese were forbidden from leaving them. Even the "hands-off" United States, which sought only trade and places to buy coal for refueling, was rebuffed—until Commodore Matthew Perry arrived in 1852 with a squadron of steam-powered frigates armed with late-model cannons.

When Japanese officials at Yokohama refused to let Perry come ashore to deliver a letter to the Shogun from U.S. president Millard Fillmore, Perry said he would bombard the defenseless port. Unsurprisingly, the officials changed their minds.

Perry then went ashore with an escort of two hundred U.S. Marines. According to one American witness, to intimidate the Japanese, Perry selected as his personal guards two tall, muscular black sailors who were "armed to the teeth." Meanwhile, the local Japanese governor mobilized thousands of soldiers and cavalry to encircle Yokohama and prevent the foreigners from infiltrating Japan. Silk screens were erected everywhere to make sure the foreigners saw as little of Japan as possible, and the only building they were permitted to enter was a temporary silk tent.

Perry entered the tent to deliver Fillmore's letter to the Japanese officials, but when they all sat down together, there was an awkward silence lasting several minutes, as neither side wanted to "go first." Through an interpreter, Prince Toda of Idzu finally told Perry to put the letter in a ceremonial wooden box; aside from that, the Japanese didn't say a single word during the half-hour meeting. The letter called for a treaty providing free trade at two Japanese ports, the establishment of a U.S. consulate, and the safe return of American sailors shipwrecked on the Japanese coast.

Perry's visit threw the Japanese government into turmoil. Realizing that Japan had fallen far behind the West, high-ranking officials grew dissatisfied with the Shogun and planned a massive modernization program. These nationalist reformers also secretly plotted a restoration of the Japanese emperor Meiji as a figurehead for their new government.

– *Revolution Watch: France France Revolution* –

In 1787, France was a total mess. Yet not too long before, everything had been golden under Louis XIV, the "Sun King." What happened? The short version is his successors began raising money through very unpopular policies. The long version is a bit, well, longer.

Since the medieval period, French society had been divided into three "estates": the clergy, the nobility, and everyone else. All commoners were lumped together in this "Third Estate," from wealthy merchants, to smalltime shopkeepers, down to the poorest peasants and artisans. The king could tax only the Third Estate, the first two estates being tax-exempt. This arrangement worked well enough in simpler times, but as France developed, the government couldn't keep up.

As the commoners' taxes got higher and higher, the nobles had their own complaints. The main issue: they had loaned the king huge

amounts of money, and by the late eighteenth century, it was beginning to look like he might not be able to pay it back. And so the French
Revolution began to unfold.

> *What is the Third Estate? Everything. What has it been up to now
> in the political order? Nothing. What does it demand? To become
> something.*
> —Abbe Sieyes, January 1789

The first phase of the Revolution, the revolt nobiliare of 1787, began
when the nobles refused to loan Louis XVI more money, and instead
demanded a set of guidelines to manage royal spending—in effect, an
American-style constitution. The nobles said that the only institution
that could set the standards was the Estates-General, a medieval assembly of all Three Estates. It hadn't met since 1614.

This turned out to be a bad move. Meeting without the other two
estates, the Third Estate concluded that France had to have a constitution dictated by the people, not the nobles. On June 17, 1789, the
Third Estate assumed a new name, the National Assembly. The regular folks were now in charge.

When Louis heard the news, he tried to dismiss the Estates-
General, but it was too late. What was supposed to be a quiet nego-
tiation between him and the nobles had suddenly become revolution.
When Louis kicked the National Assembly out of Versailles, they retreated to one of the king's private tennis courts and swore they
wouldn't leave until France had a constitution—creatively known as
the "Tennis Court Oath."

However, the National Assembly had issues of its own. The wealthy
members (upper bourgeoisie) wrote a constitution that restricted the
right to vote to property owners—meaning themselves—and the
poorer members were not pleased. In 1787–1789 Mother Nature piled
on: the harvest was destroyed by hail and drought, and the winter of
1788 was one of the coldest ever. Starving city dwellers rioted, and law
and order began to break down.

The mobs were energized by a brilliant young orator from the
National Assembly, Maximilien Robespierre, a disciple of Rousseau
who believed every adult male had a right to vote, regardless of property, and who also said that government should guarantee commoners food and shelter. This communal utopia was far more radical
than anything the upper bourgeoisie wanted, but Robespierre had a

huge following among the poor artisans of Paris. In July 1789, hungry mobs attacked soldiers guarding grain shipments arriving from the countryside. Looking for weapons, on July 14, poor Parisians seized the Bastille, an old castle used as a royal armory and prison. In August 1789 the National Assembly abolished the feudal system, distributing nobles' land to the peasants. Then, in 1790, they confiscated all the property of the Catholic Church.

Alarmed by the growing radicalism of the Revolution, nobles began fleeing France to organize resistance in other European countries. Louis himself foolishly tried to escape France in disguise in June 1791, only to be caught and accused of plotting counterrevolution with Austria, the home turf of his wife, Marie Antoinette.

In April 1792, the National Assembly voted to declare war on Austria. As war raged, the radicals executed the royals and began expelling moderates from the National Assembly, accusing them of treason. In April 1793, the radicals organized a Committee of Public Safety (warning: irony ahead) to find and execute "enemies of the people." In all, about forty thousand people fell victim to "the Terror." A few years after its birth, French democracy was snuffing itself out.

The French Revolution sent shockwaves through Europe. To destroy the Revolution where it was born, in 1793 the kings of Britain, Spain, Hanover, and Saxony joined Austria and Prussia in a giant coalition against France. But the Committee of Public Safety organized what was essentially history's first draft, and the giant Revolutionary armies, more than eight hundred thousand strong, swept the foreigners from France with ease. Then, seized by revolutionary fervor, they pursued them into their homelands.

Ironically, as the radical Revolution triumphed abroad, Robespierre wore out his welcome at home. In June 1794, 1,285 people were guillotined in a month, and the National Assembly decided they'd had enough. Robespierre was arrested and executed, along with twenty-one followers. The "radical" phase of the Revolution was ending—but the most incredible parts were still to come, thanks to a certain Napoleon Bonaparte.

·········· **WHO'S UP, WHO'S DOWN** ···············

Napoleon Bonaparte: **WAY UP, WAY DOWN, THEN REPEAT**
Although he grew up in Corsica speaking Italian, Napoleon was an ardent French nationalist with a taste for guns. In 1785, at the

age of sixteen, he graduated from the prestigious Military School in Paris but soon joined the revolutionary cause. When counterrevolutionaries attacked the National Assembly in 1795, he cleared the streets with cannons at point-blank range—typical Napoleon. In 1796 he led a Revolutionary army into northern Italy, where they defeated the Austrian army. Napoleon mixed with the grunts, who loved him, giving him the nickname "Little Corporal." He also proved his genius in battle by using cannons on horse-drawn wagons as devastating mobile artillery.

To build his empire, Napoleon appealed to French nationalism, telling the French people they had a unique historical mission to free Europe from monarchy. But he was a megalomaniac himself: in 1804 he crowned himself emperor of France, putting the crown on his own head because no mortal was fit to confer the honor—even though the pope was present. (The whole "freeing Europe from monarchy" thing? Just kidding!)

Realizing that Napoleon was bent on world domination, in 1805 Britain persuaded Austria and Russia to declare war on France again. Of course Britain was just beyond Napoleon's reach, an island fortress protected by the Royal Navy. So the Little Corporal did the next best thing, destroying the combined armies of Austria and Russia at Austerlitz on December 2, 1805, before Britain could lift a finger.

Now there was no one to stop Napoleon. He annexed southern Italy, crowned himself "King of Italy," appointed his brother Jerome king of Westphalia, and created a new federal state, the Confederation of the Rhine, in western Germany, with himself as dictator. Napoleon also forced Francis II of Austria to dissolve the Holy Roman Empire, ending the millennium-old realm with a single decree. The Brits looked on helplessly, and in 1806 the strain (and heavy drinking to cope) killed Prime Minister Pitt.

And there were still so many countries to conquer. In October 1806, after everyone else had been beaten, King Frederick Wilhelm III of Prussia finally joined the fray. Two weeks later, Napoleon stomped the Prussian armies at the Battle of Jena, and the brief adventure was over. Just for the heck of it, Napoleon also conquered Spain.

With continental Europe under Napoleon's thumb, in 1807 Czar Alexander of Russia asked for negotiations. As part of the peace terms, Alexander was supposed to help Napoleon enforce a reverse blockade of Britain, called the Continental System. Unable to defeat Britain militarily, Napoleon thought he could bring the island to its knees by cutting off all its European trade. To buy time, Alexander agreed to turn on his former ally—for now.

But Napoleon's heavy-handed approach created a backlash all over Europe, inspiring nationalist movements to combat the French "liberators" (more accurately "looters" and "rapists"). As bloody rebellions in Spain and Austria kept French troops tied down, in 1811 Czar Alexander of Russia split with France again, reopening trade with Britain and undermining Napoleon's Continental System.

Alexander's betrayal made Napoleon very, very angry, and his judgment started to slip. He decided to punish Russia—and why not? Well, it turns out there are lots of reasons. In autumn, torrential rains turn primitive roads into rivers of mud. Then winter brings feet of snow. No wonder the Russians say their best commanders are "General Mud" and "General Winter."

The French retreat from Moscow was one of history's worst military disasters. Cold, starving French troops were easy targets for Russian guerrilla fighters. Of the six hundred thousand soldiers who invaded Russia, ten thousand made it back to France. When they heard about the disaster, the kings of Prussia and Austria rejoined Britain and Russia in the fight against Napoleon. France was totally surrounded, and in April 1814, Napoleon was forced to abdicate. It was all over . . . well, almost.

Napoleon went into exile on Elba, a small island off the Italian coast, but he couldn't stand the quiet life, so in 1815 he sneaked off the island and tried conquering Europe . . . *again*. After landing in southern France with three thousand diehard followers, Napoleon marched north to Paris, cheered on by huge crowds. Thousands of veterans flocked to his cause, and in less than a month he commanded an army of one hundred thousand seasoned fighters.

With the old band back together, Napoleon was set to kick off a reunion tour of all the European capitals. And amazingly, he almost succeeded. He was mopping the floor with the Brits at Waterloo when their Prussian allies arrived to save the day. Humiliated and furious after Napoleon's "100 Days" adventure, the Brits sent him to St. Helena, a tiny rock in the south Atlantic, where he had no chance of escape. He died there in 1821.

—————— THAT'S NO GRAPE . . .

Was Napoleon's penis really removed and preserved in a jar? Probably. According to Napoleon's servant Ali, he and a priest named Vignali removed unspecified pieces of Napoleon's body during his autopsy in 1821. Later Vignali's descendants sold his various Napoleon souvenirs, including the Little Corporal's little corporal, described as "one inch long and resembling a grape." In 1977, a Columbia University urologist, John K. Lattimer, bought it for $3,000.

Napoleon's conquest of Spain created a golden opportunity for another group of revolutionaries, in South America. The educated middle class of Spain's New World territories had long resented European rule. When Napoleon conquered Spain in 1807, they seized the chance to go their own way, hoping to follow the example of the United States.

Their leader was Simon Bolivar. The son of an old Colombian family that made its fortune from mining, the teenaged Bolivar journeyed to Europe for his education and even joined Napoleon's entourage for a time. But he was disgusted by Napoleon's betrayal of the principles of the French Revolution, and when Napoleon installed his brother Joseph as king of Spain in 1808, Bolivar led the revolution (several, actually) against the puppet government.

A great leader, Bolivar efficiently liberated Venezuela, Colombia, Panama, and Ecuador in 1821. In 1824 he freed Peru and Bolivia (the latter is named after him). However, his plan for a "Greater Colombia" uniting the northern part of South America failed. And his ill-fated attempt to make himself dictator in 1828—followed by his flight to Europe in 1830—foreshadowed ugly developments in South America's future.

Still, Bolivar's accomplishments had lasting effects all over the world. The tide of revolution rippled from South America back to Europe. Together with the American and French revolutions, Bolivar's national revolutions inspired European nationalists to create two new nation-states, Italy and Germany, in the mid-nineteenth century.

EUROPE DOES THE SHUFFLE

After the defeat of Napoleon in 1815, the victorious European monarchs formed a new diplomatic club called the "Concert of Europe." To make sure France never became so strong again, this ultraconservative group decided to redraw the map of Europe. The only problem: they never consulted the "regular folks," who actually, you know, lived there. In the process, they set the stage for nationalist rebellions and the formation of Germany and Italy, which destroyed the balance of power. Smart move, guys!

First up were France's closest and smallest neighbors, Belgium and Holland. These were lumped together into a single state, even though the Belgian Walloons and Dutch Flemings have nothing in common and don't particularly care for each other. The new state was called the "United Kingdom of the Netherlands" (an optimistic name).

Poland, which had ceased to be an independent state in 1795, was due for another hundred years of getting kicked around. Most of the country was handed over to Russia as a "reward" for defeating Napoleon. The Russians also got Finland from Sweden as a buffer zone against fierce herds of reindeer, or something. And because Sweden lost Finland, it got Norway from Denmark (which had fought on the wrong side, as Napoleon's ally).

How'd all these changes turn out? The United Kingdom of the Netherlands lasted all of fifteen years, until the Belgian Revolution of 1830 (which began with a riot at an opera). The Russians brutally crushed dissent in Poland, but that didn't prevent two major rebellions in 1830 and 1863. The Finns also came to hate the Russians and declared independence as soon as they could. Norway separated from Sweden peacefully in 1905.

Germany: UP (*Everyone Else*: NERVOUS)

German nationalism began as a popular movement, before a conservative politician harnessed it on behalf of an old-school king. The politician, Otto von Bismarck, used trickery and warfare to unite eleven kingdoms in a German Empire. His boss, King Frederick III of Prussia, became the first "Kaiser" of the new German Reich.

After Napoleon's defeat in 1815, smaller German kingdoms looked to Prussia as a protector—and maybe unifier. But with the French Revolution fresh in their memories, Prussian kings still feared popular nationalism. Legitimacy must come from royal blood, not public opinion. So in 1848, when German nationalists formed a national assembly, wrote a constitution, and asked King Frederick Wilhelm IV of Prussia to rule as a constitutional monarch, he refused to accept a "crown from the gutter."

However, his successor, Frederick III, realized that national unification could make Prussia even more powerful—and no one ever said Germany had to be a *democracy*. His boy Bismarck just needed to neutralize Austria and France, which would never accept such a powerful neighbor. That's where Bismarck's brand-new Prussian army came in. In three stunning campaigns, Bismarck totally

THE QUOTABLE OTTO VON B.

"I have seen three emperors in their nakedness, and the sight was not inspiring."

"Laws are like sausages, it is better not to see them being made."

"The great questions of the day will not be settled by means of speeches and majority decisions but by iron and blood."

destroyed the armies of Austria-Hungary and France (and Denmark, for good measure). Prussian troops briefly occupied Paris in 1871, confirming that France was no longer king of the hill. To drive the point home in the most humiliating way possible, Bismarck arranged to have Frederick III crowned Kaiser of the new German Empire in the Hall of Mirrors at Versailles—Louis XIV's old stomping grounds.

In 1871 Germany had the same population as France, around forty-one million, but it also had a much higher birth rate, and its economy was developing more rapidly. Even more ominous, the aggressive Germans had a chip on their collective shoulder. More trouble was brewing . . .

Austria: DOWN

Getting slapped around by Napoleon and Bismarck wasn't Austria's only problem: it had at least twenty. The emperor of Austria presided over dozens of different ethnic groups with their own languages. In simpler times, all these groups respected the authority of the Holy Roman Emperor (the Austrian "Kaiser"). But the Magyar nobles who ruled Hungary were "hungry" (okay, that was bad) for more power, and popular nationalism gave them political leverage.

In 1867, Hungary's Magyar nobles forced Emperor Karl I to recognize Hungary as a distinct kingdom within his empire. Now he was officially called the emperor of Austria and the king of Hungary. This might not seem like a big difference, but it meant that Hungary got its own constitution and parliament, and Austria was now called Austria-Hungary.

Ironically, nationalism proved to be a double-edged sword for the Magyar nobles. The Kingdom of Hungary contained many national minorities, including Romanians, Serbians, Croatians, Slovenians, and Bosnians—and they all wanted out. Now the Magyar nobles themselves were on the defensive. In short, Austria-Hungary was an utter mess, and the stage was set for catastrophic collapse.

Italy: UP

As a Corsican, Napoleon Bonaparte was understandably sympathetic to Italian nationalism and decreed a united Italy (under his control, of course). Although the Concert of Europe split them up again, the Italians didn't forget their brief experience of national unity. After Napoleon's downfall, two Giuseppes emerged to lead Italian nationalism—one a poet, one a warrior. The poet was Giuseppe Mazzini, an essayist who began advocating an Italian republic in the 1830s. The warrior was Giuseppe Garibaldi, who led several Italian rebellions and tried to drive the Austrians out of northern Italy in the 1830s–1840s. But all these attempts failed.

Like Germany it took a bureaucrat to finally create the new Italian state. Count Camillo Cavour helped King Victor Emmanuel II of Piedmont-Sardinia conquer most of Italy's other small states and proclaim himself king of Italy in 1861, bringing the whole peninsula under a single ruler for the first time in almost fifteen hundred years. Still, Pope Pius IX was so nervous about Italian nationalism that he wouldn't let Victor proclaim Rome his capital. But nationalism was now stronger than the Church: in 1870 Victor seized Rome and confiscated most of the papal states, leaving Pius IX the Vatican City as a consolation prize.

The Ottoman Empire: DOWN

The Ottoman Empire had been declining for centuries, but the spread of nationalism made it even more decline-y. Beginning in the Napoleonic Era, the Slavic peoples were inspired by the French Revolution to fight for their freedom and embrace their national identities.

In 1821, Greek nationalists launched a rebellion with support from Western European intellectuals who admired the ancient Greeks. The cause attracted passionate artists such as Romantic poet Lord Byron, who traveled to Greece to dramatically organize supplies to the rebels before dramatically dying of fever in 1824. The Turks finally acknowledged Greek independence in 1832.

Meanwhile, the ornery Serbs were also agitating for independence, beginning with a revolt that lasted from 1804 to 1813. Serbia finally became independent in 1878, and its rebellion opened the way for other nationalist movements in Romania, Bosnia and Herzegovina, and Bulgaria in the 1870s and 1880s. By the late nineteenth century the Ottoman Empire was wheezing and coughing up blood—but it *still* wouldn't die.

BUT "SAHARA DESERT" DIDN'T RHYME . . .

The Marine Corps anthem's opening line about "the shores of Tripoli" isn't quite accurate. In 1801 Thomas Jefferson sent the United States Navy to the Mediterranean to protect merchant ships from Barbary pirates—Arab bandits operating out of the decaying Ottoman Empire in Libya and Algeria. In 1805 the ambitious American commander cut to the root of the problem by capturing Tripoli . . . not from the sea, as expected, but in a surprise attack overland across the Sahara desert.

Persia: DOWN

Persia had a little revolution of its own in 1781, but this was a far cry from the American and French revolutions. While the latter produced massive changes in government and society, the founding of Persia's Qajar Dynasty was basically a game of musical chairs before returning to business as usual. Persia was only going to get weaker.

Like most of the tribes that ruled Persia for most of history, the Qajars were semi-nomadic horsemen who overthrew another group of semi-nomadic horsemen (the Zand), who had themselves kicked out yet another group of semi-nomadic horsemen (the Safavids) in 1747. While they all despised each other, these tribes had a lot in common, including contempt for urban civilization, general viciousness, and good old-fashioned greed. The Qajar didn't really have the time or inclination for government; instead they focused on collecting tribute, hunting, and not getting killed by their cousins.

The tone was set by Agha Mohammad Khan, the dynasty's founder. Castrated by his father's enemies as a young boy, Agha apparently held a grudge against pretty much the whole world. When he blinded twenty thousand men in the city of Kerman, for example, he was just being nice: usually he killed all the inhabitants and burned the city to the ground. After Agha's assassination in 1797, the throne went to his nephew Fat'h Ali Shah, who was smarter and nicer than his uncle, but not much good at the whole government thing.

RULE BRITANNICA

After receiving the 1797 edition of the Encyclopedia Britannica, Fat'h Ali Shah read the whole thing and added a new title to his list: "Most Formidable Lord and Master of the Encyclopedia Britannica."

Fat'h recognized the threat posed to Persia by the Russian Empire, which in 1801 annexed the Kingdom of Georgia (traditionally Persian territory), but he overestimated Persia's chances against the Russians. Two wars ended in disastrous defeat, setting the stage for even more humiliation. The Brits jumped into the ring in 1856, supporting Afghan rebels against the Qajars and seizing territory in the Persian Gulf. With Russia's conquest of Turkmenistan and Uzbekistan in 1881, Persia found itself surrounded by powerful European empires. From here on out, things would only get worse.

China: DOWN (BUT HIGH)

China may be the oldest continuous civilization on earth, but the Chinese soon discovered that Westerners have no respect for age. In fact, being old and decrepit makes you an easy target—especially if you're addicted to opium!

By 1830 the British opium trade had reached 1,400 tons a year, serving about 12 million Chinese addicts. In some coastal areas, where the drug was easiest to get, as much as 90 percent of the population was addicted.

Skyrocketing Chinese addiction rates and the resulting crime wave even got the attention of the out-of-touch emperor Dao-guang. In 1839 he appointed an honest, energetic official, Lin Zexu, to halt the British opium trade. Lin Zexu sent a letter to Queen Victoria warning her that he planned to stop the flow of the drug into China, then confiscated all the opium in the British warehouse in the southern city of Canton (Guangzhou) and dumped it in the ocean.

Infuriated by the destruction of property, in 1840 the Brits dispatched an invasion force that seized Canton and forced the Chinese to make peace in 1842; as part of the peace terms, the emperor ceded them the island of Hong Kong under a long-term lease. Now the opium trade kicked into high gear, and it was just a matter of time before another "Opium War" broke out. In 1856, the Second Opium War was sparked by a Chinese pirate operating out of the new British colony at Hong Kong. The war ended in 1860, with the Chinese signing two humiliating treaties—the first of many "unequal" treaties with European powers—that legalized opium and granted the Brits extraordinary rights in Chinese ports, including exemption from Chinese laws.

Native Americans: DOWN (AND DRUNK)

One of the first orders of business for the newly created United States was settling the Louisiana Territory purchased from France by Thomas Jefferson in 1803. The only problem was there were millions of people there already: the Native Americans, who stubbornly refused to stop existing. So the U.S. government decided to give them a hand, beginning with mass deportations such as the Cherokee "Trail of Tears" in 1838, when seventeen thousand men, women, and children were force-marched from Georgia to Oklahoma, with about four thousand of them dying along the way.

The sale of liquor to Native Americans also served to speed the destruction of their society. Liquor was hardly new in the nineteenth century, but it hit Native Americans like a ton of bricks—and that was the whole point. The native trappers loved it, and it was easier to transport than other goods: fur traders could smuggle barrels of pure alcohol into "Indian Country," dilute it with river water, and trade it on the spot. To make this "firewater" look and taste like liquor, they added things like tobacco, red pepper, black molasses, and strychnine.

The U.S. government tried to cut off the liquor supply by inspecting the cargo of steamboats on the Mississippi and Ohio rivers, so the American Fur Company did the logical thing: it secretly built a distillery inside Indian Country, sending farmers to grow corn to distill into whiskey.

Mormonism (and Weddings): UP

In 1829 a farmer in upstate New York named Joseph Smith told friends and family that an angel named Moroni had guided him to two golden tablets buried in the wilderness near his home outside the small town of Fayette.

The tablets, Smith said, contained the religious writings of a lost tribe of Israel that had migrated to North America around 600 BCE, where their descendants created a great civilization. According to Smith, after his death and resurrection, Jesus Christ visited the New World to preach the gospel to the people of this civilization, who were converted and saved.

In 1830, Smith published the contents of the tablets as a new gospel of Jesus Christ called the Book of Mormon, which didn't replace the Bible, but added to and "confirmed" it. Smith also said the angel had directed him to found a new church and to baptize its members.

In 1831, after their neighbors in upstate New York harassed them for their strange ways, including polygamy, Smith led his followers to Ohio. Here the Mormons built a church or "temple" and sent out missionaries, who attracted more converts. But the Church was again attacked by neighbors. So the congregation moved to Missouri, where the real trouble started.

In a series of prolonged riots called the Missouri Mormon War, their neighbors in northwestern Missouri attacked Smith's roughly twelve thousand followers. In the end, Missouri's governor, Lilburn Boggs, issued Executive Order 44, also known as the "Extermination Order," ordering Missourians to kill any member of the Church caught in Missouri (of course, this was blatantly illegal).

To stop the killing, the Mormons signed over their property to Missouri militiamen and moved to Nauvoo, Illinois. But Nauvoo was just as bad. Here, the Illinois Mormon War of 1844 deprived the Church of its leader. After a disagreement with a local newspaper, Joseph Smith was arrested and then shot in his jail cell by an angry mob.

Now under the leadership of Smith's disciple Brigham Young, the Mormons moved again—this time to the faraway Salt Lake Valley, in Utah. After the 1,300-mile trek ended in 1847, they immediately began clearing farmland and surveying plots for Salt Lake City, with broad streets and lots of parkland. The community centered on a cathedral-like temple and an adjacent tabernacle that Joseph Smith and Brigham Young had described from visions.

Mormons have since become known for their clean living (forbidding alcohol, tobacco, and caffeine) and work ethic—the original name they chose for their state, Deseret, meaning "honey bee" and symbolizing industry.

- Revolution Watch -

American Revolution, Round Two

Though history (that's us!) has judged them harshly, the Confederate States of America were on pretty solid legal ground when they seceded from the United States in 1861. After all, there was no rule in the Constitution forbidding a state from leaving the Union if it wanted to; indeed, to Southern rebels, the American Civil War was nothing less than a "Second American Revolution," protecting states' rights against the big federal bully.

Of course, the Civil War was about a lot more than states' rights. The Northern and Southern economies had been diverging since colonial times. With smaller farms, manufacturing, and commerce, slavery didn't make economic sense in the North. The South, by contrast, was dominated by giant agricultural estates—plantations—where slaves were needed to grow labor-intensive crops such as cotton and tobacco.

But the regional economies didn't split—just the opposite. As Northern cities industrialized during the 1820s–1850s, their textile mills depended on cotton from Southern plantations. The Southern plantation aristocracy feared (correctly) that the industrial North wanted to make them political and economic vassals—just as Great

Britain, another industrial power, was subjugating less developed agricultural areas for her world empire.

Against this backdrop of economic tension, Northerners and Southerners disagreed ever more bitterly about slavery, the "real" cause of the Civil War. The Northern movement to abolish slavery was fueled by fanatical evangelical Christians, many from New England, who believed they had a divine mission to abolish slavery.

Enter Abe Lincoln, a self-taught lawyer from the Illinois frontier. In 1854 Lincoln helped found the antislavery Republican Party, and ran for senator from Illinois in 1858. (He lost.) At first Lincoln insisted he didn't want to end slavery in the South—just keep it from spreading to more states. Of course he couldn't allay the fears of Southern slave owners, and in December 1860, one month after he was elected president, South Carolina seceded from the Union, soon followed by ten other "slave" states. On April 12, 1861, the new Confederate army bombarded Fort Sumter, an island in Charleston Harbor. The Civil War had begun.

Early on, the North was defeated left and right. Virtually *all* the best generals hailed from Southern states and returned to fight for their homes. For example, the country's best general, Robert E. Lee, felt honor-bound to fight for his home state of Virginia. But in the long run, the North enjoyed key advantages with its large population, industry, and navy. As a Union naval blockade cut off cotton exports, literally starving the South, Lincoln finally found a winning commander in Ulysses S. Grant. Grant wasn't actually a very good general, but he was ready to accept unlimited casualties as he chased Lee across northern Virginia. With "Butcher Grant" (his nickname in Northern newspapers) in charge, the Union finally triumphed at a cost of at least six hundred thousand dead on both sides.

War is cruelty, and you cannot refine it.
—Gen. William Tecumseh Sherman

The Civil War saw the end of slavery with Lincoln's Emancipation Proclamation of 1863. But many freed black slaves found their position little improved, with no land, money, or education. Meanwhile, the war totally devastated the South, where defeated whites were left embittered. This foreshadowed another century of horrific racial strife throughout the United States, North and South.

Beyond the astonishing body count, the war was breathtakingly brutal in other ways: during his infamous March to the Sea, the Union general William Tecumseh Sherman burned or stole everything in his path, devastating a twelve-thousand-square-mile swathe of Tennessee, Georgia, North Carolina, and South Carolina. Meanwhile new weapons such as the Gatling gun, a predecessor of the machine gun, allowed ordinary men to mass-produce death on the battlefield. This mechanized mass killing foreshadowed the bloodiest, most destructive wars in world history, about to unfold in the heart of "civilization" itself.

········· **SO LONG, AND THANKS FOR ALL THE . . .** ·········

Canned Peaches and Condensed Milk
Napoleon Bonaparte commanded larger armies than any general in previous history, which presented a huge logistical problem. With more than 1,500,000 soldiers across Europe, Napoleon had to make sure he had enough food for his troops.

> *An army marches on its stomach.*
> —Napoleon Bonaparte

In 1800 Napoleon created a 12,000-franc prize (about $3,000 at the time, or $1.4 million in today's dollars) for anyone who invented a way of keeping food fresh indefinitely without ice or salt. Both methods were expensive, and neither prevented spoilage in the long term. That's where Nicolas Appert came in.

Although he was a candy maker, not a scientist, Appert had plenty of resources to experiment with packaging and treating food in his Paris candy factory. But one of Appert's most important observations came from a vice other than sugar: in wine making, he noticed that sealing bottles with airtight corks prevented wine from spoiling indefinitely.

Appert's stroke of genius was packaging food in airtight containers (wine bottles, in fact) and then cooking it, rather than vice versa. By sealing off food from the air before heating it to a high temperature, Appert killed whatever bacteria were present and also prevented new ones from getting a foothold.

He collected his prize in 1809, and Napoleon's troops carried with them all kinds of food preserved in wide-mouth bottles, including milk, eggs, meat, and vegetables. Appert patented the method, launching the world's first "cannery," and described his discovery in a book. In one of his bigger PR stunts, Appert once even preserved a whole sheep.

Fast Food

What do nineteenth-century Russian horsemen have to do with your hip neighborhood eatery? Well, the name, for one: *bistro*, a French word that has become common English usage, isn't really French at all. It comes from a Russian word, usually transliterated *bistra* or *bistrot*, which means "now!"

HAPPY HOUR

In the eighteenth century, tonic water containing quinine was one of the few ways to reduce malaria among British troops in Asia. Meanwhile, limes were required in sailors' diets to prevent scurvy. The British East India Company decided to mix it all up into a concoction so foul that nobody would drink it—until some clever realist suggested adding gin. Voilà! A cocktail is born.

If this seems rude, that's because it is. The word came to be associated with small street-level cafés when Russian troops occupied Paris after Napoleon's defeat and abdication in 1814. Fresh from the Russian countryside, these "rustic" Russian soldiers made a lasting impression on the French by getting belligerently drunk in restaurants and pounding on tables to encourage faster delivery of their food—shouting "Now! Now!" in Russian.

They even influenced the physical layout of cafés. Throughout the eighteenth century, restaurants and taverns were typically walled off from the street to keep out the odor of horse manure and other "bad air." But all that changed with the arrival of the Russians in 1814. The Cossacks—Russian cavalry descended from Central Asian nomads—refused to dismount to enter restaurants. They preferred to eat on horseback, so they tore down walls and rode into restaurants, where they placed their orders from the saddle. Thus the typical bistro now has large "French doors" that open on to the street.

There's an interesting parallel on the Russian side: the modern Russian term for "to beg," *sheramiz avat*, comes from the French words *cher ami*, or "good friend"—the desperate plea of French soldiers scrounging for food during Napoleon's disastrous retreat from Moscow.

Good Times with Nitrous Oxide

Anyone who's ever received nitrous oxide or "laughing gas" at the dentist's knows something about its whacky effects. The British chemist Joseph Priestly first identified nitrous oxide in 1772, but it wasn't until the 1790s that another scientist, Humphry Davy, discovered that inhaling it was, well, lots of fun. After Davy's discovery, traveling carnivals began charging a penny for a minute's worth of intoxication by laughing gas. Around the same time, Davy's student Michael Faraday also experimented with sulfuric ether, whose effects were similar (meaning, it was also good for getting high).

Both gases became important anesthetics—substances that can dull sensation and even produce unconsciousness to reduce pain during surgery. But in an age before mass communications or standardized medical language, it was hard to get the word out. So knowledge about the gases spread through "laughing gas parties" and "ether frolics," where doctors and their friends got high together. As part of their education, medical students were given doses of ether and laughing gas in the lecture hall. After all, what better way to understand the effects than experiencing them firsthand?

GOD SAVE THE QUEEN

In the Christian era, European women weren't allowed to take pain killers or anesthesia to dull the pain of childbirth, because the pain was considered God's punishment for Eve's sin. Public opinion shifted, however, when it became known that Queen Victoria asked for chloroform anesthetic during the birth of Prince Arthur in 1850. Victoria's endorsement made it acceptable for ordinary women.

Absinthe Minds

Absinthe is one of history's more "romantic" liquors, despite being known for causing blindness, insanity, and death. When it works right, it produces a sense of euphoria like that produced by opium or cocaine, with an extra hallucinogenic "kick" thanks in part to leaves of the poisonous wormwood bush (in addition to an alcohol content that varies between 45 and 90 percent). The herb anise gives absinthe an emerald green tint, so its nineteenth-century devotees called it "the green fairy." It was first distilled in Switzerland in 1792, but the classical period of absinthe use/abuse didn't begin until the second half of the nineteenth century, when French artists popularized the drug.

There's a whole ritual associated with drinking absinthe. Wormwood and anise extracts are very bitter, so drinkers (called *absintheurs*) usually mix sugar and water into the brew before drinking. Typically the person preparing absinthe puts a sugar cube in a slotted spoon, caramelizes it over an open flame, and then pours cold water over it into the drink. The cold water turns the absinthe cloudy, another integral part of the experience.

Absinthe was a big hit with intellectuals and artists living in Paris, including the Spanish painter Pablo Picasso, the French poet Guy Rimbaud, the French painter Pierre Manet, and the Irish author Oscar Wilde. The most popular absinthe brand was Pernod Fils. Of course, the drinkers weren't deterred by the occasional case of kidney failure, blindness, or death—caused by thujone, a potent neurotoxin found in wormwood that can induce fatal convulsions. Some poisonings were probably also due to knockoff brands, whose distillers added copper, zinc, and methanol.

Death Spirals

For two centuries European soldiers were armed with muskets—the firearm of choice during the wars of Louis XIV and the American Revolution. The problem with muskets is they aren't terribly accurate. In the mid-eighteenth century, a brilliant English engineer named Benjamin Robins realized that cutting spiraling lines on the inside of the gun barrel could vastly improve accuracy. While it might sound counterintuitive, "rifling" the gun barrel this way makes the bullet fly in a straight line by putting spin on it—exactly as with a football (this worked better when musket balls were replaced by elongated shells).

Robins was ahead of his time, so rifled guns were used only by sharpshooters—i.e., snipers—until 1800, when Ezekiel Baker produced the Baker Rifle, also called the Infantry Rifle. From 75 feet, the effective range of the "rifled muskets" grew to 600 feet . . . and beyond. During the war against Napoleon, one expert rifleman using the Baker Rifle killed a French general at the incredible distance of 2,400 feet. Later models, such as the Snider-Enfield, produced in 1853, were accurate up to 3,000 feet, and the Martini-Henry rifle of 1871 was good up to 4,200 feet.

Rifling also worked to improve the accuracy of cannons. The British first used rifled cannons accurate up to 3,300 feet in 1776, during the American Revolution. In 1846, Swedish and Italian engineers built rifled cannons that were loaded at the "breech" end rather than the mouth of the barrel, which made it easier and safer to load the guns. During the Franco-Prussian War of 1870, the Prussians used rifled cannons built by Krupp (still a famous German manufacturer) that were accurate up to 9,000 feet.

The American Consumerist Mind-set

The single biggest real estate buy in history was the result of an uncharacteristic decision by Napoleon Bonaparte to cut his losses.

Napoleon hoped to rebuild the French empire in the New World, with grain from the Midwestern "Louisiana Territory" feeding slaves on France's island colonies in the Caribbean. But a successful slave uprising in the French colony of Haiti and Britain's Royal Navy made his dream impossible.

This was good news for the United States, because Napoleon decided to sell the Louisiana Territory at a bargain price. In December 1803, President Thomas Jefferson bought the two-million-square-mile territory for $15 million. It was later divided into the modern American states of Louisiana, Arkansas, Oklahoma, Missouri, Kansas, Colorado, Wyoming, Nebraska, Iowa, Minnesota, Montana, North Dakota, and South Dakota. Pretty good deal.

Another good buy for the United States was Alaska, purchased from Russia in 1867 for $7.2 million—though at the time, people thought it was a waste of money.

The Russians had colonized Alaska in 1741 for one reason: otters, whose luxurious fur was turned into clothing for Europe's fur-obsessed upper classes. But the Russians never settled Alaska in force, and after the otters ran out, there wasn't much reason for them to be there at all, so they decided to get rid of the useless territory in exchange for cold, hard cash. The only problem was that most Americans thought Alaska was useless, too.

Fortunately Russia's ambassador to the United States, Edouard de Stoeckl, knew the way to U.S. senators' hearts: in 1868 he dispensed massive bribes to dozens of senators to smooth the way for the acquisition. For $7.2 million, the U.S. Secretary of State William Seward picked up territory measuring 586,412 square miles, about twice the size of Texas. That works out to about 2 cents an acre. Nonetheless many people still dismissed the deal for "Seward's Icebox" as a waste of money—until they discovered it had some delicious frozen treats. In 1896, prospectors discovered gold, triggering the great Klondike gold rush, and in the twentieth century, huge oil deposits were discovered.

Train Delays

Railroads of a sort were in use in Europe since the 1550s—rutted wagon ways lined with wood rails in Germany, later used in England, too. Wood rails were replaced with stronger iron rails by 1776, just as steam engines came on the scene.

In 1803 an English businessman Samuel Hofray offered a cash prize to any engineer who could design a steam engine to haul loads over unpaved (mud) roads, and an engineer named Richard Trevithick stepped up to the challenge in 1804. Then, in 1814, a self-taught engineer, George Stephenson, built the world's first steam locomotive for use over rails. Stephenson convinced his bosses at the Stockton & Darlington Railway to use steam power—rather than animals—to haul loads. He was quickly promoted to chief engineer.

Stockton & Darlington was soon offering regular combined passenger and freight service, and competitors began springing up. Railroads were faster, smoother, and more dependable than any system of land transportation in history, and were soon also remarkably cheap, allowing ordinary people to travel longer distances than ever.

An American example: heading west from Missouri in the mid-ninteenth century, wagon trains typically took four to five months to reach destinations in California and Oregon. Then, by two acts of Congress, the Central Pacific and Union Pacific railroads were built (the former heading east from California, the latter west from Nebraska; finally meeting up in 1869). With the first transcontinental express in 1876, the wagoneers' 4–5-month trip now took 83 hours and 29 minutes (about 3.5 days).

· · · · · · · · AND THANKS, BUT NO THANKS, FOR · · · · · ·

Death by Undergarments

You may have heard of "suffering for fashion," but in the nineteenth century, people took this expression literally. Women and men both started wearing corsets in the first half of the nineteenth century to slim their figures but often caused themselves serious medical problems in the process.

The stereotypical corset is the "under-bust" model that fits under the chest and above the hips. The corset is made of leather or cloth sewn onto a grille of metal wires or whalebone "ribs" or "stays," with a lace-up back. Because the laces were usually out of reach to the wearer, a second person had to tighten and tie it.

In the nineteenth century women, especially, strove to have very small waists—in fact, at one time the ideal waist size was considered to be under twenty inches, with some waists getting as small as fifteen inches! One "rule of thumb" measure for feminine beauty: the woman's lover should be able to put his hands around her waist and have the tips of both his thumbs and middle fingers touch, implying a waist size of sixteen to eighteen inches. Women who wore corsets regularly found they could achieve smaller waist sizes over time, as their bodies readjusted to the clothing.

ANOTHER FASHION FAUX PAS

During the Industrial Revolution, manufacturers began using chemicals to speed production of felt for hat-making. One of the most important chemicals for the process was mercury, which helped separate fur from animal skins. Unfortunately for workers in hat factories, mercury is also incredibly toxic. Even if they handled the mercury safely (they didn't) the rest of the hat-making process—which involved rinsing the felt with hot water and drying it repeatedly—ensured that workers inhaled plenty of mercury-laden steam. Many suffered from debilitating physical ailments, and some went totally bonkers. Hence the term "mad hatter."

Women weren't the only ones wearing corsets, however. Throughout the nineteenth century and into the twentieth, many men wore looser corsets to conceal their pot bellies. And from the 1820s to 1850s, men in Victorian Britain and America wore "tight-lacing" corsets to achieve the "hourglass" shape then considered attractive for men. In this period, many men's fashions, including narrow waistcoats and tight trousers, required wearers to avail themselves of a corset.

Of course, radically reducing waist size could lead to some serious health issues. Victorian doctors blamed a host of ills on overzealous corset wearers lacing their corsets too tight. Corsets compressed the liver and displaced the heart, uterus, ovaries, and kidneys. They also constricted the lungs, making breathing difficult and causing chronic pain. Finally, they impeded blood flow, leading to fainting spells.

Royal Body Parts

Think Napoleon's penis was the only famous body part preserved in this period? Think again! In another bizarre French organ-stealing scenario, a physician secretly loyal to the French royal family removed and preserved the heart of the young Louis XVII, who died at the age of ten while in a French prison.

Young Louis-Charles, son of Louis XVI and Marie Antoinette, had been imprisoned by French revolutionaries in a cold, dark cell with no toilet and no bath. The revolutionaries feared that French aristocrats might try to restore Louis-Charles to power, but couldn't bring themselves to kill an innocent child. So, instead, they indoctrinated him in revolutionary ways, forcing him to take up a trade (shoe making) and teaching him to curse the names of his dead parents. Denied medical treatment, the boy died of tuberculosis. His body was supposedly riddled with tumors, sores, and scabies.

Before the body was dumped in a mass grave, however, the examining doctor for the autopsy, Jean-Philippe Pelletan, cut out the dead boy's heart, hid it in a handkerchief, and preserved it, in keeping with an ancient royal custom calling for the heart of the king to be pickled separate from his body. After the defeat of Napoleon and the restoration of Louis-Charles's uncle as Louis XVIII, Pelletan tried to return the boy's heart to the royal family, but they refused to believe it was genuine. Later, one of Pelletan's students stole the heart. After he died, his widow gave it to the archbishop of Paris, but it was later smuggled to Spain for safekeeping. The heart currently resides in the Saint Denis Basilica near Paris.

Sharing

During the Industrial Revolution poor factory workers found hope in communism, a new system of thought that explained every aspect of reality with a single, sweeping worldview. In fact, Karl Marx and his collaborator Friedrich Engels said they could prove the theory "scientifically," with mathematical rules that predicted the future. (They couldn't.)

To explain history, Marx borrowed from Friedrich Hegel, a German Enlightenment philosopher. Like Hegel, Marx believed that history is a giant dialogue, or "dialectic," between opposing forces that unfolds in a series of cycles. But Marx said Hegel was wrong about one crucial detail: the real action doesn't take place in the world of ideas, as Hegel believed, but rather in material reality.

Innovation in the means of production of goods—not philosophical debate—is the real engine of change, because it allows individuals to accumulate wealth or capital (a concept Marx borrowed from Adam Smith) and change human society. Culture, laws, and government are just by-products of this process. In this cynical view, the ruling class—meaning, whoever controls the means of production—always creates laws and government that suit its needs, dressing them up with "ideals" to justify their oppression of other classes.

Marx and Engels grouped history into three different periods, but in each period the basic pattern was the same. First, the existing system of production was disrupted by new methods, which made innovators rich. But then "contradictions" between the new economy and the old social system eventually led to collapse. From this collapse arose a new system—and the whole thing started over again.

In the first big phase of history, the Classical Period, the big landowners of republican and imperial Rome drove smaller farmers into bankruptcy and added their land to giant plantations worked by slaves. The unemployed farmers moved to cities, where they overtaxed the welfare system—causing Rome to collapse.

In the second phase, Germanic barbarians overthrew the Roman Empire and established feudal kingdoms based on their tribal customs, with serfs supporting noble lords. Marx said the feudal system brought about its own destruction with the rise of free "bourgeoisie" (city-dwellers). Led by wealthy merchants and manufacturers, this new middle class established government based on parliaments (where only men with property could vote) and overthrew feudal power.

The bourgeoisie were the most innovative class in history, inventors of the Industrial Revolution—but also the cruelest. Pursuing efficiency, Marx predicted, bourgeois capitalists would pay workers less and less, until the latter couldn't even secure food and shelter. Marx predicted that the proletariat (workers) would eventually rebel and the system would collapse. The proletariat would abolish laws protecting property and everything, including farmland and factories, would belong to "the people."

Communism was utterly terrifying to Europe's upper and middle classes, and for good reason. To achieve this radical change in society, Marx openly advocated criminal behavior, arguing that the laws of an unjust system must be broken. In the twentieth century Marx's disciples took this to heart and implemented it on a vast scale.

Later, Taters

The Irish Potato Famine of 1845–1849 is a tragic example of the risks associated with "monoculture"—growing just one kind of crop or (even worse) just one genetic variant of one kind of crop. When the staple crop turns out to be susceptible to new disease, the food supply can collapse overnight, leading to mass starvation. Of course, in the case of Ireland, it didn't help that the Brits deliberately ignored the problem.

The potato "blight" (*Phytophthora infestans*) arrived in 1845 and spread across Ireland in just a few months. A family's crop could be wiped out in a day, forcing them to beg—but charity didn't exist when neighbors had no food to give. The Irish Potato Famine was characterized by the mass migration of starving refugees: first within Ireland, with millions of people heading to the coasts; then with secondary migrations to America, Canada, and Australia. Over the four-year period, about one million people died of starvation and disease, and another two million fled Ireland in conditions of indescribable misery. Rumors of cannibalism in more remote parts of Ireland persist to this day.

The British government's response was, well, pathetic. To justify handouts, the Brits employed starving Irishmen in make-work tasks such as flattening hills, filling valleys, and building endless stone walls that still dot the Irish landscape, serving no purpose. To be eligible for this meaningless work, poor farmers had to give up their land, which was confiscated by rich English landlords. Wages were paid on Fridays, so workers often died of starvation before payday. Interestingly, Ireland remained a net exporter of food from 1845 to 1851, with English landlords shipping abroad three million live animals that could have been used as food. The English escorted the livestock past the starving Irish under armed guard.

· **BY THE NUMBERS** ·

800,000	number of French soldiers recruited in first draft, 1793
450,000	size of the next-largest European army (Russia) at that time
6.25 million	amount of coal, in tons, mined in England in 1790
16 million	amount of coal, in tons, mined in England in 1815
31 million	amount of coal, in tons, mined in England in 1839
225 million	amount of coal, in tons, mined in England in 1900
100	miles of railroad track in England in 1830
6,600	miles of railroad track in England in 1852
22,500	miles of railroad track laid in the United States, 1850–1860
28 million	French population in 1800
39 million	French population in 1900
29 million	German population in 1800
56.4 million	German population in 1900
1.4 million	German iron production, in tons, 1870
4.7 million	German iron production, in tons, 1890
1.2 million	French iron production, in tons, 1870
2 million	French iron production, in tons, 1890
2.8 million	population of the American colonies in 1780
7.2 million	population of the United States in 1810

23.2 million population of the United States in 1850
63 million population of the United States in 1890
14 time zones covered by the Russian Empire at its
greatest extent

10

THE EMPIRES
STRIKE OUT

(1900–1930)

$\approx$

In 1900, it was still good to be the king. Or the emperor, or the prince, or the archduke, for that matter. Various empires dominated the world outside North and South America. Fortified by the largest navy in the world, Great Britain supervised one quarter of the entire globe. "The sun," went a popular saying, "never sets on the British Empire." By the end of her sixty-three-year reign in 1901, Queen Victoria ruled over the British Isles, Canada, Australia, New Zealand, India, Burma, Egypt, and a good chunk of the rest of the African continent. But the Brits were by no means alone in the ardent practice of imperialism, which could be defined as "we can run your country better than you can, we want your natural resources, and this is a good spot for our military purposes, so welcome to the empire."

The Hapsburgs sat atop the Austro-Hungarian Empire, the Romanovs over the Russian Empire, the Manchu over Imperial China, and the Ottomans over, well, the Ottoman Empire in Asia Minor. The French, Italians, Germans, Belgians, and Portuguese all had colonies. Japan, after centuries of mostly trying to avoid foreign entanglement, took control of Formosa (now Taiwan) in 1895 and Korea in 1910. Even the United States, which through the Monroe Doctrine had for seventy-seven years sternly warned Europe to stay out of the New World, held Puerto Rico, Hawaii, the Philippines, and Cuba.

Only South America was largely free of colonial influences. With the exception of small European holdings in Guiana, the rest of the continent had shed its colonial bonds by the end of the nineteenth century.

Europe had been without major conflict since 1815. But as colonialism reached its peak, the competing empires and would-be empires began bumping up against each other—and rubbing each other the wrong way.

And as industrialization continued its ascent as the dominant factor in the world's economy, some countries outstripped their neighbors. The resulting tensions escalated into various small wars around the globe, from South Africa to Korea.

But there were internal conflicts as well. Fueled by the nineteenth-century writings of a German economics philosopher named Karl Marx, socialists agitated for replacement of monarchs with the masses as the heads of government. At the same time, "colonials" were chafing at the empires' yokes. Nationalism began to take on imperialism.

These battles of "isms" boiled over in the Balkans in 1912, when Montenegro successfully rebelled against the Ottoman Empire. Serbia, Bulgaria, and Greece followed. The aftershocks rippled throughout Europe, as the flagging Romanov and Hapsburg empires tried to squeeze into the gap left by the Ottomans.

As the situation festered, nations solidified alliances, and by August 1914, Europe was at war. Horrifically effective weapons such as tanks and poison gas, coupled with disease, led to the deaths of more than eight million soldiers, and more than twenty million non-fatal casualties before the war's end in 1918.

In an effort to restore some sort of order and instill real meaning to the catchphrase "war to end all wars," the formal peace treaty eventually signed at Versailles created a League of Nations. The league lacked any military clout, but was supposed to use economic and political pressure to exert influence. It didn't work, especially when the U.S. Senate refused to authorize America's membership.

While America's politics were isolationist, its status as the world's postwar banker made it indispensable. Big U.S. banks made huge loans to foreign countries. When the countries couldn't, or wouldn't, repay the debts, the banks were left high and dry. Farm failures, a growing disparity between the rich and poor, over-reliance on personal credit, and a stock market overheated by get-rich-quick speculation all contributed to a resounding crash of the U.S. economy in 1929.

From an economic standpoint, when the United States sniffled, the world caught a cold. And at the end of the first thirty years of the twentieth century, you might say the world was on the edge of pneumonia.

.... **WHAT HAPPENED WHEN** ....

Jul. 2, 1900   Count Ferdinand von Zeppelin launches the first rigid airship. The flight lasts 18 minutes.

Jan. 1, 1901	The five British colonies in Australia are united to become a commonwealth.
1902	A 7,000-foot-long dam is completed across the Nile River near Aswan, in Southern Egypt.
Dec. 17, 1903	Ohio bicycle shop owners Orville and Wilbur Wright make several flights in a powered flying machine.
1905	German physicist Albert Einstein publishes three groundbreaking papers, including his theory of relativity.
1908	Henry Ford's factory in Detroit produces the first Model T.
Mar. 10, 1910	China abolishes slavery within the empire.
Apr. 14, 1912	The RMS *Titanic*, the world's largest passenger liner, strikes an iceberg in the North Atlantic and sinks on its maiden voyage.
Aug. 5, 1914	What are believed to the world's first traffic lights begin operating at the corner of East 105th Street and Euclid Ave in Cleveland.
Aug. 14, 1914	After a decade under construction, the Panama Canal is formally opened.
Apr. 22, 1915	The German military uses poison gas against French colonial and Canadian troops.
1918	"Spanish" influenza kills an estimated 6 million people in Europe alone.
Nov. 2, 1920	Radio station KDKA in Pittsburgh makes the first regularly scheduled commercial broadcast.
Oct. 31, 1922	A thirty-nine-year-old former draft dodger named Benito Mussolini becomes the youngest prime minister in Italy's history.
1923	The world's first domestic electric refrigerator is sold in Sweden.
1924	U.S. Congress enacts legislation that bans all immigration from Asia.

1925 The Communist Party is formed in China.

1926 Protesting a lack of influence, Brazil becomes the first country to leave the League of Nations.

Dec. 25, 1926 Hirohito, the twenty-five-year-old crown prince of Japan, becomes the country's 124th emperor.

Sept. 7, 1927 American engineer Philo Farnsworth uses electronics to transmit images on what will become known as a "television."

Oct. 24, 1929 The U.S. stock market begins a precipitous slide that will severely affect the world's economy.

~ The War to End All Wars, Until the Next One ~

The 50-cent Version

An archduke got shot; a bunch of countries chose sides and went to war; nasty weapons were used, killing lots of people; disease killed a bunch more; everyone got tired of fighting and agreed to quit; empires fell apart and dictatorships arose.

The $9.99 Version

The match that lit World War I's fuse was the June 28, 1914, assassination of the Austrian archduke Franz Ferdinand and his wife by a nineteen-year-old Serbian student/nationalist/terrorist named Gavilo Princip. After Serbia, supported by Russia, refused a demand to extradite Princip and his co-conspirators, Austria declared war. Germany joined sides with Austria and attacked Russian ally France by cutting through neutral Belgium, planning to defeat France in the west, then turn east and lick the Russians.

The plan's success hinged on a quick victory in France. But various countries then rushed in to involve themselves. When Britain entered the war on the side of France and Russia, prospects for a short war collapsed. The Austro-Hungarian Empire teamed up with Germany, later joined by the Ottoman Empire and Bulgaria, to form the Central Powers. They were opposed by the better-named Entente, composed of Britain, France, Russia, and later Italy and Greece. Both sides dug in—literally—and the conflict bogged down in a series of attacks and counterattacks along a three-hundred-plus-mile front of fortified trenches.

Modern weaponry, such as tanks and machine guns, and the-psychologically-as-well-as-physically terrifying use of poison gas, proved to be appallingly efficient. The carnage was staggering. During the six-week First Battle of Ypres in 1914, for example, Germany lost 130,000 soldiers, Britain 58,000, and France 50,000.

And diseases such as dysentery and the so-called Spanish Flu that circled the world in 1918 felled many of the men who weren't killed by their fellow men.

Civilian casualties often rivaled the military's. In the Ottoman Empire, Turkish leaders used the war as an excuse to conduct ethnic cleansing against Armenians. Hundreds of thousands were slaughtered or forcibly relocated to desert areas, where many starved to death.

> *Nobody could conceive the dimension of a world conflagration, and the misery and trouble it would bring upon the nations. All previous wars would be as child's play.*
> —German chancellor Theobald Von Bethmann-Hollweg, April 7, 1913, on the potential impact of a world war

The war's tipping point came when German submarine attacks on American shipping prodded a heretofore reluctant-to-get-involved U.S. government into joining the British and French in April 1917. Eventually realizing it could not match the other side's manpower or materiel, Germany signed an armistice on November 11, 1918, and a formal peace treaty at Versailles, France, on June 28, 1919—five years to the day after Archduke Ferdinand's assassination.

With the exception of the United States, every major country involved in the conflict had been seriously crippled. More than 8.0 million soldiers had been killed and more than 20.0 million injured. Germany lost 1.8 million men, France 1.3 million. The financial cost was enormous: an estimated total of $186.0 billion, $37.7 billion of that incurred by Germany, $35.3 billion by Great Britain. Even though the United States didn't get involved until April 1917, it still managed to spend $22.6 billion, much of it in loans to its allies.

What the world got for its lost lives and money wasn't much. An effort by U.S. president Woodrow Wilson to be magnanimous in victory was rebuffed by the other victors, who, to be fair, had suffered far more. Led by a vengeful France, the winners made Germany acknowledge that the war was its fault, disarm itself and promise to stay disarmed, and make reparations.

The Austro-Hungarian, Ottoman, and Russian empires were dismantled. More than a half-dozen new countries were carved out of the old empires in Eastern Europe, and German and Turkish territories in the Middle East and Africa were ceded to France and Britain.

But the end of the war was by no means the end of conflict. The democratic revolution that began in Russia in 1917 ended in 1922 with the world's first communist state—the Union of Soviet Socialist Republics. Dictators rose to power in Poland and Italy. Japan was asserting itself as the dominant economic, political, and military force in Asia. And dismal economic conditions threatened the republican form of government that took shape in postwar Germany—and nurtured the ambitions of a dictator wannabe named Hitler.

 ············· **SPINNING THE GLOBE** ··················

Japan:
Entering the World Stage with a Vengeance

After staying below the Western radar for centuries, Japan quickly learned to adapt the West's technology, industrial methods, and even its politics. It also embraced the West's imperialist tendencies.

In 1895, after a brief war with China, Japan secured control of the island of Taiwan. In 1905, after crushing Russia in a war, the Japanese secured more territory and concessions, which paved the way for a takeover of Korea in 1910. In 1914, after the outbreak of World War I, Japan grabbed German colonies in the Pacific, and by 1918, it controlled portions of Siberia and Manchuria. Japan was now the major power in East Asia.

In 1919, Japan was made a permanent member of the League of Nations, and in 1922 it strengthened its ties with Western nations by signing an agreement with France, Britain, and the United States to reduce naval forces, denounce the use of poison gas in warfare, and ban submarine attacks on merchant vessels.

But the Japanese did not go along with the West on everything. In 1928, when Western countries acquiesced to Chinese demands for new treaties among the nations, Japan refused. This set the stage for increasing friction between not only Japan and China, but also Japan and the West.

When hard economic times hit the country in 1929, radical nationalists and sympathetic military leaders began to assert themselves and gradually take over the government. In 1930, the Japanese began a new round of incursions into Manchuria and parts of Northern China, foreshadowing much larger conquests to come.

China:
A Series of Ineffective Revolutions

As the twentieth century began, the world's oldest empire was staggering. The Q'ing (Manchu) Dynasty had been in power since the mid-seventeenth century. Starting in 1861, it was ruled, mostly behind the scenes, by the empress dowager Cixi. But it had lost a brief war to Japan in the mid-1890s, and was torn between a conservative ruling class bent on preserving the status quo and a growing number of people calling for reforms.'

> ## NO QUALIFICATIONS NECESSARY
>
> In 1905, the Q'ing Dynasty abolished the country's two-thousand-year-old civil service system because it interfered with the regime's corrupt political patronage system.

There was also growing resentment to foreign, mostly European, incursions into Chinese culture and commerce. In 1900, a group of Chinese, angered by Christian missionary work, went on a rampage, marching on Beijing and laying siege to foreign legations there. The rebels were dubbed "Boxers," a Westernized shorthand for their Chinese name "Righteous Harmonious Fists."

Troops from the United States, Japan, and six European countries ended the sieges, and in 1901 forced China to accept the presence of foreign troops on its soil and pay huge reparations to the "Eight-Nation Alliance."

Following the death of Cixi in 1908, the last emperor in China's four-thousand-year history ascended to the throne. P'u Yi was not quite three years old when he became emperor, and his reign lasted only a little longer than that. In 1911, a revolution began, led by a forty-six-year-old doctor named Sun Yat-sen. In February 1912, the

When your nickname is the "Dragon Lady," you don't worry much about whether you can vote or not. Which is why Cixi, or T'zu-His, the de facto ruler of China for nearly half a century, didn't. "I have often thought that I am the most clever woman who ever lived," she once said. "I have four hundred million people dependent on my judgment."

Born to a middle-ranking Manchu family, Cixi became a member of the emperor Xianfeng's harem at the age of seventeen, and gave birth to the emperor's only son. That elevated her status from concubine to consort. When Xianfeng died in 1861, Cixi's six-year-old son, Tongzhi, took the throne. Cixi became empress dowager, and de facto ruler. When Tongzhi died in 1875, Cixi gave his crown to her three-year-old nephew Guangxu. But Guangxu began implementing radical reforms that alarmed China's ruling classes. So in 1898, Cixi put her nephew under arrest, quite possibly had him killed, and replaced him with her three-year-old grandnephew P'u Yi. Cixi herself died in 1908, and her tomb is now a pretty big tourist attraction.

rebels overthrew the monarchy, the Republic of China was declared, and Sun became China's first president.

In 1916, however, China's second president, Yuan Shikai, decided he'd like to name himself emperor. He died before he could pull it off, and the country fragmented into a chaotic caldron of feuding warlords and nascent political parties that included the Kuomintang, or Chinese Nationalists, and the Chinese Communist Party. By 1923, full-scale civil war had broken out.

In 1926, Chiang Kai-shek, a military man who had once served in the Japanese army, became head of the Kuomintang. Chiang led an alliance, which included the Communists, in a successful fight against warlords in Northern China in 1927. But the following year, he turned on his Communist allies and purged them from his government.

This, in turn, set off a civil war that would not end for another twenty-three years. Thus in 1930, China was in many ways just where it had been in 1900: under autocratic rule, brimming with civil unrest, economically impoverished, and dreaming of better days.

Russia (and Eventually the Soviet Union): Seeing Red

Like China, Russia went through a bewildering blizzard of brutal changes between 1900 and 1930, including a civil war, two regular wars, two revolutions, and a famine.

Also like China, Russia found itself torn between an Old Guard aristocracy and an increasingly restless peasantry. Hoping to distract his subjects from their other troubles, the largely ineffectual czar Nicholas II went to war in 1904 with Japan, nominally over territorial disputes in Manchuria and Korea.

Bad idea. Russia was severely thrashed by the Japanese, which only added fuel to the fire at home. On January 22, 1905, a very large but generally peaceful group of workers tried to present the czar with a petition calling for political and economic reforms. They were greeted with a volley of gunfire from Nicholas's guards, and more than a hundred workers were killed.

What became known as "Bloody Sunday" resulted in a revolution that failed to overthrow Nicholas but forced him to agree to make Russia a constitutional monarchy, with people guaranteed certain basic rights.

But you can't eat basic rights. In 1907, a famine struck the country, killing millions. Although Russia had become one of the world's

LENIN, TROTSKY, AND STALIN WALK INTO A BAR . . .

A trio of widely disparate men chiefly led Russia's transformation from czarism to communism: Vladimir Lenin, Leon Trotsky, and Joseph Stalin.

Lenin was a lawyer and intellectual who had been heavily influenced in his teens by the writings of Marx and Engels. In 1903, Lenin led a split from the dominant radical left party in Russia. His faction, called the Bolsheviks (from the Russian word for "majority"), advocated immediate and violent revolution.

The son of a wealthy Jewish farmer, Trotsky was at first affiliated with the more moderate Menshevik ("minority") Party, but eventually became Lenin's chief lieutenant. The son of an alcoholic cobbler, Stalin spent parts of his youth as a seminary student and a bank robber. Lenin regarded Stalin as something of a useful thug.

In late 1922, Lenin suggested Trotsky as his successor, noting that "Stalin is too rude." But Stalin was also politically cunning, and brutal. When Lenin died in 1924, Stalin elbowed Trotsky aside and assumed control. In 1929, Stalin exiled Trotsky, who was assassinated in Mexico in 1940 by a Soviet agent.

Stalin was more interested in eliminating rivals, consolidating power, and pushing his "Five-Year Plan" (which called for putting millions of peasants into factories or onto massive state-run farms) than in expanding the "People's Revolution."

Except for Mongolia, the Soviet Union would remain the only Communist state until after World War II.

biggest industrial nations, workers' wages remained microscopic. World War I turned out to be another disaster, with Russia suffering defeat after defeat, mostly at the hands of Germany. By the end of 1915, one million Russian soldiers had been killed and another one million captured.

In February 1917, another revolution broke out, and the following month, Nicholas abdicated, and he and his family were later executed. By November, the Bolshevik Party, led by Vladimir Lenin and Leon Trotsky, had taken over. The Bolsheviks quickly sued for peace and withdrew from the world war.

But their ascension touched off a civil war between the "Reds" (Bolsheviks and other communist groups) and the "Whites," a collection of nationalists and aristocrats. Several foreign countries, including the United States, sent troops to aid the Whites. The foreign interests hoped that kicking out the Bolsheviks would get Russia back into the war against Germany.

But the Whites were badly fragmented, and by 1921, Lenin's forces had won. In 1922, the world's first major Communist-controlled country was formally declared: the Union of Soviet Socialist Republics. And like other European countries by 1930, the former Russia began to rearm.

Germany:
Sore—and Poor—Losers

In 1900, Germany was as bellicose and avaricious as most of its Western European neighbors. In addition to running colonies in Africa and the Pacific, it was clamping down on the former French and Russian territory it had wrested away in the nineteenth century.

Its policies were often harsh in the areas it dominated. Poles, for example, were forbidden to speak their own language at public meetings or in classrooms. Yet at home, the German government was at times fairly progressive. In 1903, sick-leave benefits were extended to many workers, and in 1909 women were admitted to state universities.

World War I eviscerated the country economically as well as psychologically. Some 90 percent of the country's merchant fleet was lost as a result of the war, along with 75 percent of its iron ore pro-

WHEN THE WHISTLE BLOWS

Times were tough in postwar Germany, but that didn't mean there wasn't a bright spot now and then. In 1921, for instance, a factory in Westphalia manufactured thirty-six teakettles that whistled when the water was boiling. They were offered for sale in a Berlin department store—and sold out in three hours.

duction. France occupied Germany's chief manufacturing region and refused to leave.

In 1919, Germans elected a national assembly in the city of Weimar (hence the term "Weimar Republic") and crafted a new constitution that guaranteed "basic personal liberties" and universal suffrage.

But the huge reparations bill presented by the victorious countries helped drive the country deeper into the economic Dumpster. The government began to print money like crazy, and the resulting inflation was stratospheric. By 1923, it took one *trillion* marks to buy what one mark bought in 1914. It literally took a wheelbarrow full of bills to buy a loaf of bread. Unemployment rose from one million people out of work in 1923 to five million by 1930.

The economic crisis went hand in hand with political unrest. Communists stirred up trouble on the left; archconservative nationalists on the right. Among the right-wing groups was the Nationalist Socialist German Workers Party, or Nazis, founded by a former corporal and failed artist named Adolf Hitler. In 1923, Hitler brashly proclaimed a new government, and was arrested, convicted of treason, and sentenced to five years, although he served only a little more than a year.

In 1925, Germans elected a seventy-seven-year-old war hero named Paul von Hindenburg as president. He was unable to do much to address the country's deep economic woes, or stem the lingering resentment many Germans felt for being held responsible for World War I.

Hitler's Nazi Party, meanwhile, was steadily making political headway. In the 1928 elections, the Nazis held 12 seats in the Reichstag, or German parliament. In 1930, that number rose to 107, or about 20 percent. By 1932, the percentage had increased to almost one third.

Germany also began to rearm itself, in defiance of the agreements it had made with the victorious countries after the war.

United States of America:
Getting Nosy

Although perhaps not yet as greedy or grasping as other Western powers, the United States entered the twentieth century with its own yen to run other countries' affairs—and benefit from their resources—whether those countries were keen on it or not.

The first president of the century, William McKinley, lasted only until September 1901, when a self-proclaimed anarchist assassinated him during a visit to an international fair in Buffalo, New York.

McKinley's successor, Theodore Roosevelt, was positively bully on the idea of increasing America's clout in the rest of the world. In 1903, he encouraged Panama to revolt against Colombia, and then grant the United States rights to build a canal across the Panamanian Isthmus, thus linking the Atlantic and Pacific oceans.

In 1905, he brokered a peace treaty between Russia and Japan that earned him the Nobel Peace Prize. And he sent the U.S. Navy fleet around the world on a mission of "goodwill"—which also served to give other countries a glimpse of what they would be messing with if they messed with the United States.

ONE RARE BEAR

Theodore Roosevelt is the only man to be awarded both the Nobel Prize for brokering peace, and the Congressional Medal of Honor for waging war.

Born in 1858 into a prosperous New York merchant family, Roosevelt was a sickly child. To buck up his health, his father pushed him into a lifestyle built around strenuous exercise and constant activity. After a brief career as a cattle rancher and part-time lawman in the Dakota Badlands, Roosevelt returned to New York and entered politics, eventually being named assistant secretary of the Navy by President William McKinley.

When the U.S. war with Spain began in 1898, Roosevelt organized a cavalry unit known as the Rough Riders. His daring exploits in Cuba brought him national fame, helped him get elected governor of New York, and earned him the Medal of Honor (posthumously, in 2001).

It also secured Roosevelt the 1900 vice presidential nomination under McKinley on the successful GOP ticket. In 1901, after McKinley was assassinated, Roosevelt became, at forty-three, the youngest U.S. president.

As chief executive from 1901 to 1909, Roosevelt greatly expanded the role of the office, created most of the federal government's important environmental programs, and pushed major consumer protection and monopoly-fighting acts through Congress. He often quoted an old African adage: "Speak softly and carry a big stick."

And he found time to write books, hunt big game, explore the Amazon, design a simplified spelling system (that failed to catch on), and lend his name to one of the world's most popular children's toys, the Teddy Bear.

Roosevelt died of a coronary embolism at the age of sixty. "Death had to take Roosevelt sleeping," Vice President Thomas Marshall said, "for if he had been awake, there would have been a fight."

The presidents who followed Roosevelt—William Howard Taft, Woodrow Wilson, Warren Harding, and Calvin Coolidge—had their own versions of "gunboat diplomacy." U.S. troops were dispatched on several occasions to various Latin American nations to "protect American interests," which was generally understood to mean "protect American business interests."

But Americans were by no means united in support of imperialism. An Anti-Imperialist League was formed, led by such disparate and celebrated figures as author Mark Twain and industrialist Andrew Carnegie. And when World War I broke out, most of the country was solidly for the United States minding its own business. In 1916, in fact, Wilson won reelection with the slogan "He kept us out of war."

This changed, however, due mainly to German submarine threats against U.S. shipping and clever Allied anti-German propaganda that galvanized American sentiment in favor of England, France, and to a lesser extent, Russia.

In April 1917, the United States declared war on Germany, and by the end of the war had dispatched 1.4 million troops to European battlefields. Although it spent a large amount of money, U.S. casualties—about 48,000 killed in battle and 56,000 lost to disease—were trifling when compared with the stupendous carnage suffered by other nations.

Moreover, no battles were fought on U.S. soil. As a result, the country was uniquely poised to help the world heal after the war. For the most part, however, America said "no thanks."

It wasn't from lack of trying on the part of Woodrow Wilson. Even before the war ended, Wilson proposed a plan of "14 points" that outlined what he thought would be a lasting peace. Other nations' leaders, however, found the plan naïve: "Moses brought down Ten Commandments," sniffed French premier Georges Clemenceau. "Wilson needed fourteen."

Wilson also failed to persuade the U.S. Senate to approve America's membership in the League of Nations, crippling the fledgling organization's chances of success.

And fearful of being flooded with a massive human wave of refugees from the rest of the war-torn world, Congress turned down the heat under America's "melting pot" by approving measures in 1921, 1924, and 1929 that severely limited immigration.

One thing America continued to do after the war for much of the world was lend it money. But many of the borrowers couldn't pay it back.

Coupled with a combination of farm failures, bad loans, and an over-inflated stock market in the United States, the rest of the world's economic troubles finally caught up with Uncle Sam.

In late October 1929, the U.S. stock market crashed. Investors lost $15 billion in one week, and the country was plunged into the deepest and longest economic morass in its history.

Latin America:
It's Not That We Don't Appreciate
Your Shameless Interference, but . . .

By the beginning of the twentieth century, almost all of Central and South America had already shrugged off the yoke of European empires. But the omnipresent shadow of the United States was still, well, omnipresent.

U.S. interference was often designed to head off political instability that might threaten American business investments in the region. If autocratic in its methods, the United States was democratic in its targets. U.S. troops went into Colombia in 1902 to help put down a revolt, and then backed rebels in Panama against Colombia the following year, when the rebels seized control of the Panamanian Isthmus. Cuba, Nicaragua, and Haiti also played unwilling hosts to U.S. soldiers and Marines.

America's closest Latin American neighbor, Mexico, went through some big changes all by itself. In 1911, an odd coalition of intellectuals, peasants, Indians, and urban radicals coalesced to overthrow the dictatorship of Porfirio Diaz.

But the revolutionaries soon splintered, and the country was plunged into chaos. One of the revolution's leaders, Francisco Madero, was elected president in 1911, then overthrown and killed in 1913. He was followed by Victoriano Huerta, who resigned in 1914 and was replaced by Venustiano Carranza, who was killed in 1920 and re-

COME, MR. TALLY MAN, TALLY ME BANANA

Sometimes American businesses eliminated the middleman. In 1911, for example, Samuel Zemurray, the owner of the Cuyamel Fruit Company, didn't like the U.S.-backed government of Nicaragua. So he sponsored a revolution that put in charge someone who was more to his company's liking. In the mid-1920s, Zemurray tried unsuccessfully to get Honduras to invade Guatemala so he could gain control of a prime banana-growing area. In fact, Latin American countries run by dictators, often in cahoots with Yankee businessmen, became widely known as "banana republics," a phrase first coined by the American writer O. Henry in 1904. (And you thought it was just the name of a store!)

placed by Álvaro Obregón. Obregón made it through most of the 1920s as president, and actually accomplished a few things before he was killed in 1928.

As if the domestic side of being president of Mexico during this time weren't rough enough, there were also troubles on the foreign front. In 1915, U.S. troops entered Mexico, chasing the revolutionary leader Francisco "Pancho" Villa, who had raided into U.S. territory. The following year, it was revealed that German emissaries had tried to entice Mexico into an alliance against the United States. Although Mexico had rejected the overture, the incident wasn't exactly a relations booster between the two countries.

BANDITO TO HERO

The son of a horse trainer, Emiliano Zapata was born in 1879 in southern Mexico. After a brief—and involuntary—military stint, Zapata organized an army of five thousand peasants in 1910 and backed the revolutionary efforts of Francisco Madero against the dictator Porifirio Diaz. After Madero won, however, Zapata and Madero had a falling-out.

For most of the next decade, and under the motto "*Tierra y Libertad*" (Land and Liberty), Zapata battled for sweeping land reforms that would end the country's semi-feudal system. He also established commissions that were charged with distributing land equitably, and set up a bank to make loans to small farmers.

During most of the decade, Zapata's forces in the south were allied with the rebel forces of Francisco "Pancho" Villa in the north. In 1917, however, federal troops defeated Villa and increased the pressure on Zapata.

In April 1919, a federal officer ingratiated himself into Zapata's confidence and lured him into an ambush, where he was gunned down. He was buried in Morelos, in southern Mexico.

A snappy dresser with a trademark drooping moustache, Zapata was often vilified during his life as a "common bandit" by Mexico's upper crust and in the American press. It didn't faze him.

"It is better to die on your feet," he once remarked, "than to live on your knees."

While largely uninvolved in World War I, Latin American countries did not escape the social unrest that swept through much of the rest of the world. Intellectuals, laborers, and peasants pecked away at the aristocracy that controlled most of the region's land and resources.

This unrest sometimes ripened into revolution, and the winners were often military leaders who sided with the revolutionaries—until the dust had settled. The period saw military revolts, and subsequent dictatorships, in Ecuador, Peru, Brazil, and Chile.

Africa:
Ready to Break Up with Europe Already

European countries continued to milk their African colonies before, during, and after World War I, a continuation of what historians have called "the Scramble for Africa." And their colonies covered almost the entire continent.

By the time the war began in 1914, only Ethiopia, which had soundly defeated Italy's takeover bid in 1896, and Liberia, which had been established as a home for freed slaves from America in the mid-nineteenth century, enjoyed independence from European domination.

Naturally that sometimes led to fights between the conquering powers. In South Africa, Dutch settlers, who had developed their own language, called Afrikaans, and British settlers, who had come in droves after the discovery of diamonds in the region, squared off in a series of fights that sometimes involved the Zulu nation. The Brits won.

But the European powers didn't always fight over the continent. Sometimes they just traded territory. King Leopold II of Belgium was so anxious to have a piece of Africa that he used personal funds to buy a huge section of the Congo River Basin. His overseers were appallingly brutal in forcing the locals to work. Some estimates put the death toll from starvation, disease, and outright murder at as many as ten million in the early part of the century—as much as half the population. So excessive was his exploitation of the region that even the other rapacious nations were repulsed. In 1908, bowing to international pressure, he was forced to cede the colony to the Belgian government.

Leopold, however, was by no means alone when it came to bad behavior. When various groups of native Africans revolted, the reaction was almost always brutal reprisals. The Herero tribe of southwest Africa, for example, numbered eighty thousand in 1900. By 1910, dis-

PIXLEY STICKS

In 1912, an Oxford-educated South African named Pixley ka Isaka Seme called a meeting of black leaders in a shack in the town of Bloemfontein. The meeting eventually resulted in formation of the African National Congress, which would help overturn white supremacist governments on the continent.

ease, starvation, and fights with German troops had reduced their number to fifteen thousand.

After World War I, France and Britain split up German holdings in Africa. At the same time, resistance to the "Europeanization" of the continent began to take on more formal trappings. Native political groups were organized, such as the African National Congress in 1923.

But it would be well into the twentieth century before much of Africa would shake off the oppression of colonialism.

·············· **WHO'S UP, WHO'S DOWN** ··········

Ottoman Empire: DOWN AND OUT

For the better part of six centuries, the Ottoman Empire had been a major force in the world. It was an Islamic dynasty that in some ways was a successor to the Roman and Byzantine empires, and was the major Muslim threat to the rising influence of Western European countries. With its capital at the Turkish city of Istanbul (the former Constantinople), it dominated the Middle East, parts of Eastern Europe, and North Africa.

But by 1900, the empire was down on its luck. The rising tide of nationalism in the nineteenth century had led to revolts in parts of the empire. Western powers had nibbled away at others, and the Ottomans had been defeated in a war with the Russians in 1877–1878 and lost even more territory. Its economy was in such bad shape that the empire was dubbed "the sick man of Europe."

In 1909, liberal reform groups referred to as Young Turks teamed with military officers to depose the Ottoman sultan Abdul Hamid II, and a constitutional monarchy was declared. But as in so much of history, the new bosses turned out to be pretty much the same as the old bosses: despotic, autocratic, and brutal.

This was particularly true for the empire's estimated two million Armenian Christians. The Armenians had hoped to win equality after the 1909 revolt. What they got was a severe increase in persecution.

Meanwhile, the empire continued to crumble. Montenegro declared itself independent in 1910. Italy took Libya in 1911, and Serbia, Bulgaria, and Greece broke free as independent states in 1912.

When World War I broke out, the empire sided with Germany and Austria-Hungary. Turkish rulers, hoping the war would serve as a distraction, ordered the massacre or forced deportation of hundreds of thousands of Armenians in the first large-scale genocide of the century.

After the war, Britain and France divvied up most of the Ottoman territories and Allied forces occupied Istanbul. But in 1919, a career army office and war hero named Mustafa Kemal began efforts to drive out the Allied forces and set up a new government. In 1922, the Ottoman Empire's last sultan, Mehmed Vahiduddin, was dethroned, and the following year the Republic of Turkey came into being.

ATTA TURK!

Kemal, who assumed dictatorial powers, made vast changes. He greatly secularized the government, introduced a new alphabet with Latin, rather than Arabic, characters, and set up a national railway system. In 1934, the national parliament gave him the name Atatürk, or "Father of the Turks." He died in 1938.

American Bootleggers: **UP**

Americans are an opportunistic lot. So when the Eighteenth Amendment to the U.S. Constitution went into effect in January 1920, banning the sale of alcoholic beverages, it wasn't all that surprising that an illicit liquor industry would spring up to replace the legal one.

What might have been surprising were the scope of the bootleg business and the spectacular failure of Prohibition. The U.S. government apparently thought it would be fairly easy to enforce, hiring only 1,500 special agents to police a nation of 106 million liquor-loving citizens. The feds had counted on help from local law enforcement, but in many areas the local cops were either apathetic—or sympathetic, to the bootleggers: Midwest bootlegger George Remus once boasted he had 2,000 law enforcement officers on his payroll.

Moreover, the courts only diffidently prosecuted those who were arrested. In New York City, for example, there were 514 arrests for bootlegging in 1926 and 1927. Only 5 of those arrested were held for trial.

The most notable booze organization was the operation run out of Chicago by the gangster Al Capone, who was widely seen as the most powerful man in the country's second-largest city. The business methods of Capone and other bootleggers were often brutal: bombings in Chicago increased from 51 in 1920 to 116 in 1928. Their product was often dangerous: More than 50,000 deaths from alcohol poisoning were reported nationwide during the 1920s. And arrests for driving drunk and public drunkenness soared: in Philadelphia, alcohol-related arrests grew from 23,740 in 1919 to 58,517 in 1925.

But bootlegging was extraordinarily lucrative. Capone's Chicago mob was reported to have taken in $60 million a year, and it's estimated that the total amount of illegal booze business during the era reached $2 billion.

Actually, there is some statistical evidence that Prohibition did reduce the per capita consumption of alcohol. But the attendant social problems—not to mention the loss of taxes on alcohol the government no longer collected—eventually soured reformers who had originally pushed for it. The law was repealed in late 1933.

Buggies: DOWN

Although automobiles were being manufactured as early as the late 1880s in Europe and the United States, they were mostly considered either as novelties or nuisances at the start of the twentieth century. Cars were expensive, noisy, smelly, and unreliable, and their owners were often greeted by derisive calls of "get a horse," in various languages.

But as the technology of components—such as brakes—improved, and as the more dependable gasoline-powered internal combustion engine beat out electric and steam-powered motors, the public's interest was piqued.

European companies tended to make each car as a stand-alone effort, and emphasized speed. Italy produced a model in 1908 that could reach 56 miles per hour, and the French made a car in the 1920s that topped out at 130 mph.

After experimenting with making fairly expensive custom cars, however, a Detroit-born inventor named Henry Ford decided in 1903 to concentrate on cars that the average working guy could afford. In 1913, Ford's company adopted a moving assembly line that could turn out a whopping one thousand cars a day. Mass production meant that prices of Ford's Model T dropped from $950 in 1908 to less than $300 by 1920.

Of course at that price, there weren't a lot of options. "Give them any color they want," Ford was once quoted as saying, "as long as it's black."

Almost as important long-term was Ford's institution of a better wage system for his workers, starting with a five-dollar-a-day rate in 1914. The higher wages meant a more stable workforce for Ford—and also that workers could afford to buy the cars they were building.

By the 1920s, the U.S. economy was humming along enough to provide a market for luxury cars, while the expanding view that a car was a necessity rather than a luxury pushed many European manufacturers into producing smaller and more affordable models.

The automobile had a galvanizing effect on many aspects of life. It spurred the growth of ancillary industries, from tires to road building. It also made it easier for people to routinely travel longer distances, to spread out in terms of where they lived, and to close the gap between rural and urban areas.

While the number of cars grew exponentially, however, the number of automakers shrank as the century progressed. In the early 1900s, there were an estimated two thousand U.S. companies making cars. By 1929, the number had dropped to forty-four.

Suffrage: UP

Although women had fought for equal voting rights for centuries, the movement really took hold in the early twentieth century. The arguments for women being given the right to vote ranged from the philosophical (all human beings should have equal rights) to the chauvinistic (as the gentler sex, women would bring a "civilizing" tone to elections).

Whatever the reasons, it caught on. In 1897, women won the vote in New Zealand, followed by their sisters in Australia (1902), Finland (1906), and Norway (1913). By 1930, Canada, Soviet Russia, Germany, Austria, Poland, the United States, Hungary, Great Britain, Ecuador, and South Africa had extended the franchise to women.

As women gained the right to vote, they also began to gain the right to seek votes. In 1907, women in Norway were permitted to stand for election. In 1917, a Montana woman named Jeannette Rankin became the first female elected to the U.S. Congress.

And in 1929, the Privy Council (the United Kingdom's highest appeals court) overruled the Supreme Court of Canada and declared that women were "persons," and thus eligible to run for the Canadian Senate. (Which had the additional benefit of establishing that, legally speaking, senators were people too.)

Buttered Popcorn Consumption: UP

Technological advances in making pictures move were occurring in several countries in the decade before the twentieth century. In France, Louis and Auguste Lumière were developing a combination movie camera and projector; in Germany, Emil and Max Skladanowsky created a film projection device; in England, Birt Acres and Robert Paul made strides in the field, and in America, Thomas Edison and William K. Dickson came up with a motor-driven camera and a method of showing the films it took.

But things really took off after the turn of the century:

1902 French filmmaker Georges Méliès produces a 14-minute, 30-scene science fiction film called *A Trip to the Moon*, with pioneering special effects.

1903 American filmmaker Edwin S. Porter makes *The*

Great Train Robbery, the first "blockbuster" movie. It's a Western, filmed in New Jersey.

1905   The first small theater converted to view films opens in Pittsburgh. Admission price is a nickel, so the place is called a "nickelodeon."

1906   Australian filmmaker Charles Tait releases a biopic of Aussie outlaw Ned Kelly, called *The Story of the Kelly Gang.* It's the first full-length feature film, with a running time between 60 and 70 minutes.

1911   *Motion Picture Story Magazine,* the first movie fan mag, begins publication.

1913   A company that will become known as Universal Pictures makes *Traffic in Souls,* the first film to boldly use steamy sex in its ads. The $5,700 film makes $450,000.

WHO KILLED OSWALD RABBIT?

One of the world's most beloved animated characters debuted in 1928, after his creator lost a legal fight with his former partners for the rights to a cartoon rabbit named Oswald. Bereft of the rabbit, Walt Disney tied his future to a mouse named Mickey.

1918   Charlie Chaplin signs the industry's first million-dollar contract, with First National Pictures.

1920   The population of Hollywood, California, reaches 35,000, a hefty increase from the 5,000 of a decade earlier. Almost 75 percent of U.S. films are now made in Hollywood.

1926   *Don Juan,* the first feature-length film accompanied by synchronized sound effects and musical soundtrack (but no dialogue) debuts.

1927   *The Jazz Singer* is released. It features 350 spoken words, six songs, and Al Jolson.

Wait a minute, wait a minute, you ain't heard nothing yet!
—First line spoken in *The Jazz Singer,* the first feature-length "talking picture," 1927

1927 Los Angeles movie house owner Sid Grauman comes up with the idea of having movie stars put their handprints and footprints in wet cement outside his theater.

A Sub Is Not Always a Sandwich

Although the first military submarine debuted in 1775 (an American-made one-man sub tried and failed to sink a British warship), most navies around the world didn't consider them big deals as weapons at the start of World War I.

The exception was the German navy, which was heavily outmatched when it came to surface ships. So the Germans countered with the U-boat, whose name was derived from the German word *Unterseeboot*, or "undersea boat." The standard sub was slightly more than two hundred feet long and displaced about one hundred tons. But as the war progressed, the Germans developed a boat close to three hundred feet long, with bigger deck guns and more torpedo capacity.

SINK THIS!

Among the Brits' countermeasures against the U-boats were the "Q-ships." These were decoy vessels, such as fishing boats, armed with concealed weapons and designed to engage U-boats when they surfaced and moved in close to sink what looked like an easy target.

The Germans' first U-boat efforts were disastrous—for the Germans. One boat hit a mine, another was rammed and sank, and a third sank for no apparent reason. But as the boat's technology improved, it had better hunting. U-boats generally cruised on the surface using diesel engines, then submerged during attacks, using electric power.

Once the war's pace sputtered to a crawl a few months after it began, both the Allies and the Central Powers began to consider harsher measures. The British navy clamped an effective blockade on German ports. The Germans countered with U-boat attacks on non-military targets. In 1917, the Germans adopted a policy of "unrestricted warfare," which meant that any ship in certain areas of the high seas was considered fair game.

The policy may have made sense militarily, but not politically. The bad feeling it caused among Americans was a significant factor in the United States' entry into the war.

Plastic . . . Fantastic!

What do elephants, billiards, and a Belgian scientist looking for a better way to insulate wire have in common? Right, plastic.

In the 1860s, people were looking for an inexpensive substitute for ivory to make billiard balls, since most ivory came from elephants, and it was a nuisance to have to go shoot an elephant just to be able to play pool. One of the first attempts, by an American printer named John Wesley Hyatt, was a substance that used cellulose and camphor. Hyatt called it "celluloid."

It turned out that celluloid wasn't great for making billiard balls because the balls tended to shatter. It was also highly flammable. But celluloid proved to be very useful for a host of other things, such as shirt collars that could be easily cleaned, corset stays that wouldn't rust, and motion picture film.

In 1909, while looking for a synthetic substitute for shellac to insulate wires in electric motors and generators, a Belgian-born scientist named Leo Baekeland developed the first true plastic—that is, a substance made entirely from synthetic ingredients.

He somewhat immodestly called it Bakelite: a cheap, strong, and moldable substance that quickly

> ### OFF HER CHEST
>
> In 1913, a New York society matron named Mary Phelps Jacobs put together two handkerchiefs and some ribbons and cords, and used it to keep from revealing too much of herself under a sheer evening gown. Other women liked the invention so much that Phelps patented the device the following year—and gave the world the modern bra.

became used in thousands of ways, from toys to weapons—and also billiard balls, which made it very popular with elephants.

Firebirds, Rites—and Riots

Like most nine-year-olds taking piano lessons and forced to practice their scales, Igor Stravinsky sometimes got bored. Unlike most nine-year-olds, he amused himself by noodling out his own scales.

Russian born and the son of an opera singer, Stravinsky earned a law degree and then began focusing seriously on a music career. He studied under the master composer Nikolai Rimsky-Korsakov, and got his big break in 1910, at the age of twenty-eight, when the director of the world-famous Ballets Russes commissioned him to compose a piece for the ballet troupe's performance at the Paris Opera.

The result was *The Firebird*, a suite written for a very large orchestra that included four times as many woodwinds as customary and three harps. It was a huge success, and Stravinsky followed it with a piece called *Petrushka*. Then, in 1913, Stravinsky composed the third of what would be a trilogy of pieces for the ballet that were based on Russian folk themes.

On May 29, 1913, *The Rite of Spring* opened at the Theatre des Champs-Elysees, and caused a riot—literally. Some audience members were a little disquieted by the fact that the piece ended with the depiction of a human sacrifice. Others were put off by its primitive rhythms, dissonance, or the fact that it opened with just about the highest notes it's possible to play on a bassoon.

Whatever the cause, some patrons stormed out, others got into fistfights, and others booed and hissed so loudly the performers missed their cues. Police were called in to settle things down.

Critics initially ripped the piece for wildly diverging from the expected. But *The Rite of Spring* eventually came to be recognized as the birth of modernism in music.

"There is not a composer who lived during his time or is alive today who was not touched, and sometimes transformed, by his work," wrote composer-performer Philip Glass, in a 1998 *Time* magazine piece that named Stravinsky one of the twenty greatest artists of the twentieth century.

Monet! (That's What I Want)

Oscar-Claude Monet set out to make an impression with his art—and succeeded. The son of a prosperous grocer, Monet found initial success as an artist at the age of fifteen, when he sold a series of well-crafted caricatures.

After two years in the military, Monet and several contemporaries spent the 1860s developing a style of painting that didn't attempt to faithfully reproduce a scene, but instead tried to record a more visceral and less cerebral image.

"I want the unobtainable," Monet said. "Other artists paint a bridge, a house a boat, and that is the end . . . I want to paint the air which surrounds the bridge, the house, the boat . . ."

Monet often chose simple subjects, such as haystacks or buildings, and then painted the same scene at different hours or different seasons to capture the effects of varying light on colors and shapes.

The Impressionist style (so dubbed by a French journalist after viewing a Monet painting named *Impression: Sunrise*) was not well received by critics or the art-buying public. During the 1870s, Monet moved around a good deal, sometimes destroying his own work rather than see it seized by creditors.

In the 1880s, however, Monet's paintings began to sell, particularly to American collectors. By the end of the decade, he was financially secure enough to settle into a farmhouse in the rural hamlet of Giverny, establish an elaborate water-lily garden, and create some of his most famous work.

Despite being almost completely blind at the end of his life because of cataracts, he continued to paint until his death in 1926 from lung cancer, at the age of eighty-six. His grave is now a French national landmark.

Air Mail

In 1919, a New York hotel owner named Raymond Orteig offered a $25,000 prize for the first person or persons to fly from New York to Paris. Several tried, and failed.

But a twenty-five-year-old flying mailman named Charles Lindbergh figured he could pull it off if he could get the right plane. The son of a former Minnesota congressman, Lindbergh dropped out of college to indulge his passion for flying. In 1923, he bought a World War I plane, took some lessons, and got a job with the U.S. Post Office, flying a mail route between Chicago and St. Louis.

In 1927, Lindbergh won financial backing from a group of St. Louis businessmen. Then he went to San Diego, where a small firm named Ryan Aeronautical put together a specially designed craft, under Lindbergh's supervision.

It was, in the words of one observer, "a two-ton flying gas tank." There was no radio, no parachute, no brakes, and no front windshield. To test it, Lindbergh flew the plane, dubbed *Spirit of St. Louis,* from San Diego to New York.

On May 20, he took off from New York, with quiet confidence, and five sandwiches. "If I get to Paris, I won't need any more," he told reporters who questioned his lack of provisions. "And if I don't, I won't need any more either."

The 3,600-mile trip took Lindbergh 33.5 hours. He sometimes flew less than 100 feet above the waves. Lanky, handsome, and affably laconic, "Lucky Lindy" captured the fancy of virtually the entire world, and was arguably its most famous personage after his feat. He also showed he was fairly prudent: on the return trip to New York, he hitched a ride on a U.S. Navy cruiser.

> *Which way to Ireland?*
> —Aviator Charles Lindbergh to a boat of startled fishermen off the Irish coast, on his solo transatlantic flight, May 20, 1927

Burning Down Tokyo

Japan's capital had suffered earthquakes before, even bigger ones in terms of magnitude. But very few were as devastating. The Great Kanto Quake (named after the region that surrounds Tokyo) struck a little before noon on September 2, 1923. It measured 8.3 on the quake scale in use in Japan at the time; estimated at 7.4 on the Richter scale.

The quake itself, which lasted more than four minutes, did enormous damage, as did the landslides it triggered. But the fires it sparked did far more. Since it was lunchtime, thousands of charcoal and coal cooking stoves had been lit, along with gas ovens. The results were scores of small fires that quickly joined into major conflagrations. In the most horrible incident, more than thirty thousand people who gathered in or near a supposed shelter were suffocated or incinerated in a firestorm.

More than eighty-eight major blazes broke out in the city of Yokohama, about seventeen miles south of Tokyo. Burst water mains hampered fighting the fires, and people who gathered on ships in Tokyo Bay had to quickly put to sea when oil on the water began to burn.

The death toll has been put at more than 130,000, with as many as 50,000 injured and more than 700,000 residences destroyed.

In the aftermath of the quake and fires, rumors spread that foreigners were invading the area. Vigilante mobs formed and began beating or killing non-Japanese, particularly Koreans. In an effort to stop the violence, the Japanese army opened a shelter in which Koreans could seek protection. On September 8, the city was put under martial law.

If there was a bright side to the disaster, it was the quick and generous response by other countries to provide aid, particularly Great Britain and the United States.

The Mummy's Curse

The Egyptian expedition's financial angel dies suddenly. At the time of his passing, his dog suddenly dies—thousands of miles away. The lights in the city of Cairo go out. A cobra eats a canary.

Sounds like a curse.

At least that's what much of the world's media decided in April 1923, after a British earl named George Herbert, Lord Carnarvon, died in Cairo.

Carnarvon had financed the explorations of American archeologist Howard Carter, which resulted in the fabulous discovery of the tomb of Tutankhamen in November 1922. Carnarvon had been one of the first to enter the tomb.

The official cause of his death was listed as pneumonia, brought on by an infection caused by a mosquito bite. But imaginative writers put together a few facts, a few rumors, and a little speculation, and came up with another cause: a three-thousand-year-old curse:

- A cobra ate Carter's pet canary the day the tomb was opened.
- There was an inscription above the tomb entrance that vaguely resembled a warning.
- The power in Cairo may or may not have gone out at the time of Carnarvon's death.
- His dog may or may not have died in England about the same time.

Somber statements by "experts" such as Sir Arthur Conan Doyle, the creator of Sherlock Holmes and a leading exponent of spiritualism, fueled the media frenzy.

"The pharaohs were very anxious to guard the tombs of their kings," Conan Doyle explained the day after Carnarvon died. "There is reason to believe they placed 'elementals' there and such may have caused his death."

The curse story grew over the years, as various members of the expedition died, sometimes in accidents or as a result of suicide or mysterious illness.

Studies, however, have shown that there was no statistically significant difference between the life span of the two-dozen Westerners at the tomb's opening and that of the general population.

That didn't stop a San Francisco policeman from citing the curse as the cause of a mild stroke he suffered in 1982 while guarding a display of Tut artifacts.

A judge dismissed the cop's disability claim.

Curses.

The Kansas Flu

Popular history recalls it as the Spanish flu epidemic. But the evidence is that it more likely started at U.S. Army camps in Kansas in the spring of 1918 than in Spain. And it was really a pandemic, because it wasn't localized, but occurred all over the world.

Did it ever. The estimates are that at least twenty-five million people—and maybe as many as fifty million—were killed during the three main waves of the flu. Virtually every area of the world was hit, with as many as one third of the planet's human population being infected. India lost more than twelve million people. In the United States, more than half a million died. Entire villages from Alaska to the Amazon were wiped out.

The flu hit in three stages: the spring of 1918, the summer of 1918, and the winter of 1918–1919. By the summer of 1919, it had all but disappeared, although there were minor outbreaks during the 1920s.

It was often a swift death: victims might be dead within twenty-four hours of being stricken, their lungs wracked by violent hemorrhaging. One of the more unusual things about this flu, aside from its stunning virulence, was that its victims were often people in the prime of life instead of the very young or very old that influenza usually targets.

Although its origins are still something of a mystery, the pandemic is believed to have started at Camp Funston and Camp Riley, Kansas. It may have been passed on to humans from birds, and almost certainly was hastened in its trip around the world by troop movements during World War I.

And the "Spanish" moniker it acquired? Various theories ascribe it to the fact that since Spain was neutral during the war, its media were freer to report about the flu; that among its early victims were members of the Spanish royal family, and that it killed a lot of Spaniards in a very big hurry in May 1918.

· · · · · · · · · · · · · · · · · · · **BY THE NUMBERS** · · · · · · · · · · · · · · · ·

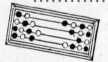

0 number of passenger pigeons left in the world in 1915. The last member of a species that once numbered in the tens of millions died at the Cincinnati Zoo in 1914

1 number of pounds of bread rationed daily to Russian soldiers by late 1916

4:19:52 record time, in days, hours, and minutes, it took the British liner *Lusitania* to cross the Atlantic in 1907

6 number of Western Front battles during World War I in which at least 250,000 people were killed

11 number of revolutionary movements against the Manchu Dynasty in China between 1895 and 1911

12 size, in horsepower, of motorcycle engine that powered the Wright Brothers' flying machine at Kitty Hawk

42	number of countries that were charter members of League of Nations in 1920
56	combined number of battleships in German and Austro-Hungarian fleets, 1914
74	number of battleships in British fleet, 1914
90	percentage of Austro-Hungarian military personnel killed or disabled in the war
340	weight, in pounds, of U.S. president William Howard Taft in 1912
728	number of minutes it took to build a Model T Ford in 1913
93	number of minutes it took to build a Model T Ford in 1915
452	U.S. stock market industrial index in September 1929
58	U.S. stock market industrial index in July 1932
3,000	number of people killed in earthquake and fire in San Francisco in 1906
10,000	number of people killed by typhoon in Tahiti in 1906
250,000	estimated number of people killed by bubonic plague in India in 1901
48,909	number of U.S. soldiers killed in action during 1917 and 1918
55,985	number of Americans killed in motor vehicle accidents during the same period
8,500,000	number of soldiers killed in World War I
21,000,000	number of soldiers gassed, wounded, or shell-shocked in World War I
20,000,000	number of telephones in the United States in 1929, twice as many as the rest of the world combined
186,000,000,000	estimated cost, in U.S. dollars, of World War I

11

TO THE BRINK OF
THE ABYSS

(1931–1962)

The collapse of the U.S. economy in late 1929 greatly exacerbated the rest of the planet's financial woes. By 1932, the world's economic output had dropped 40 percent, and it would take five more years for the global economy to reach 1929 levels again.

Human nature being what it is, people looked around for someone to blame. In the Soviet Union, it was the capitalists of the West. In the United States, it was the Republicans. In China, it was the Communists. In Germany—most ominously—it was the Jews. The blame game combined with the post–World War I decline of monarchies to open the door for waves of nationalism. Countries increasingly hungered for their own identity, a hunger often whetted by individuals' hunger for power: former schoolteacher Benito Mussolini in Italy; military officer Francisco Franco in Spain; military officer Hideki Tojo in Japan; failed painter Adolf Hitler in Germany; and seminary student turned bank robber Joseph Stalin in the Soviet Union.

So, you combine a crippled world economy, a hunger for national identity, and a collection of monsters masquerading as men, and what you ultimately get is a very big war.

The group that would become known as the Axis Powers—Germany, Italy, and Japan—warmed up for war with fighting in Manchuria, China, Ethiopia, and Spain. In 1939, after rolling over Austria and Czechoslovakia, Germany finally ignited the firestorm by invading Poland.

Allied against the Axis were, well, the Allies. Led by Britain, the United States, and the Soviet Union, the allied forces turned the tide of war by the end of 1943. Before the war's end in 1945, however, the world would endure two of history's worst nightmares: the use of nuclear weapons, and the Holocaust.

After the war, most of Eastern Europe fell under an "iron curtain" of Soviet control. In Asia, meanwhile, Communists under Mao Zedong finally won their twenty-five-year struggle with the Nationalist government and took control of the world's most populous nation in 1949.

Western powers dug in to confront the spread of communism. In 1948, the USSR blockaded land routes into the city of Berlin and eventually built a wall cutting the city in half. One side was controlled by the Communist government of East Germany and the other by West Germany.

A much more violent confrontation occurred on the Korean Peninsula. Korea had been partitioned after the war into two countries, with a Soviet-backed Communist state in the North and a U.S.-backed capitalist state in the South. After three years of intense fighting, the two sides agreed in 1953 to an armistice, redrawing the border almost exactly where it had been when the fighting started.

By the end of the 1950s, the world had divided itself politically into three basic groups: Communist, capitalist, and non-aligned nations, labeled the third world. But not every conflict revolved around Communist versus anticommunist.

India, the world's second most populous nation, finally won its independence from the British Empire in 1947 after decades of often violent civil unrest. In the Middle East, the creation of the Jewish state of Israel triggered a war with neighboring Islamic countries and kicked off what proved to be a more-or-less continual conflict in the region.

To be fair to the species, mankind did make some pretty impressive scientific and medical strides during the period. There was the invention of the transistor and the first electronic computer, the discovery of vaccines for the dreaded childhood disease of polio, the refining of the use of antibiotics to fight infections, the development of synthetic fibers such as nylon, the launching of the first manmade earth-orbiting satellites—and the blossoming of television.

But there was a mushroom-shaped shadow constantly hanging over the planet. By 1949, thanks in large part to successfully spying on U.S. programs, the Soviet Union had its own nuclear weapons. Great Britain had them by 1952, France by 1960, and China by 1964.

The mushroom shadow was perhaps at its darkest in the fall of 1962, when U.S. spy planes discovered that Soviet missiles were being deployed in the Communist island nation of Cuba. For the better part of two weeks, the world held its breath, poised on what seemed to be the brink of nuclear war. Fortunately, both sides kept their cool. The Soviet missiles were removed from Cuba, the U.S. missiles from Turkey.

Life went somewhat nervously on.

··················· **WHAT HAPPENED WHEN** ··············

Sept. 23, 1932	The kingdom of Saudi Arabia is founded.
Jan. 30, 1933	Adolf Hitler begins 12-year span as dictator of Germany.
Mar. 4, 1933	Franklin D. Roosevelt begins 12-year span as U.S. president.
Oct. 16, 1934	Chinese Communist forces begin what will be a year-long, 6,000-mile retreat from Nationalist forces.
Sept. 15, 1935	Germany adopts the Nuremberg Laws, which strip German Jews of most of their legal and human rights.
Nov. 11, 1935	The first official trans-Pacific airmail flight leaves San Francisco. It arrives in Manila a week later.
Sept. 1, 1939	World War II begins as Germany attacks Poland.
June 4, 1940	The last of 340,000 French and British troops are evacuated from the French beaches of Dunkirk.
Apr. 1, 1940	The world's first electron microscope is demonstrated at the RCA laboratories in Camden, New Jersey.
June 22, 1941	German troops invade the Soviet Union, ending the two nations' alliance of convenience.
June 6, 1944	D-Day: More than 170,000 Allied troops land on beaches in France's Normandy province.

Apr. 12, 1945	President Roosevelt dies of a cerebral hemorrhage.
Apr. 30, 1945	Adolf Hitler commits suicide as Soviet troops converge on Berlin.
May 8, 1945	World War II ends in Europe.
Aug. 10, 1945	Japanese leaders sue for peace. U.S. president Harry Truman declares victory on August 14.
Jan. 10, 1946	The United Nations opens its first General Assembly session, in London.
Aug. 29, 1949	The Soviet Union successfully detonates an atomic bomb at a test site in Kazakhstan.
Oct. 1, 1949	The People's Republic of China is proclaimed.
Oct. 2, 1952	Britain joins the United States and the Soviet Union as a nuclear power.
Mar. 6, 1957	Ghana, formerly called the Gold Coast, becomes the first sub-Saharan African state to win independence.
Oct. 4, 1957	The Soviet Union launches Sputnik I, the world's first man-made earth-orbiting satellite.
Jan. 1, 1959	Cuban dictator Fulgencio Batista flees the island and is replaced by rebel leader Fidel Castro after a two-year civil war.
Feb. 13, 1960	France explodes an atomic bomb at a test site in the Sahara Desert.
Apr. 17, 1961	Cuban exiles trained by the CIA in Florida invade the Caribbean island.

- *The Next One* -

The 50-cent Version

Germany started taking over parts of Europe; Japan started taking over parts of Asia. France and Great Britain objected, militarily, and formed the Allied Powers. Italy lined up with Germany and Japan to form the Axis Powers. The Soviet Union allied itself with Germany, until it was double-crossed, then it switched to the Allies. Japan goofed big-time by attacking the United States, which joined the Allies. The Axis Powers eventually ran out of gas—and other things. Germany and Italy surrendered. The U.S. dropped two atomic bombs on Japan, and it surrendered. World War II was over. The Cold War started almost immediately.

The $9.99 Version

The first dress rehearsal for World War II took place in Ethiopia in 1935, when Italian forces invaded what was one of the very few independent African states. In 1936, a rebellion in Spain led to a three-year civil war that was eventually won by forces under dictator-in-waiting Francisco Franco. Franco's forces were backed by military support from Germany and Italy.

As in Ethiopia, the Spanish conflict emboldened the most rapacious of the nationalist leaders, Germany's Adolf Hitler. Starting in 1936, Germany began a series of moves on other people's territory: a demilitarized area between France and Germany called the Rhineland, followed by Austria, then Czechoslovakia. All the while, European powers Great Britain and France dithered and hesitated, while the United States clung to the hope that it could stay out of another European war, as it had not been able to do in 1917.

In Asia, Japan was every bit as aggressive as Germany. In 1931, the Japanese invaded the Chinese province of Manchuria, and in 1937 began the conquest of large sections of China. Three years later, Japan expanded its hostile takeover bids into French Indochina (now Vietnam).

In the fall of 1939, Hitler moved into Poland, which finally proved a country too far for France and Britain, who declared war on Germany.

> *Take a good look around Warsaw. This is how I can deal with any European city.*
> —Adolf Hitler on a tour of the conquered Polish capital with foreign journalists, October 5, 1939

After six months of diplomatic posturing, Germany invaded France in May 1940, and World War II was on in earnest.

The final major players entered the fray in 1941, when Germany launched a surprise attack on its erstwhile ally, the Soviet Union, and Japan tried to destroy the U.S. Pacific fleet by bombing the naval base at Pearl Harbor, Hawaii.

While the Axis Powers—Italy, Germany and Japan—initially had the best of things, the tide began to turn in 1943 in favor of the Allies, led by the United States, Britain, and the Soviet Union. The Germans were driven out of North Africa and suffered tremendous losses in the Soviet Union after invading that country. In the Pacific, U.S. aircraft carriers that had escaped destruction at Pearl Harbor led decisive victories over the Japanese at the battles of the Coral Sea and Midway Island.

> *Nuts.*
> —U.S. Gen. Anthony McAuliffe, responding to German demands that he surrender his 101st Airborne Division during the Battle of the Bulge at Bastogne, France, on December 24, 1944. The 101st held until relieved.

By mid-1944, Allied forces had established a foothold in France, and by mid-1945, Germany and Italy were defeated. Japan, which had been steadily retreating since the beginning of 1943, continued to fight. But a weapon developed in America—in large part by scientists who had fled the totalitarian regimes in Europe—would take the fight out of the Japanese.

On August 6, 1945, a U.S. atomic bomb obliterated the city of Hiroshima, killing seventy thousand people. Three days later, the city of Nagasaki met a similar fate. Five days after that, Japan unconditionally surrendered, making it formal on September 2. World War II was over.

The cost of the war was literally incalculable. Estimates of the total number of military personnel and civilians killed have ranged as high as seventy million. More than 20 percent of the entire prewar

THE NUCLEAR RACQUET

On December 2, 1942, on a racquet court under a football stadium at the University of Chicago, scientists fired up the world's first artificial nuclear reactor—a harbinger to building atomic weapons—for thirty-three minutes. The lead scientist, Enrico Fermi, had fled Italy because his wife was Jewish.

population of Poland, and 10 percent of the prewar populations of Yugoslavia and the Soviet Union died. Nearly ninety thousand Soviet cities and villages were destroyed.

Many of the civilians killed were the "incidental" victims of the various countries' brutally efficient war machines. But millions were the victims of deliberate and horrific murder. The most atrocious acts were committed by Hitler's Nazis, whose "Final Solution" saw the systematic extermination of six million Jews and millions of other "undesirables," who ranged from the disabled and infirm to Gypsies and Jehovah's Witnesses.

· · · · · · · · · · · · · · · · **SPINNING THE GLOBE** · · · · · · · · · · · ·

Africa:
One Step Forward, Two Steps Back

While the fervor for nationalism continued to ferment on the African continent after the end of World War I, there was little significant progress toward independence during the 1920s and 1930s. In fact, during these decades the most significant movement along these lines was backward.

In October 1935, Italy used a border dispute between its Italian Somaliland colony and Ethiopia as an excuse to invade. Ethiopia was one of the few African nations not then under a European country's thumb, and had rebuffed an Italian conquest attempt in the 1890s.

The war pitted Italian fighter planes and poison gas against Ethiopian warriors armed with spears. Predictably, the fight was over in eight months. Italian dictator Benito Mussolini declared the conquest the beginning of what would be a new Roman Empire. It turned out to be a short-lived empire. British troops pushed the Italians out of Ethiopia in 1941.

Most of the rest of the fighting in Africa during the war occurred in the northern part of the continent. The fighting seesawed: The British pounded the Italians; the Germans beat up the British; and the British and United States eventually smashed the Germans. By May 1943, the war was effectively over in Africa.

After the war's end, Africans' unrest began to grow in earnest. In 1946, an uprising broke out in Algeria against French rule. In 1952, the Mau Mau Rebellion in Kenya triggered a four-year fight between native Kenyans and the British.

> *When the reed buck horn is blown, if I leave a European farm*
> *before killing the European owner, may this oath kill me.*
> —From the oath taken by members of the Mau Mau secret society

In 1956, the Israeli, British, and French forces invaded Egypt after the Egyptians, armed by the Soviet Union, decided to nationalize the Suez Canal. Under intense political pressure, the three countries eventually withdrew, and the canal, which links the Red and Mediterranean seas, fell under the supervision of the first-ever United Nations peacekeeping force.

The Suez mess greatly weakened the international standing of Britain and France, and encouraged nationalism movements in other parts of Africa. Most European countries began to relinquish most of their holdings on the continent. In 1960 alone, France, Italy, Great Britain, and Belgium granted independence to sixteen African colonies. In 1962, after eight years of strife, France let go of Algeria.

There were holdouts. Portugal did not give up its colonies in Angola, Guinea-Bissau, or Mozambique until the mid-1970s, and the British did not leave Rhodesia (now Zimbabwe) until 1980. But for the most part, Africa's colonial days were over by the beginning of the 1960s.

Japan:
On the Attack!

The economic woes of the late 1920s and early 1930s gave greater voice to the nationalist movement in Japan, which wanted to break away from decades of emulating Western ways. After wresting power from pro-West politicians and businessmen (many of whom were killed after being wrested), nationalist radicals gave way to military leaders who rapidly built a formidable war machine.

Japan's first target was neighboring China. The Chinese province of Manchuria was taken in 1931, and a full-scale war was launched in 1937. Angered by a U.S. decision in mid-1941 to stop selling Japan oil and scrap metal, Japanese leaders attempted in December to cripple the U.S. Navy and/or discourage the Americans from getting involved in a Pacific war by attacking the U.S. base at Pearl Harbor. Both goals fell short, however, and by the end of 1942, Japan was in retreat.

After the war, the United States initially wanted to keep Japan weak both militarily and industrially. The Korean War and the threat of a spread of communism changed America's mind, however, and Japan was encouraged to rebuild its economy. Japanese labor and management cooperated with each other to an extent unknown in

BURNING DOWN TOKYO (AGAIN)

Although the nuclear bombings of Hiroshima and Nagasaki are more remembered by the world, the firebombing of Tokyo on March 9–10, 1945, has to rank as one of the most horrific experiences any city has ever suffered.

Taking off from the Marianas Islands, 334 U.S. B-29 Superfortress bombers—stripped of guns and some of their armor to make room for Napalm and more than 1,500 tons of incendiary bombs—swept over the Japanese capital in the darkness at altitudes between 4,000 and 9,000 feet.

Two hours later, Tokyo was afire. The brisk winds whipped the flames from building to building, and the heat was so intense that steel beams melted. People who hurled themselves into the city's canals to escape the fire were boiled, or asphyxiated by the smoke.

More than fifteen square miles of the city were destroyed, and estimates of the death toll ranged from eighty thousand to two hundred thousand, more than were killed by either of the two atomic bombs. After the bombing of Tokyo, similar sorties were conducted by U.S. bombers against three other Japanese cities. Fewer than forty U.S. planes were lost in all the raids combined.

---

the West, and the country's economic output grew at a handsome 9.5 percent annual average during the 1950s.

China:
Look Before You Leap

In China, the Nationalist government of Chiang Kai-Shek had broken in the mid-1920s with its former allies, the Communists. Under their charismatic leader Mao Zedong, the Communists embarked on a six-thousand-mile exodus to the northern province of Shensi. There they waited.

After an alliance of convenience during the war, Mao's forces resumed their fight with the Nationalist government, which was nominally a republic but in reality a dictatorship. The Communist forces were swelled by millions of disaffected peasants, and by 1949, the Communists had driven Chiang Kai-Shek's forces out of mainland China and onto the island of Taiwan, about one hundred miles off the coast.

Mao quickly began looking to export the new government's influence to neighbors. China took over Tibet in 1950, backed North Korea in its war against South Korea, and supplied Communist rebels in French Indochina.

Mao had less luck at home, however. In 1958, the Chinese government launched what it called the "Great Leap Forward." This consisted of redistributing farmland, "collectivizing" villages, and redirecting the workforce into industry. The effort turned into a great flop backward. So much effort was put into the industrial push that not enough people were growing food. The result was a famine that killed an estimated thirty million people. The Great Leap was called off in 1961, and Mao was shunted aside for several years from the Chinese leadership.

French Indochina (aka Vietnam-to-Be):
Carping with Diem

In what was then called French Indochina, the aforementioned French returned after the Japanese departed. It wasn't their best idea. Vietnamese nationalists, and Communists called the Viet Minh, began rebelling, with Chinese and Soviet support. The French were driven out in 1954, and the country was partitioned as Korea had been. A Communist state, led by a sixty-five-year-old former cook named Ho Chi Minh, was in the north; an anticommunist state, led by a fifty-five-year-old civil servant named Ngo Dinh Diem, was in the south.

The international accord that had divided the country after the French left called for a 1956 election to reunify it. But Diem, figuring he would lose in the election to Ho, reneged on the deal. Ho promptly organized an army that was part militia, part guerillas, and part terrorists, called the Viet Cong. By 1962, Ho's forces controlled a big part of South Vietnam, and U.S. forces that had served largely as advisers to Diem's army began to take a more direct role in the fighting.

IN NAME ONLY . . .

In 1949, the country of Siam officially changed its name to Thailand, meaning "land of the free." That's the same country that went through a dozen military dictatorships and seventeen constitutions between 1932 and 2007.

Europe:
Welcome to Financial Rehab

Recovery from the Great Depression in Europe was fragmented, with some countries rebounding faster than others. Germany, which had probably been hit hardest by the global economic collapse, actually was one of the first to recover. Hitler's government pumped public money into programs such as the construction of a highway system, creating lots of jobs. By the eve of the war, Germany's economy was one third bigger than it had been in 1929.

> *That man for chancellor? I'll make him a postmaster, and he can lick the stamps with my head on them.*
> —German president Paul Von Hindenburg on Hitler's demand that he be made chancellor, August 13, 1932

In addition to economic troubles, much of Europe was under the shadow of despotism even before World War II broke out. Although most of the continent's nations were democracies after World War I, only eight—the United Kingdom, France, Switzerland, Czechoslovakia, Denmark, Finland, Sweden, and Norway—were still democracies in 1939. The rest had repressive governments or were outright dictatorships.

After the war, most of the Continent was in shambles. More than twenty-five million European military personnel and civilians had been killed, and another sixteen million permanently displaced from their homes. The most influential part of the world before the war, Europe lost its military, political, and economic clout to the new superpowers, the Soviet Union and the United States.

In spring 1947, U.S. secretary of state George Marshall persuaded President Harry Truman and Congress to generously finance Europe's economic recovery. Under the Marshall Plan, nearly $13 billion was provided between 1948 and 1952.

But the shifting power base had effectively divided the continent. Eastern Europe became dominated by the USSR. In 1947 and 1948, Poland, Hungary, Czechoslovakia, Romania, Bulgaria, and Yugoslavia all became Communist states. With the exception of Yugoslavia, all of them were under the Soviet thumb. Because the USSR blocked the Eastern European countries from taking part in the Marshall Plan, the Western European countries' postwar recovery was in most cases much faster.

ONE SORE LOSER

Adolf Hitler hoped to use the 1936 Summer Olympics, held in Berlin, to showcase his "Master Race" athletes. His plans were upset, however, by an African American named Jesse Owens, who won four gold medals, and by other black athletes with good results. When the Olympic Committee requested that Hitler either congratulate all athletes or none, Hitler chose none.

Fearing the potentially violent spread of the Soviet sphere of influence, Western nations established the North Atlantic Treaty Organization in 1949. Members were pledged to mutual defense against Soviet aggression. The Communist countries countered in 1955 with formation of the Warsaw Pact.

Membership in the Pact was not optional. In 1956, after Hungary quit the Warsaw Pact and demanded that the USSR remove its troops from inside the country, Soviet tanks rumbled into Hungary. Thousands were killed before the Hungarian Revolt was suppressed, and thousands more fled to the West.

The Hungarian expatriates had plenty of company. Between 1949 and 1961, an estimated twenty-five million Germans left the Eastern part of the country, which was controlled by a Communist regime, for the West. On August 13, 1961, exasperated at the embarrassing exodus, East German police began building what they called an "antifascist protection wall" between East and West Berlin. In West Berlin, it was called the "wall of shame."

Soviet Union:
I Don't Care What My Teachers Say, I'm Gonna Be a Superpower

After consolidating his power in the 1920s, Stalin began pushing hard to industrialize the country. Millions of farmers were turned into factory hands, seldom by choice. In 1926, about 80 percent of the population worked on farms. Within thirteen years, the percentage had fallen to slightly more than half. The effort met with some success, and by 1939, the USSR was one of the world's leading industrial powers.

Stalin pursued his reign of terror against political enemies—real and imagined—as vigorously as he pushed for industrialization. Opponents who weren't killed—and millions were—were pushed into prison camps known as gulags, where they were used as slave labor. It's estimated that in 1930, Soviet gulags contained 179,000 prisoners. By 1934, the number was 500,000; by the time of Stalin's death, in 1953, it was close to 2 million.

In June 1941, less than two years after its invasion of Poland started the war, Hitler's Germany launched Operation Barbarossa, an all-out, fast-moving assault against its until-then ally. The Red Army, though larger than the German invasion force, was poorly trained and badly equipped, and German forces rolled quickly into Soviet territory. Hundreds of thousands of civilians and prisoners of war were systematically murdered by the Germans as troops pushed one thousand miles into the USSR.

But by the winter of 1942, bad weather, a stubbornly courageous Soviet military, and a young general named Georgiy Zhukov combined with overextended German supply lines to halt the advance. By November 1944, the tide had turned and the badly beaten Germans were in full retreat.

Though victorious, no country suffered more in World War II than the Soviet Union. An estimated twenty-six million-plus military personnel and civilians were killed. The country's meat and grain production was cut to half of prewar levels.

Any progress the Soviet economy had made before the war was wiped out by the conflict, and Stalin reinstituted the forced modernization of industry and agriculture. Most of the industrial work focused on military equipment and heavy machinery rather than consumer goods.

In March 1953, Stalin died. After three years of rule by a three-person collective, a sixty-two-year-old longtime Communist Party official named Nikita Khrushchev took over. Khrushchev adopted much less harsh governing methods than Stalin.

> *To American production, without which this war would have been lost.*
> —A toast by Joseph Stalin at the Tehran conference with Churchill and Roosevelt, November 30, 1943

> *History is on our side. We will bury you.*
> —Soviet premier Nikita Khrushchev to Western diplomats at a Moscow reception, November 17, 1956

The emergence of the USSR and the United States as the world's two superpowers led to an intense rivalry between the two in areas outside the political and military realms. Both countries spent billions in a race to dominate the exploration, and possible exploitation, of outer space, a race led mostly by the USSR during the 1950s.

The two nations even argued about kitchen appliances. In 1959, U.S. vice president Richard Nixon visited the Soviet Union to serve as host at an exhibition of Western consumer goods. The visit was marked by a debate between Nixon and Khrushchev about the relative merits of Soviet washing machines and blenders versus their U.S. counterparts, which culminated in the two world leaders poking each other in the chest with their fingers.

But the "kitchen debate" blustering notwithstanding, the Soviet Union was in reality a superpower with a very strong military backbone and a very weak domestic economy.

United States:
Booming Economy, Booming Babies, Booming Anticommunism

With the onset of the Great Depression, American voters decided to try a Democratic president for a change. Their choice was a New York politician who was crippled with polio and was a distant cousin of Theodore Roosevelt.

The biggest attributes Franklin Delano Roosevelt brought to the White House were boundless optimism and seemingly limitless energy. In his first one hundred days, Roosevelt pushed through a plethora of programs designed to get the U.S. economy back on track: jobs for youths, bank reforms, civic redevelopment, massive public works projects, and wage and price controls.

Historians still argue about how effective FDR's New Deal programs were. But it's undeniable that they cheered people up, enough that they reelected Roosevelt in 1936, and gave him unprecedented third and fourth terms in 1940 and 1944.

While trying to right the economy, Roosevelt and Congress also strove during the 1930s to keep the United States out of the looming conflicts in Asia and Europe. By 1940, however, it had become apparent to FDR that American involvement was inevitable. Somewhat reluctantly, he prodded Congress into approving a peacetime draft, doubling the size of the navy, and okaying the sale of military hardware to countries whose interests seemed aligned with those of the United States.

After Pearl Harbor, U.S. industry began to flex its muscle. In 1942, for example, Roosevelt called for the production of fifty thousand planes a year. By 1944, Americans were building ninety-six thousand annually. Wartime production, in turn, heated up the economy, providing jobs and boosting wages.

The economic good times continued after the war. Buffered by the vastness of the Atlantic and Pacific oceans, the United States suffered the least of all the major combatants during the war. There were plenty of jobs for returning servicemen, and $13 billion worth of educational and investment capital available to them through the GI Bill. From 1946 to 1960, the gross national product jumped from $200 billion to $500 billion a year.

The GNP wasn't the only thing jumping. The two sexes, largely separated during the war, overcompensated somewhat after the war was over. The U.S. population grew from 150 million to 180 million during the 1950s, and the "Baby Boom" generation would have social and economic impacts on the country for the rest of the century (and beyond).

All this prosperity was accompanied by an unhealthy dose of paranoia, brought on by both the hot war in Korea and the cold war in Europe. Anticommunist feelings flourished, fueled in large part by an alcoholic U.S. senator from Wisconsin named Joe McCarthy. The demagogic senator wildly charged that Communists had infiltrated nearly every level of American life, from the government and military to classrooms and the entertainment industry.

While McCarthy was eventually discredited and shunned, the anticommunist feelings lingered. They were heightened on October 16, 1962, when U.S. intelligence services reported to President Kennedy that Soviet missile-launching sites were under construction in Cuba, less than one hundred miles from the Florida coast.

> *It shall be the policy of this Nation to regard any nuclear missile launched from Cuba against any nation in the Western Hemisphere as an attack by the Soviet Union on the United States, requiring a full retaliatory response upon the Soviet Union.*
> —President John F. Kennedy, in a nationwide address on October 22, 1962

For the next eleven days, the world teetered as close as it had ever come to nuclear war between the two superpowers. On October 22, Kennedy publicly revealed the presence of the sites, ordered a U.S. naval blockade of Cuba, and stepped up intense one-to-one negotiations with Soviet premier Nikita Khrushchev.

FIRST AMONG FIRST LADIES

Her mother thought she was ugly, her maiden name was the same as her married name, and she was six feet tall. It's a bit of an understatement to say that Anna Eleanor Roosevelt was in many ways an extraordinary woman.

She was born in 1884 in New York, the niece of Theodore Roosevelt. Both of her parents died before she was ten—but not before her mother had time to ridicule her publicly for her plain appearance.

In 1905, she married Franklin D. Roosevelt, a very distant cousin. The couple had six children. It was an often painful marriage for Eleanor. FDR had a long and not very well concealed affair with Eleanor's social secretary. In 1921, he was stricken with polio, and Eleanor became his legs, making political trips for him when he couldn't travel.

When Franklin won the presidency in 1932, Eleanor threw herself into the role of First Lady with zeal heretofore unseen. She held regular press conferences, but for women correspondents only. News organizations that had never hired female reporters were thus pushed into doing so. She also wrote a syndicated newspaper column that recounted life in the White House, and doled out advice.

Eleanor toured the country extensively, reporting directly to FDR about Depression-era conditions. And she was an outspoken champion of civil rights and women's issues. Although her activism earned her praise, it also made her the target of often vicious and personal criticism.

On October 28, Khrushchev blinked. The Soviet missiles would be removed and the sites dismantled. In return, the United States promised not to invade Cuba, and eventually removed American missiles from sites in Turkey.

Coupled with Soviet advances in space and military technology, however, the Cuban missile crisis fed into a new feeling among many Americans: Maybe those oceans weren't going be enough to protect the country in the next world war.

·········· WHO'S UP, WHO'S DOWN ··············

The Subcontinent: UP

It took decades of sit-ins, boycotts, and turning the other cheek—along with more than a few violent confrontations—but the Indian subcontinent bore two new nations after World War II.

India had been under the thrall of Great Britain since the eighteenth century, and not surprisingly, the natives weren't happy about it. In 1919, after a British massacre of Indian demonstrators, the Indians took a different tack: civil disobedience, coupled with nonviolent resistance.

Leading the effort was a British-educated lawyer named Mohandas Gandhi. When the British instituted a new tax on salt in 1930, for example, Gandhi led thousands of Indians on a 250-mile march to the sea to gather salt for themselves. The Brits responded by jailing 60,000 Indians, including Gandhi.

> Nonviolence and truth are inseparable and presuppose one another. There is no god higher than truth.
> —Mohandas Gandhi, 1939

After a few years of on-again-off-again tactics like this, the British agreed in 1935 to allow Indian provinces to govern themselves on matters within the provinces, but the country itself remained under

THE GANDHI MAN CAN

One of Mohandas Karamchand Gandhi's early report cards rated him "good at English, fair in arithmetic and weak in geography." He turned out to be pretty good at political science, too.

Born in 1869 near Bombay, Gandhi studied law in England and became an attorney. In 1893, he signed a one-year contract to practice law in South Africa. The country's segregated policies helped transform him from a mild-mannered lawyer into a mild-mannered but determined civil rights leader. He became the guiding light of a two-decade-long, partially successful struggle to win legal and political rights for Indians and "people of color" in South Africa.

Equipped with political tools such as civil disobedience and passive resistance, Gandhi returned to India in 1914 to take up the fight for independence from the British Empire. He organized boycotts of British goods and businesses, and advocated avoidance of the empire's legal system. In 1930, he led a much-heralded 250-mile march to protest a tax on salt, which resulted in one of his several prison stretches.

By 1931, Gandhi was *Time* magazine's "Man of the Year" and had earned the nickname Mahatma, or "Great Soul." In his personal life, Gandhi was a stirring example of humility. He was a strict vegetarian, wove his own clothes, and lived as simply as a national leader could.

By the time India finally won its independence in 1947, Gandhi's primary mission had shifted to trying to quell the bloody violence between Hindus and Muslims on the subcontinent.

On January 30, 1948, while on his nightly stroll, Gandhi was shot and killed by a Hindu fanatic who was furious at the Mahatma's efforts to reach an accord with Muslims. His October 2 birthday has become a national holiday in India.

British control. It was a half-a-loaf approach that pleased almost no one. When World War II began, the Indian leaders refused to take part or encourage Indians to help, because they hadn't been consulted about the Allies' decision to declare war on the Axis powers.

In 1946, a rebellion in the Royal Indian Navy set off widespread violence, and the British government, weary after years of war, decided that enough was enough. Prime Minister Clement Atlee announced in March that the empire would agree to full Indian independence.

Gandhi and nationalist leader Jawaharlal Nehru (who would become India's first prime minister) wanted to preserve the subcontinent as a unified nation, with equal rights for the country's Hindu and Muslim populations. But Indian Muslims, led by Mohammad Ali Jinnah, wanted their own piece of real estate. The result was a series of violent clashes between the two religious groups.

On August 15, 1947, Hindu India and Muslim Pakistan became separate nations. The fighting, however, intensified as members of the two religions moved to and from the two states. More than five hundred thousand people died as Muslims fled west and Hindus moved east. A full-fledged, albeit brief, war broke out between the two fledgling states over who would have authority over the region of Kashmir. It was settled, at least temporarily, by a United Nations mandate. But the fight would prove to be only the first of several wars between the two nations separated at birth.

Jews: DOWN, BUT NEVER OUT

Anxious to keep Russia fighting during World War I, British officials came up with a strategy to encourage Russia's Jews to support the Allied effort: promise them a Jewish homeland in Palestine after the war. After the war, the League of Nations picked up the idea, proclaiming that Jews had a right to immigrate to the Middle Eastern region then controlled by Great Britain.

But nothing much came of it. And through the 1920s and 1930s, Europe's Jews became the primary target of Adolf Hitler's Nazism as Hitler gradually gained power in Germany. The Jews, he charged, were conspiring with the Communists to stamp out Hitler's mythical Aryan race.

"There is no such thing as coming to an understanding with the Jews," he wrote in his book *Mein Kampf.* "It must be the hard-and-fast 'either-or.'"

Formal persecution of Jews in Germany began almost as soon as Hitler assumed control. In April 1933, Jews were banned from all civil service and teaching positions. By the end of 1935, they had lost their German citizenship and virtually all other rights. Hitler initially wanted to expel Jews from the Continent, but the outbreak of the war thwarted his plan. Then he attempted to isolate them in ghettoes, where they could be used as a source of labor. But by late 1941, a "Final Solution" had been formed. Eight major extermination camps were set up. An estimated 6.0 million Jews were systematically murdered, 1.5 million of them children.

The end of the war and the Holocaust did not end persecution of Jews in Europe; more than a thousand were murdered in 1946 in Poland alone. So it wasn't surprising that many European Jews wanted to go elsewhere. Many of them did—to the Palestinian "homeland" the British had dangled before them in 1917.

But Great Britain, facing economic troubles at home, wanted nothing to do with sorting out differences between Jews and Muslim

Annelies Marie "Anne" Frank was born in Frankfurt in 1929. Her father, Otto, had been a decorated German officer in World War I. But he was also a Jew.

Fearful of what the Nazi ascension to power portended for Jews, Frank moved the family to Amsterdam when Anne was four. An energetic girl who yearned to be a published writer, Anne had what seemed like a bright future. In May 1940, however, Germany invaded the Netherlands.

In the summer of 1942, the Franks went into hiding, in rooms at the back of Otto Frank's office building. Friends supplied the family with food and other necessities. In an autograph book she had been given for her birthday, Anne began keeping a diary. Her entries varied from schoolgirl observations to abstract thoughts about God and somber reflections on her family's plight.

"In spite of everything," she wrote in one entry, "I still believe that people are really good at heart."

In August 1944, German security police raided the Franks' hiding place, apparently having been tipped off by an informant. The family was sent first to the Auschwitz concentration camp, then to Bergen-Belsen. There Anne died, apparently of typhus, a few weeks before the camp was liberated by British troops.

After the war, Anne's father, the only family member to survive, recovered her diary from friends who had found it in the hiding place. He had it published, first in Dutch in 1947, then in English in 1952.

Since then, the diary has been published in more than fifty languages, become the subject of plays and movies, and been widely praised for bringing to life the individual horrors of the Holocaust in a way that mind-numbing statistics might not.

Arabs in Palestine. More than fifty thousand European Jews were intercepted by the Brits and placed in camps on the island of Cyprus. Finally, Britain lobbed the issue to the fledgling United Nations. On November 29, 1947, the UN narrowly voted to partition Palestine into Jewish and Arab states.

On May 14, 1948, the last British troops pulled out of the region. About ten minutes after the withdrawal—literally—the United States formally recognized the new nation of Israel. The Soviet Union quickly followed suit. And the new nation's Arab neighbors promptly attacked. A year-long war ensued before the Arab nations grudgingly—and only temporarily—gave up the fight. More than six hundred thousand Palestinian Arabs fled Israeli territory to refugee camps in Jordan, Egypt-controlled Gaza, and Syria.

The Jews had a homeland—and a whole new set of problems in the decades to come.

Communists: **UP AND ALL OVER**

On March 5, 1946, British leader Winston Churchill gave a speech in Fulton, Missouri. "From Stettin in the Baltic to Trieste in the Adriatic," he said, "an iron curtain has descended across the Continent." Churchill's reference to the postwar spread of communism marked what many historians cite as the formal beginning of the cold war.

Prior to World War II, the apostles of the Communist political philosophy had either been stymied by nationalist and/or fascist governments, or had confined themselves to consolidating power within the Soviet Union. But even before the war ended, Soviet troops were already positioning Communists into power in Poland and Romania. After the war, the Soviets, and eventually China's Communist government, began to seek to expand their influence even farther into countries that had been freed of Japanese and German authority.

Some of the expansion was internal. In China, for instance, the Communist Party's membership grew from 4.5 million in 1949 to 17.5 million in 1961. But most of the expansion was directed outward. By 1961, Communist governments controlled not only the Soviet Union and China, but also most of Eastern Europe and much of Southeast Asia.

Naturally, the capitalist West, led by the United States, took umbrage. The threat of the use of nuclear weapons by one side or the other—or both—made the cold war potentially the most deadly and horrific of all of mankind's conflicts. But the very threat of a nuclear "hot" war reined in both Communist and capitalist interests from pushing the other side too far or too hard.

Instead of face-to-face confrontations, the two sides more often used proxies, backing factions in various third world countries, particularly in Africa, Latin America, and Asia. Both sides plied the nonaligned nations with economic, military, and technological aid. Somehow, the third world countries rarely seemed to profit from all this attention.

Soviets: **WAAAY UP**

One of the hottest fronts in the cold war was the competition between the USSR and the United States to conquer space. In 1957, the Soviets had jumped in the lead by successfully launching Sputnik, an unmanned orbital satellite. And on April 12, 1961, they decisively won the first-man-in-space leg of the race.

At 9:07 a.m., Moscow time, a 4.75-ton spacecraft called Voltok 1 was launched from a field in Kazakhstan. In it was a twenty-seven-year-old Russian Air Force second lieutenant named Yuri A. Gagarin.

Born on a collective farm, this son of a carpenter was selected for the flight in part because at five feet, two inches tall, he was a good fit for the tiny capsule. Another reason was his outgoing personality. During the flight, he whistled a Russian tune called "The Motherland Knows," the lyrics of which include "the Motherland knows where her son flies in the sky."

By the time the capsule landed 108 minutes later, Gagarin had been promoted to major, a rank Soviet leaders thought more befitting the first human to fly into space and come back alive.

Gagarin's feat not only sped up the space race, but also made him a Soviet hero and a worldwide celebrity. Monuments were raised in his honor, and streets—and eventually his hometown—were renamed after him.

The Soviet success, while an inspiration to much of mankind, was unquestionably a black eye to the United States in its quest to win the hearts and minds of third world nations. "America must wake up completely to the challenge," declared U.S. senator Hubert Humphrey on the day of Gagarin's flight.

On May 5, the United States sent navy commander Alan Shepard into space, albeit for only 15 minutes and 115 miles. And on May 25,

ANOTHER RACE TO THE TOP

When the Tibetan government granted access to the tallest Himalayan peaks to the outside world in 1921, the climbers came calling. By 1953, seven expeditions had tried and failed to reach the tip of Mount Everest.

In 1951, a British reconnaissance team found what looked like a promising route to the top, up the south face of the summit. Two years later, under the leadership of a masterful organizer named Colonel John Hunt, a team of British climbers and Sherpa guides prepared to try the route.

After establishing nine camps along the way, the first two-man assault team gave it a try, using a closed-circuit breathing system that circulated pure oxygen. But the system apparently leaked, and they came up short.

Two days later, on May 28, 1953, a team consisting of Edmund Hillary, a beekeeper from New Zealand, and Tenzing Norgay, a Sherpa guide, began a final push from a camp at 27,900 feet. Unlike the previous team, they used an open-circuit breathing system, which was much lighter.

At 11:30 a.m., on May 29, Hillary and Norgay reached the summit. They shook hands, embraced, ate some sweets, left a food offering for the gods, and started down again after fifteen minutes.

When they reached the base camp, according to expedition member George Lowe, the first thing Hillary said was "Well, George, we've finally knocked the bastard off!"

As of mid-2007, more than two thousand people from around the world had followed in their footsteps up Mount Everest.

President John F. Kennedy announced that America would land a man on the moon by the end of the decade.

The Soviets followed their satellite and spaceman successes on March 17, 1965, with the first spacewalk, when cosmonaut Alexei Leonov spent ten minutes outside his spacecraft.

In 1968, Gagarin was killed when his plane crashed during a routine training flight while he was re-qualifying as a fighter pilot. The following year, his outer space accomplishment was eclipsed somewhat when the United States successfully landed men on the moon.

Still, first is first, and Gagarin was first. Plus he was well named for his feat: *Gagarin* is derived from the Russian word for "wild duck."

International Teamwork: UP(ISH)

While the League of Nations had been largely a failure (mostly because it lacked any way to enforce sanctions or crack down on rogue countries), the anti-Axis states decided to give a nation co-op another try.

As the war wound down, representatives from fifty nations met in San Francisco in April 1945. The conference hammered out a charter for a multinational group and called it the United Nations Organization (UNO). Apparently that acronym didn't work for the member nations, and it became known simply as the UN.

The organization's formal birthday was October 24, 1945, after its charter was ratified by the Security Council, which was composed of the five big winners of the war: the Republic of China, the Soviet Union, Great Britain, France, and the United States.

THE LAST WORD

The United Nations has been the scene of some pretty memorable rhetoric over the years, but few have had as much wit and drama as this October 25, 1962, exchange between U.S. ambassador Adlai Stevenson and Soviet ambassador Valerian Zorin:

"Do you, Ambassador Zorin, deny that the U.S.S.R. has placed and is placing medium- and intermediate-range missiles and sites in Cuba? Yes or no—don't wait for the translation—yes or no?"

"I am not in an American courtroom, and therefore I do not wish to answer. In due course, sir, you will have your reply."

"You are in the courtroom of world opinion right now, and you can answer yes or no."

"You will have your answer in due course."

"I am prepared to wait for my answer until hell freezes over."

"The charter of the United Nations which you have just signed," U.S. president Harry Truman told the assembled delegates, "is a solid structure upon which we can build a better world."

How accurate Truman was is of course in the eye of the beholder. There's no question the UN has been far more effective than the League of Nations. For one thing there hasn't been a major worldwide conflict since World War II. On the other hand, the UN has failed to stop several genocides and more than a few regionalized wars.

The number of UN Member States has grown from 51 to 192, but not without controversy. In 1971, for example, the United States finally gave in to pressure and agreed to admit the People's Republic of China and throw out Nationalist China (Taiwan), which had been an original member of the Security Council.

Polio: DOWN

Give a University of Pittsburgh doctor some monkey kidneys, and you just might start stamping out a nasty contagious disease that particularly stalks children.

Of course there are a few steps in between. The disease in question is polio, a viral illness that in about 98 percent of cases produces either no or only mild symptoms. In the other 2 percent, however, the disease can permanently cripple and kill.

Although the disease dates back at least to ancient Egypt, its most extensive outbreaks occurred—unexpectedly enough—in industrialized countries during the twentieth century. The theory is that since it is most readily spread through contact with fecal matter, generations of hand-washing kids didn't get exposed to it at an early age, when symptoms were likely to be less severe.

The result was that by the early 1950s, there was a very big population susceptible to polio. In 1952, there were sixty thousand cases in the United States alone, with three thousand deaths. Millions of dollars in research funds were invested, and by 1955, an injectable vaccine developed by University of Pittsburgh scientist Jonas Salk was licensed for use.

Salk's vaccine, grown in kidney tissue from rhesus monkeys, was used in mass immunization campaigns. By 1957, the annual number of polio cases in the United States had dropped to 5,600.

In 1961, an oral vaccine developed by Dr. Albert Sabin was introduced. Worldwide vaccination campaigns through the World Health Organization have almost eradicated polio around the globe. In 1988, 355,000 cases in 125 countries were reported. By 2006, the total had dropped to fewer than 2,000, and was endemic in only 6 countries.

The Mighty Pen

For dozens of years, mankind had searched for a reliable writing tool that used a quick-drying ink, didn't have to be refilled all the time, and wasn't too messy.

Enter Lazlo Biro. In 1938, Biro was a thirty-nine-year-old Hungarian newspaper editor who had observed that newspaper ink dried fast but wouldn't work well in a fountain pen. Working with his chemist brother Georg, Biro came up with a pen featuring a tip with a freely revolving ball, and ink in a cartridge. They patented the idea in Paris in 1938.

In 1940, the brothers, who were Jewish, fled Europe to Argentina, where they opened a ballpoint pen factory. A few years later, a vacationing American named Milton Reynolds saw the Biro brothers' pen and decided to bring it back to the United States—albeit without their permission. On October 29, 1949, the Reynolds pen went on sale at Gimbels department store in New York. It was a smash hit, with 10,000 pens sold in a single day—at $12.50 each.

But the unreliability and expense of the pens cried out for further innovation. In 1949, two guys named Patrick Frawley, Jr., and Fran Seech came up with a pen that used no-smear ink and had a retractable tip. They called it the Papermate. In 1952, a French guy named Marcel Bich came up with a smooth-writing pen in a clear plastic barrel, dropped the last letter of his last name, and gave birth to the Bic.

But the Biro brothers were not forgotten. In many countries, ballpoint pens are still called biros, and September 29—Lazlo's birthday—is celebrated in Argentina as Inventors' Day.

A Famous Formula

He had the most illustrious brain of the twentieth century—so maybe it was fitting that when he died, they took it out of his head to study it. In fact, it's just what Albert Einstein wanted.

Einstein was born in 1879 in Germany. As a boy, he later recalled, his future course in science was set by two events. One was being mystified at the age of five by a compass. The other was an encounter—and subsequent fascination—with a geometry book at the age of twelve.

After a circuitous education that saw him fail to finish high school but eventually allowed him to graduate from a Swiss university, Einstein tried and failed to get a job as a teacher or assistant to a scientist. He finally took a job as a clerk in a Swiss patent office.

In 1905, while still working for the patent office, Einstein earned a doctorate from the University of Zurich. He also published four astonishing papers on physics that year. Among other things, he posited that time slows down for an object at high speeds relative to a fixed point on earth, and that mass is just energy in another form, and energy is equal to mass times the speed of light squared ... or $E=mc^2$. (Remember what that stands for, and you'll be a hit at cocktail parties.)

Einstein eventually returned to his native Germany. In 1921, winning the Nobel Prize in Physics enhanced his worldwide fame. But Einstein was Jewish, and after Hitler came to power, the physicist and mathematician was certainly smart enough to know that his days in Germany were numbered. He accepted a job at Princeton University in New Jersey in 1933, eventually becoming a U.S. citizen.

Although Einstein urged President Roosevelt as early as 1939 to develop a nuclear weapon—as a defense against the possibility Germany would develop a similar weapon—he was an ardent opponent of war. "I do not know how the Third World War will be fought," he once said, "but I can tell you what they will use in the Fourth—rocks."

ELEMENTARY, MY DEAR WATSON

In 1953, British physicist Francis Crick and U.S. biochemist James Watson used beads, wire, and cardboard to build their famous three-dimensional model of deoxyribonucleic acid, or DNA.

At the time of his death from a heart attack in 1955, Einstein was one of the most famous men in the world. His casual attire, wild hair, and eccentric persona made him, in the words of one biographer, "a cartoonist's dream," and his very surname became a synonym for intelligence.

By his own request, Einstein's body was cremated and his brain donated to scientific study. Like everything else, he wanted to find out what made himself tick.

Good Things in Small Packages

Next time an annoying telephone commercial has you on the brink of madness, you might take comfort in the fact that competition between phone companies just might have given us the most important invention of the twentieth century.

In 1906, as Alexander Graham Bell's telephone patents were expiring, different phone companies were looking for an edge. At America Telephone & Telegraph (AT&T), they decided to focus on development of a vacuum tube that would amplify phone signals and allow them to be transmitted long distances. The tubes worked, but they were expensive, short-lived, got hot, and needed vast amounts of electricity.

Although some German scientists made strides in developing a viable substitute to the tubes, the real breakthrough came after World

War II, at AT&T's Bell Laboratories. On December 23, 1947, three physicists—William Shockley, John Bardeen, and Walter Brattain—demonstrated a new device, called a transistor, that let weak electronic signals control much stronger signals, sort of like a faucet on a water line, without needing a vacuum tube.

The invention wasn't made public until June 25, 1948, and didn't make much of an impression. Shockley, who later shared a 1956 Nobel Prize with Bardeen and Brattain, eventually developed an even better transistor. But while they were a vast improvement on tubes, individual transistors still had to be connected to other components such as resistors and capacitors, and there were still limits to circuit construction.

In 1959, however, U.S. scientists came up with an "integrated" circuit, which put multiple transistors and other components on a single chip of silicon (which, as a semi-conductor, both allows the flow of electrons and acts as insulation).

Since the early 1960s, the number of circuits that can be placed on a single chip has doubled every eighteen months, leading to the development of microprocessors—so you can just blame your Internet addiction on phone companies trying to get an edge.

Cars for the "Volks"

It was commissioned by a monster, designed for the common man, and became the single most popular car model in the history of automobiles.

The lowly Volkswagen Beetle came about when in 1933 German dictator Adolf Hitler told auto designer Ferdinand Porsche that he wanted an affordable car for the average German, one that would seat five, get good gas mileage, and be capable of going sixty miles per hour on the system of freeways he was building, called the Autobahn.

SOME OTHER ADDICTIVE INVENTIONS

While in New York to attend a toy fair, in 1957, Southern California toy makers Richard Knerr and Arthur "Spud" Merlin heard about a kids' craze in Australia that involved rotating a wooden hoop around the hips.

In 1958, they began producing a three-foot-in-diameter plastic hoop. They couldn't patent the device, since kids had been playing with hoops since at least the days of ancient Egypt. But they did trademark the name: Hula Hoop.

By the end of 1959, the Wham-O Company had sold more than 100 million of the $1.98 hoops around the world.

And even when the craze ended, Knerr and Merlin doubtless found consolation in another plastic toy they had actually come up with the year before the Hula Hoop: a plastic disc called the Frisbee.

Porsche came up with a round-topped two-door auto with a four-cylinder, air-cooled, rear-mounted engine and a four-speed manual transmission. Hitler wanted to call the vehicle the *Kraft durch Freude Wagen*, meaning "Strength-through-Joy car," or *KdFwagen*. But the name didn't catch on, and the vehicle eventually became known as "the People's Car," or "Volkswagen."

The Volkswagen factory opened in 1938 and Germans were encouraged to make weekly deposits into a savings plan that would eventually be enough to buy a car. But the war kept car production to a minimum, and Allied bombing destroyed two thirds of the factory.

After the war, British and U.S. automakers turned down the chance to take over the plant, and most of the few Beetles that were made went to the British Army and the German Post Office.

By 1948, however, a British major named Ivan Hirst and a German engineer named Heinrich Nordhoff had rallied the factory into accelerating production. More than 500,000 had been built by 1953, and 5 million by 1961. In 1972, the Beetle passed the Ford Model T as the most-built model, and by the time the last one rolled off a Mexican production line in 2003, more than 22 million had been sold in more than 140 countries.

By the way, Hitler, who did not drive, most often rode around in a Mercedes-Benz.

The Devil's Music

It was a uniquely American sound, an amalgam of blues, folk, gospel, and country music, with roots that were decidedly African American. Its name came from an African American slang term for sex. It was hated by adults and adored by teenagers, and by the end of the twentieth century, it could be reasonably argued that it was the most dominant form of popular music in the world.

While rock 'n' roll's roots were many and varied, its rise after World War II had as much to do with postwar American affluence as with the music itself. White teenagers had an average of ten dollars a week to spend, and they increasingly spent it on what had been referred to first as "race music" and then "rhythm and blues."

In 1952, however, a savvy Cleveland disc jockey named Alan Freed began calling it "rock 'n' roll," a term that allowed whites to more comfortably embrace—and co-opt—the sound. By 1955, rock 'n' roll was beginning to have a major influence on popular culture, from dress and hairstyles to movies.

It also inexorably, if inadvertently, blurred U.S. racial divisions. In fact, it's been argued that rock 'n' roll's ascension in the 1950s was a key ingredient in making integration efforts more acceptable to younger Americans.

Ministers, educators, and parents decried it as immoral, disrespectful, and potentially anarchistic. Music critics sneered it as ephemeral: "It has a clanking, socked-out beat, a braying, honking saxophone, a belted vocal, and, too often, suggestive lyrics," a *Time* magazine critic sniffed in 1955.

No matter. Led by a former truck driver from Memphis whose real name was Elvis Presley, rock 'n' roll musicians became demigods to millions of teens. Presley alone had six major hits in 1956, and at one point was selling a staggering seventy-five thousand records a day.

In 1957, rockers Buddy Holly and Jerry Lee Lewis toured Australia, and Bill Haley and the Comets toured Europe. Rock 'n' roll was here—and there—to stay.

Dirty Books

When Alfred Kinsey graduated from high school in New Jersey in 1910, they put a line from *Hamlet* under his yearbook photo: "Man delights not me; no, nor woman."

Boy, were they wrong.

True, Kinsey initially went on to become a zoologist who specialized in the characteristics of gall wasps, not people. But in 1938, goaded by his students at the University of Indiana, Kinsey began a ten-year study of human sexual behavior.

In 1948, he published an 804-page work called *Sexual Behavior in the Human Male*. Based on 12,124 case histories, Kinsey's report stunned Americans with its findings: 85 percent of American males had sex before marriage; 70 percent had visited a prostitute; 33 percent had had a homosexual experience.

Almost as stunning as Kinsey's conclusions were the book's sales. Despite its leaden, scholarly format, in just a few months it sold 250,000 copies—at $6.50 apiece. In 1953, Kinsey released a similar report on female sexuality (50 percent of U.S. females had sex before marriage; 26 percent fooled around after marriage), and that one sold even better.

Kinsey's methodology was criticized for relying on samples that while large, were not randomly selected enough to ensure they were reflective of the entire population.

The most virulent criticism, however, was on moral grounds. The *Chicago Tribune*, for example, labeled it "a real menace to society" on the grounds it would lower moral standards. Others condemned it for dehumanizing human sexuality by reducing it to a mere physical function.

But history has since credited Kinsey with greatly contributing to an understanding of human sexuality by dragging the subject from behind closed doors.

"If I had any ulterior motive in making this study," said Kinsey, who died in 1956 at the age of sixty-two, "it was the hope that it would make people more tolerant."

········ **AND THANKS, BUT NO THANKS, FOR** . . . ·····

The 411 on Hitler's Naughty Bits

Adolf Hitler was a sexually repressed incestuous gay or bisexual sadomasochist with an Oedipus complex and only one testicle and probably had syphilis. At least that's the amalgamated opinion about the German dictator propagated by amateur and professional head shrinkers. How much, if any, of this is true is unknown, but it hasn't stopped a vast herd of people from trying to find a sexual explanation for Hitler's monstrous behavior.

For example, the U.S. Office of Strategic Services (OSS), the predecessor of the CIA, speculated in 1943 that Hitler had "possibly even a homosexual streak in him." The report also stated Der Fuehrer liked to have women urinate on him.

The famed psychoanalyst Carl Jung speculated that Hitler had "characteristics of a man . . . with female instincts." The famed Nazi hunter Simon Wiesenthal theorized that Hitler's hatred of Jews stemmed from his contracting syphilis from a Jewish prostitute in Vienna before World War I.

Other observers noted that most of the women Hitler hung out with looked at least a little like his mom. A 2001 book by German historian Lothar Machtan concluded that Hitler was gay. And a widely reported story is that Soviet medical examiners conducted an autopsy of Hitler's body after the war and found that he had only one testicle.

While this is titillating historical fodder, there isn't a lot of evidence to support it. Hitler's contemporaries recalled more than anything that he was a loner, with no real interest in people as a species or individually. He is believed to have had an affair with a niece named Geli Raubal, who subsequently committed suicide. In 1935, his long-time mistress and very short-time wife, Eva Braun, wrote "he needs me only for certain purposes," but she didn't elaborate. (She did say that Hitler liked Valkyrie-proportioned women.)

That Hitler had some kind of testicular abnormality, however, was probably true. Of course most any Allied soldier from World War II could have attested to the Fuehrer's lack of balls.

Backstabbing In-Laws

Nothing like a brother-in-law to steer you wrong. At least that was U.S. Army sergeant David Greenglass's story. A machinist at the top-secret Los Alamos nuclear laboratory, Greenglass was busted in 1950 for passing atomic secrets to the Soviet Union.

Greenglass promptly ratted on his sister, Ethel Rosenberg, and her husband, Julius. The couple were arrested and charged with espionage. At their trial, Greenglass testified that Julius had recruited him to steal secrets in 1944. He later also testified against his sister.

Greenglass got fifteen years in prison, and was released in 1960. The Rosenbergs, however, got the electric chair. Their execution at New York's Sing Sing prison, on June 19, 1953, made them the only American civilians to be executed for espionage during the cold war.

"I consider your crime worse than murder," Judge Irving Kaufman said in handing down the sentence. The judge blamed the Rosenbergs for encouraging Communist aggression in Korea. "By your betrayal," he charged, "you undoubtedly have altered the course of history to the disadvantage of our country."

During the two years between their sentencing and their execution, supporters of the couple hollered long and loud that (1) the Rosenbergs had been railroaded because of the near-hysterical anti-communist fervor in the country at the time; (2) even if they were guilty, the stuff they passed on wasn't worth much; and (3) their sentence was way too severe. But those arguments were lost in the uproar of anticommunist hysteria, which was fueled by the demagogic rants of Wisconsin senator Joe McCarthy.

Subsequent events—including the posthumously published memoirs of Soviet premier Nikita Khrushchev in 1990 and security documents declassified in 1995—seemed to indicate pretty conclusively that Julius was certainly guilty of helping to operate a Soviet spy ring. But it's also likely that Ethel, while cognizant of her husband's activities, did very little actual espionage. In 1996, in fact, Greenglass admitted in a book that he had lied about his sister's involvement to protect his own wife and children.

And with the aid of historical hindsight, the sentence of the Rosenbergs today seems like, well, overkill.

· · · · · · · · · · · · · · · · · · · BY THE NUMBERS ·

3	number of American soldiers in the famous photo depicting the raising of the U.S. flag on Mount Suribachi during the battle for the island of Iwo Jima who were later killed in the battle
6	number of soldiers in the photo
8	weight, in tons, of UNIVAC, or the Universal Automatic Computer (the first electronic digital computer designed for commercial use)
18	cost, in cents, of a gallon of gasoline in the United States in 1933
30	age of American singer and bandleader Bill Haley when "Rock Around the Clock" became the first truly international rock 'n' roll hit song in 1955
33	number of whooping cranes left in the world in 1959
~260	number of whooping cranes estimated in the world in 2007
43	age of John F. Kennedy at his inauguration as U.S. president in 1961, making him the youngest elected president in the country's history
45	number of revolutions per minute (rpm) completed by a recording format introduced by RCA in 1949
68.4	life expectancy, in years, of human being in United States in 1953
<50	life expectancy, in years, of human being in China or India in 1953
2,294	number of U.S. banks that failed in 1931
2,400	number of Germans who fled East Berlin on a single day, August 12, 1961
5,000	range, in miles, of U.S. and Soviet intercontinental ballistic missiles by the late 1950s
10,000	estimated number of Austrian Jews who committed suicide after being forced into Nazi concentration camps

33, 514	number of "enemies of the people" killed by Soviet secret police in 1937 and 1938
150,000	number of British officials in India in 1931
353,000,000	number of Indians in India in 1931
179,000	number of people in Soviet slave labor camps, or gulags, in 1930
1,700,000	number of people in Soviet gulags in 1953
836,255	number of women's dresses found by Russian troops after liberating the Auschwitz concentration camp in late January 1945
23,000,000	number of Americans receiving some form of government aid in 1938
2,300,000,000	the world population in 1940, about 25 percent of whom lived in China

12
ONE WORLD

(1963—2007)

In the space of just a few weeks in the summer of 2007, British scientists in Antarctica appeared in a globally televised environmental awareness concert; a major French bank triggered a plunge in the U.S. stock market, and Chinese restaurateurs prepared for the 2008 Summer Olympics by translating their menus into English—and learning the difference between *carp* and *crap*.

It's a small world, after all.

In fact, as the twenty-first century plowed through its first decade, technological innovation, environmental challenges that transcended geopolitical borders, and an increasingly intertwined international economy combined to shrink the planet considerably.

Following the Cuban missile crisis, both of the world's super powers, the United States and Soviet Union, took a step back from the abyss, and settled into ideological combat by proxy in other countries. But by the end of the 1980s, the Soviet Union's faltering economy betrayed its military and political aspirations, and the cold war was over.

Unfortunately, there were plenty of other wars: in Vietnam, the Middle East, East Africa, Eastern Europe, and on the Indian subcontinent.

In 1991, the United States, now the world's sole superpower, led an international force against Iraq to drive dictator Saddam Hussein's invading forces out of Kuwait. In 2001, following a massive terrorist attack on American targets, the U.S. led another international force to overthrow the religious dictatorship of the Taliban in Afghanistan, followed by the U.S. invasion of Iraq in 2003. And so on. Clearly, the fall of communism did not presage a Pax Americana.

In the Middle East, an abundance of disparate ingredients—economic feuds over the area's bountiful oil supplies; bitter sectarian disputes between Sunni and Shiite Muslims, and the Arab world's antipathy toward Israel—worked to keep the region a seething cauldron of unrest.

Racial, ethnic, and religious differences sparked fights in other areas as well, from Northern Ireland to South Africa to East Timor. Predictably, the unrest triggered massive waves of migration, more often forced than voluntary.

The collapse of communism ended third world nations' roles as colonial pawns, but post-colonialism did not equate to post-poverty. By 1998, Africa contained 10 percent of the world's population, yet only 1 percent of its industrial output.

Latin America had reasonably good success in industrializing and relatively poor results in securing political stability. During the first decade of the twenty-first century, highly centralized governments that were either socialist or bordered on socialism took control in Venezuela, Bolivia, and Ecuador, countering moves toward democracy in countries such as Chile, Brazil, and Argentina.

In China, the disintegration of the Soviet Union left the world's most populous nation as the only large Communist country. Years of often violent internal unrest finally gave way to a more stable, if still repressive, government. The Chinese economy began to modernize, and the country entered the new century as a dominant player in the global marketplace.

In Europe, at least in Western Europe, cold war tensions between the USSR and the United States served to push countries toward greater cooperation. The European Economic Community was formed in 1957 on the Continent, joined in 1969 by England and Ireland. Other countries joined what became the European Union in 1995. By 2002, twelve European countries had adopted a unified currency, the euro.

While each region of the world was struggling with its own problems and enjoying its successes, advances in technology and science were making the world more interesting, more accessible—and smaller. Man walked on the moon; a sheep was successfully cloned; a human baby was conceived in a laboratory dish. Personal computers evolved from simple word processors to marvels of calculation and information, which expanded exponentially with the development of the Internet. Cellular and satellite telephones meant there was virtually no place on earth that was out of earshot.

The communications revolution helped spur a more fluid world economy. Goods and money moved more easily over oceans and across borders. Multinational groups such as the European Union and participants in the North American Free Trade Agreement fostered international cooperation on issues such as tariffs. The number of multinational firms went from thirty-seven thousand in 1983 to more than sixty-three thousand in 2000.

But there were downsides to the global economy too. Inequities in earnings meant that high-wage countries shipped jobs to low-wage nations. Foreign capital could be fickle and withdrawn precipitously, leaving new industries in developing countries in the lurch, or at the mercy of corporate interests in other nations that swooped in to take advantage of the situation.

Economic interests weren't the only things countries shared with one another. Highly communicable viruses such as HIV and SARS replaced the plague and smallpox as epidemics that traveled without passports. Environmental problems, ranging from global warming to the destruction of rainforests to air and water pollution, all transcended borders.

As the twenty-first century began to gather steam, mankind's best hope for solving the daunting environmental, economic, political, and social problems might well lie in an adage coined by the American statesman Benjamin Franklin in 1776: "We must all hang together, or assuredly we shall all hang separately."

·············· **WHAT HAPPENED WHEN** ··············

June 16, 1963 The United States and Soviet Union agree to ban testing nuclear arms aboveground and orbiting nuclear weapons in space.

Apr. 6, 1965 The world's first global telecommunications satellite, EARLY BIRD, is launched from Cape Canaveral, Florida.

July 20, 1969 U.S. astronaut Neil Armstrong sets foot on the Earth's moon.

Jan. 15, 1973 The United States suspends all military action against North Vietnam to concentrate on peace talks.

Aug. 9, 1974 After the Watergate scandal Richard M. Nixon becomes the first U.S. president to resign from office.

Jul. 25, 1978 A healthy 5-pound, 12-ounce baby girl is born in London from an egg that is fertilized outside her mother's body—history's first "test-tube baby."

Oct. 16, 1978 Cardinal Karol Jozef Wojtyla of Poland becomes Pope John Paul II, the first non-Italian pontiff since 1522.

May 3, 1979 Margaret Thatcher becomes Britain's first female prime minister.

Dec. 26, 1979	Soviet troops invade Afghanistan.
Sept. 17, 1980	Iraq declares war on neighboring Iran.
Dec. 3, 1985	Poisonous gas leaks from a pesticide plant near Bhopal, India, killing 2,500.
Nov. 9, 1989	Guards throw open the gates at the Berlin Wall.
Aug. 6, 1991	A young British scientist named Tim Brenners-Lee posits an idea for using the Internet to share information called the "World Wide Web Project."
Dec. 26, 1991	The Supreme Soviet, which had ruled over the USSR since 1917, dissolves itself, completing the breakup of the Soviet Union.
Apr. 25, 1994	The all-white parliament of South Africa also dissolves itself, ending 342 years of white rule.
Jul. 1996	A United Nations report reveals that 385 people control about half of the world's personal wealth.
Aug. 1999	The population of India reaches 1 billion. Overall, the world's population reaches 6 billion.
Mar. 29, 2004	NATO formally admits seven new countries that were once part of the Soviet Union or Soviet-dominated.
Aug. 24, 2006	Pluto is reclassified as a dwarf planet, shrinking the solar system's full planet roster to eight.

 ············· **SPINNING THE GLOBE** ··················

Africa:
Free(ish) at Last

By the 1960s, most African countries had achieved independence, or were on their way to doing so. But once the colonial powers departed, Africans were left to hastily put together their own governments, something they were often ill prepared to do.

The result in many cases was either a military coup or civil war, sometimes accompanied by genocide. In Libya, Colonel Moammar al-Gaddafi seized power in 1969, followed by General Idi Amin in Uganda in 1971. Civil wars erupted in the Sudan (1956 and 1983), Nigeria (1967), and Liberia (1990).

In 1974, a Soviet-backed Marxist coup toppled the venerable leader Haile Selassie in Ethiopia, and a decade later the region of Eritrea broke off from Ethiopia. A nine-year civil war ended with Eritrean independence in 1993.

In famine-ridden Somalia, troops from the United States and other countries tried both humanitarian and military aid to stop a civil war in the early 1990s. In 1995, however, they gave up the military efforts and the war continued into the 2000s.

In April 1994, ethnic violence broke out in Rwanda between members of the Hutu and Tutsi tribes. Within three months, an estimated one million Tutsi and moderate Hutus had been shot, clubbed, or hacked to death by Hutu gangs and members of the Rwandan military. When the genocide finally ended, more than two million Hutu, fearing reprisals, had fled the country to refugee camps in neighboring nations.

In Sudan, the largest country in Africa, a civil war raged between

YOU CAN CALL ME AL(-GADDAFI)

Although he has been ruler of the country since 1969, Libya's Muammar al-Gaddafi holds no official public office and lacks a formal government title. Heck, he's not even a general, he's a colonel.

"Arab" Sudanese in the north and "African" Sudanese in the south. From 1956 to 1972, and then from 1983 to 2005, the fighting killed more than 2.0 million and displaced another 4.5 million. Even as an uneasy peace was worked out between north and south, the Arab-dominated government was using militia groups and mercenaries to wage war on residents of Darfur in western Sudan. More than 2,000 villages were destroyed and more than 400,000 people killed.

Not all the fighting was African on African, and not all Europeans bowed out gracefully as the post-colonial era dawned. In Rhodesia, a minority white government led by a politician named Ian Smith broke away from British rule and established its own whites-in-charge government. Eventually bowing to international pressure, the white government held elections in 1980, which resulted in the election of a black-majority government led by a Marxist politician named Robert Mugabe. Mugabe rapidly became dictator of what was renamed Zimbabwe.

In South Africa, whites' control of the government began to slip in the 1980s. Widespread riots broke out in 1985, followed a year later by an economic boycott of the country by the United States and the

European Economic Community. By 1994, black civil rights leader Nelson Mandela, who had spent more than twenty-seven years behind bars, was elected the country's president.

Even the relatively stable and democratic East African country of Kenya had its share of political unrest, including an attempted 1982 military coup and ethnic violence following a controversial 2007 election.

In addition to a high degree of political unrest throughout much of the continent, Africa also suffered from a severe case of empty wallet. Both the West and the Communist bloc had shown interest in currying the emerging nations' favor through economic aid. But the collapse of the Soviet Union made Africa less interesting to Western leaders. Direct economic aid from Western governments gave way to loans from organizations such as the World Bank or the International Monetary Fund, and the result was that many African nations rolled up heavy debts, with little economic growth to show for it.

While the economies stagnated, however, population growth did not. With the highest birthrate of any continent, Africa's turn-of-the century population of about 750 million was expected to nearly triple by 2050. The continent also led the world in another most unwelcome category: with 13 percent of the earth's population, Africa was home to nearly 70 percent of the earth's HIV/AIDS victims.

Soviet Union:
Refragmented

While the breakup of the Soviet Union seemed to happen overnight, it actually began to show signs of cracking decades before it occurred.

In 1964, Premier Nikita Khrushchev was forced from office after his efforts to reform the nation's moribund economic system failed. Leonid Brezhnev, an old-school, hard-line Communist, replaced Khrushchev. Brezhnev wasted no time slapping down attempts to liberalize Communist regimes in Czechoslovakia in 1968 and Poland in 1981.

The country continued its full-court press in the contest with the United States for supremacy in space; in 1971 the Soviets launched Solyut I, the first in a series of permanently manned space stations. The USSR also continued to encourage the spread of communism in other countries and continued to economically prop up those countries that already had it.

All that, plus trying to keep up in the arms race and fight a war in Afghanistan, put a heavy strain on the Soviet economy. In addition,

Soviet leaders just wouldn't stop dying. In 1982, Brezhnev expired and was replaced by sixty-eight-year-old Yuri Andropov, who died in 1984. He was replaced by seventy-two-year-old Konstantin Chernenko, who died in 1985. Chernenko's replacement was fifty-four-year-old Mikhail Gorbachev, who pledged to revitalize the economy, modernize Soviet communism, and improve relations with the West.

In 1988, Gorbachev introduced major economic and political reforms, dubbed "perestroika" (restructuring) and "glasnost" (openness). He also urged other Warsaw Pact nations to follow the USSR's lead. They did so with enthusiasm. The Berlin Wall came down in 1989, as did Communist governments in country after country. This included the Soviet Union itself in 1991, but only after Boris Yeltsin, president of the Russian Republic, thwarted a Communist coup attempt in that state.

The USSR was dissolved into a collection of autonomous states that enjoyed varying degrees of success on their own. The Russian Republic remained a considerable world presence; due in large part to its wealth of natural resources, including oil. In 1999, Vladimir Putin, a former KGB official, succeeded Yeltsin as Russian leader, and Russian relations with the West took a decidedly frostier turn.

Putin agreed to step down as president in 2008—after hand-picking his successor, Dmitry Medvedev—but made it clear he intended to continue to be the dominant figure in Russian government, even without the title.

China:
Off to a Slow Start, but Picking Up Steam

The world's largest nation had ended the 1950s with one of the world's most ironically named failures, the Great Leap Forward. So, in 1966, Mao Zedong tried launching another big-name program, the Cultural Revolution.

Enforced by a newly formed paramilitary organization called the Red Guard, Mao wanted to root out all deviation from Communist ideals. Led by Mao's wife, Chiang Chi'ing, the Red Guard hunted down "counterrevolutionaries," who were punished with penalties that ranged from being forced to wear a dunce cap in public to being executed. By the time of Mao's death in 1976, the fanatical movement, in which as many as five hundred thousand people were killed, threatened to crumble Chinese society.

Chiang tried to rule in her husband's place with a quartet of henchmen known as the Gang of Four, but most Chinese officials had had enough of her and the Cultural Revolution, and she and the gang were thrown out.

Mao's successor, Deng Xiaoping, began a serious reform of China's economy, mostly by loosening up overbearing governmental controls and taking advantage of the country's huge size. It worked. Between 1978 and 1998, the gross national product grew at an average annual rate of 10 percent. Exports soared a staggering 2,000 percent during the same period. It didn't hurt things that China regained control of the economic dynamo of Hong Kong from the British in 1997.

Political reform, however, lagged. Efforts to democratize were vigorously thwarted and dissent stifled, most notably demonstrated by the crushing of a student demonstration in 1989 at Beijing's Tiananmen Square.

Still, as the twenty-first century began, China was poised to become more of a world force than it had been in centuries, and had emerged as America's chief rival for the preeminent position in the world economy.

Elsewhere in Asia:
Changing Times

Other Asian countries steered similar courses to China's, without the Cultural Revolution part. In the Philippines, a lawyer named Ferdinand Marcos was elected president in 1965, was reelected in 1969, declared martial law in 1972, and stayed in office until he was ousted in 1986.

One of the reasons Marcos gave for seizing power was the fear of a Communist takeover. It wasn't a wholly unwarranted fear. After North Vietnamese Communists took South Vietnam in 1975, Laos and Cambodia followed.

In Cambodia, the ruling Khmer Rouge party, under Communist dictator Pol Pot, undertook one of the century's most horrific regimes. More than 1.5 million people—as much as 20 percent of the country's entire population—were worked to death, starved to death, or executed for offenses as mystifyingly petty as wearing eyeglasses.

The Khmer Rouge was toppled in 1979 by invading Vietnamese troops, who withdrew in 1989. Although Vietnam remained as one of the world's few Communist nations in 2007, democratic governments were restored in Laos in 1989 and in Cambodia in 1991.

While much of the rest of Asia was quarreling with neighbors or fighting internally, Japan was continuing its amazing postwar economic recovery. Through the 1960s, its economy grew at an average annual clip of 11 percent. In the 1970s, Japan responded to the global oil crisis by shifting its focus from heavy industry to high-tech electronics. This consolidated its position as an economic heavyweight.

But it also became a victim of its own successes. Rapid growth and continual innovation raised expectations of financial markets to unreasonable levels. Other Asian states—most notably Singapore, Hong Kong, South Korea, and Taiwan—emulated Japan's methods and provided stiff competition. By the end of the twentieth century, Japan's remarkable economic run had ended.

LORDS OF THE RINGS

In 1964, Japan hosted the Summer Olympics, marking its full reemergence onto the world scene after World War II. The hosts didn't do badly in the games, either: Japan won sixteen gold medals, behind only the USSR and the United States.

In South Asia, the world's largest democracy, India, struggled through the 1960s like a gawky adolescent trying to figure out how to harness his developing strength. It found itself frequently at odds with its neighbors—China in the early 1960s, Pakistan almost continually—and dealing internally with sectarian and religious strife among the Hindu, Muslim, and Sikh elements of its population.

As a leader of the world's nonaligned nations, India became a nuclear power in the 1970s and played both sides of the cold war against each other, siding often with the Soviet Union and occasionally with the West. Beginning in the 1980s, India also undertook a series of ambitious economic reforms. By the first decade of the new century, its economy was one of the fastest growing in the world.

The Middle East:
Shifting Sands

If you had to pick just one word to describe the Middle East from the 1960s on, *unstable* would be a good one. At least four complex and deep-rooted conflicts intertwined into a Gordian knot of, well, instability:

- fundamentalist Islamic antipathy toward the West;
- sectarian feuds between Shiite and Sunni Muslims;
- differences between Islamic countries with more secular governments and those with religious bases; and

the Arab world's ever so mild (he said, sarcastically) dislike of Israel.

The very existence of Israel, in fact, was enough to send many Arab leaders scurrying for their helmets in the 1960s. In 1967, fearing an attack was imminent, Israel launched a preemptive strike on Egypt and quickly routed Arab forces, which were indeed planning an attack. The so-called Six-Day War ended with Israel seizing Arab territories that included the Sinai, the Gaza Strip, the West Bank of the Jordan River, and the city of Jerusalem. It also ended with a three-year-old group called the Palestine Liberation Organization (PLO) taking the lead in seeking the destruction of Israel.

In 1973, Egypt and Syria struck first and pushed into Israeli territory before an Israeli counterattack drove them back. Under pressure from both the United States and Soviet Union, the Arab nations gave up the fight. (But the Arab-dominated Organization of the Petroleum Exporting Countries (OPEC) retaliated by cutting oil supplies. Prices around the world tripled, effectively ending the globe's post–World War II economic surge.)

Weary of the violent approach, Egyptian president Anwar Sadat decided to seek peace with the Israelis. In 1978, at the U.S. presidential retreat at Camp David, in Maryland, Sadat and Israeli prime minister Menachem Begin signed a peace treaty brokered by President Jimmy Carter.

Peace didn't catch on. In 1981, Sadat was assassinated for his efforts, and Israel invaded Lebanon in an effort to root out PLO terrorists who were using the country as their base. Israeli troops stayed four years. In 1993, however, Israeli and PLO leaders met secretly in Oslo, Norway, and came up with a tentative plan for semi-autonomy for Palestinians in some of the territory Israel had seized in 1967. Like Sadat, Yitzhak Rabin, the Israeli prime minister who oversaw the Oslo peace effort, was assassinated.

Although some progress was made as a result of the Oslo Agreement, violence and unrest continued in the region and most major issues remained unresolved.

Not all of the Middle East's problems involved Israel. In 1980, Iraqi dictator Saddam Hussein launched an attack on neighboring

ONE WACKY IRAQI

According to U.S. journalist Mark Bowden, Iraqi dictator Saddam Hussein had the chefs at each of his twenty-plus palaces prepare three elaborate meals each day, whether he was there or not, to lessen the chances of his being poisoned.

Iran. Financially drained by the war, which basically ended in a tie, Saddam demanded tribute from the small oil-rich country of Kuwait in the fall of 1990, and then invaded. But a U.S.-led coalition responded with massive force, crushing the Iraqi army in less than six weeks and forcing Saddam to sign a humiliating peace treaty. He was allowed, however, to continue in power.

In Iran, meanwhile, the corrupt-but-pro-U.S. Shah of Iran, Reza Pahlavi, had been overthrown in a 1979 coup led by a Muslim cleric, Ayatollah Ruhollah Khomeini. After the United States gave refuge to the shah, Iranian students retaliated by seizing the U.S. embassy in Tehran and holding sixty-seven Americans hostage, fifty-two of them for more than a year.

In Afghanistan, a fundamentalist Islamic group called the Taliban had ruled the country since 1996. After the September 11, 2001, attacks on American targets by members of the al-Qaeda terrorist group, U.S. officials charged that the group's leaders were being harbored in Afghanistan. When the Taliban refused to hand over the terrorists, U.S. and British forces attacked Afghanistan, forced out the Taliban, and occupied the country as part of a multinational force.

In 2003, the United States followed up by accusing Iraq of developing "weapons of mass destruction." After Saddam refused to acknowledge the weapons' existence, the United States and some other countries invaded Iraq.

Saddam was overthrown, eventually captured, tried for crimes against humanity by an Iraqi court, and executed. No weapons of mass destruction were found, and the country continued to be occupied by Western, mainly U.S., troops and wracked by sectarian terrorism and civil war.

United States of America:
Lonely at the Top

The United States faced two main demons as the 1960s unfolded, one foreign and one domestic. In 1963, South Vietnam's dictator, Ngo Dinh Diem, was assassinated. Although the United States had propped up Diem's dictatorship, it wasn't really sorry to see him go. After his death, the United States stepped up its military support of the country in its fight with Communist North Vietnam.

By the time he was assassinated himself that November, President John F. Kennedy had sent sixteen thousand U.S. military "advisors" to Vietnam. Kennedy's successor, Lyndon Johnson, accelerated the pace. By March 1965, more than one hundred thousand U.S. troops were in the country and U.S. aircraft were heavily bombing targets in

North Vietnam. By the beginning of 1968, the U.S. troop count had reached five hundred thousand.

But it was a confusing war for the American people. Relatively few knew exactly what the war's objectives were, beyond defeating Communists. Watching the horrors of the war on television every night didn't help, and opposition to American involvement grew so intense that Johnson chose not to run for reelection in 1968.

> *All Vietnam is not worth the life of a single American boy.*
> —U.S. senator Ernest Greuning (D-Alaska), during debate on the Gulf of Tonkin Resolution, which gave President Lyndon Johnson congressional authority to commit U.S. forces to "defend" Southeast Asian countries threatened by communism, August 6, 1964

The country elected Richard Nixon, a veteran Communist fighter. Nixon tried several methods to force the North Vietnamese to negotiate a settlement, ranging from heavy bombing to invading Cambodia. But nothing worked. In January 1973, after years of fighting and the deaths of fifty-eight thousand American soldiers, the United States signed a "peace treaty" with North Vietnam and pulled out. In April 1975, North Vietnam overran its southern counterpart and took control.

The demon on the home front was racial discrimination. Although the American civil rights movement had its roots in the 1950s, it picked up speed in the 1960s. Tactics borrowed from India's Gandhi supplied part of the momentum: sit-ins, marches, and strikes. Political leadership—first by Kennedy and his attorney general brother, Robert, and then by Johnson, as well as by civil rights leaders such as Martin Luther King, Jr.—also played a significant role.

> *If physical death is the price I must pay to free my white brothers and sisters from a permanent death of the spirit, then nothing can be more redemptive.*
> —Dr. Martin Luther King, Jr., on June 5, 1964, a few months before the year he was awarded the Nobel Peace Prize for his work toward racial equality. He was assassinated four years later.

In 1964, Johnson pushed a bill through Congress that banned racial discrimination in public places such as hotels and restaurants and broadened federal authority to enforce civil rights laws. The following year, Congress approved another bill that safeguarded the voting rights of African Americans.

But white resistance and black impatience combined in an explosive mix. Race riots broke out across the country in 1965, 1967, and

1968. Black leaders Malcolm X and the Rev. King were murdered. The streets eventually cooled, but race relations remained one of America's most vexing problems.

If the 1960s were turbulent, the 1970s were sort of depressing in America, despite its two hundredth birthday in July 1976. Nixon was driven from office by a political scandal; the Arab-pushed oil embargo inflicted major damage on the economy, and U.S. prestige suffered a humiliating blow when the president was unable to rescue the hostages held in Tehran by Iranian students.

"WHAT I MEANT TO SAY WAS . . ."

I don't give a shit what happens, I want you all to stonewall it, let them plead the Fifth Amendment or anything else.
—President Richard M. Nixon, discussing the Watergate cover-up with aides, March 22, 1973

There is no Soviet domination of Eastern Europe.
—President Gerald R. Ford, during a 1976 presidential debate with Jimmy Carter

I've looked on a lot of women with lust. I've committed adultery in my heart many times.
—Democratic presidential candidate Jimmy Carter, in a 1976 *Playboy* magazine interview published just before the election

Trees cause more pollution than automobiles do.
—President Ronald Reagan in 1981

I'm going to say this again. I did not have sexual relations with that woman, Miss Lewinsky.
—U.S. President Bill Clinton, issuing a forceful denial at a White House press conference, January 26, 1998

We found the weapons of mass destruction. We found biological laboratories . . . and we'll find more weapons as time goes on. But for those who say we haven't found the banned manufacturing devices or banned weapons, they're wrong, we found them.
—President George W. Bush to a Polish television interviewer, May 29, 2003, in justifying the U.S. invasion of Iraq

But in 1980, an improbable hero showed up in the form of a former Hollywood actor. Ronald Reagan, a charismatic B-movie star and two-term California governor, was elected president. While personally affable and self-deprecating, Reagan was steadfast and stubborn when it came to pushing his political ideas. Domestically, he believed that if business thrived, the benefits would "trickle down" to everyone. Internationally, Reagan was a "big stick" man. He heated up the cold war by calling the Soviet Union amoral and evil, and by building up U.S. missile defenses.

But his tough talk also helped the USSR realize that America was not going to slow down in the arms race, and helped bring about the end of the cold war and the United States' emergence as the only true superpower.

As the world's cop, the United States led international coalitions into wars in Kuwait, Afghanistan, and Iraq. The actions, particularly the highly controversial decision by President George W. Bush to invade Iraq in 2003, led to a tidal wave of international criticism.

The attacks on September 11, 2001, also rammed home a chilling reminder that even the biggest dog on the block is vulnerable. Economic globalization and technological innovation challenged America's place in the world marketplace. As the twenty-first century dawned, the United States was finding that a smaller world didn't necessarily mean a better one.

– Name That War! –

Keeping all those wars straight can be a tough job, especially when there are so many repeat offenders. Lucky for you, here's a quick cheat sheet to the major wars since 1962.

Sudan: North Sudanese vs. South Sudanese, 1956–1972, 1983–2006. As many as 2 million dead, mainly civilians. Ended in uneasy peace between North and South, but did nothing to end violence in Western province of Darfur.

Rwanda: Hutu vs. Tutsi, 1959–1994, off and on. More than 1 million killed, overwhelmingly civilian. Ended in uneasy peace between two feuding tribal groups.

Vietnam: United States and South Vietnam vs. North Vietnam, 1962–1973. As many as 1.1 million North Vietnamese soldiers, 58,000 U.S. soldiers, and 1 million to 4 million civilians dead or missing. The United States stopped fighting in 1973; North Vietnamese took over South Vietnam in 1975.

India-Pakistan: India vs. Pakistan, 1965 and 1971. The 1965 war killed a total of about 6,500 on both sides; ended in a draw. The 1971 war's military casualties were more than 8,000; civilian deaths at more than 400,000. Resulted in East Pakistan becoming nation of Bangladesh.

Israel I: Israel vs. Egypt, Jordan, and Syria, 1967. About 19,000 deaths on all sides. Israel ended up with triple the territory it had when the Six-Day War started.

Israel II: Israel vs. Egypt, Syria, and others, 1973. About 20,000 total military deaths. Israel gained some territory, but generally it was a draw.

Afghanistan I: Afghans vs. Soviet Union, 1979–1989. Soviets lost about 14,500; Afghans more than 1 million soldiers and civilians. Afghan rebels won; last Soviet troops pulled out in February 1989.

Iraq I: Iraq vs. Iran, 1980–1988. Deaths uncertain, but estimated at as many as 500,000 on each side. Basically ended in a draw.

Iraq II: Iraq vs. United States, 1991. United States and allies lost about 200; Iraq about 24,000 military personnel and 6,000 civilians. Iraq's invasion of Kuwait was thwarted and the country severely damaged by U.S. bombing.

Balkans: Slovenia, Croatia, Serbia, Montenegro, and Bosnia vs. various combinations of each other 1991–2001. As many as 250,000 deaths, most of them civilians. Resulted in dissolution of former Yugoslavia into several independent states.

Afghanistan II: United States vs. Taliban, 2001–present. United States and allies lost 758 through December 2007; Taliban casualties unknown. United States succeeded in overthrowing terrorist-supporting Taliban theocracy, but through early 2008 was unable to completely secure the country.

Iraq III: Iraq vs. United States, 2003–present. Through January 2008, American casualties were at about 4,000; Iraqi civilian deaths at more than 30,000. As 2008 began, United States had yet to stabilize Iraqi government.

·············· **WHO'S UP, WHO'S DOWN** ············

Drug Traffickers: UP

Humans' use of drugs, at least for mystical and medicinal reasons, dates back at least fifty thousand years, according to archaeological finds in the Shanidar cave in Iraq. Use of the opium poppy dates back to 10,000 BCE. And drugs certainly played an occasional role in international relations. In the mid-nineteenth century, for instance, the French and English used military force to push China into legalizing the use of opium from British-ruled India.

But drug trafficking really began to play an increasing role in geopolitics in the latter half of the twentieth century. In the 1960s and 1970s, both U.S. and Chinese spy operations alternately fought and propped up drug warlords and drug-financed regimes in Southeast Asia. Drug cartels in Colombia and Mexico grew to exert substantial influence on those countries' political and legal systems.

In Afghanistan, the radical Islamic group the Taliban played both sides: When they were in charge of the country, the Taliban cited Islamic tenets against drug use and dealt harshly with Afghanistan's prolific opium poppy farming. After being overthrown by a U.S.-led military coalition in 2002, the Taliban formed a coalition with the country's opium smugglers to finance the group's comeback efforts. By the end of 2004, an estimated 75 percent of the world's opium came from Afghanistan.

There were plenty of customers for it. A 2004 United Nations report estimated the world's drug-abuser population at around 185 million people. Another report estimated that the illegal drug black market had grown from $450 billion a year to $900 billion a year from 1992 to 2002, making illegal drugs the single most lucrative commodity in the world. Traffickers often invested drug profits in legitimate enterprises. In Colombia, for example, drug lords poured millions into the country's cattle business.

In addition to its role as a source of governmental and legal corruption, drug trafficking also played an increasing role during the last part of the twentieth century in the spread of other illicit goods internationally, such as Ukrainian gangs trading guns to Colombian cartels for cocaine. Intravenous drug use also contributed to the spread of HIV.

Like legitimate enterprises, drug dealing profited from economic globalization. The Internet, satellite phones, lowered tariffs, and relaxed currency controls all made it easier to move goods and money. At the same time, despite spending huge sums of money on interdiction, the restrictions of geographic borders and sometimes uneven levels of cooperation with police in other countries hampered law enforcement authorities. At best, the international war on illegal drugs was an ongoing stalemate as the twenty-first century began.

Communists: DOWN

Despite its heady success in the fifteen or so years after the end of World War II, the Communist ideology, particularly as espoused by the Soviet Union, wasn't able to make as much headway as the 1960s unfolded.

One reason was the sobering effect of the Cuban missile crisis. Both sides in the cold war recognized there was a limit to how much they could push each other without risking dire consequences. Rising nationalism in third world countries in Latin America and Africa resisted influence from both sides. Some countries, such as India, played both sides against each other. And the resurgence of Islam as a driving political force in the Middle East hampered Communist efforts to expand its influence in that region.

The United States also played a role. Determined to slow down revolutionary activities often financed by the USSR and other Eastern European Communist states, the United States began funneling arms and money to anticommunist forces in nations such as Angola, El Salvador, Guatemala, and Afghanistan. In the fall of 1983, U.S. troops were directly involved when they invaded the tiny Caribbean island of Grenada to topple a Communist-backed regime.

Meanwhile, the natives were getting restless at home inside the European Communist Bloc. In 1968, Soviet tanks rolled into Czechoslovakia to suppress an effort by the Czech government to liberalize judicial and other policies. In 1981, the Soviets intervened in Poland to head off similar attempts at reform. Soviet troops were also sent to Afghanistan in 1979 to prop up a Communist regime there.

Such intervention was costly—and the Soviets just didn't have the dough to pay for it, keep up with the West in the increasingly expensive modern arms race, and fulfill basic government jobs such as feeding its people.

In Asia, China was going through its own cultural and economic upheavals and paid less attention to extending the reach of communism. Vietnam, exhausted from its long war, began seeking to normalize relations with the West, and in 1991 it withdrew from neighboring Cambodia.

By the middle of the 1980s, Soviet leaders were openly encouraging other European Communist nations to stop looking to the USSR for everything and to start developing their own political and economic reforms. They did so with enthusiasm.

In August 1989, Poland convened its first non-Communist government since 1948. By the end of 1990, governments in Romania, Bulgaria, Czechoslovakia, Albania, and Hungary had followed suit. And by the end of 1991, the Soviet Union had itself dissolved.

As of 2007, only five states controlled by a single-party Communist system—the People's Republic of China, Cuba, Laos, North Korea, and Vietnam—still existed.

Terrorists: **ALL OVER THE PLACE**

Defined by the CIA as "the premeditated use or threat of extra-normal violence or brutality by sub-national groups to obtain a political, religious or ideological objective through intimidation of a large audience," terrorism has been around in one form or another at least as long as have government and organized religion.

But in the latter half of the twentieth century and into the twenty-first, terrorist groups had changed in several ways from their predecessors. They became less tightly knit organizations and more loosely affiliated networks; less political and more religious in their motivations; more likely to be international in their memberships; slower to take credit for their actions; more indiscriminate in their choice of targets, and less clear in what they wanted to accomplish through a specific terrorist act.

> *"Today's terrorists don't want a seat at the table, they want to destroy the table and everyone sitting at it."*
> —Member of the U.S. National Commission on Terrorism in 2000

Starting in the late 1960s, the targets of terrorism seemed to gravitate from the specific to the general. In 1978, the Red Brigade kidnapped and killed the Italian interior minister; in 1979, the Irish Republican Army assassinated Earl Mountbatten of England; in 1985, the Palestinian Liberation Front seized an Italian cruise ship and murdered a wheelchair-bound American tourist.

In 1983, a suicide bomber killed 63 people at the U.S. Embassy in Beirut, Lebanon; this was followed by a similar attack that killed 240 U.S. Marines in a barracks in the same country. In 1988, bombs believed to have been planted by Libyan terrorists destroyed a passenger airliner over Lockerbie, Scotland, killing 269 people. In 1995, a religious cult used nerve gas on a Tokyo subway, killing a dozen people and sickening hundreds more.

And on September 11, 2001, nineteen terrorists armed with box cutters and affiliated with the radical Islamic group al-Qaeda hijacked four U.S. commercial airliners. One crashed into the Pentagon in Washington, D.C.; one into a Pennsylvania field as passengers tried to retake control; and two into the twin towers of the World Trade

Center in New York City. Nearly three thousand people were killed in the worst terrorist incident in history.

> *America, you lost. I won.*
> —9/11 terrorist Zacarias Moussaoui shouting after he was sentenced to life in prison for his role in the attacks, May 3, 2006

The attack on the Pentagon and World Trade Center underscored the ability of terrorists to take advantage of modern communications and transportation systems to export terror to virtually anywhere. It also demonstrated the "trans-nationalism" of modern terrorists. By 2005, according to the CIA, the group responsible for the attack, al-Qaeda, led by the charismatic fanatic Osama bin Laden, had branches or allies in sixty-eight countries.

In response to the September 11 attacks, the U.S. declared a "war on terrorism" that eventually led to American invasions of Afghanistan and Iraq. But the effectiveness of the effort was debatable. In September 2006, a National Intelligence Estimate compiled from sixteen U.S. spy agencies concluded that the U.S. effort, particularly in Iraq, had only fueled the idea of jihad, or holy war against the U.S. in the Middle East, and encouraged the formation of more terrorist cells and groups.

THE BREAST MILK IS OKAY, THE LIP GLOSS ISN'T GOING TO FLY

Most people don't get any closer to the front lines of the war on terrorism than an airport terminal—and that's plenty close for most people. In the wake of the 9/11 attacks, the Transportation Security Administration was formed in the United States to ferret out potentially dangerous items before they could be smuggled aboard flights.

What's considered "potentially dangerous" ebbs and flows with the times. After abortive attempts to smuggle liquid explosives aboard flights from London to New York in August 2006, for example, virtually all liquids were banned. This was later amended to allow things such as small amounts of baby formula and breast milk. In 2006, TSA agents confiscated 11.6 million cigarette lighters. Then the rules were changed in August 2007 to allow most normal lighters to be carried on.

Still, confiscated items, almost all of which are thrown away, do add up: Between 2002 and 2005, sixteen million "potential weapons," ranging from chain saws to plastic swords from Disneyworld, were seized by the forty-three thousand folks who make up the TSA. That's an average of fourteen thousand a day.

While the vigilance has certainly played a part in preventing any new 9/11-type occurrences, the system isn't foolproof. In March 2007, an airline employee managed to smuggle a duffel bag onto a flight from Orlando, Florida, to Puerto Rico. It contained thirteen handguns, an assault rifle, and eight pounds of marijuana.

Oil Prices: UP

It was a classic example of economic coercion—or a textbook case of international pouting. Either way, the 1973 world oil crisis had impacts that lasted far beyond the decade of the seventies.

It began in mid-October, with the announcement by oil-producing countries in the Middle East that they were cutting off oil shipments to countries that had either supported Israel in the Yom Kippur War, or had declined to support Egypt and Syria. Sensing an opportunity, other oil-producing nations who were members of the Organization of Petroleum Exporting Countries (OPEC) decided to jack up their prices.

The result was a severe oil shortage in many Western countries that had since the end of World War II become increasingly dependent on imported oil to fuel industry and transportation. And the impacts of this were immediate and widespread.

In the United States, the world's largest consumer of oil, the price of gasoline rose by mid-1974 to an average of 55.1 cents a gallon ($2.29 in 2007 dollars), a 43 percent increase from mid-1973. Overall inflation soared, and the world was pushed into a general economic recession.

Not all countries suffered. In the Soviet Union, which actually exported oil, higher prices meant increased foreign currency, which propped up the USSR's sagging economy. In Japan, the shortage spurred Japanese automakers to focus on more fuel-efficient cars and turned manufacturers' attention from heavy industry to electronics. Brazil began to focus on developing fuel from sugar (which it had in abundance) instead of oil (which it didn't).

Industrialized nations also either began or accelerated ways to conserve energy (the United States, for example, dropped the freeway speed limit to fifty-five miles per hour), increase domestic oil production, and develop alternative energy sources.

In 1979, OPEC nations took advantage of the uncertainty of oil supplies from the Middle East because of the revolution in Iran to again jack up oil prices. The action again jarred many industrialized nations.

Throughout the 1980s and 1990s, increased oil production—spurred in part by some OPEC nations getting a bit greedy—resulted in something of a glut on the world market, and prices were relatively stable.

As the twenty-first century moved through its first decade, however, demands for oil surged as giant countries such as China and India began developing their industries and transportation systems. At the beginning of 2008, the price of oil broke the one-hundred-dollar-a-barrel mark, and declining reserves made it increasingly unlikely that the world's supply would meet future demands.

Technology: OUT OF SIGHT

Shortly after assuming the papacy in April 2005, Benedict XVI issued a "thought of the day" to the Roman Catholic faithful—via a text message on his cell phone.

Yup, communications had come a long way since an April day in 1973 when a forty-four-year-old electrical engineer named Martin Cooper hefted a thirty-ounce apparatus to his ear while walking along the street in New York City and made a telephone call, to an engineer who worked for a rival company.

In fact, the last half of the twentieth century and the first decade of

> **ERROR, ERROR ERR . . .**
>
> The first attempt to send a message via the Internet was between scientists at UCLA and Stanford University in 1969. The system crashed when the sender got to the *g* in *login*.

the twenty-first saw a vast herd of technological advances that simultaneously made life simpler and easier, and more maddeningly complex:

- The development of the microprocessor paved the way for the manufacture and sale of "personal" computers that could be used in the home. By 2007, nearly 270 million personal computers were being sold throughout the world each year.
- Originally designed to be a tool for military and scientific intelligence sharing, the Internet became the twentieth century's version of the telegraph. Only the Internet was much more. Coupled with the personal computer, the Internet allowed the development of e-mail and the World Wide Web, a vast electronic compendium of information, opinion, and ideas (oh yeah, and porn.)
- The development of incredibly powerful microscopes and other tools in the 1980s led to a new scientific field: nanotechnology, which allows scientists to manipulate individual molecules and atoms. Want a stereo system that can sit on the head of a pin? They can do that. Just don't drop it.
- Of course all that technology advancing can make one hungry. So in 1967, a U.S. company began marketing a

microwave oven that could fit on a countertop and was reasonably safe. By 1975 in the United States, microwave ovens were selling faster than gas ranges, and popcorn has never been the same.

Back to the cell phone. By 1970, scientists had figured out a way to hand off calls from tower to tower. By 1980, the U.S. Federal Communications Commission got around to allocating enough bandwidth to accommodate the growing demand for cell phones, despite their cumbersome size and high price. By 1987, cellular phone subscribers in the United States had reached more than a million.

DOES THIS COME WITH A WAGON TO CARRY IT IN?

A 1983 Motorola model cell phone weighed nearly two pounds, was shaped like a brick, and cost $3,500.

In Great Britain, meanwhile, engineers were developing a system that allowed cell phone users to send text messages by tapping in letters on the phone's keypad. The first system was in place by 1995; by 1999, more than a billion messages a year were being sent.

By 2005, it was estimated about seven hundred million cell phones were being sold each year around the world, with the number expected to top one billion by 2009—meaning that about 40 percent of the world's population would be using the ubiquitous little buggers.

Accessorized with cameras, digital music players, and access to the World Wide Web, cell phones had revolutionized modern life, from papal text messages to warning entire populations of looming disasters.

In fact, according to a 2004 survey by the Massachusetts Institute of Technology, the cell phone was the invention people hate the most—but can't do without. Incredibly (or not) it beat out alarm clocks and television.

– Major Assassinations of the Late Twentieth – and Early Twenty-first Centuries

Assassinations have been viewed throughout human history as an expedient and emphatic—if brutal—method of making a political statement, and the last sixty years have been no different. Here are a few you should probably know something about:

John F. Kennedy. The thirty-fifth U.S. president was shot and killed while traveling in a motorcade in Dallas, Texas, on November 22, 1963. A crazy former U.S. Marine named Lee Harvey Oswald was arrested after the shooting. Two days later, Oswald was shot and killed by a Dallas nightclub owner named Jack Ruby as Oswald was being moved from the Dallas jail.

Martin Luther King, Jr. The Nobel Peace Prize–winning minister and U.S. civil rights leader was in Memphis, Tennessee, on April 4, 1968, to support striking sanitation workers. He was shot and killed while on the balcony of a Memphis motel. An escaped convict named James Earl Ray was convicted of the murder. Ray died in prison in 1998.

Anwar Sadat. President of Egypt beginning in 1970, Sadat was the first Arab leader to officially visit Israel. In 1978, he and Israeli prime minister Menachem Begin reached an accord that earned them a shared Nobel Peace Prize. It also earned Sadat an assassination, on October 6, 1981, by a squad of insurrectionists. Several hundred were implicated in the assassination, but no one did much prison time.

Indira Gandhi. The prime minister of India made the country a nuclear power in 1974. But she also came down hard on dissenting groups. Two Sikhs who were part of Gandhi's bodyguard unit machine-gunned her down in a garden on October 31, 1984, to avenge an army raid she had ordered on a Sikh temple to dislodge extremists. Her murder sparked anti-Sikh riots across India that resulted in the deaths of more than a thousand people.

Yitzhak Rabin. The two-time prime minister of Israel was yet another Nobel Peace Prize winner who ended up assassinated. Rabin was shot and killed on November 4, 1995, at a peace rally, by a right-wing Israeli law student who opposed the peace accord Rabin had reached with Palestinian leaders. The student, Yigal Amir, was sentenced to life in prison.

Benazir Bhutto. The daughter of a Pakistani prime minister who was executed after a military coup, Bhutto was herself twice elected that country's prime minister. She returned from exile in 2007 to again run for prime minister. But on December 27, 2007, she was killed while leaving a campaign rally. As of early 2008, her killers had not been caught.

Some others:

Ngo Dinh Diem (1963): first president of South Vietnam

Malcolm X (1965): black Muslim leader

George Lincoln Rockwell (1967): founder of the American Nazi Party

Robert F. Kennedy (1968): U.S. senator and presidential candidate

Wasfi al-Tal (1971): prime minister of Jordan

Faisal (1975): king of Saudi Arabia

Mujibur Rahman (1975): president of Bangladesh

Harvey Milk (1978): gay rights leader and San Francisco supervisor

George Moscone (1978): mayor of San Francisco

Rajiv Gandhi (1991): Indian prime minister, son of Indira Gandhi

Mohamed Boudiaf (1992): president of Algeria

Zoran Dindijc (2003): prime minister of Serbia

········ **SO LONG, AND THANKS FOR ALL THE** ... ········

Change of Heart

As early as the 1700s, scientists had experimented with the idea of replacing damaged human organs with new parts, either organic or mechanical. In 1954, surgeon Joseph Murray conducted the first successful human kidney transplant, and in 1960, Stanford University doctors Norman Shumway and Richard Lower transplanted a heart into a dog, which lived for three weeks.

But the first human heart transplant was left to a fifty-five-year-old South African surgeon who had trained with Shumway's Stanford team. Christian Neethling Barnard had become interested in repairing or replacing organs early in his career, after a patient gave birth to an infant with a fatally irreparable heart. On December 3, 1967, Barnard's team took nine hours to move the heart of Denise Ann Darvall, twenty-five, who had been struck by a car, into Louis Washkansky, a fifty-five-year-old businessman who suffered from gross heart failure and was dying.

BAD NEWS/BAD NEWS

In 1964, the U.S. Surgeon General confirmed the link between tobacco smoking and lung cancer. And the Nobel Prize for Chemistry went to an English scientist who determined the structure of cholesterol. Turned out it builds up from eating anything that tastes good.

While the transplant was an initial success, Washkansky died of pneumonia eighteen days after the operation. Although other surgeons rushed to emulate Barnard, so many transplant patients' bodies rejected the foreign organs that the number of heart transplants dropped from one hundred in 1968 to eighteen two years later.

But in the 1970s, researchers found that a compound called cyclosporine, made from a fungus, helped calm the body's natural rejection tendencies. Survival rates greatly improved, and the survival rate today is about 84 percent at one year and 77 percent at three years after surgery.

Barnard, who died in 2001, lived long enough to see the world's first successful heart-lung operation performed at Stanford University in 1981 and the first successful pediatric heart transplant in 1984.

A Mother Like No Other

She was a tiny bundle of positive energy who started as a novice nun and wound up being lauded as a twentieth-century saint.

Agnes Gonxha Bojaxhiu, better known to the world as Mother Teresa, was born on August 26, 1910, in Macedonia. At the age of seventeen, she became a novice nun, taking the name Sister Teresa. In 1929, Teresa was sent to Calcutta, where she taught high school. She lived a relatively comfortable life teaching middle-class students and living in a convent.

But on September 10, 1946, during a train trip on her way to a retreat, she later recalled, she received a call "to serve the poorest of the poor."

Teresa eventually received a papal dispensation to pursue her charge. She founded her own religious order, the Congregation of the Missionaries of Charity, and opened a school for poor children. A hospice, an orphanage, and a leper colony followed the school.

> *Do not wait for leaders; do it alone, person to person.*
> —Mother Teresa.

Teresa's efforts went largely unrecognized outside the subcontinent. In 1969, however, a BBC documentary brought her efforts to international attention. A decade later, she was awarded the Nobel Peace Prize.

Teresa's charitable acts, which eventually expanded to more than one hundred countries, were paralleled by her crusade for conservative religious values that included opposition to abortion, contraception, and divorce.

Barely five feet tall and frail, Teresa spent most of her last decade battling injury and illness. When she died in Calcutta in 1997, India declared a national period of mourning. She was buried in a grave at one of her charity houses. The inscription, from the Gospel of St. John, reads, "Love one another as I have loved you."

From White to Right

It was the equivalent of a political miracle. Over a four-day period in April 1994, tens of thousands of black South Africans waited patiently in lines that stretched for as long as a mile for a chance to vote. The event capped a decades-long struggle to end apartheid, which was an Afrikaner word for "apartness" and the name of a political system that gave legal sanction to a brutally segregated society.

South African apartheid began after World War II, when the country won independence from the British Empire and the National Party won control of the South African government. The new government quickly put into law what had been practice in the region since the white man arrived. Blacks and whites were required to use different transit systems, schools, hotels, restaurants, restrooms, and park benches. Interracial sex was outlawed. Beginning in the 1970s, the government created tribal homelands in the crummiest areas of the country. Blacks were assigned citizenship in them, and had to have passes to travel through or work in any area outside these "homelands."

Protests against the system were dealt with harshly, and dissenting political parties were outlawed. The repression triggered opposition that often turned violent. To justify its actions, the government argued that it was protecting itself from infiltration by Communists.

But the rest of the world wasn't buying it. South Africa was banned from the Olympic Games in 1984, and in 1986 both the United States and the European Economic Community instituted economic sanctions against it. Once one of the most thriving nations on earth, South Africa began to suffer financially.

> *I have just got to believe God is around. If He is not, we in South Africa have had it.*
> —Anglican bishop Desmond Tutu, accepting the Nobel Peace Prize, December 10, 1984

In response, the government agreed to abolish the "pass" laws in 1986. In 1989, an attorney named F. W. de Klerk was elected president. De Klerk realized that if apartheid continued, the country was headed for civil war. In 1990, he freed a black lawyer and civil rights leader named Nelson Mandela, who had been in prison for twenty-seven years.

Mandela and de Klerk negotiated an agreement in 1991 to end white rule through elections. The two men won the 1993 Nobel Peace Prize for their efforts; South Africans of all colors won the right to choose their government. Nearly twenty-three million turned out at the polls in 1994, seventeen million of them black. Mandela's African National Congress party won 63 percent of the vote and Mandela was elected president.

"The nation that once was a pariah," U.S. vice president Al Gore observed at Mandela's inauguration, "will now become a beacon of hope."

No-Hands Football

Up until the end of the twentieth century, the average American might have been hard pressed to name the most-watched sporting event in the world.

The answer, of course, is the World Cup, a quadrennial event that pits teams from thirty-two nations in a multi-round soccer tournament to win a sleek solid-gold cup and international bragging rights.

Although soccer (known outside the United States as football) has its antecedents in games played in ancient Japan, China, Greece, and Rome, the modern version was pretty much born in nineteenth-century Britain.

By the late 1920s, the game had spread to other countries and had attained status as an Olympic event. So the sport's international governing body, the Fédération Internationale de Football Association, decided that soccer, uh, football, should have its own tournament. The first was held in Uruguay in 1930. Except for a twelve-year stint between 1938 and 1950 because of World War II, the World Cup has been held every four years ever since.

The current format involves teams facing off over a three-year period in an effort to qualify for one of 32 berths in the actual tournament, which rotates to different host countries. In 2006, 198 nations tried out; in 2010, that number is expected to reach 204.

That same year, an estimated 715 million people around the world (about 11 percent of humanity) tuned in to watch the final game between Italy and France, and the total number of viewers for all televised games was an impressive 26 billion.

And in the United States, viewing jumped 38 percent as the number of hours of games televised by U.S. channels more than doubled. The Yanks were catching on.

Contraception has been around since people figured out that sex sometimes resulted in babies. In ancient Egypt, for example, women used a *pessary* composed of honey, sodium carbonate—and crocodile dung.

But it took a root used by the Aztecs, an heiress to a farm machinery fortune, and a couple of determined scientists to come up with perhaps the most effective contraceptive in history.

Katharine Dexter McCormick was one of the first women to graduate from the Massachusetts Institute of Technology and was heiress to the International Harvester fortune. In 1950, after the death of her husband, McCormick agreed to finance research by two Massachusetts scientists. The scientists, John Rock and Gregory Pincus, combined estrogen and progestin (extracted from a wild yam, called Barbasco root, that had been used as a contraceptive by Aztec women), and came up with a contraceptive that could be taken in pill form.

The pill was manufactured and marketed by the Searle company after receiving approval from the U.S. Food and Drug Administration in May 1960. Despite concerns from time to time about side effects, the pill sold well. By 1963, thirteen major drug companies around the world were working on their own versions, and by 1967, more than twelve million women were using the contraceptive.

In 1971, a version that didn't have to be taken every day was on

FOR PREVENTION OF DISEASE ONLY

Early feminists had opposed abortion and contraception, on the grounds that if men could have sex without the responsibility of reproduction, they would exploit women. By 1900, however, feminist attitudes had begun to shift. If women could not protect themselves from unwanted motherhood, the argument went, they would never be able to achieve parity with men in public life and the workplace. However, at the beginning of the twentieth century, a federal law had been passed banning contraception sales through the mail, and most states prohibited it.

In 1914, a New York woman who had trained as a nurse opened a family planning and birth control clinic in Brooklyn. Margaret Sanger's clinic was open only nine days before police shut it down and she was arrested and served thirty days in jail.

But in 1918, probably spurred by wartime concerns about the spread of venereal diseases, an appeals court justice in New York ruled that contraceptive devices could be legally sold, if they were prescribed by a physician, and only in packages marked "for prevention of disease only." Many such products still carry those words.

the market most everywhere in the world except the United States (which took until 1996 to approve it.) Other contraceptive forms that were improvements on historical methods were also developed in the last part of the twentieth century. These included intrauterine devices, vasectomies, and post-sex contraceptive pills. None of them used excrement from reptiles.

Lyrical Liverpudlians

John met Paul, who brought along George, and eventually they picked up Ringo, and that's how the Beatles were born.

Or something like that. Actually it began in the hardscrabble English port town of Liverpool on October 9, 1940, when a kid named John Lennon was born.

In 1957, Lennon formed a group called the Quarrymen and met a couple of other teenagers named Paul McCartney and George Harrison, who joined the band. After playing nightclubs in Germany, the group, now called the Beatles, returned to England, added a drummer named Ringo Starr and began their rise to international stardom.

Fueled by songs written by Lennon, McCartney, or both, the Beatles leaped to the top of the pop musical world during the 1960s. They had forty number-one singles and albums, sold more than one billion records, tapes, and discs, and in 2004 were named the greatest rock artists of all time by *Rolling Stone*.

> *Christianity will go. It will vanish and shrink . . . I don't know what will go first, rock 'n' roll or Christianity. We're more popular than Jesus now.*
>
> —Musician John Lennon, commenting on the popularity of his group, the Beatles, March 4, 1966

The group's musical influences were enormous, ranging from lyric writing to layering instrumental tracks atop one another to create a more complex sound. They shaped hair and clothing styles, and language and advertising, and introduced the West to Eastern music and philosophy.

Personal differences and business pressures broke up the Beatles in 1970, and all four went on to successful solo careers. Lennon moved to New York City, where he was shot and killed by a crazy fan in 1980. Harrison, who in his post-Beatles career was more reclusive than the others, died of lung cancer in 2001. McCartney, who was knighted in 1997, and Starr were still active musicians in 2008.

Total Meltdown

If Swedish nuclear power plant workers hadn't noticed some radioactivity on their clothes, the world might *still* be waiting for news of the meltdown of the Chernobyl nuclear power plant, not far from the city of Kiev.

Okay, that's a gross exaggeration. But the fact is Soviet officials uttered not a peep about the accident until other countries, starting at a Swedish nuke plant, began detecting radiation in the air and deduced it was coming from the USSR.

The accident, which began at 1:23 a.m. on April 26, 1986, took place during an experiment at the Chernobyl plant's Reactor 4, in which plant workers shut down the regulating and emergency safety systems and withdrew most of the control rods while letting the reactor continue to run.

Firefighters from the nearby village of Pripyat joined with plant workers to try to stem the damage, but it was too little too late. Radiation on the scene quickly killed thirty-two people, a number that eventually rose to fifty-six direct deaths. Within a week, forty-five thousand people in the area were evacuated; the number eventually climbed to more than three hundred thousand. Millions of acres of forests and farmland were contaminated in the Ukraine, and radiation, though not at fatal levels, spread as far west as France, Italy, and Ireland.

Soviet officials buried radioactive debris from the site in hundreds of "temporary" sites, and enclosed the reactor core in a tomb of concrete and steel. Because of a desperate need for energy, Ukrainian officials allowed three other reactors at the site to continue operating. The last of these wasn't shut down until 2000.

The total impact of the Chernobyl disaster is still being tallied. Various studies have estimated the eventual number of deaths from radiation-caused illnesses will reach anywhere from four thousand to fifty thousand people. The current structure entombing the damaged reactor is not a permanent solution, and an effective shelter is expected to cost more than $1 billion.

MUSHROOMING PLANTS

As of mid-2007, there were 437 operating nuclear power plants throughout the world, with an additional 30 under construction, 74 in the planning stage, and 182 proposed.

Tastes Like Chicken

To much of the outside world, Ugandan dictator Idi Amin seemed at times to be a charming and witty leader in Africa's emergence from its colonial chains, and at times to be an amusing buffoon. His background was certainly interesting enough: a former soldier in the British Army, a heavyweight boxing champion, a convert to Islam who had five wives.

But to people inside Uganda, he was a terrifying thug. During his eight-year reign, which began in 1971, Amin, through his "State Research Bureau" and "Public Safety Unit," carried out the murders of as many as two hundred thousand political enemies. Amin was deposed and fled the country in 1979. He lived in exile in Libya and Saudi Arabia until his death in 2003.

The rumors about Amin's personal excesses were legion. There were reports he had personally decapitated some foes, and kept their heads in cold storage. In one case, he was said to prop up severed heads at the dinner table for a mock "farewell supper." He was also said to have had one of his wives killed and dismembered, then sewn back together and displayed to their children. And, it was rumored, he was a cannibal.

Whether he really was has never been documented. In a 1979 interview with a French magazine, Amin denied he was a cannibal, but added that he once had been forced to eat human flesh when he was captured by Mau Mau rebels while fighting with the British Army.

"We risked death if we refused," he said. "We ate human meat only in order to accomplish our military mission."

In a 1981 interview with Associated Press, Amin again denied that he occasionally had people for dinner. "I am a simple human being, not the eater of human flesh," he said. "Do I look like a cannibal?"

Well, now that you mention it . . .

A New Plague in Town

In 1981, researchers at the Centers for Disease Control and Prevention in Atlanta noticed something strange about reports coming out of California and New York. An abnormally large number of cases of a rare form of cancer were showing up in homosexual males.

Within a year, groups that seemed especially susceptible to the disease included intravenous drug users, immigrants from Haiti, and hemophiliacs and others who had received blood transfusions. By the end of 1982, fourteen nations had reported cases. By the end of 1983, the number of reporting countries was up to thirty-three, and a French doctor had isolated the retrovirus that caused acquired immune deficiency syndrome, or AIDS.

Because of the stigma attached to some of the disease's most common victims, such as gays, prostitutes, and drug users, governments were slow to respond to the threat. By 1987, when U.S. president Ronald Reagan declared the disease "public health enemy No. 1," AIDS was killing twenty thousand Americans a year, and millions more around the world in every demographic group.

A POX ON POX

In 1979, after more than a century of vaccination campaigns around the planet, the World Health Organization certified that smallpox had been eradicated. To date it is the only human infectious disease to be wiped out.

Where AIDS came from is still not entirely certain, although there is some evidence that it may have originated in Africa after World War II, possibly contracted first by people who ate infected monkeys and chimps.

Whether it came from Africa or not, it hit that continent harder than anywhere on earth. A United Nations report in 2004 estimated that 70 percent of the 38 million people living with HIV were residents of sub-Saharan Africa. In some African countries, one third of the adult males were infected.

In the 1990s, researchers found that a combination of drugs was effective in slowing the disease. But the drug "cocktail," as well as tests used to detect HIV, were expensive, and thus out of reach for many people. The World Health Organization estimated that 90 percent of people who needed treatment could not afford it.

Hot Times Ahead

In 1896, a Swedish scientist named Svante Arrhenius published a novel idea: the burning of fossil fuels such as oil and coal might someday put enough carbon dioxide into the atmosphere so that more infrared radiation from the sun would be absorbed, and global temperatures would rise.

It was an interesting theory, but most scientists at the time figured that the oceans would absorb any extra carbon dioxide and that the earth's climate was a pretty stable deal. By the 1950s, however, research had shown that the oceans couldn't hold more than a third of the CO_2 being produced.

Still, not everyone thought that meant the world was warming up, and if it was, so what? There was evidence that the earth had gone through some fairly drastic climactic changes in the past. And who really likes winter that much anyway?

In fact, some scientists in the 1970s postulated that all the dust and smog particles humans were spewing into the atmosphere might actually block sunlight and trigger a new ice age. Analysis of weather statistics from the Northern Hemisphere, in fact, showed that since the 1940s, the world had been cooling down.

But by the end of the century, things were heating up again. In fact, the ten warmest years in recorded world history occurred after 1990. Using voluminous amounts of gathered data and improving computer models, many scientists in the 1980s and 1990s began warning that nations needed to cut back on activities that emitted greenhouse gases, most notably in manufacturing and transportation, which were dependent on fossil fuels.

In 1988, the world's scientific community formed an international organization of climatologists, economists, geologists, oceanographers, and other scientists. The Intergovernmental Panel on Climate Change (IPCC) had more than 2,500 representatives from 113 countries, and was charged with providing political leaders with sound scientific information on global warming.

In 1992, officials from 154 nations meeting in Rio de Janeiro signed a convention calling for the voluntary restriction of greenhouse gas emissions. The accord was followed in 1997 by the Kyoto Protocol, an agreement reached in that Japanese city that called for specific reductions in greenhouse gas emissions by 2012.

While hailed as one of the most significant international environmental treaties ever, the Kyoto Protocol's success seems unlikely: the world's largest greenhouse gas producer, the United States, refused to sign it, and the second-largest, China, was exempted because it was classified as a "developing country."

It might not matter anyway. In February 2007, the IPCC reported that it was likely higher temperatures and rising sea levels "would continue for centuries" no matter how much greenhouse gas emissions were reduced. Just one more thing to look forward to!

· · · · · · · · · · · · · · · · · · BY THE NUMBERS · · · · · · · · · · · · · · · · · ·

8 number of weeks of unbroken bombing by U.S. forces of targets in North Vietnam, beginning in February 1965. Over the next three years, the United States dropped more bombs than were dropped over Asia and Europe during World War II.

800 bombs, in tonnage, being dropped per day in August 1966

45 life expectancy, in years, of a male resident of Rwanda in 1994

52 number of U.S. senators who voted in 1991, to authorize military action against Iraq

47 number of senators who voted against it in 1991

77 number of U.S. senators who voted in 2002 to authorize military action against Iraq

23 number of senators who voted against it in 2002

192 number of Member States in United Nations as of June 2006, with admission of Montenegro

537 number of votes by which Republican presidential candidate George W. Bush won the 2000 election in Florida over Democratic candidate Al Gore, thus winning the U.S. presidency

2,195 cost, in dollars ($3,878 in 2006 dollars) of an Apple McIntosh computer in 1984. It comes with 128 kilobytes of RAM.

1,999 cost, in dollars ($1,999 in 2006 dollars) of an Apple notebook computer in 2006. It comes with 512 megabytes of RAM, about 400 times more powerful than the 1984 model.

5,000 number of people estimated to be starving to death in Somalia in July 1992

40,000 number of children estimated by the United Nations International Children's Emergency Fund to be dying each day in 1984

10,000,000 number of refugees estimated by the United Nations to be scattered throughout the world

560,000,000 number, in dollars, pledged for refugee aid by 99 nations at a UN conference in 1981

5,600,000,000 estimated number, in dollars, spent on arms and military by the world's nations in 1981

IF YOU THOUGHT THE LAST DEPRESSION WAS GREAT ...

As the first edition of this book went to press in September 2008, the United States was entering one of the biggest economic. downturns in decades, dragging the rest of the world with it. Reaching for comparisons, economists have been warning that the recession could turn into Great Depression, Part 2. But if we look to history, it's likely things won't get as dismal as before, so don't start stockpiling guns and canned food just yet (unless that's your thing).

There's no denying it's really bad this time around: from a peak of 14,164.53 on October 9, 2007, the Dow Jones Industrial Average plummeted to 6,547.05 on March 9, 2009, a 54 percent decline in a year and a half. What caused the stampede? While the technical details are ludicrously complicated (which was part of the problem), the basic dynamics are easy enough to understand. During the first years of the third millennium, American real estate values grew rapidly (much like the Dutch tulips of the 1630s), attracting more buyers, mostly ordinary people who were betting the market would continue to go up—and it did. As real estate prices climbed higher, banks started lending money to less-qualified home buyers using "sub-prime" mortgages, many of which began with low "teaser" rates that later reset to unmanageably higher rates. The borrowers were convinced that they wouldn't have to worry about the higher rates because the value of their home would continue to increase, and they would be able to refinance before the higher rates kicked in.

Meanwhile, mortgage lenders "sold" these mortgages to banks, hedge funds, and other investors, mixing the good loans in with the bad and spreading the contagion. Then the investors used these mortgages as collateral to finance other deals. When some sub-prime borrowers began missing payments and defaulting on their mortgages, the bankers and everyone else suddenly realized that most of their worth was in bad loans that weren't going to be repaid—in other words, worthless. Banks discovered they didn't have

Yep. There are plenty of similarities between the 2008 crisis and the Great Depression. Both were caused in part by easy access to credit: where in the 2000s the culprit was sub-prime loans, in the 1920s it was "no money down" purchase plans for the new must-have items of the day, like automobiles and home appliances. Both followed a surge of investment in the stock market by ordinary Americans and financial services companies, contributing to a stock market bubble; in both cases the effects of corporate bankruptcy were worsened by decades of prior consolidation. And both saw big American banks go bust or almost go bust, triggering a financial meltdown around the world, with the United States as the global leader.

The Great Depression was, as the saying goes, no joke: from a peak of 381.17 on September 3, 1929, over three successive crashes and a long slide the stock market sank to a low of 41.22 on July 8, 1932, having shed 89 percent of its value. American banks failed left and right, with the total number of banks falling from around 30,000 in 1925 to about 16,000 in 1935. Meanwhile unemployment soared from 3.2 percent in 1929 to 24.9 percent in 1933. No surprise, huge drops in consumer spending followed, gutting demand. This situation caused a collapse in production: gross national product fell 40 percent from 1929 to 1933.

The most visible sign of the Great Depression, however, was the real human misery it inflicted on the American people. At its height, 30 percent of Americans were living below the poverty line and 1.6

DUST BUSTED

The nation's economic woes were further compounded by an ecological disaster, the Dust Bowl, in which a drought and poor farming techniques caused billions of tons of topsoil to blow away across 300,000 square miles of the Great Plains, damaging or entirely destroying 160 million acres and adding 3.5 million farm workers to the ranks of the unemployed; in 1935 the police chief of Los Angeles County illegally sent 125 officers to the borders of Arizona and Oregon to stop displaced rural refugees from entering the state. Labor disputes became the norm, with 2,000 strikes in 1934 alone. As more people went hungry, violence and civil disorder increased as well: after six major riots from 1920 to 1928, there were fourteen violent incidents between 1929 and 1937, all of them labor-related.

percent were homeless. In Chicago, 40 percent of the workforce was unemployed, and in New York City, one out of five children suffered from malnutrition. A quarter million teenage boys wandered the country in search of work or charity, hitching rides on trains and living "on the bum" alongside several million adult men; in 1931 the Southern Pacific Railroad said it threw 683,000 hobos off its trains.

Recovery finally began in 1934—five years into the downturn—but it was slow and painful: in the words of the American economist Richard M. Salsman, "Anyone who bought stocks in mid-1929 and held onto them saw most of his or her adult life pass by before getting back to even". . . in 1954. Although Franklin Delano Roosevelt did his best to turn things around with mass employment programs funded by the government, the truth is the economy only really improved with America's entry into World War II, which provided a massive stimulus to production and employment.

the money they needed to back their loans, so they screamed for government bailouts or went bust. Ordinary companies that rely on credit to do business abruptly found the bank vaults closed; even healthy companies started laying people off, and many less-healthy companies just went bankrupt. In the worst-case scenario, which looks pretty likely, in 2009 bankruptcies and layoffs will put even more people out of work, leading to more mortgage defaults and drops in consumer spending, causing more banks and companies to go bust, and so on.

But don't let the bad news depress you too much: there are a couple of bright spots. Unlike those living through the 1930s, we're the beneficiaries of seven decades of more or less consistent economic growth, and we already have social welfare programs in place —none of which existed when the Great Depression began. Our standard of living and level of education have soared, with 80 percent of Americans currently holding high school diplomas, compared to only 24.5 percent just eighty years ago. Even if life does get worse, it would be tough for the level of human misery to come anywhere near the Great Depression, with its iconic bread lines and convoys of homeless families.

Even though 2008 might not earn the title of "best year ever," a few good moments in history lie scattered among the ruins of the world economy. Among them:

- America elected a man named Barack Hussein Obama as the first African American president, despite the similarity of his name to certain *personae non gratae*.
- The planet was not sucked into a giant black hole, which some had feared the Large Hadron Collider at CERN in Geneva, built to simulate the Big Bang, would cause to happen.
- China hosted its first Summer Olympics, marking its official "coming out" as a great power (think debutante ball, not "out of the closet").
- A few years after suffering civil war and genocide, Kosovo declared its independence from Serbia and was officially recognized by fifty countries, including the United States.
- The Mars *Phoenix* lander touched down successfully near Mars's north pole, a totally unexplored region, where it is searching for water in the form of ice and sending back photos of the Red Planet (it's really more dunn-colored).
- For the first time in more than twenty-five years, the percentage of American adults reading literature went up instead of down.
- Researchers proved that happiness is contagious among social networks, and that having happy friends increases your odds of personal contentment more than having some extra cash. Now that's good news for hard times!

OH YEA, CANADA

They haven't gotten much of a mention so far, but even a super-condensed version of history should include the plucky, sensible Canadians. For one thing, there's the sheer size of the place: at 3.8 million square miles, it's the largest country in the world after Russia (100,000 square miles larger than the United States). And this vast expanse holds untold treasures of oil, gold, silver, diamonds, and industrial metals, as well as some of the most fertile land on the planet.

But, darn it, it's cold up there. So over the last four hundred years, this treasure trove and cornucopia has attracted just a fraction of the settlers who came to the United States. Today Canada has a population of less than 33.5 million, about a tenth the size of the U.S., at 300 million, and smaller, in fact, than California, with roughly 36.5 million; what's more, 90 percent of its small population is concentrated in a narrow band, one hundred miles wide, hugging the U.S. border.

Despite the size difference, Canada enjoys an unprecedented degree of security, especially compared to other countries with small populations next to big neighbors (think: Belgium). This security is symbolized by the "longest unfortified border in the world," 3,145 miles long from the Atlantic to the Pacific, policed only by customs officials—and rather casually at that. It's also cited as proof that democracies usually pursue pacifist policies toward other democracies.

It wasn't always this way, however. In its infancy, the United States looked on Canada with deep suspicion, fearing it could be a launching pad for the British to regain control of its wayward colonies.

Canada and the thirteen colonies, both originally ruled by Britain, parted ways during the American Revolution. Even before the beginning of hostilities, American rebels tried to spread revolutionary fervor north to Canada, but got a rather frosty reception, for a couple reasons. For one thing, the 13 colonies attracted a lot of Puritans and poor Scots-Irish, who both had their reasons for loathing the Brits. More importantly, however, Canada included a sizeable French contingent: in 1763 Britain's defeat of France in the Seven Years' War (or "French-and-Indian War") gave it possession of Quebec, previously the largest French colony in the New World.

— LEAVE IT FOR BEAVERS

The French settlement of Canada began with Acadia, founded in 1604 near the modern border between Maine and New Brunswick. Like the English settlements at Roanoke and Jamestown (during its early days), Acadia was a miserable failure. A mere four years after its founding, the French colonists gave up, letting the explorer Samuel de Champlain lead them north to Quebec, which was more of a success, thanks to the thriving beaver pelt trade.

The English and French coexisted uneasily, and the tension between them forced the English to rely on the British crown for security and authority. Meanwhile, the French *Canadiens* harbored no illusions about their fate if they joined the American Revolution: they would simply be absorbed into a new English-speaking country. Better to stay with the Anglophone devil they knew.

When it became clear the Canadians weren't going to join the Revolution, American rebels decided to "liberate" them anyway . . . whether they liked it or not. But the assault on Quebec City in the winter of 1775–1776 ended in complete disaster for the Americans, who had neglected to bring a single cannon to besiege the walled city. Much the same fate awaited the next American invasion of Quebec during the War of 1812, when four highly disorganized American "armies," with no real strategy or even common goals, proved no match for the British Redcoats and Canadian militias. The ill-conceived war ended with Canada still British and Washington, D.C., a smoking ruin (down south, New Orleans somehow ended up in American hands, even though the United States basically lost).

There would be a few more skirmishes that for some reason centered on pigs, including the absurd, undeclared Aroostook War of 1839 (casualty: one pig) and the also undeclared "Pig War" of 1859 (triggered by the shooting of a pig near Vancouver), but the Americans eventually realized that Canada was, actually, not an easy country to conquer, being so huge and all; and anyway it wasn't worth antagonizing Great Britain over.

The American Revolution made a big impression in Britain, of course. To keep Canada in the imperial fold, the British made a number of extraordinary concessions in the 19th century, which became models for self-rule in other parts of the Empire. Many of these concessions were linked to popular movements in Britain that undermined the old Liberal system (where only property-owners could vote) and extended the vote to the working class. In light of this, it's no surprise that Canada paralleled Britain's development into a parliamentary democracy with a pronounced socialist sensibility.

Canadians also seem to have retained some of the best parts of British culture: its absurd humor and dry wit, which Americans love—but can't necessarily "do." Happily, they're more than ready to come south and make millions of dollars amusing Americans. The list of famous Canadian comedians who made it big in the United States includes Dan Aykroyd, John Candy (RIP), Jim Carrey, Tommy Chong, Michael J. Fox, Tom Green, Phil Hartman (RIP), the comedy troupe The Kids in the Hall, Eugene Levy, Norm MacDonald, Howie Mandel, Rick Moranis, Mike Myers, Leslie Nielsen, and Martin Short. While not particularly funny himself, Lorne Michaels, producer of *Saturday Night Live* and The Kids in the Hall, is also a Canuck.

INDEX

Abbasid Dynasty, 130, 146
Abelard, Pierre, 175
abortion, 388
Abraham, 6, 16, 30, 130
Adams, John, 263
Adams, Samuel, 260
Adena culture, 108
Afghanistan, 371
Africa, 3, 106–7, 310–11, 333–34, 364–66. *See also specific countries*
agriculture, 3, 5–6, 8, 15, 44–45, 47, 106
air travel, 319
Akbar, 204–6
Alcibiades, 68, 76
alcohol, 26. *See also* beer; gin; U.S. Prohibition; vodka; wine-making
  absinthe, 284–85
  cocktails, 283
  Native Americans and, 278–79
Alexander I, 271–72
Alexander the Great, 77, 87
  Alexandria designed by, 79
  death of, 80–81

Greece defeated by, 78
in India, 79
Persian empire conquered by, 67–68, 78–79
tutoring, 78
Allies, 327, 331–33
American Revolution, 257, 259–61
Americas, 107–8, 137–38, 165–66, 219. *See also* Latin America; North America; South America
Amin, Idi, 391
Ammon, 9–10
Amyitis, 59–60
Anasazi, 129, 166
Andropov, Yuri, 367
anesthesia, 283–84
Anglican Church, 198, 225
antibiotics, 328
anticommunism, 340
apartheid, 44, 386–87
Appert, Nicolas, 282–83
Arab Empire, 17, 130–32
Aradashir I, 104–5
Aristotle, 77, 86
Ark of the Covenant, 61–62

Arrhenius, Svante, 392
Art of War (Sun Tzu), 87
Ashanti Empire, 258, 265–66
Ashoka, 71–72, 93
assassinations, 382–83
Assyrians, 8, 17, 24, 36, 51–52
astronomy, 127, 176
Athens, 39–41, 64, 68, 74–77
Attila, 98, 113
Augustine of Hippo, 122–23
Aurangzeb, 205–6
Australia, 13–14, 264
Austria, 275
automobiles, 313–14. *See also*
    Volkswagen Beetle
Avery, Henry, 236
Avicenna, 148–49
Axis Powers, 327, 331–33
Aztecs, 159, 165, 201–2

Babar, 205–6
Babylon, 6, 8, 54, 56. *See also*
    Hanging Gardens of Babylon
Bacon, Nathaniel, 224, 228
Baghdad, 129–30
ball-point pens, 350
banquets, 91–93, 100
Bantu people, 36, 44–45, 61, 106
barbarians, 110–12. *See also*
    Huns
Basil II, 128, 136, 164
Beatles, 389
beer, 26, 215–16
Bell, Alexander Graham, 351
Berbers, 106, 132
Berlin Wall, 338
Beserkers, 140
Bhutto, Benazir, 383
Bich, Marcel, 350
bikinis, 355
Biro, Lazlo, 350

Black Death, vii, 164, 172, 181–82,
    185, 212, 218
blunderbuss, 247
boats/ships, 25, 208, 236. *See also*
    sea navigation; Spanish
    Armada; submarines
Bolivar, Simon, 257, 273
Bonaparte, Napoleon, 257,
    270–72, 282–83
Book of Common Prayer, 199
bows and arrows, 23–24, 129,
    138
bras, 317
Brattain, Walter, 352
bronze, 23, 60
Buddha, 88–89
Buddhism, 88–89, 106, 115–17,
    128, 134
Bush, George W., 374
Byzantine Empire, 127–28,
    134–36, 151, 164. *See also*
    Constantinople; Justinian

Caesar Augustus, 90, 115
caesaropapism, 164
calendars, 48, 142, 153
Caligula, 90, 100
Calvin, John, 196
Cambodia, 368
Canada, 399–401
cannons, 206, 246–47
Capone, Al, 312
Carnarvon, George Herbert,
    320–21
Carraza, Venustiano, 308
carsus publicus, 115
Carter, Howard, 321
Carter, Jimmy, 370
Carthage, 43, 69
Castro, Fidel, 330
Catal Huyuk, 5–6

Catholic Church, 191, 194–95, 212, 223. *See also* popes
Caucasians, 17
Caucasus Mountains, 17, 236
cell phones, 382
Chandragupta Maurya, 67–68, 71
chariots, 24, 52, 144
Charlemagne, 128–29, 132, 137, 154
Charles I, 223–24, 226
Charles V, 199–200, 207
chastity belt, 184–85
Chernenko, Konstantin, 367
Chian Chi'ing, 367
Chiang Kai-shek, 302, 335–36
chiles, 242
Chimu culture, 138, 159, 165, 168
China, 12–13, 45–47, 186. *See also* Great Wall; Qin Shi Huang; Silk Road
    banquets, 92–93
    cities, 12–13
    creation myth, 21
    divorce in, 151
    dress in, 251–52
    feudal system, 70
    first civilization, 5
    Grand Canal, 128, 133, 154
    Han Dynasty, 67–68, 70, 102–4
    hemp in, 28
    Jin Dynasty, 104
    language in, 12
    legalism, 70
    Manchus, 224, 231–32
    Ming Dynasty, 189, 190, 203–4, 219, 224
    modernization in, 362, 367–68
    money in, 204
    nationalistic movement, 335–36
    Opium Wars, 277–78
    population, 203
    porcelain, 242
    Q'ing Dynasty, 224, 232, 258, 301
    rebellion in, 301–2
    Shang Dynasty, 13, 19, 93
    silk from, 49
    Song Empire, 159, 161–62
    Szechuan cooking style, 242–43
    Tang Dynasty, 123, 128–29, 133–34, 153
    unification, 68, 70
    warlords, 104
    warring states, 68–69
    weapons from, 86–87
    women rulers, 123
    Xia Dynasty, 6
    Yuan Dynasty, 161–62, 189, 203
    Zhou Dynasty, 36, 45–47, 69
Christianity, vii, 97, 116, 128–29
    church-state relations, 172–73
    Monophysitism, 144
Churchill, Winston, 346
Cicero, 92
circumcision, 113
cities, 3–5, 12–13. *See also specific cities*
city-states, 6–8, 39, 97, 107. *See also* Athens; Sparta
civilizations, 108. *See also specific civilizations*
    agriculture and, 47
    in Americas, 138
    first in China, 5
    spread of, 8
Cixi, 301–2
Classical Age, 97, 103, 113, 127, 164
Cleopatra, 69, 87–88
Coaticue (goddess), 201–2
cocoa, 201
coffee, 151
cold cream, 117–18
Coleridge, Taylor, 177–78
Columbus, Christopher, 200
communications revolution, 362

communism, 289–90, 328, 340, 346, 376–78
computers, 328. *See also* microprocessors
Concert of Europe, 273–74
condoms, 245–46
Confucianism, 134, 161
Confucius, 70, 102
Constantine, 110, 115, 149
Constantinople, 100, 135, 164, 207
contraception, 388–89
Cook, James, 251
Coolidge, Calvin, 307
Cooper, Martin, 381
Corcyra (ancient name for Corfu), 75
Corinth, 75
corn, 57–58
Corpus Juris Civilis, 143–44
corsets, 287–88
Cortéz, Hernando, 190, 202
Crab Nebula, 176
creation myths, 20–21
Crick, Francis, 351
Cromwell, Oliver, 226
crossbows, 86–87, 183. *See also* gastrophetes
crucifixions, 93
Crusades, 158–59, 170, 186
 Children's Crusade, 171
 end of, 171
 Goose Crusade, 171
 Muslims and, 163
Cuban missile crisis, 329, 341, 361, 377
Cyrillic alphabet, 149
Cyrus the Great, 36, 54–56, 73
czars, 229–31. *See also specific czars*

Daijosai, 28
Dante, 185, 192

Darius I, 56, 58, 63, 68, 73
Dark Ages, 36, 39, 127, 137
David, 53
Deborah, 53
de Gama, Vasco, 209, 219
de Klerk, F. W., 386
de la Boë, Franciscus, 245
Delian League, 75
democracy, 40, 274
Democritus, 84–85
Deng Xiaoping, 368
deoxyribonucleic acid (DNA), 351
Descartes, René, 238–39
de Stoeckl, Edouard, 286
Dialogues (Plato), 63
Diaz, Porfirio, 308–9
dice, 56–57
Dinonysius, 90
Diocletian, 109–10
Diodorus Siculus, 59–60
disease. *See specific diseases*
The Divine Comedy (Dante), 185
divorce, 151
DNA. *See* deoxyribonucleic acid
Dorians, 38–39, 60
Drake, Francis, 209, 215, 236
drinking, 18–19. *See also* alcohol
drug trafficking, 375–76

East India Company, 231
Edison, Thomas, 314
Egypt, 32, 370. *See also* Cleopatra
 Assyrians conquering, 36
 as first state, 5, 9
 food of, 10
 incest in, 31–32
 Jews as slaves in, 52
 Jews fleeing, 36, 53
 pharaohs of, 9–11
 plagues in, 53
Einstein, Albert, 239, 350–51

Eleanor of Aquitaine, 167–68
electron microscope, 329
Elizabeth I, 191, 198–99, 215, 217, 236
Engels, Friedrich, 303
England, 129, 198–99, 225–28, 231, 264–65. *See also* London
Enlightenment, 238–42
Ericsson, Leif, 129, 141
Eric the Red, 129, 141
Ethiopia, 50, 107, 310, 331
Etruscans, 80, 97
Europe. *See also specific countries*
    Concert of Europe, 273–74
    economic rehabilitation, 336–38
    plagues in, 160
explorers, 207–9. *See also specific explorers*
Exquemelin, Alexandre, 237
eye glasses, 179–80

Szechuan cooking style, 242–43
    tamales, 57–58
    wheat, 14–15
forks, 180
fountain pens, 350
France, 160–61, 197–98, 228. *See also* Louis XIV; Notre Dame, Cathedral of
    India colonies, 231
    North American colonies, 229
Franco, Francisco, 327
Frank, Annelies Marie ("Anne"), 345
Franklin, Benjamin, 262
Franks, 111–12
Frederick III, 274–75
French and Indian War, 259–60, 396
French Indochina, 336
French Revolution, 257, 268–70

Fallopius, Gabriello, 245
Faraday, Michael, 284
Ferdinand, 189–90, 199–200
fertile crescent, 6–8
feudalism, 152–53. *See also* serfs
fire, 5
firecrackers, 134
foederati, 111
food, 3. *See also* agriculture; hunger; restaurants
    bread, 172
    of Egypt, 10
    flour, 186
    insurance system, 4
    maize, 165
    mare's milk, 113
    packaging, 282–83
    potatoes, 215, 290–91
    pretzels, 150–51

Gagarin, Yuri A., 346–48
Gaius Caesar Germanicus, 100. *See also* Caligula
Galeazzo, Gian, 190, 192–93
Galen of Pergamum, 117–18
Galileo, 224, 238
gambling, 56–57. *See also* dice; playing cards
Gandhi, Indira, 383
Gandhi, Mohandas, 342–43, 372
Garibaldi, Giuseppe, 275–76
gastrophetes, 87
Genghis Khan. *See* Temujin (aka Genghis Khan)
George III, 245, 260
Germany, 274–75, 304–5, 329, 331–33
Ghana, 330
gin, 245

gladiators, 117
global warming, 392–93
Godiva, Lady, 161
Gorbachev, Mikhail, 367
Grant, Ulysses S., 281
Great Flood, 21–22
Great Mosque of Al-Mutawakkil, 154
Great Schism, 194–95
Great Wall, 93, 112, 204, 219
Great Zimbabwe, 185
Greece. *See also* Athens; Sparta
  Alexander the Great defeating, 78
  city-states, 39
  creation myths, 20–21
  Dark Ages of, 39
  invasion of, 68
  at war with Persian empire
    (Persian Wars), 73–75
Greenglass, David, 356–57
gunpowder, 134
Gupta, Chandra, 105–6
Gutenberg, Johann, 214

Hadad, 8
Hadrian, 100, 113
Hagar, 16
Hagia Sophia cathedral, 153
Hamilton, Alexander, 262
Hammer of Witches, 210
Hancock, John, 260
Hanging Gardens of Babylon, 59–60
Hannibal, 68, 81
Hapsburgs, 233–34. *See also* Thirty Years' War
Harappan civilization, 5–6, 11–12, 17
Harding, Warren, 307
Harrison, John, 244–45
heating systems, 100

Hegel, Georg Wilhelm Friedrich, 240, 289
heliocentric theory, 224
Heloise, 175
hemorrhoids, 61–62
hemp, 27–28
Henry, Patrick, 260
Henry II, 159, 167, 184
Henry the Navigator, 208
Henry VIII, 198, 225
Hercules, 38–39
Herodotus, 54, 58–59, 63
Hetepheres, 30
Heyn, Piet, 238
Hideki Tojo, 327
Hillary, Edmund, 347
Hinduism, 22
Hispaniola, 219
Hitler, Adolf, 17, 305, 329–31, 337–38, 355–56
Hittites, 24, 36–38, 51, 60
HIV/AIDS, 363, 391–92
Hobbes, Thomas, 240
Hofray, Samuel, 286
Holocaust, 327, 344
Holy Land, 53, 164, 170
Holy Roman Empire, 137, 160, 185, 219
Homer, 42, 80
homo habilis, 5
homo sapiens, 5
homosexuality, 62, 218
Hongwu, 203
Hopewell culture, 108
horses, 17, 22–25, 52, 248–49
Huang Chang, 153
Huari culture, 137–38
Huerta, Victoriano, 308
Hula Hoop, 352
humanists, 127, 192
human sacrifice, 48, 97
Hume, David, 170
Humphrey, Hubert, 347

Hundred Years' War, 161, 189
hunger, 15
Huns, 98, 111–13
Hunt, John, 347
Huss, Jan, 194–95
Hussein, Saddam, 371

iconoclasm, 146
Iliad (Homer), 42, 80
Inca Empire, 202–3
incest, 30–31
India, 11–12, 17, 68
    Alexander the Great in, 79
    economic growth in, 369
    English colonies, 231, 264–65
    French colonies, 231
    "Golden Age," 106
    Gupta Empire, 105–6, 119
    independence, 328, 342–44
    Kushan Empire, 106
    Maurya Empire, 68, 71
    Moghul Dynasty, 191, 204–6,
        258
India-Pakistan war, 374–75
Indo-Europeans, 17, 36
Indus River, 11, 17
Industrial Revolution, 263–64
infanticide, 97–98
Inferno (Dante), 192
Innocent III, 171
Internet, 381
Iran, 17, 104, 371
Iraq War, 375
Irish Potato Famine, 290–91
iron, 60–61
iron curtain, 328, 346
Isabella, 189–90, 199–200
Ishmael, 16
Ishtar, 8
Isis, 9, 31
Islam, 105, 117. *See also*

Muhammad (the Prophet);
    Muslims; sects; Shiites;
    Sunnis
    Jerusalem captured by armies of,
        128
    rise of, 129–32
    spread of, 127–28
Israel, 50, 344–45, 370
Italy, 275–76
Ivan III, 223
Ivan the Great, 209–10
Ivan the Terrible, 229–30

Jacobs, Mary Phelps, 317
Jainism, 106
James I, 250
Japan, 25, 27–28, 46, 120, 162, 169,
        186, 331–33
    Buddhism, 128
    closing of, 232
    conquests, 300–301
    earthquakes, 320
    economic run-in, 368–69
    nationalistic movement in,
        334–35
    opening of, 267–68
    Samurai, 162
    shoguns, 159, 232, 267–68
    Tokyo firebombing, 335
Jeanne d'Arc, 211
Jefferson, Thomas, 261, 276, 278
Jericho, 5–6
Jerusalem, 36, 54, 113, 128
Jesus Christ, 51, 116
Jews, 15–16, 17, 113–14, 182, 185.
        See also Ark of the Covenant;
        Holocaust; Judaism
    Babylonian exile, 54
    blackmailing, 212
    dying from Black Death, 212
    fleeing Egypt, 36, 53

Jews (*continued*)
  freed from Babylon, 56
  in Israel, 344–45
  judges, 53
  Nazi extermination, 329, 333, 344
  as slaves in Egypt, 52
Jimmu, 46
Johnson, Lyndon, 371–72
John VIII, 139
John XII, 196
John XIII, 196
Jomon culture, 25
Joshua, 53
jousts, 184
Juan-juan, 132
Judaism, 16, 30, 113
judges, 53
Julius Caesar, 69, 82–83, 88, 91–92
Jung, Carl, 355
justice system, 183–84
Justinian, 128, 143–45
Juvenal, 109

Kallinikios, 151
Kama Sutras, 119
Kant, Immanuel, 240
Karl I, 275
Kemal, Mustafa, 312
Kennedy, John F., 341, 348, 371, 383
Khan, Agha Mohammad, 277
Khayyam, Omar, 174
Khfare, 29
Khmer, 128–29
Khmer Empire, 159
Khmer Rouge, 368
Khrushchev, Nikita, 339, 342
Khufu, 29–30
King, Martin Luther, Jr., 372–73, 383

kings, 3–4. *See also specific kings*
  of Babylon, 6
  of England, 198–99
  of France, 197–98
  Parthians as, 104
  Sumerian, 7–8
Kinsey, Alfred, 354–55
kissing, 101
Kitab al-shifa, 148
Knerr, Richard, 352
Knickerbockers, 228
Koran, 153
Korean War, 328, 334
Kublai Khan, 159, 161, 169, 177–78, 180, 185
Kushan Empire, 106
Kyoto Protocol, 393

Lackland, John, 159
language. *See also* Cyrillic alphabet; writing
  Bantu, 45
  in China, 12
  English, 213–14
  French, 213–14
  Greek, 98, 115
  Latin, 98, 115
Laos, 368
Lao Tzu, 70
Latin America, 308–10. *See also specific countries*
lead, 216–17
League of Nations, 296, 307
Lee, Robert E., 281
Lenin, Vladimir, 303–4
Leo III, 146, 153
Leonidas, 74, 78
Leo VII, 196
Leo X, 195–96
Leo XI, 146
Leucippus, 85

Leviathan (Machiavelli), 240
Liberia, 310
life expectancy, 31
Lincoln, Abraham, 281
Lindbergh, Charles, 319
Li Si, 70
Li Tian, 134
Liu Bang, 68, 70
Loch Ness Monster, 139
Locke, John, 241
London, 153, 172
longbows, 182–83
Longshan culture, 12
Louis-Charles, 288–89
Louisiana Territory, 278,
    285–86
Louis VII, 167
Louis XI, 197–98
Louis XIV, 223–24, 228, 247–48,
    257, 268–70
Louis XVI, 260
Louis XVIII, 289
Lower, Richard, 384
lugal, 7–8
Luther, Martin, 190, 195–96
Lysis, 63

Macedonia, 77–78
Machiavelli, Niccoló, 193, 240
Machu Picchu, 202
Madero, Francisco, 308
Madison, James, 262–63
Magellan, Ferdinand, 209
Magyars, 152
Mahenjo-Daro, 11–12
Malcolm X, 373
Mali, 212–13
Malleus Maleficarum, 210
Mamelukes, 157, 163, 181
Mandela, Nelson, 387
Mani, 121–23

Manichaeism, 121–23
Mao Zedong, 328, 335–37
Marc Antony, 69, 87–88
Marcos, Ferdinand, 368
Marcus Agrippa, 88
marijuana, 27
Marshall, George, 337
Martel, Charles, 132
Martin V, 194
Marx, Karl, 289–90, 296, 303
mathematics, 127
    algebra, 97–98
    geometry, 86, 238–39
Mau Mau Rebellion, 333
Mayan Empire, 68, 72–73, 97, 121,
    138
    agricultural exhaustion, 143
    calendars developed in, 142,
        153
    city-states of, 107
    collapse of, 143
    peak of civilization, 127–29,
        143
Mazzini, Giuseppe, 275–76
McCarthy, Joe, 340–41
McCormick, Katharine Dexter,
    388
McKinley, William, 305
medicine, 97, 127, 179. *See also*
    anesthesia; organ transplants;
    vaccines
Mediterranean basin, 18
Medvedev, Dmitry, 367
Mehmet II, 219
Mehmet IV, 235
Menelik I, 50
mercury poisoning, 288
Merlin, Arthur ("Spud"), 352
Mesoamerica, 47–49
Mesopotamia, 6–8, 17
Mexico, 3
mice, 61–62
Michael III, 149

microprocessors, 352, 381
microwave ovens, 382
Middle Ages, 108, 127, 152, 157, 164
    jousts in, 184
    justice system, 183–84
Middle East, 369–71. *See also specific countries*
milla passum, 115
Mississippians, 165–66
Mithradates the Great, 104
Moche people, 108
monasteries, 138–40
Monet, Oscar-Claude, 318–19
money, 264
    Carthaginian coins, 43
    in China, 204
    silver, 219
Mongols, 157, 168–70, 189–90, 203–4, 209–10. *See also* Kublai Khan
monks, 129, 138–40, 147, 150, 153. *See also* monasteries
monsoon winds, 98, 107
Montezuma II, 202
Morgan, Henry, 237
Mormonism, 279–80
Moses, 52–53
Mother Teresa, 385–86
Mount Everest, 347
Mount Vesuvius, 118
movies, 314–15
Muhammad (the Prophet), 128, 130
mummies, 29
music, 26–27. *See also* Beatles; Presley, Elvis; rock 'n' roll; singing; Stravinsky, Igor
muskets, 247, 285
Muslims, 128, 132, 163
al-Mu'tasim, 131
Mycenaean civilization, 17, 36, 38–39

Nabonidus, 55
Nabopolassar, 52
Napier, Charles, 265
Native Americans, 227, 248–49, 278–79
NATO. *See* North Atlantic Treaty Organization, (NATO)
Natufian culture, 5, 15
natural law, 84
Nazca culture, 107–8
Nazi Party, 305, 329, 333–34
Nebuchadnezzar, 54, 56, 59
necrophilia, 31
Nehru, Jawaharlal, 343
Neoplatonist school, 120
Nero, 101
Newton, Isaac, 224, 239
Ngo Dinh Diem, 336, 371
Nile River, 9–10, 38
Nintoku Tenno, 120–21
Nixon, Richard, 339, 372
Nok civilization, 61
nomads, 3–5, 158
Norgay, Tenzing, 347
Normans, 161
North America, 158, 165–66, 224, 226–29, 235. *See also specific countries*
North Atlantic Treaty Organization (NATO), 337
Notre Dame, Cathedral of, 159, 176–77
nuclear power, 330, 390

Obregón, Álvaro, 308
obsidian, 108
Octavian, 69, 83, 88. *See also* Caesar Augustus
oil, 370, 380–81
Old Copper Complex, 23
Old Testament, 19–20, 32, 61

Olmecs civilization, 36, 47–48, 57–58
OPEC. *See* Organization of the Petroleum Exporting Countries (OPEC)
opium, 250–51, 258, 264, 277–78
Opium Wars, 277–78
Optiks (Newton), 239
Organization of the Petroleum Exporting Countries (OPEC), 370
organ-stealing, 288–89
organ transplants, 384–85
orgies, 90
origins of universe, 20. *See also* creation myths
Orthodox Christian Church, 136
Osiris, 9, 30
Ostrogoths, 111–12
Ottoman Empire, 163, 190, 206–7, 235–36. *See also* sultans
    decline of, 257, 276, 311–12

Pahlavi, Reza, 371
Palace of Versailles, 247–48
Palestine Liberation Organization (PLO), 370
Papal Schism, 190. *See also* Great Schism
paper, 97, 103
Parsis, 50
Parthians, 104
"parting shot," 104
Paul II, 196
Paul VI, 139
Pax Romana, 83
pedophilia, 62–63
pellagra, 58
Pelletan, Jean-Philippe, 289
Peloponnesian War, 75–77, 93
Pepin the Short, 132, 154

pepper, 124, 219, 231
Pericles, 77
Perry, Matthew, 267–68
Persian empire, 54–56, 236, 257. *See also* shahs
    Alexander the Great conquering, 67–68, 78–79
    kingdoms in, 63
    postal service, 59
    Qajar Dynasty, 257, 277
    span of, 58–59, 63
    vassals in, 73
    at war with Greece (Persian Wars), 73–75
Peter the Great, 224, 229–31
Peter the Hermit, 171
Petrarch, 192
pharaohs, 9–11, 31–32, 78. *See also* specific pharohs
Philip II, 68, 77–78, 161, 223, 225
Philippines, 368
Philistines, 38, 53, 61
Phoenicians, 43–44, 64, 81
physics, 238
pirates, 236–38, 276
Pi Sheng, 161
Pius IX, 276
Pizarro, Francisco, 191, 203
plagues. *See also* Black Death; HIV/AIDS; SARS; Spanish flu epidemic
    in Athens, 76–77
    in British Isles, 129
    bubonic, 145, 190
    in Egypt, 53
    in Europe, 160
    population and, 160
    rapid spread of, 158
plastic, 317
plastic surgery, 71
Plato, 63
playing cards, 180–81
Pliny the Younger, 119

PLO. *See* Palestine Liberation Organization (PLO)
poetry, 153, 174
pok-a-tok, 121
Poland, 331–33
polio, 349
Polo, Marco, 178, 180, 185
Polynesians, 127, 141
Pompeii, 118–19
popes, 139, 146, 196. *See also specific popes*
population, 31, 47, 64, 160, 172, 203
Portugal, 207–9
power loom, 263
Presley, Elvis, 354
Priestly, Joseph, 283
printing press, 214–15
prose, 174–75
Ptolemaic Dynasty, 87
Ptolemy, 81, 87
Punic Empire, 43
Punic Wars, 81
Puritans, 225–26
Putin, Vladimir, 367
pyramids, 5, 10–11, 29–30, 48, 108, 123
Pythagoras, 86

Al-Qanun fi'l-tibb, 148
Qin Shi Huang, 68–70, 87, 93
Quan Tan Shi, 153
Queen Makeda (aka "Queen of Sheba"), 49–50

Rabin, Yitzhak, 370, 383
racism, 17. *See also* apartheid
railroads, 286–87
Raleigh, Walter, 215

Ramesses II, 52
Ramesses III, 38
Rankin, Jeannette, 314
al-Rashid, Harun, 146
Reagan, Ronald, 373–74
Reformation, 194–96, 198
religions, 115–17. *See also* Anglican Church; Buddha; Catholic Church; Christianity; Confucius; Jesus Christ; Jews; Orthodox Christian Church; popes; sects; *specific religions*
clash of, 158
monotheistic, 16, 50–51, 105
polytheistic, 15, 130
Renaissance, 127, 189–93, 212
representative government, 147
restaurants, 283
Reynolds, Milton, 350
Richard I, 167
rifles, 285
roads, 58–59, 114–15. *See also* Royal Road
Robert Bruce VIII, 186
Roberts, Bartholomew (aka Black Bart), 237
Robespierre, Maximilien, 269
Robins, Benjamin, 285
Rochambeau, 261
rock 'n' roll, 353–54
Roman empire
banquets, 91–92
collapse, 127, 136–37
crucifixions, 93
as dictatorship, 83
economy, 109
emperors, 110
expansion, 82
founding, 68, 80
Greek language in, 82
orgies, 90
political instability, 109
roads, 114–15

senate, 80–81
size, 109
slaves, 83–84
women rulers, 123
Rome, 99–101
burning of, 101–2
"navel" of, 115
sacking of, 110
Romulus Augustus, 111
Roosevelt, Eleanor, 341–42
Roosevelt, Franklin Delano, 329, 339–40
Roosevelt, Theodore, 306
Rosenberg, Ethel, 356–57
Rosenberg, Julius, 356–57
Rostislav, 149
Rousseau, Jean-Jacques, 241
Royal Road, 58–59, 63
Rubiyat of Omar Khayyam (Khayyam), 174
Russia, 223, 224, 229–31. *See also* Soviet Union
dress in, 252
revolution in, 302–4
Rwanda civil war, 374

Sabin, Albert, 349
Sadat, Anwar, 370, 383
Saladin (aka Salah-al-din Yusuf ibn Ayyub), 157, 159, 163, 171
Salk, Jonas, 349
Salutari, Coluccio, 192–93
Sanger, Margaret, 388
SARS, 363
Sassanians, 104–5
Saudi Arabia, 329
Saul, 53–54
Savery, Thomas, 263
Saxons, 129
Scandinavia, 127, 140
sea navigation, 242–45

Sea Peoples, 36–37, 42–43, 51
sects, 145–46
Seech, Fran, 350
Seljuk Turks, 157–58, 163
Seme, Pixley ka Isaka, 310
semi-conductors, 352
Seneca, 92
Sepoy Mutiny, 265
Serbia, 276
serfs, 152–53
Seward, William, 286
sex, 146–47, 196, 245–46, 354. *See also* chastity belt; condoms; contraception; homosexuality; incest; kissing; necrophilia; pedophilia
Sexual Behavior in the Human Male (Kinsey), 354
Shah, Fat'h Ali, 277
shahs, 236. *See also specific shahs*
Shaka, 266–67
Shakespeare, William, 252–53
Sherman, William Tecumseh, 281–82
Shiites, 128, 146
Shikibu Murasaki, 158
Shintoism, 28
Shockley, William, 352
Shona Empire, 159
Shovel, Cloudesly, 244
Shumway, Norman, 384
Shushruta, 71
Siam, 217–18. *See also* Thailand
Siddhartha, 88–90. *See also* Buddha
silk, 49, 135
Silk Road, 98, 99, 116–17, 124, 133
Simon Bar Kochba, 114
singing, 26–27
slavery, 234–35, 280–82
slaves, 74, 83–84, 235, 237
smallpox, 392
Smith, Adam, 241–42

Smith, Joseph, 279
smoking, 384
soccer, 387
Socrates, 63, 68, 85
Solomon, 49–50
Songhai people, 213
South Africa, 44, 386–87
South America, 273. *See also specific countries*
Soviet Union, 327
    collapse of, 362, 366–67
    industrialization of, 338–39
    in space, 330, 346–48
    as superpower, 339
Spain, 199–200
Spanish Armada, 223–25
Spanish flu epidemic, 321–22
Sparta, 36, 41–43, 64, 68, 74–77
Spartacus, 83–84
spinning jenny, 263
Spinoza, Baruch, 239
Stalin, Joseph, 303, 338–39
steam engines, 263, 286–87
Stephenson, George, 287
stirrups, 118
Stone Age, 23–24
Strang, James, 280
Stravinsky, Igor, 317
submarines, 316
Sudan civil war, 374
Suetonius, 90
Suez Canal, 334
sugar, 150
Sui Dynasty, 132
Suleiman the Magnificent, 207
sultans, 131, 235–36. *See also specific sultans*
Sumerian civilization, 7, 19–21, 26
    Great Flood myth, 21–22
    incest in, 30
Sunnis, 128, 145
Sun Tzu, 87
Sun Yat-sen, 301

Sushruta Samhita, 71
Synod of Whitby, 129
syphilis, 217
Syrians, 104, 157, 370

Tacitus, 91, 119
Taft, William Howard, 307
The Tale of Genji (Shikbu Murasaki), 158
Talib, Ali Ibn Abi, 145
Taliban, 361, 371
Tamerlane (aka Timur), 170, 190, 204–6
Taoism, 70
Tartars, 182
taxes, 161, 241–42
Taylor, John, 237–38
tea, 133, 243
Teach, Edward (aka Blackbeard), 236
technology, 381–82. *See also* automobiles; cell phones; computers; Internet; microprocessors; nuclear power; telephone; transistors; weapons
telephone, 351
telescope, 238
Temujin (aka Genghis Khan), 157, 159, 169–70, 186, 204
Teotihuacán, 97, 107–8
terrorism, 361, 378–80
tetrahydrocannabinol (THC), 27
Thailand, 336
THC. *See* tetrahydrocannabinol (THC)
Themistocles, 74–75
Thera, 36–37
Third Estate, 268–69
Thirty Years' War, 223–24, 233–34. *See also* Hapsburgs
Thutmose III, 27

Thycydides, 76
Tiberius, 90
Tigris River, 8
Timur. *See* Tamerlane
    (aka Timur)
tobacco, 249–50. *See also* smoking
Tokugawa Ieyasu, 232, 267
Toltec Empire, 158, 165
toolmaking, 23, 45
transistors, 328, 352
trepanning, 28–29
Trevithick, Richard, 286–87
Trojan War, 42
Trotsky, Leon, 303
Truman, Harry, 330, 337
tsunami, 18, 37
Tuareg people, 213
tulip bulbs, 234
Tutankhamen, 60, 321
Tutu, Desmond, 386
typhoons, 169. *See also* monsoon
    winds
Tyre, 78

Uganda, 391
Umayyad Dynasty, 146
United Nations, 330, 348–49
United States, 280–82, 305–6,
    331–33
    economic crisis of 2008–09 in,
        395–98
    Great Depression in, 308, 327,
        395–97
    gunboat diplomacy, 307
    racial discrimination in,
        372–73
    in space, 347–48
    as superpower, 339–42, 361,
        371–74
Ur, 7–8
Urban II, 170

Urban VIII, 238
U.S. Civil War, 280–82
U.S. Prohibition, 312–13

vaccines, 349
Vandals, 111–12
vassals, 64, 73
Vedic civilization, 60
Victor Emmanuel II, 276
Victoria, 295
Viet Cong, 336
Vietnam War, 371–72, 374
Vikings, 129, 140–42, 148, 152. *See
    also* Beserkers
Villa, Francisco ("Pancho"), 309
Visigoths, 111–12
vodka, 216
Volkswagen Beetle, 352–53
Voltaire, 160
vomitoria, 92
von Bismarck, Otto, 274
von Hindenburg, Paul, 305, 336

Walter of Malvern, 159
War of Spanish Succession, 224, 228
War of the Roses, 198
wars, 87, 91, 98, 104, 302–4, 333,
    374–75. *See also* Crusades;
    specific wars
Warsaw Pact, 33, 337
Washington, George, 260–61
Watson, James, 351
weapons, 23, 44, 285. *See also*
    specific weapons
    from China, 86–87
    incendiary, 151–52
    nuclear, 327, 328, 332
    small firearms, 159, 247
Western philosophy, 84

Westminster Abbey, 185
William I, 129, 161, 186
William the Conqueror, 166, 172, 213
Wilson, Woodrow, 307
windows, 137
wine-making, 18–19
witches, 210–12
women
    empowerment in Siam, 217–18
    rulers, 123, 153
    suffrage, 314
    as witches, 210–12
World War I, 296, 298–300
World War II, 329–30, 331–33
writing, 4. *See also* poetry; prose
Wycliffe, John, 194–95, 214

Xerxes, 67–68, 73–75
Xibo, 13
Xipe Totec (god), 202

Yang Chien, 132
Yangdi, 133
Yaroslav I, 161
Yeh Shen, 150
Yellow River, 12, 19
Yeltsin, Boris, 367
Young, Brigham, 280
Yuanzhang, 203. *See also*
    Hongwu

Zapata, Emiliano, 309
Zealots, 113
Zemurray, Samuel, 308
Zhao, 45, 47
Zhukov, Georgiy, 338
Zhu Yuanzhang, 189
ziggurat, 8
Zoroaster, 36, 50–51, 54, 105
Zoroastrianism, 50–51
Zulu Empire, 258, 266–67, 310

ABOUT THE AUTHORS

An award-winning political journalist and history writer for more than three decades, **Steve Wiegand** has worked as a reporter and columnist for the *San Diego Evening Tribune*, the *San Francisco Chronicle*, and the *Sacramento Bee*, where he currently covers state government and politics.

During his career, he has interviewed four presidents and six California governors—and has the dubious distinction of once being airsick and throwing up on the shoes of the state attorney general's wife.

It may have been his greatest personal contribution to world history.

Wiegand is a graduate of Santa Clara University, where he majored in American literature and U.S. history. He also holds a Master of Science degree in Mass Communications from California State University, San Jose.

In addition to *The mental_floss History of the World*, Wiegand is the author of *U.S. History for Dummies, Sacramento Tapestry*, and *Papers of Permanence*, a contributing author to *mental_floss presents: Forbidden Knowledge*, and a frequent contributor to *mental_floss* magazine.

He lives in Northern California.

Erik Sass is a journalist who covers the media business from his main base of operations in Los Angeles, with branch offices around the country. When not writing for *mental_floss*, he reports on magazines, newspapers, radio, and billboard advertising for MediaPost.com.

A shy, withdrawn child ("loser"), Erik spent many of his formative years reading about history. Ironically, the knowledge he acquired transformed him from mopey misfit to man-about-town; now much sought after for his historical anecdotes, he is considered an indispensable conversational ornament to any party attended by persons of substance.

A giver, Erik also works with *mental_floss* to share these benefits with others. In addition to the present volume, he was a contributing author for *mental_floss presents: Forbidden Knowledge*, and also writes about history for *mental_floss* magazine.

Erik has not vomited on the shoes of government officials or their spouses; however, he has vomited on his own shoes more than once.

Will Pearson and **Mangesh Hattikudur** met as first-year students at Duke University. Ignoring the lures of law school and investment banking, the pair cofounded *mental_floss* in 2001 and have been grinning ever since.

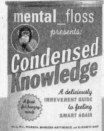